ANCIENT ROME

OTHER TITLES IN THE
GREENHAVEN ENCYCLOPEDIA OF SERIES:

Greek and Roman Mythology
Witchcraft

THE GREENHAVEN ENCYCLOPEDIA OF

ANCIENT ROME

Don Nardo

Daniel Leone, *President*
Bonnie Szumski, *Publisher*
Scott Barbour, *Managing Editor*

Greenhaven Press, Inc., San Diego, California

The author wishes to express his gratitude to University of Louisville scholar Robert B. Kebric, author of the widely popular Roman People, *for his kind input in the selection of topics for this volume.*

Library of Congress Cataloging-in-Publication Data

Ancient Rome / Don Nardo.
   p. cm.
  Includes bibliographical references and index.
  ISBN 0-7377-0551-5 (lib. bdg. : alk. paper)
  1. Rome—Encyclopedia. I. Title: Greenhaven Press encyclopedia of ancient Rome. II. Nardo, Don, 1947–

DG16 .A53 2002
937'.003—dc21

2001033754

Cover photo credit: © Archivo Iconigrafico, S.A./CORBIS

Copyright © 2002 by Greenhaven Press, Inc.
10911 Technology Place, San Diego, CA 92127

Printed in the USA

CONTENTS

Chapter 2: Important Geographical Places

Chapter 3: Gods and Religion

Chapter 4: Government and Law

Chapter 7: Enemies, War, and Military Affairs

To ignore the ancient Romans would be nothing less than to deny and lose touch with a piece of ourselves. Though many people in Western countries today are scarcely aware of it, much of the spirit of this long vanished people dwells, still very much alive and vital, within them. Profound in its influence, that spirit, like a silent and faceless engineer, busies itself in the ongoing elaboration of the structure we call Western civilization.

To the ancient Romans, Rome was not merely a city or the center of the greatest empire on earth, but also "an idea in the mind of God." Indeed, Roman civilization lasted so long that it and its culture and ideas seemed to have a timeless quality that the ancients put into words in the phrase *Roma aeterna,* "eternal Rome." As it turns out, there was a strong element of truth in this concept. Although the Roman Empire did eventually pass away (in the fifth and six centuries A.D.), it was mainly its government that perished. Rome's cultural heritage lived on and became deeply imbedded in the thinking and everyday habits of European life. Over the ensuing centuries, that heritage was quietly and steadily transmitted to future generations of Europeans and eventually reached the modern world. Thus, as noted historian R.H. Barrow points out, in a sense "Rome never fell," but merely "turned into something else." After its physical decline, it "passed into even greater supremacy as an idea. Rome, with the Latin language, has become immortal."

One needs only a cursory glance at today's social and political institutions to appreciate the enormity of Rome's heritage. The contribution its legal system made to European law courts and justice systems, including such concepts as trial by jury, impartial justice, and unwritten "laws of nature," is enormous to say the least. No less influential was the means of expressing these laws—the Latin language. Adapted by different peoples in different areas, Latin gradually developed into French, Spanish, Portuguese, Italian, and Romanian, the so-called "Romance" languages. And even after it had ceased to be widely spoken, Latin survived as the leading language of European scholars, as well as the official language of the Roman Catholic Church.

Christianity itself, of course, is among the most important of Roman cultural survivals. It was born in a Roman province, spread throughout the Empire, and eventually became the realm's official religion. Later, as antiquity gave way to the Middle Ages, it was the Church that became the chief unifying force of European civilization, influencing and often controlling most aspects of daily life.

Through the efforts of its monk-scribes, the Church also performed the vital service of copying ancient manuscripts and thereby preserving for future ages the ideas and writings of Greco-Roman civilization. Indeed, as the modern nations of Europe began to emerge in the fourteenth and fifteenth centuries, their cultures were at first fascinated by and then relentlessly and subtly reshaped by the classical works they had found stored on the dusty shelves of churches, monasteries, and libraries. Some of the ideas contained in these works became the principal inspiration for the Renaissance, Europe's widespread cultural flowering in those centuries.

Meanwhile, even though Roman political power itself was long since dead, Roman political ideals survived among the

Germanic kingdoms that grew on the wreckage of the western Empire. Many Roman concepts and institutions (or Greek, Egyptian, or Persian ones that Rome had adopted) survived Rome's fall and are today woven, often imperceptibly, into the fabric of modern life. Only a partial list includes: banks, hospitals, the postal system, fire brigades, bakeries, hair-dressing shops, glass windows, central heating, apartment buildings, public sanitation (including drainage, sewers, and public toilets), the social welfare system, historical treatises and novels, the theater, the circus (which evolved from Roman games and theatricals), and public education.

The story of Rome, therefore, is the story of a great civilization that created a blueprint for later civilizations to build on. No single book can convey the full enormity of that story, including Rome's origins, leaders, institutions, beliefs, arts, wars, and other endeavors. Thousands of books and articles have already been written on these topics. And archaeologists and historians constantly add new knowledge and reinterpret existing evidence, so that new books and articles appear on a regular basis. Needless to say, the process of keeping track of and sorting out all of this information is difficult even for scholars, not to mention students and general readers.

The *Greenhaven Encyclopedia of Ancient Rome* attempts to help in this process by providing nonscholarly readers with an overview of ancient Roman civilization that is not only thorough and accurate but also easy to access and readable. For convenience, the hundreds of topics are broken down into chapters, each covering a major aspect of Roman history and society—for instance, a chapter on Roman people, one on religion, and others on arts and literature, warfare and enemies, and so on. Most entries are carefully cross-referenced, guiding the interested reader to related topics or expanded discussions. In addition, the extensive bibliography directs the serious reader to further exploration of ancient Rome in the writings of today's leading scholars as well as the ancient authors.

As long as books like this one continue to illuminate "the grandeur of Rome," as one prominent modern writer called Roman civilization, awareness of the link between ancient and modern times will remain clear and sharp. People will continue to appreciate that Rome is, if not an idea in the mind of God, at least a spirit alive in the mind of humanity. As the late historian Max Cary so aptly observed:

> Rome was the principal channel through which the modern world has entered on the heritage of the ancient. If "all roads lead to Rome," they also lead out again *from* Rome. For those who have learned to think beyond yesterday, Rome is the focusing-point of the world's history.

CHAPTER 1
PROMINENT PEOPLE

Aeneas

The legendary prince of the city of Troy (in northwestern Asia Minor) whom Roman tradition viewed as the founder of the Roman race. According to the legend, as told most completely in Virgil's epic poem, *Aeneid*, when the Greeks sacked Troy, Aeneas escaped and sailed to southwestern Italy. There he met and married the daughter of a local king, and from their union sprang the lineage that led to Romulus, founder of the city of Rome. **See** Romulus; **also** *Aeneid* (Chapter 6).

Aëtius, Flavius

(mid–fourth century) The *magister militum* and most powerful military figure in the western Empire during the reign of the emperor Valentinian III. As a youth, Aëtius was held hostage by the Huns and got to know them; later, after becoming a Roman general, he enlisted their aid in fighting the Visigoths and other barbarian groups. When the Hun warlord Attila led his hordes into Gaul in 451, Aëtius turned on his old allies in an effort to save the Empire from them. With the help of his former enemies, the Visigoths, he narrowly defeated Attila at Chalons (or the Catalaunian Plain), in northeastern Gaul. But Aëtius did not destroy the Huns for fear of upsetting the balance of power among the German tribes. Although he served Valentinian faithfully, he incurred the hatred of some of the emperor's most influential relatives and associates, including Galla Placidia, Valentinian's mother. By failing to eradicate Attila, who invaded Italy soon after the Battle of Chalons, Aëtius angered the emperor as well, and the last great Roman general was assassinated, possibly by Valentinian himself, in September 454. **See** Attila; Valentinian III; **also** Battle of Chalons (Chapter 7).

Agricola

For this noted first-century A.D. Roman general and governor of Britain, **see** Tacitus, Publius Cornelius; **also** Britain (Chapter 2).

Agrippa, Marcus Vipsanius

(64–12 B.C.) The closest friend and adviser of the emperor Augustus (Octavian), as well as a gifted military leader and prolific builder. At Octavian's bidding, Agrippa defeated a rebellious Gallic tribe, then returned to Rome in 37 B.C. and attained the office of consul. After defeating Octavian's republican enemy, Sextus Pompeius, the following year, Agrippa largely engineered the victory over Antony and Cleopatra at Actium in 31 B.C. As a builder, Agrippa erected the famous Pantheon, as well as roads, aqueducts, and the capital city's first large public baths. His first wife was Attica, daughter of Cicero's friend Atticus; his second wife was Augustus's niece Marcella; and his third wife was Augustus's daughter, Julia. **See** Augustus; **also** Battle of Actium (Chapter 7).

Agrippina the Elder

(ca. 14 B.C.–A.D. 33) The daughter of Marcus Agrippa and Julia (and therefore the granddaughter of the first emperor, Augustus), she is best known for her avid dislike for and hostility toward the second emperor, Tiberius. Agrippina married the talented and popular general Germanicus, Tiberius's nephew, and had nine children by him, including the third emperor, Gaius Caligula. Devoted to her husband, she joined him on his campaigns in Germany's Rhine frontier and showed both courage and generosity by personally distributing food and clothing to the soldiers during a time of crisis. Along with Germanicus, she held dear Rome's old republican ideals, which put them on a collision course with Tiberius and his henchman, Sejanus. When the emperor ordered Germanicus to a post in faraway Syria, Agrippina followed her husband; after he died under mysterious circumstances, she became convinced that Tiberius had arranged his murder. She thereafter became openly hostile to the emperor, who finally exiled her to the island of Pandateria in the Bay of Naples, where she starved herself to death at the age of forty-seven. **See** Germanicus, Nero Claudius; Tiberius.

Agrippina the Younger

(A.D. 15–59) The daughter of Germanicus and Agrippina the Elder, sister of the emperor Caligula, and mother of the notorious emperor Nero, Agrippina became one of the most powerful and infamous women in Roman history. In the year 28, she married an unsavory nobleman, Gnaeus Domitius Ahenobarbus, and nine years later gave birth to Nero, whom she thereafter schemed to put on the throne. When her husband died in 39, Caligula suspected her of plotting against him and exiled her. But his successor, Claudius, her uncle, recalled her in 41 and in 49 married her. Thereupon she became unusually influential in the royal bureaucracy, even assuming a role in distributing funds. In 54, Agrippina apparently poisoned Claudius and fulfilled her dream of making her son emperor. Because of Nero's youth (he was only seventeen when he ascended the throne), during the early years of his reign she practically ran the Empire single-handedly. Eventually, though, he grew tired and jealous of her and began plotting her death. After a failed plot to drown her by rigging her ship to sink, he sent soldiers to stab her to death. Supposedly she challenged them to strike first in her abdomen, in which she had carried her ungrateful son, and they did so. **See** Claudius; Nero.

Alaric

(late fourth–early fifth centuries A.D.) A powerful king of the Visigoths, he came to power sometime after that tribe's defeat of the emperor Valens at Adrianople in 378. Because of the deal made later with the Visigoths by the emperor Theodosius I, allowing them to settle in Thrace permanently, Alaric was for a time a Roman ally. But after Theodosius died and the Empire was divided between his sons, Alaric could not reach an agreement with the government. Circa 402, the Visigoths marched on Italy, but a Roman army led by the general Stilicho halted their advance. Undaunted, in 408 Alaric regrouped his forces and this time marched straight to Rome almost unopposed, besieging and sacking the city in 410, an event that sent shock waves through the Mediterranean world. He died shortly afterward.

Ambrose

(later Saint Ambrose, ca. A.D. 339–397)
One of the most powerful and controversial Christian leaders of the fourth century, he was born at Trier and educated in law at Rome. He became bishop of Milan in 374; and in the coming years he exercised profound influence over a series of Roman emperors, including Gratian, Valentinian II, and Theodosius I, urging them to discourage and if possible eradicate pagan beliefs and worship. In 382 he convinced Gratian to remove the statue of Victory from the Senate and vehemently fought attempts by the noted senator Symmachus to restore it. Ambrose, who also convinced Theodosius to close the pagan temples, was a prolific writer; his surviving letters, sermons, and other works are an important source of information about the period.

Ammianus Marcellinus

(ca. A.D. 330–395) The finest Latin historian produced in the so-called Later Empire, he was born a Greek at Antioch (in Syria) and served in the army in Gaul and Persia under the future emperor Julian. In 378, Ammianus settled in Rome and began writing his now famous history, which covered events from 96 to 378. His honesty, balanced judgment, and elegant writing style rank him with the great Roman historians Livy and Tacitus, to the latter of whom he is often compared. Unfortunately, only a few sections of his masterwork have survived, specifically those covering the years 353–378, but these contain valuable information about Julian's reign, the Battle of Adrianople, and Roman society in his day, among other things.

Anthemius

For this royal regent to the emperor, **see** Theodosius II.

Antiochus III

For this Greek king who opposed the Romans in the second century B.C., **see** Scipio, Publius Cornelius "Africanus"; **also** Seleucid Kingdom (Chapter 2), Battle of Magnesia (Chapter 7).

Antonia Minor

(36 B.C.–A.D. 37) One of the most highly respected Roman women of the early Empire, she was the daughter of Mark Antony and Octavian's sister, Octavia. Antonia married Drusus the Elder, brother of the future emperor Tiberius, and reportedly loved her husband so much that after he died in 9 B.C., she never remarried. One of her sons, Claudius, later became emperor, as did her grandson, Gaius (Caligula, son of her other son, Germanicus, who died in A.D. 19). **See** Drusus the Elder.

Antoninus Pius

(A.D. 86–161) The fourth of the so-called five good emperors, he was one of Rome's most talented, efficient, and beloved rulers. Born in Gaul, he served as praetor and also as proconsul of Africa before the emperor Hadrian adopted him as his son and heir in 138. That same year Hadrian died and Antoninus ascended the throne. Among his first official acts were the donation of most of his large personal fortune to the state treasury and the pardoning of a group of condemned men; such unselfish and kind acts soon earned him the nickname of Pius ("good," "dutiful"). Indeed, he was a just, hardworking, and patient individual who dedicated himself almost entirely to the welfare of the Roman people. Another of his admirable achievements was the upbringing and training of his own adopted son, Marcus Aurelius, who succeeded him on his death in 161.

Antony, Mark

(Marcus Antonius, ca. 82–30 B.C.) A Roman military general and statesman who played a pivotal role in the fall of the Roman Republic. The son of an admiral who died when Antony was a boy, he acquired a reputation for heavy drinking and womanizing in young manhood. In about 57 B.C. Antony enlisted in the army and served in Egypt and Palestine before joining Julius Caesar's staff in Gaul in 54. He soon became one of Caesar's most trusted right-hand men. In the subsequent civil war with Pompey, Antony commanded the left wing of Caesar's army in the Battle of Pharsalus in 48 and Antony and Caesar served as consuls together in 44. On March 15 of that year, Caesar was assassinated in the Senate; Antony gave the funeral oration, which not only represented him as the dead man's heir but helped turn public opinion against the conspirators. For a while, these men, along with Caesar's adopted son, Octavian, and many senators, opposed Antony. But he regained the initiative when he, Octavian, and Lepidus established the Second Triumvirate in November 43 B.C. The following year, they smashed the conspirators' forces at Philippi (in Greece) and, following the terms of a deal struck by the triumvirs, Antony took control of most of the eastern portion of the realm.

In 41 B.C., Antony summoned the Greek queen of Egypt, Cleopatra, to his headquarters in Tarsus to enlist her aid in his plans to invade Parthia, and they became lovers. Meanwhile, as the triumvirate steadily disintegrated, his wife, Fulvia, and brother, Lucius, challenged Octavian's power; but soon Fulvia died and in 40 Antony and Octavian made a treaty at Brundisium, the latter giving his sister, Octavia, to Antony in marriage to seal the bargain. All of this seeming unity came to nothing, however. Antony's Parthian campaign in 36 was a failure and he thereafter permanently allied himself with Cleopatra, who bore him three children. (He divorced Octavia in 33.) As the lovers came increasingly into opposition with Octavian, each side vilified the other in a propaganda war; after actual war commenced, each hoped to gain mastery of the entire Roman world. Surprisingly, the outcome of the

Roman notable Mark Antony pays a visit to the court of Egypt's Queen Cleopatra VII. The two later became lovers and allies.

conflict was decided by a single battle—a sea fight near Actium (in western Greece) in September 31 B.C., where Antony and Cleopatra were defeated. The lovers escaped, fled back to Egypt, and committed suicide there the following year. **See** Augustus; Caesar, Gaius Julius; Cleopatra VII; **also** Battle of Actium (Chapter 7).

Appian

(Appianos, mid–second century A.D.) A Romanized Greek scholar, he wrote a history of Rome summarizing its conquests from its earliest days to the late first century A.D. Of the original twenty-four books, substantial parts of eleven survive complete, along with fragments of a few others. Books 13 to 17, commonly referred to or published separately as *The Civil Wars,* cover in some detail the strife of the first century B.C. and fall of the Republic.

Apuleius, Lucius

(mid–second century A.D.) Author of *The Golden Ass,* the only complete surviving

Latin novel, he was born in North Africa. After he married, his wife's relatives sued him, charging that he had used magic to seduce her. In his *Apologia* (which has survived), a speech in his own defense, he insisted that he was innocent and was duly acquitted. Thereafter, he traveled around North Africa lecturing and writing about Platonic philosophy. His most famous and enduring work, however, is *The Golden Ass,* a fantastic romance about a man who is transformed into a donkey. **See** *The Golden Ass* (Chapter 6).

Arcadius

(d. A.D. 408) Emperor of eastern Rome from 395 to 408, he was the eldest son of Theodosius I, who divided the realm between Arcadius and his other son, Honorius, who ruled in the west. Arcadius, who was only about seventeen when he ascended the throne, faced many troubles, including infighting among older, power-hungry advisers and strict domination of his court and personal life by his wife, Aelia Eudoxia, daughter of a prominent military leader. Eudoxia died in 404 and Arcadius followed her four years later, leaving their son, Theodosius II (then only seven) on the eastern throne.

Ardashir

For this third–century A.D. Persian ruler who attacked Roman-controlled Mesopotamia, **see** Arsacids; Sassanids.

Ariovistus

(flourished mid–first century B.C.) King of the Suebi, a Germanic tribe, he crossed the Rhine River in 71 B.C. and defeated the Aedui and other Gallic tribes. At first, Rome did not object to his conquests, which lessened the threat posed by the Gauls. But when his ambitions grew larger and he himself appeared to be a threat to the stability of the region, Julius Caesar (who had recently begun his renowned conquest of Gaul) engaged and defeated

him in 58 B.C. Ariovistus reportedly escaped back into Germany and died soon afterward.

Arrian

(Flavius Arrianus) A Romanized Greek born about A.D. 90 in the Roman province of Bithynia (in Asia Minor), Arrian is renowned for his *Anabasis Alexandri (Alexander's March Up-Country)*, the most complete and reliable surviving source chronicling the campaigns of Alexander the Great. Unfortunately, most of Arrian's other works, including *Events After Alexander* (in ten books), are either lost or survive only in fragments. His *Anabasis* was based largely on now lost histories by Alexander's general Ptolemy, and by Aristobulus, an engineer under Alexander. Therefore, historians consider much of Arrian's well-written account to be reasonably accurate.

Arsacids

A dynasty of Parthians who ruled much of the Near East for some five centuries during Rome's late Republic and early Empire, constituting the Romans' chief rivals and enemies in that region. In the early third century B.C., the heart of the old Persian Empire, encompassing what are now Iran and Iraq, was controlled by the Greek Seleucid Kingdom. The small region of Parthia, lying southeast of the Caspian Sea in Iran, rebelled circa 250 B.C. under a local leader, Arsaces, who defeated the Seleucid ruler Antiochus II and thereafter expanded Parthian territory at the Seleucids' expense. By the end of the following century, the Parthian Arsacids had absorbed most of the Seleucid lands; in the coming centuries they periodically fought the Romans for control of Armenia, western Mesopotamia, and especially Syria, each side tasting both success and failure. In 53 B.C., the Parthian general Surenas defeated and killed the Roman nobleman Marcus Crassus at Carrhae, in Mesopotamia. Soon afterward, an Arsacid invasion of Syria failed, and in 36 B.C., another Roman notable, Mark Antony, failed in his own attempt to invade Parthia.

Meanwhile, frequent court intrigues and rounds of civil strife continued to weaken Parthia. In A.D. 113 the emperor Trajan was able to capture the Arsacids' capital of Ctesiphon, and much of Mesopotamia. However, Trajan's successor, Hadrian, gave most of this territory back in his quest to make Rome's borders more defensible and stable. Regaining control of the lost lands did not help the Arsacids, for in 224, one of their subject peoples, the Persians, led by a local ruler named Ardashir, defeated and killed the Arsacid ruler Artabanus V. Soon afterward, the Arsacid dynasty was extinguished and replaced by the Persian Sassanid line of rulers. **See** Crassus, Marcus Licinius; Sassanids.

Atticus, Titus Pomponius

For this noted Roman aristocrat and friend of the orator Cicero, **see** Cicero, Marcus Tullius; **also** *Letters* of Cicero (Chapter 6).

Attila

(d. A.D. 453) Known as the "Scourge of God" because of his ferocity and cruelty, he was king of the Huns from 434 to 453. His empire, which he steadily expanded at Rome's expense, encompassed a large portion of Dacia and other lands bordering the Danube River in central and eastern Europe. In 447 Attila threatened Constantinople, but wisely refrained from attacking so formidable a bastion; the following year he turned on the less well defended western Empire. His initial invasion of Gaul was successful, but in 451 he met defeat at Chalons at the hands of a combined army of Romans and Goths led by Flavius Aëtius. Undaunted, Attila next descended into Italy and destroyed the city of Aquileia. But in a now famous meeting, Leo, the bishop of Rome, managed to persuade the Hun leader to spare Rome, and for reasons

that remain unclear, Attila soon led his army out of Italy. About a year later he died, and as noted historian J.B. Bury memorably puts it, "the empire of the Huns . . . was soon scattered to the winds" (*History of the Later Roman Empire,* vol. 1, p. 296). **See** Battle of Chalons (Chapter 7).

Augustine

(Aurelius Augustinus, later Saint Augustine, A.D. 354–430) The most important of the late Latin Christian writers, especially to later ages, he was born at Thagaste, in North Africa, the son of a pagan father and Christian mother, Monica. Thanks to his parents, Augustine received a thorough classical education and for a while taught rhetoric in both Rome and Carthage. Long a follower of a heretical Christian sect, the Manichaeans, in 387, inspired by the influential bishop Ambrose, he converted to Catholicism; in 395 Augustine became bishop of the North African port town of Hippo. There he spent the rest of his life,

Augustine of Hippo (later St. Augustine), the most influential writer of later Roman times, appears with his mother in this modern painting.

dying in 430 while the Vandals were attacking the town.

A brilliant thinker and writer, Augustine helped to crystallize and institutionalize many existing or developing aspects of church doctrine, including that of original sin, the notion that human beings are born as sinners because of Adam's transgressions against God in the Garden of Eden. Only by gaining God's grace through the sacrament of baptism, said Augustine, could a person be accepted into heaven. Indeed, Augustine is second only to Paul as a shaper of Christian thought. Augustine's writings, including some ninety-three books and numerous sermons and letters, exerted a profound influence on medieval and early modern thinkers and theologians, particularly the sixteenth-century Protestant thinker John Calvin. Prominent among Augustine's works are *On the Trinity* (completed in 419), discussing God's threefold nature; and the *Confessions* (ca. 397–400), an autobiographical account up to the time of his conversion. By far his greatest and most influential work is the monumental *City of God* (completed in 426), in which he criticizes Greco-Roman culture and paganism and defends Christian ideals. **See** *City of God* (Chapter 6).

Augustus

Born Gaius Octavius the Younger in Rome on September 23, 63 B.C., he later became Augustus, the first and arguably the greatest Roman emperor. Known simply as Octavian throughout his youth and early manhood, he was short, very slight of build, and prone to sickness. His great-uncle and adoptive father, the powerful and influential Julius Caesar, early took a liking to him and the two became close after the young man accompanied the general on a campaign in Spain. During the winter of 45–44 B.C., Caesar sent Octavian to Greece to study under the distinguished scholar Apollodorus of Pergamum.

There, a few months later, the young man received the news of Caesar's murder in the Senate. This event changed the course of Octavian's life, as he was thrust, at age nineteen, into the power struggle that erupted after Caesar's death. Shrewdly realizing that his dead relative's name still held prestige and authority, especially among Caesar's soldiers, Octavian immediately began calling himself Gaius Julius Caesar. Most leading Romans of the day, including Mark Antony, Caesar's chief military associate, failed to recognize the young man's abilities and at first treated him with disdain. But Octavian soon proved himself a worthy opponent by acquiring the backing of a small army of Caesar's troops and forcing Antony to flee Rome.

Octavian next boldly suggested that he, Antony, and the powerful general Marcus Lepidus should become allies. The other two men accepted and the three formed the Second Triumvirate in the winter of 43 B.C. After murdering many of their political opponents, including the great orator and senator Cicero, they defeated Caesar's leading assassins (Brutus and Cassius) in Greece in October 42. Not long afterward, however, the triumvirate disintegrated. First Octavian and Antony pushed the weaker Lepidus aside; then they faced off in still another round of civil strife, in which Octavian defended Italy and Rome's western territories against Antony, who held sway over the Roman lands and troops of the eastern Mediterranean. Supporting Antony in his bid for ultimate power was his lover, Cleopatra VII, queen of Egypt, who threw her country's vast resources of money and grain behind the effort. But though their forces were formidable, the lovers had met their match in Octavian. Aided by his friend, the gifted military leader Marcus Agrippa, Octavian decisively defeated them at Actium (in Greece) on September 2, 31 B.C., finally ending Rome's destructive cycle of civil wars.

These events left Octavian, now thirty-two, the most powerful figure in the Roman world. In the years that followed, he used that power to bring about profound and lasting changes in Rome's political, administrative, and social systems. Tired of the suffering, destruction, and uncertainty the many years of civil strife had brought, most Romans longed for peace and were now willing to follow the lead of one powerful individual, as long as he was capable, fair, and loyal to Rome and its cherished ideals. Realizing this, slowly and shrewdly Octavian consolidated a wide array of the former Republic's powers, always in what appeared to be full accordance with established Roman law and tradition. He did not attempt to confer any powers or titles on himself. Indeed, he saw no need, since the senators were more than happy to do so, giving him the title of Augustus, the "revered one" in 27 B.C. He himself used the unofficial and more modest name of *princeps,* meaning "first citizen," bolstering his image as a simple man of the people. But though he and his intelligent, dignified, and faithful wife, Livia, lived in a small house and rejected a lavish lifestyle, he was nothing less than an emperor with far-reaching powers.

The hallmark of Augustus's long and constructive reign proved to be the concept of positive reform—of healing the nation's wounds, of building anew, and of restoring lost values. This policy was most evident in his impressive public building programs. Believing that the Roman Empire needed a capital that would stand as an example of the wealth, nobility, civility, and other "superior" qualities of the Mediterranean's so-called master race, he undertook a mighty burst of urban renewal and large-scale municipal reorganization. As the Roman historian Suetonius sums up: "Augustus so improved [Rome's] appearance that he could justifiably boast: 'I found Rome built of bricks; I leave her clothed in marble'" (*Augustus* 28, in *The Twelve Caesars*). Augustus also significantly reorganized and improved the military, creating a standing, permanent army and providing the troops adequate rewards and pensions to keep them more loyal to him and the state than to their generals. In addition, he built two large imperial navies and several smaller provincial navies. His other achievements included the creation of a police force for the capital city, substantial and efficient administrative and tax reforms, and steadfast financial and moral support for the arts and literature. He listed these and many other deeds in his *Res gestae,* a synopsis of his accomplishments.

Overall, Augustus became such a constructive, effective, and beloved ruler that when he died on August 19, A.D. 14 at the age of seventy-six, the Roman nation grieved more solemnly than it had for any other leader. More than a hundred thousand people, many of them weeping openly, marched in his magnificent funeral procession, at the climax of which a lone eagle was released, symbolizing his soul ascending to heaven. Truly one of the most remarkable rulers in human history, as a young man he had risen ruthlessly through the corridors of power to become an all-powerful dictator; but unlike most other absolute rulers, once he achieved that position he displayed uncommon wisdom, compassion, and justice. **See** Antony, Mark; Livia; **also** Augustan Age of literature; *Res gestae* (Chapter 6); **and** Battle of Actium (Chapter 7).

Aurelian

(Lucius Domitius Aurelianus, ca. A.D. 215–275) Emperor of Rome from 270 to 275, he was one of a handful of strong and talented military leaders who managed to save the Empire from collapse during the anarchy of the mid–third century. From humble origins, he rose through the ranks, becoming *magister equitum* (cavalry commander) under Claudius II Gothicus. When Claudius died in 270, Aurelian, whom the soldiers nicknamed "Hand-on-Hilt," became emperor and almost immediately defeated a German tribe near the Danube River. The following year he crushed a Vandal army and won other victories over the Germans. Aurelian's best-known victory, however, was over the forces of Zenobia, queen of the Near Eastern city-state of Palmyra; he captured her and on returning to Rome marched her in his triumph. But she outlived him, for in 275 an assassination plot engineered by members of the Praetorian Guard succeeded. **See** Zenobia.

Ausonius, Decimus Magnus
(ca. A.D. 310–ca. 393) A Latin poet who hailed from Gaul and served as tutor to the emperor Gratian. After the latter ascended the throne in 367, Ausonius rose rapidly in the government, eventually attaining the rank of consul in 379. Soon after the emperor's murder in 383, the poet returned to Gaul, where he apparently spent the rest of his life. He wrote numerous poems with diverse themes, perhaps the best known being the *Ephemeris* (*A Day's Events*), which describes in detail a typical day in his life.

Bar Cochba
For this Jewish rebel leader who challenged the Romans in the second century A.D., **see** Hadrian.

Benedict
(A.D. 480–547) One of the principle figures in the Christian monastic movement in its formative years and founder of the Benedictine order of monks, he was born in the Italian town of Nursia. At about age twenty, he became a hermit, but after a few years he attracted a group of disciples and founded a monastery in the remote village of Monte Cassino (between Rome and Naples). Benedict is best known for his *Rule,* a document outlining the expected rules and daily disciplines of monastic life; it became a model widely followed by European monks in the centuries that followed. **See** Christianity (Chapter 3).

Boethius, Anicius Manlius Severinus
(ca. A.D. 476–524) A noted public official, philosopher, and Christian writer, he hailed from a prominent Roman family and headed the civil service in Rome under Theodoric the Ostrogoth beginning sometime after 510. Suspected of treachery, Boethius was imprisoned in 523 and executed the following year. The last major Latin writer with a mastery of Greek, he set out to translate and comment on all of Plato's and Aristotle's works; although he did not complete this grandiose project, the portions he did finish, along with his handbooks on geometry, music, and astronomy, were widely used in medieval schools. His most famous work, the *Consolation of Philosophy,* written in his jail cell shortly before his death, became one of the most widely translated and beloved works of the Middle Ages and Renaissance.

Boudicca
(mid–first century A.D.) A renowned "warrior woman," who for a time led the Iceni, a Celtic tribe of central Britain. When her husband, the king, died about A.D. 60, he left half his kingdom and royal treasury to Nero, then Rome's emperor. But Britain's governor arrogantly plundered the dead man's kingdom and flogged his widow, Boudicca. In response to this outrage, the Iceni, with Boudicca as their war leader, launched a full-scale rebellion, which tens

of thousands of warriors from neighboring tribes eagerly joined. She led them against the Roman stronghold of Londinium (now London), utterly destroying it, and went on to massacre more than seventy thousand Roman settlers. But soon afterward a Roman army defeated her and she may have committed suicide to avoid capture. **See** Britain (Chapter 2) **and** Iceni (Chapter 7).

Brutus, Lucius Junius

(late sixth century B.C.) According to tradition, Brutus, the pivotal figure in the establishment of the Roman Republic, opposed the rule of his uncle, King Tarquinius Superbus. When Lucretia, wife of Brutus's friend, the nobleman L. Tarquinius Collatinus, was raped by the king's son and soon afterward killed herself, Brutus vowed to topple the monarchy. With the aid of other leading citizens, he led a revolution that ousted the royal family and founded a republican form of government (ca. 509 B.C.). One of the Republic's first two elected consuls (with Collatinus), Brutus became known for his strong sense of justice. He died while resisting an invading Etruscan army. The main source of his story is Livy's history of Rome. **See** Monarchy **and** Republic, Roman (both Chapter 4).

Brutus, Marcus Junius

(ca. 85–42 B.C.) A prominent senator and one of the two leaders (along with Cassius) of the conspiracy to murder Julius Caesar, Brutus fought for Pompey against Caesar at the Battle of Pharsalus (48 B.C.). Following Pompey's defeat, Brutus asked for and received the pardon of the victorious Caesar, who appointed him praetor early in 44. But soon afterward, perhaps upset by the thought that Caesar's cronies would rule Rome while the dictator was away on an upcoming campaign, Brutus joined the murder plot. According to the Roman historian Suetonius, when Brutus plunged his dagger into Caesar, the dying

man uttered the words "Even you, Brutus!" (later immortalized by Shakespeare as "Et tu, Brute!"). The quotation has been interpreted as a reference to the possibility that Brutus was actually Caesar's son, since it was rumored that Caesar had once had an affair with the younger man's mother. After the assassination, Brutus fled to Greece, where he and Cassius raised an army to resist Caesar's successors, Antony and Octavian. At the Battle of Philippi, fought in northern Greece in 42, the conspirators lost and Brutus took his own life. He was known for his love of learning and oratorical skills, and his friend, the great statesman Cicero, made him one of the main speakers in the treatise titled *Brutus*. **See** Caesar, Gaius Julius; Cassius, Gaius Longinus; **also** Battle of Philippi (Chapter 7).

Caesar, Gaius Julius

Perhaps the most famous of all Roman figures, without doubt one of the greatest military leaders of all times, and the man who brought the Roman Republic to its knees, Gaius Julius Caesar was born on July 12, 100 B.C. His parents, Gaius and Aurelia, were well-to-do patricians who traced their family lineage back to Julus, a son of the legendary hero Aeneas. Not much is known about Caesar's childhood, but he no doubt witnessed or heard firsthand about the exploits of his uncle, the successful general Gaius Marius; and as a young man he supported Marius after the aging general took control of Rome while his powerful rival, Sulla, was on a military campaign. But Marius died suddenly in 86 B.C. and Sulla returned in 83 and seized the capital, killing thousands of Marius's sup-

According to the Roman writer Suetonius, Caesar was a tall, imposing, and very well groomed individual.

porters. Probably because Caesar was a fellow aristocrat, Sulla at first spared him. But when the dictator demanded that the youth divorce his wife, Cornelia, to show his allegiance, Caesar refused and went into hiding.

Five years later, when Sulla died unexpectedly, Caesar returned and began to make a name for himself. He threw lavish parties and did favors for acquaintances, calculating correctly that in this way he could build a strong political reputation; and in 69 B.C. he secured the office of quaestor. The following year he married Pompeia, an aristocratic young woman related to the former dictator, Sulla (Cornelia having died three years earlier). Caesar next became aedile (an official in charge

of public buildings and games), a job in which he outdid himself, staging the most spectacular gladiatorial fights Rome had ever witnessed. This made him a household name and significantly contributed to his election as praetor in 63 B.C.

Many senators saw the brilliant and ambitious Caesar as a threat and sought to keep him from gaining more power, especially the consulship. But he shrewdly outmaneuvered them. In the summer of 60 B.C., he engineered a major political alliance, later called the First Triumvirate, with the two most powerful men in Rome, the noted general Pompey and the wealthy financier Crassus. With their backing, he easily became consul and used, or more accurately misused, his authority to intimidate and silence almost all opposition. Already, he was thinking ahead, reasoning that to maintain his power base when no longer a consul, he would need an army more loyal to him than to the state. So he used his consular influence to gain the governorship of Cisalpine Gaul (in northern Italy), as well as the Gallic province—the Narbonese.

When Caesar took charge of these provinces in 58 B.C., he found about twenty-four thousand troops at his disposal and immediately began raising more recruits. He needed as large a force as he could muster, for his real interest was not in administering the Narbonese, but in conquering Transalpine Gaul, the then little known lands encompassing what are now France and Belgium. Caesar launched campaign after campaign against the tribal peoples of this region in a series of conquests spanning almost eight years. Along the way, he won the admiration and devotion of his troops and also gained much prestige and power for greatly expanding the Roman realm. As gifted a writer as he was a general, he also kept a log of his exploits, the *Commentary on the Gallic War,* which provides modern scholars with a wealth of information about these events and the peoples of Gaul in that era.

Returning from his Gallic conquests in 50 B.C., Caesar camped his army in Cisalpine Gaul and contemplated his next move. Crassus had died in 53, the triumvirate had fallen apart, and the Senate now ordered Caesar to relinquish command of his armies. Refusing to do so, on January 10, 49, he led his men across the Rubicon River, plunging the Roman world into a devastating civil war. As his forces marched on Rome, Pompey and many senators fled to Greece, but Caesar followed, and in August of the following year, on the plain of Pharsalus (in east-central Greece), he won a stunning victory over Pompey and the senatorial forces. Thereafter Caesar won one victory after another, defeating adversaries in Egypt, Asia Minor, Africa, and Spain. When he finally and triumphantly entered the capital in September 45 B.C., he was the undisputed master of the Roman world and quite literally the most powerful human being who had ever lived.

Now firmly in control of the government, Caesar surprised those who saw him as nothing more than a brutal warmonger by proving himself a civil administrator of extraordinary skill, perhaps even of genius. His adept handling of problems ranging from the national debt to an inaccurate and confusing calendar suggested that he might lead Rome into a bright and constructive future. But in his rise to power he had made many enemies, and he now proceeded to make more. He firmly believed that the best way to achieve permanent peace and prosperity was to abandon many of the old republican ways and to place most state power in the hands of a benevolent dictator. Accordingly, in February 44 B.C. he took the bold and fateful step of declaring himself dictator *perpetuo* ("for life"). Fearing that his absolute rule might spell the end of the Republic, a group of senators stabbed him to death in the Senate House on March 15 (the "Ides of March").

However, this rash act not only did not bring back the Republic, but ignited another ruinous civil war, from which eventually emerged the same sort of benevolent dictator Caesar had envisioned (namely, his adopted son, Octavian, who became Augustus, the first Roman emperor). By leaving behind the blueprint from which his immediate successors constructed the immensely successful Roman Empire, the irrepressible Caesar had attained an even greater triumph in death than he had in life. **See** Augustus; Pompey; **also** Gaul (Chapter 2); *Commentaries on the Gallic and Civil Wars* (Chapter 6); **and** Battle of Pharsalus; Battle of Thapsus; civil wars; siege of Alesia (all Chapter 7).

Caligula

(Gaius Julius Caesar Germanicus, A.D. 12–41) A Roman emperor notorious for his corruption of imperial power, he was the son of the noted general Germanicus and his wife, Agrippina the Elder. The boy accompanied them on campaign, living in army camps, where he acquired the affectionate nickname of Caligula, meaning "Little Boots," which he later professed to hate, but which stuck nonetheless. Succeeding to the throne in 37, he was at first popular with both the senators and the populace. But a few months later he had a bout of serious illness, which may have affected his mind, for afterward his personality and behavior became increasingly unbalanced, deranged, and corrupt. Disregarding the public good, he spent most of the state treasury on public games and personal luxuries, including enormously lavish banquets. Moreover, to raise the money to support his extravagant lifestyle, he demanded expensive gifts from wealthy Romans (often including their entire estates) and imposed several heavy and unfair taxes. He also began executing people for the slightest infraction and, perhaps worst of all, suggested that statues of himself, a "living god," replace those of Jupiter in temples. Considering these and other excesses, it is hardly surprising that assassination plots were hatched; one of these, carried out by the Praetorian Guard, succeeded in January 41.

Camillus, Marcus Furius

(d. ca. 365 B.C.) A noted early Roman general and statesman, most of his real deeds are obscured by legend and tradition. According to the Roman historian Livy, he commanded the army that captured the Etruscan city of Veii in 396 B.C. and not long afterward overcame another Etruscan town, Falerii. In 391 B.C., Camillus went into exile, but the following year his countrymen recalled him and made him dictator to deal with the crisis resulting from the Gauls' sack of Rome. Supposedly, he defeated the invaders and went on to be appointed dictator four more times. Camillus is also credited with several crucial military innovations, including the abandonment of the phalanx and adoption of maniples, although in reality he was probably just one of a succession of reformers who instituted these changes over the course of several decades.

Caracalla

(Marcus Aurelius Antoninus, A.D. 188–217) Emperor of Rome from 211 to 217, he was the eldest son of the strong emperor Septimius Severus. In the late 190s, Severus openly groomed both Caracalla and his younger brother Geta for the throne, which led to enmity between the two royal siblings. On Severus's death in 211, it was proposed that the brothers divide the Empire, but Caracalla foiled this plan by murdering Geta the following year. Seeing himself as a reincarnation of the Greek conqueror Alexander the Great, the new emperor concentrated most of his en-

The magnificent baths of Caracalla, a mediocre leader best known for granting citizenship to all free adults in the Empire.

ergies on military matters and large-scale construction projects. These endeavors were very expensive; to help pay for them he raised taxes. He also made a grand show of granting citizenship to all free adult inhabitants of the Empire in 212, but this was mainly a ploy to increase the number of taxable citizens. Caracalla's most imposing building project was his public baths, among the most grandiose ever erected in the Roman capital. In 213 he launched military campaigns that took him from the borders of Germany, through Greece and Egypt, and on into Mesopotamia. During these journeys, he increasingly displayed the unbalanced, cruel sides of his character, until the powerful Praetorian prefect Macrinus killed him in April 217 and took his place on the throne.

Carus, Marcus Aurelius

(d. A.D. 283) Rome's emperor from 282 to 283, he was born in Gaul and became Praetorian prefect in 276. When the emperor Probus was killed by his own troops in 282, Carus took the throne and soon bestowed the title of Caesar on his own two sons, Carinus and Numerian. Carus then aggressively campaigned along the northern borders, decisively defeating the barbarian Sarmations and Quadi. Carus's armies were also victorious on the Persian front, where the province of Mesopotamia was restored to Rome in 283. At the height of the campaign, however, he died, perhaps of illness, and his son Numerian succeeded him.

Cassiodorus, Flavius Magnus Aurelius

(ca. A.D. 490–583) A noted Roman statesman and writer, he served as head of the civil service under the Ostrogothic ruler Theodoric and also as a consul and senator before retiring to his rural estates in Calabria (in southeastern Italy). There, Cassiodorus, a devout Christian, founded a monastery at Vivarium, where his monks diligently copied manuscripts, helping establish a tradition that over time transmitted pieces of classical culture to medieval and early modern European society. Among his major written works were his *History of the Goths,* a history of the known world to the year 519, and the *Institutiones,* a guide to both religious and secular education. The latter work was based largely on the "seven liberal arts"—grammar, rhetoric, dialectic (discussion or dialogue), arithmetic, geometry, music, and astronomy—which became standard in later European education.

Cassius, Gaius Longinus

(d. 42 B.C.) Best known as one of the leaders of the conspiracy to assassinate Julius Caesar, Cassius, a prominent senator, earlier served with distinction in the military. He fought in the Battle of Carrhae in the Near East in 53 B.C. and supported Pompey in the civil war against Caesar in the early 40s B.C. Cassius received a pardon from Caesar, but turned on him soon after the latter declared himself dictator for life. After the assassination, Cassius fled to Greece, where in 42 B.C. he suffered defeat at the hands of Antony and Octavian at Philippi and immediately afterward committed suicide.

Catiline

(Lucius Sergius Catilina, d. 62 B.C.) A Roman nobleman who early in his career earned a reputation for dishonesty and shady dealings, he served as praetor in 68 B.C. and then became governor of the province of Africa. Defeated by Cicero for the consulship of 63 B.C. (in the elections held the year before), Catiline made another unsuccessful bid for the consulship, after which he decided to stage a coup. The plot—to kill the consuls and seize control of the government—was not well organized or concealed, however. Learning of it, Cicero exposed Catiline in the Senate, forcing him to flee the capital. Soon afterward, Cicero's fellow consul, Antonius, assembled an army and defeated and killed Catiline. **See** Cicero, Marcus Tullius.

Cato the Elder

(Marcus Porcius Cato, 234–149 B.C.) One of the most prominent statesmen and writers of republican times, he fought as a military tribune in the Second Punic War against Carthage's Hannibal. After the war, Cato served as praetor in 198 B.C., consul in 195, and then governor of Spain. He is most famous for his very conservative, traditional social and political attitudes, which earned him the permanent nickname of "the censor" long after he actually served in that office (in 184). Indeed, perceiving that Roman morals had become lax, he worked, rather unrealistically as it turned out, for a return to the so-called simplicity of the small agricultural state Rome had once been. Cato also displayed his conservative bent in his attitude toward Carthage. As an old man he made an official visit, as a senator, to that former Roman enemy and was shocked and disturbed that the Carthaginians had managed to regain so much prosperity after losing the Second Punic War. Thereafter, Cato made it his business to see that Carthage, which he perceived as a serious potential danger to his own country, was eliminated; for the rest of his days, whenever he spoke in the Senate, no matter what the topic being discussed, he ended his speeches with the phrase "Carthage must be destroyed!" He was likely pleased when the Third Punic War, which would ultimately end with Carthage's obliteration, began just prior to his death in 149 B.C.

Cato's writings were wide-ranging and influential. His *Origines,* which has not survived, covered Rome's foundation and other historical events. It was notable because it was composed in Latin, rather than Greek, as had been the custom of earlier Roman historical writers, and also because it inspired other Romans to write about their history. His *On Agriculture,* parts of which have survived, gives advice to estate owners on growing crops, managing slaves, and other farming matters. The section in which he describes slaves as objects to be discarded when they are no longer useful is often quoted to show the more conservative, heartless side of Roman slavery. Another of his works, *The Sayings of Marcus Cato,* a collection of moral adages, became extremely popular in European schools during the Middle Ages.

Cato the Younger

(Marcus Porcius Cato "Uticensis", 95–46 B.C.) The great-grandson of Cato the Elder, he was, along with Cicero, one of the last great senators and republican champions during the years in which the Republic was crumbling. Cato backed Cicero in the decision to execute Catiline's supporters (who had attempted to topple the government) in 63 B.C. Later, Cato became the chief opponent of the so-called First Triumvirate and a thorn in the side of Julius Caesar, continually speaking out against and hindering the ambitions of both. Though he distrusted Pompey, Cato took his side against Caesar in the civil war of the early 40s B.C. Early in 46, in despair after Caesar's victory at Thapsus, Cato, now residing in Utica (in Africa), committed suicide.

Catullus, Gaius Valerius

(ca. 84–ca. 54 B.C.) A distinguished and popular Roman poet, Catullus was born at Verona (in northern Italy) into a wealthy family. About 62 B.C. he journeyed to Rome and joined a circle of poets known as the *neoterics* ("moderns" or "young ones"). Eventually, he fell in love with a married woman whose name was likely Clodia, but whom he referred to in twenty-five of his poems as Lesbia. The poems trace his relationship with her from the ardor of first infatuation to the pain of final parting, a literary model that influenced many of his successors, including Ovid, Propertius, and Tibullus. Catullus's other poems cover a wide range of subjects and genres, among them friendship, political satire, and wedding songs. **See** poetry (Chapter 6).

Celsus, Aulus Cornelius

For this first-century A.D. Roman medical writer, **see** medicine (Chapter 5).

Chrysostom, John

(later Saint John, ca. A.D. 346–407) Known as one of the four great "eastern fathers" of the Christian Church, he was a prominent religious leader and renowned orator. He was born in Antioch and as a young man became a monk, living in solitude in the Syrian mountains. After six years he returned to Antioch, became ordained as a presbyter (elder) in the local church, and began preaching. His fame as an orator became so great that he was known as the "golden-mouthed." In 398 the eastern emperor Arcadius and his grasping palace chamberlain, Eutropius, forced him, evidently against his will, to become bishop of Constantinople. Once in the post, John refused to be a lackey to the royal court and courageously spoke out against its corruption and overindulgence in luxury, which brought him into conflict with the emperor, empress, and other leading political figures. Eventually, Arcadius banished him to a bleak town on the shores of the Black Sea, where the great preacher died of illness in 407.

Cicero, Marcus Tullius

(106–43 B.C.) More is known about this great statesman, who gave his life trying to preserve the disintegrating Roman Republic, than about any other person of the ancient world. His prominence as a lawyer, orator, consul, senator, patriot, and prodigious and gifted writer made him loom large in the Roman consciousness, both in his own and later eras. After his death his speeches became textbooks for the teaching of oratory and his ideas and deeds were retold and discussed by scholars and writers of all kinds and nationalities. Most of what is known about him comes from his own writings, a mammoth literary output that includes fifty-eight lengthy speeches, over eight hundred letters, and some two thousand pages of philosophical and rhetorical tracts, including the monumental *On Duties, On the Republic,* and the *Tusculan Disputations.* Overall, his works comprise a treasure trove of information about himself, his friends, his society, and the Roman character. The letters are especially telling and timeless; about half of them are addressed

to Cicero's intimate friend Titus Pomponius Atticus (110–32 B.C.), a wealthy and prominent figure whose daughter, Attica, married Augustus's adviser Marcus Agrippa, and whose sister, Pomponia, married Cicero's brother, Quintus.

Cicero was born on January 3, 106 B.C. in Arpinum (sixty miles southeast of Rome). Well-bred, he received an excellent education, studying with the legendary Apollonius Molo (from the Greek island of Rhodes), who taught him rhetoric, and the greatest lawyer of the day, Mucius Scaevola. Under the guidance of these men, Cicero's considerable innate talents quickly matured and his rise to public prominence was nothing less than meteoric. In 80 B.C., when he was twenty-six, he attracted much attention in his first big case, in which he successfully defended a man named Roscius, who had been accused of killing his own father. Cicero went on to serve as quaestor in 75 B.C., became a senator in 74, and was elected aedile in 69. Shortly before his aedileship, he acquired added fame for his vigorous prosecution of Gaius Verres, governor of the province of Sicily, who stood accused of mismanagement of funds while in office. The prestige gained from the case helped Cicero to become praetor in 66 and eventually consul. The Romans came to see that he was a patriotic man who genuinely believed in the republican system and hated to see it exploited and corrupted, as it had increasingly come to be, by rich, powerful men. And many people found him a refreshing and reassuring representative of old-fashioned Roman values of honesty, unselfish service to the state, and duty to country.

These personal and patriotic qualities shone most brightly in the crisis that gripped Rome in the months following his election as consul in 63 B.C.—the infamous Catilinian conspiracy. On learning that Catiline was plotting to kill him and his fellow consul and then take over the government, Cicero acted swiftly and boldly. In a magnificent speech to the Senate, with Catiline himself sitting before him in the chamber, Cicero exposed the scheme and the coup quickly collapsed. For rescuing the government, Cicero was applauded as a hero and acclaimed "father of his country."

Cicero naturally opposed the coalition (the First Triumvirate) formed by Caesar, Pompey, and Crassus in 60 B.C. and remained a thorn in the side of these strongmen, who proceeded to run roughshod over the state. But in later years, as they steadily gained the upper hand, he became increasingly disillusioned. Time and again he found his efforts to reinstate the Senate's authority impeded by Caesar and Pompey. When civil war erupted in 49, Cicero held himself and his colleagues partly to blame, mainly for their failure to stop the rise of the generals in the first place. "Do you see," he asked in a letter to Atticus, "the kind of man into whose hands the state has fallen? . . . It pains me to think of the mistakes and wrongs of ours that are responsible for this" (*Letters to Atticus,* 8.13). Later, in 46, by which time Caesar had become a virtual dictator, Cicero retired from politics, feeling his voice was no longer effective.

However, in 44 B.C., after Caesar's assassination and the assumption of his dictatorial powers by his associate, Mark Antony, Cicero felt compelled to reenter the political fray. To this end, the sixty-two-year-old statesman composed several speeches denouncing Antony (the *Philippics*). Antony took revenge for these attacks after he joined with Lepidus and Octavian in the winter of 43 to form a new triumvirate. Their first order of business was to eradicate their enemies; not surprisingly, Cicero's name appeared at the top of Antony's list. The triumvir's henchman caught up with the great orator at his country house at Astura (about fifty miles south of Rome), cut off his head and hands, and nailed them to a platform in Rome's main square, a barbaric act that exemplified the depths of self-serving ambition and brutality to which many Roman leaders had sunk. Indeed, in a very real sense the Roman Republic and its noblest qualities died with Cicero. **See** Caesar, Gaius Julius; Catiline; **also,** *Letters* of Cicero; *On Duties; On Oratory; On the Republic;* orations of Cicero; *Tusculan Disputations* (all Chapter 6).

Cincinnatus, Lucius Quinctius

(fifth century B.C.) A semilegendary hero of early Rome, of whom it was said that he accepted the office of dictator in 458 B.C. to deal with a threat posed by a neighboring Italian tribe (the Aequi). Having defeated the enemy army, he dutifully resigned his office after only sixteen days and returned to his farm. Cincinnatus later became a model of old-fashioned Roman agrarian simplicity and virtue.

Claudian

(Claudius Claudianus, d. ca. A.D. 404) One of the last great Latin poets, he was born in Alexandria and traveled to Rome in the mid–390s. Soon he became a successful court poet under the young western emperor Honorius, extolling his virtues and those of his leading ministers in various verses. Claudian also composed works that severely criticized Honorius's enemies, notably in the eastern Roman court. *The Rape of Proserpine,* telling the famous story of a young maiden's abduction by the god of the underworld, of which about eleven hundred lines survive, was Claudian's greatest work.

Claudius

(10 B.C.–A.D. 54) A son of Drusus the Elder and the uncle of the emperor Caligula, he was one of the most notable and accomplished emperors of the early Empire. As a young man, Claudius was thought by most people at court to be mentally slow and not

"ruler material"; therefore he spent most of his time in scholarly pursuits, writing histories (none of which have survived), including one chronicling the reign of his illustrious predecessor, Augustus. When Caligula was suddenly assassinated in A.D. 41, however, the Praetorian Guard unexpectedly proclaimed him, as the last surviving male adult in the family, emperor. Rising to the occasion, Claudius showed that he was not only competent but quite an able and popular ruler. He built hundreds of roads, temples, aqueducts, and other public works; expanded the civil service in the provinces; and extended the Empire's frontiers, making Lycia (in Asia Minor) and Thrace (in northern Greece) new provinces. In addition, in 43 he ordered the invasion of Britain, which subsequently became a prosperous province.

Unfortunately for Claudius, he was not so accomplished in managing his own family affairs. His third wife, Messalina, plotted to kill him, forcing him to execute her in 48. Next, he married the scheming Agrippina the Younger, Caligula's sister and therefore Claudius's niece, and mother of the future corrupt emperor Nero. In 51, she persuaded Claudius to adopt Nero formally as his son and heir; three years later she reportedly (though not conclusively) poisoned her husband, allowing Nero to ascend the throne. **See** Agrippina the Younger; Caligula; Nero; **also** Britain (Chapter 2).

Claudius II, "Gothicus"

(A.D. 214–270) One of the stronger emperors of the later years of the so-called third-century anarchy, he was a general under the emperor Gallienus in 268. When Gallienus died that year, the troops chose Claudius for the throne. He pushed back the Alamanni tribe, which had invaded northern Italy, then turned farther north and defeated the Goths along the Danube frontier, earning the nickname of "Gothicus." Claudius, who showed the potential of a great leader, was unable to tend to a number of other crises in

This fanciful later depiction of the emperor Claudius shows him with European-style clothes and mustache.

other parts of the Empire, for he died of the plague early in 270.

Claudius Caecus, Appius

(flourished late fourth century B.C.) A noted Roman censor, he is most famous for his sponsorship of the construction of Rome's first aqueduct, named the Aqua Appia after him. He also backed the building of the famous Via Appia (or Appian Way), one of the major roads of Italy. A broad-minded individual, he used his influence to make it possible for well-to-do members of the middle and lower classes to become members of the Senate. In addition, he was an orator, some of whose speeches survived until Cicero's time, and the first known Roman prose writer. **See** aqueducts; roads (both Chapter 6).

Clement of Alexandria

(Titus Flavius Clemens, ca. A.D. 150–ca. 203) One of the most prominent and influential of the early Christian Church fathers, he was born a pagan in Athens. As a young man he moved to Alexandria, where he eventually became head of a noted Christian school. In that capacity he wrote several theological works, including *Exhortation to the Greeks,* which advocated the superiority of Christian over pagan ideas, and *Stromateis,* which explored the philosophical basis of Christian thought. In 202, Clement fled Alexandria during a Christian persecution instigated by the emperor Septimius Severus and soon afterward died in Palestine.

Cleopatra VII

A Greek queen of the Egyptian Ptolemaic Kingdom and one of the most famous women in history, she was born in 69 B.C., the daughter of King Ptolemy XII Auletes. When he died in 51, his will stipulated that she should rule jointly with her ten-year-old brother, Ptolemy XIII; however, the boy and his regent soon forced her to flee into the desert. She was reinstated in 48 by the Roman general Julius Caesar, with whom she had a love affair and a son (Ptolemy XV, or Caesarion). In 41, three years after Caesar's murder, Cleopatra became the lover and ally of his former assistant, Mark Antony. In the years that followed, hoping to gain dominance in the Roman world, they engaged in a propaganda war with Caesar's adopted son, Octavian (the future emperor Augustus); when the conflict erupted into violence at Actium (in western Greece) in 31 B.C., they were defeated. The following year, after Octavian landed his forces in Egypt, the proud queen, last of the Ptolemies and also the last major independent Greek ruler in antiquity, took her own life. **See** Egypt (Chapter 2); **and** Antony, Mark; Augustus; Caesar, Gaius Julius; Ptolemy XII Auletes; **also** Battle of Actium (Chapter 7).

Columella, Lucius Junius Moderatus

(first century B.C.) Hailing from Roman Spain, he is best known for writing an in-fluential treatise about farming, *On Agriculture,* in twelve books. The work, composed in simple, straightforward prose (except for Book 10, which is set in verse), covers most aspects of farm life, including livestock, beekeeping, and the duties of the farm manager (bailiff) and his wife. Columella also wrote a shorter agricultural work, of which only one section—about trees—survives.

Commodus

(A.D. 161–192) The son of the emperor Marcus Aurelius, he ruled the Empire from 180 to 192. In character the opposite of his illustrious father, Commodus was vain, selfish, spoiled, and lazy, and in general neglected his public responsibilities, choosing instead to indulge in personal luxuries and pleasure. Fancying himself a great warrior, he courted scandal by fighting in the arena as a gladiator (although always protected by his guards); it is said that he fought wild animals as well as men, killing a hundred tigers with bow and arrow in a single exhibition. On the political front, Commodus, unwilling to interrupt his comfortable lifestyle with time-consuming military campaigns, struck a deal with some barbarian tribes, allowing many of their number to settle in the northern provinces and some thirteen thousand of them to enlist in the Roman army. He also initiated a reign of terror in the capital, executing many prominent people on flimsy charges. Few were surprised or sorry when one of the several plots to assassinate him succeeded in 192.

Constantine I

Known to history as Constantine "the Great," his reign as emperor of Rome marked one of the major turning points in the Roman saga and in European history as a whole. This was chiefly because of his steadfast support and promotion of Christianity, which up to his day had been a minor, hated, and often persecuted faith. He was born in about 285 at Naissus (in the province of Upper Moesia) and was very close to his mother, Helena, originally a barmaid, whom many years later, after her death, the Christian Church would declare a saint. His father, Constantius, was an outstanding professional soldier and close associate of Diocletian, who became emperor in 284. Thanks to Constantius's connections, Constantine grew up in the privileged, splendid, but often volatile and dangerous imperial court. When Constantius was chosen as one of the four rulers in Diocletian's Tetrarchy in 293, the former took charge of Gaul and Britain and ruled from Trier (in northern Gaul). To ensure Constantius's allegiance and good behavior, Diocletian kept the youthful Constantine in the eastern capital of Nicomedia.

In the complex political intrigues and civil wars that followed Diocletian's abdication in 305, Constantius died and Constantine gained both the allegiance of his father's troops (in 306) and the title of western emperor (in 307). Eventually, Maxentius, son of the retired tetrarch Maximian, seized the city of Rome and illegally declared himself emperor; in 312 Constantine marched his army into Italy, intent on unseating the usurper. According to Constantine's contemporary biographer, the Christian bishop Eusebius, on October 27, as the army neared Rome, Constantine beheld a miraculous vision—a shining cross in the sky. Interpreting this as a sign of support from the Christian god, the next day Constantine had his soldiers paint on their shields a Christian symbol; then, at Rome's Milvian Bridge, he won a stunning victory, killing Maxentius and several thousand of his men, many of whom fell into the Tiber and drowned.

This statue of Constantine I was created about A.D. 337, the year of his death. He is known to posterity principally as a champion of Christianity.

Constantine's seemingly Christian-aided victory seems satisfactorily to explain the favor and support he showed the Christians thereafter. Like nearly all other people of his day, he was both deeply religious and highly superstitious, and he could be expected not only to attribute his win to the Christian god, but also handsomely to repay that deity by helping its followers. Constantine did not actually convert to the faith at this moment. For a long time he remained a pagan who accepted the existence of and showed favor and gratitude to the Christian god. The first and perhaps most momentous demonstration of that gratitude was the Edict of Milan, a decree of toleration for all Christians in the Empire, issued jointly with the eastern emperor Licinius in 313. Despite the good relations the two rulers initially established, their alliance rapidly deteriorated. Disputes over succession and territorial borders led to open warfare in 316; soon afterward Licinius unexpectedly violated the toleration decree by launching an anti-Christian persecution, giving Constantine additional motivation to oppose him. The final showdown took place at Adrianople (in northern Greece) on July 3, 324. Licinius went down to defeat and for the next thirteen years Constantine reigned as sole emperor, the first man to rule both western and eastern Rome since Diocletian had first divided the leadership in 286.

Both during these power struggles and throughout the rest of his reign, Constantine's fascination with and support for Christianity remained steadfast. He granted its clergy, led by the bishops, government subsidies. He invited leading bishops to attend him at the imperial court, where they joined the impressive retinue of nobles, scribes, clerks, and other officials that always surrounded him when he appeared in public. Constantine also acted as mediator of several serious disputes that arose among the bishops. The most famous example was the council held in 325 at Nicaea (south of Nicomedia). More than two hundred bishops attended, establishing important points of church doctrine. Both Christianity and the Empire as a whole also benefited from Constantine's prodigious building programs, particularly his founding of the city of Constantinople (on the Bosporus) in 330. His principal motivation was to establish a strong base from which to defend the Empire's eastern sphere against attacks from the north and east. But because of the emperor's support of the Christians and their increasing power and influence, Constantinople also grew into a mighty Christian bastion. Constantine also erected numerous Christian churches, not only in Constantinople but in other important cities across the Empire as well.

Among the largest were those in his former Gallic capital of Trier, and in Rome, where work began on the original version of St. Peter's Basilica in about 332.

Constantine evidently had more grand architectural, administrative, and religious plans for his vast realm; however, he did not live to carry them out. Shortly before Easter in 337 he became seriously ill and, feeling that death was near, asked to be baptized. He died shortly afterward. **See** Diocletian; Eusebius; **also** Constantinople (Chapter 2); **and** Christianity (Chapter 3).

Coriolanus, Gnaeus Marcius

(early fifth century B.C.) One of Rome's greatest early heroes, he supposedly received the name Coriolanus after capturing the enemy Volscian town of Corioli in 493 B.C. After exhibiting an arrogant attitude toward the people during a corn shortage, he was accused of having tyrannical ambitions; he fled to his old enemies, the Volscians, and marched on Rome at the head of their army. At the last moment, however, he refused to attack his native city, pulled back, and as a result the Volscians executed him. Both Livy and Plutarch tell his story; Plutarch's version is that on which Shakespeare based his play *Coriolanus*.

Cornelia

(second century B.C.) The second daughter of the renowned general Scipio "Africanus" and mother of the famous Gracchi brothers (Gaius and Tiberius), she became the model for the ideal, virtuous Roman matron. After the death of her husband, Sempronius Gracchus, in 153 B.C., she managed the estate and educated their twelve children with such skill and fortitude that she remained a strong influence on all of them throughout their lives. According to Plutarch, when someone asked to see her valuable gems, she summoned her sons and declared them to be her jewels. **See** Gracchus, Gaius Sempronius; Gracchus, Tiberius Sempronius.

Crassus, Marcus Licinius

(ca. 115–53 B.C.) A wealthy Roman financier and politician, he is best known as one of the members of the so-called First Triumvirate, the powerful political alliance that also included Caesar and Pompey. The young Crassus served under the general and dictator Sulla, who rewarded him with estates confiscated from rich enemies. The younger man then continued to amass wealth through silver mining and the slave trade. Crassus earned further notoriety in 72–71 B.C. when, through his political connections, he obtained command of an army and put down the slave rebellion led by the infamous Spartacus. Despite this success, thereafter Crassus felt himself overshadowed by the military brilliance and popularity of Pompey and the two became rivals. Caesar managed to get both men to reconcile long enough to form the Triumvirate in 60, but Crassus could not match the growing reputations of the other two men; seeking more military glory of his own, he put all of his energies into a military campaign against the Parthian Empire. In 53 B.C., at Carrhae (in Mesopotamia), Crassus suffered resounding defeat and death. Reportedly, his head and right hand were severed and sent to the Parthian king. **See** Caesar, Gaius Julius; Spartacus.

Curtius Rufus, Quintus

(first century A.D.) A Roman historian and biographer about whose life virtually nothing is known, he is noted for his history of the exploits of Alexander the Great. Eight of the work's ten books have survived. They display a narrative filled with detail and drama but generally lacking in critical analysis.

Decius, Gaius Messius Quintus

(ca. A.D.190–251) Emperor of Rome from 249 to 251, he was a capable administrator and general who, serving under the emperor Philip the Arab, pushed back a group of invading Goths. Decius's troops then demanded that he become emperor. Now rivals for the throne, Decius and Philip met in battle in 249; Philip was defeated and killed, leaving his opponent firmly in charge of the Empire. Decius's reign is noted for his initiation of a major persecution against the Christians and for his continued campaigns against the Goths, who killed him in battle in June 251. **See** Philip the Arab.

Dio Cassius

(ca. A.D.150–235) This noted Greek-born historian, who is sometimes referred to as Cassius Dio, hailed from the province of Bithynia. He had a distinguished political career as a Roman official, serving as a senator, twice as consul in Rome (in 205 and 229), and also as governor of the provinces of Dalmatia and Africa. The work for which he is best known is a large-scale history of Rome in eighty books (written in Greek), which reportedly took him a total of twenty-two years to complete. Books 36 to 54, covering the events and figures of the mid-to-late first century B.C., survive complete; parts of seven other books are extant. Of the lost books, many are summarized in the works of later, especially Byzantine, historians. Dio's writing is clear and detailed, but like that of other ancient historians, his accuracy varied according to the quality of his sources. Of considerable value to modern historians are his descriptions of and commentaries on political developments, especially during the reign of Augustus and in his own day.

Diocletian

(Gaius Aurelius Valerius Diocletianus, d. A.D. 316) Emperor of Rome from 284–305 and one of its most pivotal rulers, he hailed from Split (or Spalato) in Dalmatia. Of humble origins, he enlisted in the army as a young man and through a combination of talent and hard work rose steadily through the ranks. On becoming emperor after the death of Numerian in 284, Diocletian began to transform the Roman court into an eastern-style absolute monarchy, using Sassanian Persia as a model, calling himself *dominus* (lord) and holding himself aloof, secluded from all but a privileged few. In his new bureaucracy, he grouped the provinces into thirteen regional dioceses, each administered by a vicar (*vicarius*). He also appointed an officer named Maximian "Caesar," second in command and heir to the throne. Later, in 293, Diocletian went further and created the Tetrarchy, a four-man ruling coalition with himself as senior member.

Among Diocletian's other sweeping reforms, he made military service for the sons of veterans compulsory in order to keep troop numbers up. He is also famous for his attempt to keep inflation down and the economy moving on an even keel by strictly regulating prices and wages, an effort that ultimately failed. To make sure that the flow of goods and services continued uninterrupted, he ordered that nearly all workers remain in their present professions for life, which contributed to the ongoing transformation of poor tenant farmers bound in service to wealthy landlords into hapless and hopeless "slaves of the soil" (*coloni*). Overall, Diocletian's reforms created what was in effect a new Roman realm, which modern scholars often call the Later Empire. His last unprecedented move was to abdicate the throne (in 305) and go into retirement. He hoped that a new tetrarchy would maintain the peace and was disappointed when his successors fell into civil discord. **See** Tetrarchy (Chapter 4).

Diodorus Siculus

(flourished ca. 60–30 B.C.) A Sicilian Greek, Diodorus traveled extensively around the Mediterranean world and collected many ancient documents and histories that are now lost. His massive *Library of History* (also called the *World History* or *Universal History*), covering some Greek but mostly Roman historical events, was originally composed of forty books, about fifteen of which survive complete or almost so. (Supposedly, the last complete copy of the work was destroyed when the Ottoman Turks sacked Constantinople in 1453.) As a writer, Diodorus was largely unoriginal, uninspired, uncritical, and tended frequently to repeat and even to contradict himself; also, he sometimes failed to credit his sources. Nevertheless, his history is important because it preserves material from the lost histories he used as sources, works that covered time periods and events that would otherwise remain undocumented.

Dionysius of Halicarnassus

(d. ca. 7 B.C.) A noted Greek orator and historian, he resided in Rome at the height of the Augustan Age and was undoubtedly acquainted with Livy, Virgil, and other prominent writers of that golden literary era. Impressed by Rome and its civilization, he composed a twenty-two-volume history, the *Roman Antiquities,* covering events from the traditional founding date (753 B.C.) to the start of the Punic Wars (264 B.C.). About half of this large work has survived, providing modern historians with a valuable supplement to Livy's massive Roman history. **See** Livy.

Domitian

(Titus Flavius Domitianus, A.D. 51–96) The younger son of the emperor Vespasian, he remained in Rome when his father and brother (Titus) went to Judaea to put down the Jewish rebellion. Jealous of Titus, who had received more praise than he for years, on ascending the throne in 81 (after Titus's untimely death) Domitian attempted to outdo his father and brother, who had been great generals and builders. Whether he succeeded is a matter of opinion, but he did prove himself a competent military commander in some campaigns against the Germans (83–85), finished the Colosseum, and erected the Domus Flavia, an imperial palace used by numerous succeeding rulers. In addition, he was an able and efficient administrator, especially in the early years of his rule. Over time, however, Domitian revealed the cruel and twisted dimensions of his personality. Increasingly insecure and paranoid, he eventually initiated a reign of terror in which he murdered and exiled numerous senators and public officials and alienated the rest. Finally, many in high places, including his wife, Domitia, decided it was in Rome's best interests to be rid of him. Following a carefully orchestrated plot, on September 18, 96, a group of palace attendants stabbed him to death in his own quarters.

A young Domitian (center) greets his father, the emperor Vespasian, in A.D. 69. Domitian later ascended the throne.

Donatus

For this fourth-century A.D. Christian bishop whose views were at odds with the mainstream church, **see** Donatism (Chapter 3).

Drusus, Marcus Livius

(flourished early first century B.C.) The grandfather of Augustus's wife, Livia, Drusus served as a plebeian tribune in 91 B.C. He proposed a number of democratic measures, among them that Rome's Italian allies (the *socii*) should be granted citizenship and the right to vote. His position was seen as dangerously radical at the time and

he was assassinated, but soon the Social War brought about the very outcome he had died for. **See** Social War (Chapter 7).

Drusus the Elder

(Nero Claudius Drusus, 38–9 B.C.) Son of Livia, brother of the future emperor Tiberius, and the stepson of Augustus, Drusus was the father of the noted general Nero Claudius Germanicus and the future emperor Claudius (both of whose mother was Mark Antony's daughter, Antonia Minor). Drusus himself became an accomplished military leader. Beginning in 15 B.C., he and his brother Tiberius pushed back the Raetians, a tribal group that had invaded parts of northern Italy and Gaul. Between 12 and 9 B.C., Drusus pushed into Germania, reaching the Rhine and Elbe Rivers and defeating groups of tribal Chatti and Suebi. On route home, he fell from his horse and soon afterward died, plunging the Roman populace into deep mourning. After a huge, solemn funeral ceremony in Rome's Forum, he was buried in the Campus Martius. **See** Claudius; Tiberius.

Drusus the Younger

(Drusus Julius Caesar, ca. 13 B.C.–A.D. 23) Son of the emperor Tiberius (and nephew of Drusus the Elder), he served as consul in A.D. 15 and again in 21. When Augustus died and Tiberius succeeded him as emperor in 14, Drusus, then twenty-seven, began to be groomed for the succession. However, the impetuous Drusus increasingly found himself at odds with Sejanus, Tiberius's grasping chief adviser and henchman. The hatred between the two men became so pronounced that Sejanus used a slow-acting poison to murder Drusus in 23.

Elagabalus

(Varius Avitus Bassianus Marcus Aurelius Antoninus, A.D. 204–222) Emperor of Rome from 218 to 222, he was born in Syria, the son of the niece of the emperor Caracalla's mother, Julia Domna. At a young age, Elagabalus became a leading priest of the local sun-god, Elah-Gabal, from which his popular nickname derived. After succeeding the emperor Macrinus in 218, Elagabalus traveled to Rome and immediately shocked polite society with his unusual and reportedly excessive sexual and other personal habits. (Supposedly, he was bisexual and a cross-dresser.) He also spent a great deal of time attending to the religious rituals of his Syrian god, unwisely leaving the administration of the Empire to his grandmother, Julia Maesa, and the Praetorian prefect. Eventually, thanks to Ju-

lia Maesa's scheming, the emperor's young cousin Severus Alexander gained favor at the court. When, in March 222, the jealous Elagabalus tried to remove Severus from the scene, the Praetorians rebelled and killed the unpopular young emperor. They mutilated his body, threw it into the sewer, and proclaimed Severus emperor. **See** Severus Alexander.

Ennius, Quintus

(239–169 B.C.) A major early Roman poet and playwright, he was later seen as the "father" of Roman literature and exerted considerable influence on the poets Lucretius and Virgil, as well as the orator Cicero. Ennius was born in southeastern Italy, where he learned Greek, along with Latin, and was heavily exposed to Greek cultural influences. Sponsored by the noted politician Cato the Elder, he journeyed to Rome and in the 190s B.C. earned a reputation for writing tragedies. He composed at least twenty of them (none of which have survived complete), basing their plots and styles on Greek models, especially the plays of Euripides and Aeschylus. (Like Euripides, Ennius wrote a version of *Medea.*) Ennius also wrote comedies (only four lines of which survive), satires, books of verse (of which some seventy lines are extant), and numerous other poems of varying styles and lengths. Next to his tragedies, his greatest work was said to be his *Annals,* an epic poem in eighteen books, chronicling Roman history from the legendary days of Aeneas to the early second century B.C.; fewer than six hundred lines of this notable work survive.

Epictetus

(ca. A.D. 50–ca. 120) Born a Greek slave in Phrygia (in Asia Minor), he later became a highly influential Stoic philosopher. After his master, a secretary to the emperor Nero, freed him, he studied in Rome under the noted Stoic philosopher

Musonius Rufus. About the year 89, Epictetus moved to Greece, where he spent the rest of his life lecturing. One of his ardent admirers, the historian Arrian (famous for his history of the conquests of Alexander the Great), recorded many of these lectures, publishing them in four books. Later, Arrian also published the *Manual,* a summary of Epictetus's philosophy.

Like other Stoics, Epictetus taught that the universe is controlled by providence or a greater intelligence and that all people are brothers; however, based partly on his own experiences as a slave, he aimed his message at common folk rather than the intellectual and social elite, as most other Stoic teachers did. Above all, he stressed the power of the human mind and will to overcome most of life's problems. The second-century emperor Marcus Aurelius was particularly moved and influenced by him. **See** Stoicism (Chapter 6).

Eusebius

(ca. A.D. 260–ca. 340) A noted Greek Christian writer, he served as bishop of Caesarea (in Palestine) beginning in 314 and later became a close friend of the emperor Constantine I. Eusebius's biography of that pivotal ruler, composed just after his death in 337, was designed to glorify its subject and also to show that God had worked through Constantine to bring about the triumph of Christianity; therefore, the work is of questionable authenticity in its depiction of many events. Nevertheless, it proved highly inspirational to later generations of Christians. Even more influential was Eusebius's *Ecclesiastical History,* in ten books, which chronicles the rise of the church from its early days in Palestine to the year 324. Greek, Latin, and Syriac versions of the work have survived, earning him the title of the "father" of church history. Eusebius also composed an eyewitness account of the Christian persecution insti-

gated by Diocletian and Galerius, and the *Chronicle,* containing the histories of several ancient nation-states and a chronological list of rulers supposedly starting in 2016 B.C. and ending in his own day. **See** Constantine I.

Fabius Maximus

(Quintus Fabius Maximus Verrucosus, "Cunctator," ca. 275–203 B.C.) Long remembered as a leader of vision and honor and a savior of the state, he hailed from the distinguished Fabii family, which traced its descent from Hercules. According to Plutarch, the young Fabius bore two affectionate nicknames—Verrucosus (meaning "wart-covered"), because of a small but prominent wart on his upper lip, and Ovicula ("little lamb"), because of his quiet and gentle manner. Almost nothing is known of Fabius's early career. His first recorded political distinction was his election in 233 B.C. to the consulship, the first of five times he would be so honored.

The chain of events that led to Fabius's most impressive and famous deeds did not begin until 218 B.C., when he was almost sixty years old. After Carthage's Hannibal invaded the Po Valley and defeated the Romans at the Ticinus and Trebia Rivers and Lake Trasimene, he was in a strategic position to strike at Rome. Faced with this dire emergency, in the spring of 217 the Romans chose Fabius as dictator because of his reputation for honesty and sound judgment. He immediately destroyed the bridges leading to Rome and burned all the crops in the vicinity, to deny Hannibal the use of these resources. When the Carthaginian did not attack the capital but instead began moving freely through the

Italian countryside, Fabius instituted a cautious and very shrewd policy. According to Plutarch, Fabius "was determined not to fight a pitched battle, and since he had time and manpower . . . on his side, his plan was to exhaust his opponent's strength . . . by means of delaying tactics, and gradually to wear down his small army and meager resources" (*Life of Fabius* 5). These tactics, which earned Fabius the nickname of Cunctator, or "the Delayer" (and which have been called Fabian tactics ever since), were effective; but they grew increasingly unpopular among his own people. Often, Hannibal's soldiers ravaged farms and villages in plain sight of Roman troops, who were forbidden by the dictator from interfering. Many Romans became increasingly convinced that Fabius was refusing to engage the enemy because he was afraid to fight.

When Fabius dutifully laid down his six-month appointment at the end of 217 B.C., the new consuls, Varro and Paullus, reversed Fabius's policy in dealing with Hannibal. They attacked the enemy at Cannae, in southeastern Italy, and were disastrously defeated; thus the Romans learned the hard way that Fabius's attempt to wear Hannibal down while sparing Roman lives had been the wiser approach. In the years that followed, they relied on his proven policy of delaying, harassing, and containing Hannibal, which proved effective, and came to call Fabius Rome's "shield." When he died in 203 B.C. at the age of about seventy-two, the heartbroken citizens paid for his burial out of their own pockets, each of them contributing a single coin. **See** Punic Wars (Chapter 7).

Fabius Pictor, Quintus

(third century B.C.) The earliest known Roman historian, he was a senator who fought in the Second Punic War. His history of Rome, which has not survived, was written in Greek, partly because Latin was not yet widely used for literature. Both Livy and Polybius used the work as a reference in writing their own histories.

Flaccus, Gaius Valerius

(late first century A.D.) A Roman epic poet, he composed a work titled the *Argonautica,* telling the story of the Greek heroes Jason and the Argonauts and their search for the fabulous Golden Fleece. His main source appears to have been the epic poem of the same name written by the third-century B.C. Greek poet Apollonius of Rhodes, but Flaccus also drew inspiration from Homer's *Odyssey* and Virgil's *Aeneid,* as well as other works. Nothing is known about Flaccus's life, and the general era in which he lived has been inferred by a historical reference in the introduction to his masterwork.

Flamininus, Titus Quinctius

(d. 174 B.C.) An illustrious Roman statesman and military leader, Flamininus was most famous for his exploits in the Second Macedonian War (200–197 B.C.). In 197 B.C., he took charge of Roman forces in Greece and decisively defeated the army of Macedonia's King Philip V at Cynoscephalae (in Thessaly). The event was notable in that it pitted the dreaded Macedonian phalanx against the Roman legions and maniples for the first time since Pyrrhus had fought the Romans almost a century before. This time the Roman formations proved much more flexible and effective, ensuring Flamininus's victory. **See** Pyrrhus; **also** battlefield tactics; Battle of Cynoscephalae (both Chapter 7).

Flaminius, Gaius

(d. 217 B.C.) Born a pleb, he rose through the ranks to serve as a tribune, censor, and twice as consul (in 223 and 217 B.C.). After winning fame by defeating a force of Gauls in the Po Valley in 223, he went on to sponsor the construction of the Circus Flaminius, in the Campus Martius in

Rome, and an important road, the Via Flaminia, which ran northward from Rome to Ariminum (on the Adriatic coast). In 217 B.C., as the Carthaginian invader Hannibal moved through northern Italy, Flaminius met him in the Battle of Lake Trasimene, where Flaminius was decisively defeated and killed. **See** Battle of Lake Trasimene (Chapter 7).

Frontinus, Sextus Julius

(ca. A.D. 30–ca. 104) A noted public official and writer, he served as consul about the year 74 and then as governor of the province of Britain, where he distinguished himself as a military leader. In 97, the emperor Nerva appointed him water commissioner (*curator aquarum*) of Rome; during this service Frontinus composed his best-known work, *The Aqueducts of Rome.* Modern historians find the book very valuable for its detailed histories and lists of physical specifications for all of the capital city's aqueducts. Another of Frontinus's works, the *Stratagems,* a manual for military strategists, has also survived.

Fronto, Marcus Cornelius

(ca. A.D. 100–ca. 176) Probably the greatest Roman orator of the second century, he hailed from Numidia (in North Africa) but long resided in Rome. From a literary standpoint, he is most important for his surviving letters (discovered in the early 1800s), which reveal a good deal about his personal life, particularly his friendship with the future emperor Marcus Aurelius. Fronto tutored the young Aurelius and thereafter stayed in touch with him, offering him advice and even criticism, which was well received. As an orator, Fronto was influenced by Cicero and Sallust.

Fulvia

(mid–first century B.C.) The first wife of the powerful general and triumvir Marcus Antonius (Mark Antony), she played a prominent part in the power struggles following the assassination of Antony's mentor, Julius Caesar. When Antony was away from Rome, she acted as one of his principal agents in the capital and worked diligently to promote his interests. Eventually, she came to grips with Caesar's adopted son, Octavian, whom she rightly viewed as a political threat to Antony's future. After she and Antony's brother, Lucius, launched a failed military campaign against Octavian in 41 B.C., they fled to Athens. There, Fulvia met with Antony, who sternly condemned her feud with Octavian. She died soon afterward. **See** Antony, Mark.

Gaiseric

For this fifth-century A.D. barbarian leader who sacked Rome, **see** Vandals (Chapter 7).

Gaius

(second century A.D.) A noted Roman jurist, his full name is unknown, as are most of the events of his life. His fame rests on his composition of the *Institutes* (completed ca. 161), in four books, a compilation of all the Roman laws known in his day. Of little interest to his contemporaries, the work remained obscure until the sixth-century eastern emperor Justinian I adapted it in compiling his own *Institutes,* part of the *Corpus Juris Civilis,* the massive law code he commissioned and many European kingdoms subsequently adopted. In this indirect way, Gaius proved immensely influential to the later Western world. **See** *Corpus Juris Civilis* (Chapter 4).

Gaius Caesar

For this notorious Roman emperor, the first to be assassinated, **see** his popular nickname, Caligula.

Galba

For this Roman general who became emperor for a short time in the first century A.D., **see** Vespasian.

Galen

(ca. A.D.129–199) A Greek physician and scientist, he was the foremost medical practitioner in the Roman Empire. Galen started out as a doctor to gladiators in his native town of Pergamum (in Asia Minor) and, thanks to his consummate skills as physician and medical writer, his reputation steadily grew. Ultimately he became the highly trusted and respected personal physician to the emperor Marcus Aurelius and some of his successors. Galen passed along much information from earlier Greek physicians, most notably Hippocrates, including the idea of the four humors regulating health and illness. However, Galen did much experimentation of his own and was also adept at diagnosis, distinguishing between pneumonia and pleurisy, and accurately describing pulmonary tuberculosis (three serious lung conditions or diseases).

Ironically, Galen inadvertently contributed to a steady decline in medical science in the centuries that followed. He was so skilled a doctor, researcher, and writer that later Greek and Roman physicians regarded him as an unerring authority, in a very real sense the last word in medicine. So they saw no need to carry on investigations of their own and medical experimentation largely ceased for over a thousand years. Yet his eighty or so surviving works (out of some five hundred penned in less than fifty years), including *On the Natural Faculties* and *On the Usefulness of the Parts of the Body,* preserved most of the medical knowledge of classical antiquity. Educated people in the Middle Ages and Renaissance held him in awe and he remained one of the two preeminent physicians of history (along with Hippocrates) until the dawn of the modern sciences of anatomy and physiology in the

Galen was held in awe by later European scholars. Most studied and quoted his ideas instead of performing their own experiments.

sixteenth and seventeenth centuries. **See** medicine (Chapter 5).

Galerius

(d. A.D. 311) One of the coemperors in Diocletian's Tetrarchy, he is best known for his vehement anti-Christian sentiments and policies. As a youth, Galerius joined the army and worked his way up through the ranks, attaining sufficient prominence for Diocletian to select him as junior emperor (Caesar) in the eastern half of the Empire in 293. In the next few years, Galerius distinguished himself on the battlefield, leading successful campaigns along the Danube frontier and in Syria and Mesopotamia. In 298, he took up residence in Thessaloniki (in northern Greece) and soon began influencing some of Diocletian's decisions. In particular, the younger ruler convinced Diocletian to initiate what turned out to be the most severe Christian persecution in Rome's history, in which many of the faithful were executed and Christian churches and holy writings were burned. When Diocletian retired the throne in 305, Galerius became senior emperor in the east and continued his anti-Christian crusade. In 311, however, Galerius fell gravely ill and, believing rumors that he was being punished by the Christian god, he signed a decree calling for an end to the persecution. He died soon afterward. **See** Diocletian; **also** Christianity (Chapter 3) **and** Tetrarchy (Chapter 4).

Gallienus, Publius Licinius Egnatius

(d. A.D. 268) A Roman emperor during the chaotic, perilous years of the third-century anarchy, he ruled as coemperor with his father, Valerian, beginning in 253. From 254 to 260, Gallienus fought, with some success, to keep numerous Germanic tribes at bay along the northern borders. When word came that his father had been captured by the Persians in the east, he faced renewed barbarian incursions, as well as the rebellions of several Roman generals who proclaimed themselves emperor. Gallienus was able to stop only some of these usurpers, and in 268 some of his own officers assassinated him. **See** Valerian.

Germanicus, Nero Claudius

(15 B.C.–A.D. 19) The eldest son of Drusus the Elder, he was formally adopted into the Julian clan (*gens*) in A.D. 4 by his uncle, the future emperor Tiberius. From 14 to 16, Germanicus proved himself an able general in fighting the Germans on the northern frontier. In 17, he took command of all the eastern provinces, but Tiberius soon appointed one G. Calpurnius Piso as governor of Syria, and Germanicus and Piso did not get along. In 19, Germanicus became seriously ill and on his deathbed accused Piso of poisoning him. Immensely popular with

the Roman populace, Germanicus was deeply mourned. One of his surviving children, Gaius (called Caligula), later became emperor. **See** Caligula.

Geta

For this brother of and for a short time coemperor with the third-century A.D. ruler Caracalla, **see** Caracalla.

Gracchus, Gaius Sempronius

(ca. 153–121 B.C.) The son of Tiberius Sempronius Gracchus, the noted censor, and his wife, Cornelia, and also the younger brother of the famous tribune Tiberius Sempronius Gracchus. The young Gaius Gracchus served in the army of Scipio Aemilianus in Spain, where the news came in 133 B.C. that his brother Tiberius had been assassinated in Rome. Returning to the capital, Gaius at first wisely stayed safely out of the public spotlight. In 123, however, he, like his brother before him, gained election as a plebeian tribune and proposed a series of new laws designed to reduce poverty and help the common people. Gaius also proposed laws aiming to limit the authority of senators. History now seemed to repeat itself as violence broke out between the senatorial class and the Gracchian supporters. This time the Senate issued an emergency order (*senatus consultum ultimum*) to quell the disturbance and, as his enemies closed in on him, Gaius ordered one of his slaves to kill him. **See** Cornelia; Gracchus, Tiberius Sempronius; **also** *senatus consultum ultimum* (Chapter 4).

Gracchus, Tiberius Sempronius

(ca. 164–133 B.C.) The eldest son of the noted censor of the same name and Cornelia, daughter of Scipio "Africanus," he was a prominent Roman politician and social reformer. After serving in the army as a young man, he was elected as a tribune of the people in 133 B.C. Disturbed that a mere handful of wealthy individuals owned and controlled most of the land in the realm, he proposed and saw passed a law redistributing public lands to greater numbers of people, thereby helping to alleviate poverty. In his zeal, however, Gracchus made some political mistakes, including seeking reelection in an unconstitutional manner, and his enemies, mostly senators and other members of the upper classes, branded him a dangerous radical. Consequently, he and several of his supporters were attacked and killed on the Capitoline Hill. In the long run, he did not die in vain, for later generations of Romans remembered him and his brother, another social reformer, as heroes of the common people. **See** Cornelia; Gracchus, Gaius Sempronius.

Gratian

(Flavius Gratianus, A.D. 359–383) The emperor of the western Roman sphere from 367 to 383. The son of the emperor Valentinian I, he was named coruler at the tender age of eight. In 375, Valentinian died, leaving Gratian and his younger half-brother, Valentinian II, ostensibly as corulers; but Gratian exercised the real power. Gratian attempted to join forces with the eastern emperor, Valens, at Adrianople (in Greece) in 378 to repel the Visigoths. However, Valens acted too hastily and the western army did not reach the scene in time to avert disaster. (Valens and more than half of his troops were slain.) In Valens's place on the eastern throne, Gratian appointed Theodosius I in 379. In 383, while attempting to stop a rebellion in Britain, Gratian was assassinated by one of his own officers. The capable but ill-fated young emperor, a Christian, is also remembered for giving in to the demands of the Christian bishop Ambrose to step down from the pagan post of *pontifex maximus* and to remove the statue of the goddess Victory from the Senate. **See** Ambrose; Valens, Flavius Julius; **also** *pontifex*

maximus (Chapter 3) **and** Battle of Adrianople (Chapter 7).

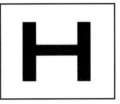

Hadrian

(Publius Aelius Hadrianus, A.D. 76–138) The third of the so-called five good emperors, Hadrian ruled the Roman Empire from 117 to 138. Born in Spain, his father died when he was a child and the emperor Trajan took him in and eventually adopted him as his son and heir. Ascending the throne at age forty-one, Hadrian devoted all his energies to running a fair and efficient government. Among his many reforms was a requirement that all senators and many other public officials receive training in government administration, and he built up a large pool of well-trained officials to carry out his policies. He also expanded the Roman welfare system, opening free schools for poor children and strengthening laws protecting slaves from abuse.

Preferring to base his provincial policies on firsthand information, Hadrian traveled extensively throughout the Empire, actually spending more of his reign abroad than in Rome. Unlike some of his predecessors, he felt the realm was already too large to administer efficiently, which explains why he refrained from invading Scotland and instead built a long defensive wall ("Hadrian's Wall") separating that territory from Roman Britain. Perhaps the most cultured of the emperors, Hadrian was fascinated by Greek history and culture and spent a great deal of time in Greece, where he generously restored many fine buildings that had fallen into disrepair. He also erected numerous notable structures in Rome, including a new version of the Pantheon (originally built by Augustus's close colleague, Agrippa). At Tivoli (about fifteen miles from Rome), Hadrian built an enormous villa, enriching it with art treasures from across the known world. Shortly before his death in 138, he named Titus Aurelius Antoninus (who would come to be called "Pius") as his heir. **See** Tivoli (Chapter 2); **also** forts, fortresses, and fortifications (Chapter 7).

Hamilcar Barca

For this noted third-century B.C. Carthaginian general, see his even more illustrious son, Hannibal.

Hannibal

(247–183 B.C.) One of the greatest military generals of all time, he was the leader of the main Carthaginian forces in the Second Punic War, fought between Rome and Carthage from 218 to 201 B.C. Hannibal was the eldest son of the noted Carthaginian leader Hamilcar Barca, who fought against the Romans in the First Punic War. After losing that conflict, Hamilcar began building a new base of operations in Spain, from where he hoped eventually to launch another war against Rome. He is said to have hated the Romans so much that he made the young Hannibal swear he would never hold friendship with them. In 229 B.C., Hamilcar died in a drowning accident, and in 221 his successor, Hasdrubal, was assassinated, which left Hannibal, at age twenty-six, in command of the Carthaginian forces.

Carrying on his father's expansion in Spain, in 219 B.C. Hannibal attacked Sa-

At his father's request, young Hannibal faithfully swears an oath never to trust or make friends with the Romans.

guntum, Rome's only ally in the region, and Rome soon declared war. Executing a brilliant and daring plan, he marched his army, which included several elephants, north through Spain, southern Gaul, and over the Alps into northern Italy, taking the Romans by surprise. He then won a stunning series of victories, including one over the consul Gaius Flaminius at Lake Trasimene. His greatest victory was in 216 B.C. at Cannae (in southeastern Italy), where his army annihilated more than fifty thousand Romans.

In the years that followed, however, Hannibal was unable to press his advantage effectively, for most of Rome's Italian allies, whom he had hoped would come over to his side, remained loyal. In 204 B.C., the Romans carried the war to Africa and he was forced to return to defend his native land. On the plain of Zama (southwest of Carthage), in 202, he was finally defeated by Scipio "Africanus." After the war, the Romans tried to hunt Hannibal down, forcing him to flee first to Syria, and later to Asia Minor. There, with his enemies closing in on him, he committed suicide in 183 B.C. **See** Scipio, Publius Cornelius "Africanus"; **also** Battles of Cannae, Lake Trasimene, Trebia, and Zama; **and** Punic Wars (all Chapter 7).

Herod the Great

(ca. 73–4 B.C.) The Jewish king of Judaea (then a Roman client state in Palestine) from 37 B.C. until his death, he was elevated to the throne after the Romans captured Jerusalem. Ruling the area much like a Greek kingdom, Herod erected a number of cities and refurbished and expanded the great and sacred Temple in Jerusalem. Under his rule, the Jews enjoyed considerable prosperity and religious freedom. Yet he was also a cruel and unscrupulous person. Many Jews disliked him, partly because he was from Idumaea, south of Judaea, which in their eyes made him less Jewish than they; and also for his importation of Greek and Roman ideas, which they felt threatened to dilute local Jewish culture. There were, therefore, several uprisings against him, which he put down by force. Herod is best known today for the biblical story in which he had all of the male children in Bethlehem killed to ensure the death of Jesus. After Herod's death, the Romans divided Palestine among his three sons— Archelaus, Philip, and Herod Antipas. **See** Judaea (Chapter 2).

Honorius

(A.D. 383–423) The western Roman emperor from 395 to 423, this son of Theodosius I and brother of Arcadius (emperor of eastern Rome) was largely a weak ruler who presided over a realm in serious decline. When Theodosius died in 395, leaving his young sons in charge of the now divided Empire, Honorius came under the influence of the powerful general Stilicho (whose daughter married Honorius that year). Eventually, Stilicho's political intrigues and failure to stop some of the barbarian incursions in the north turned the young emperor against the older man, whom Honorius personally killed in August 408. Soon afterward, in 410, the Visigoths sacked Rome, but Honorius and his court were safe in the new capital of Ravenna, in northeastern Italy. During the rest of his reign, barbarian groups continued to settle in Roman lands, usually through deals struck with the Roman government, a process that steadily whittled away at the Empire's fabric. He died childless in 423. **See** Arcadius; Stilicho, Flavius; Theodosius I.

Horace

(Quintus Horatius Flaccus, 65–8 B.C.) Born the son of a financially successful ex-slave, Horace was one of Rome's greatest poets. He studied in the best schools in Athens and Rome. Then he entered the republican army raised in Greece by Brutus and Cassius (leaders of the conspiracy against Julius Caesar). At the Battle of Philippi (42 B.C.), the poet, who later admitted that he was not soldier material, was so afraid that he fled the field in terror. Soon afterward he went to Rome and there had the good fortune to meet the great poet Virgil, who recognized his talents and introduced him to the literary patron Maecenas and rising political star Octavian. About the year 37 B.C., Horace achieved financial independence and all the leisure time he needed for writing when Maecenas provided him with a country estate staffed by an overseer, five tenant farmers, and eight slaves.

In contrast to the lofty, heroic, and generally serious tone of Virgil's works, Horace's poetry explored and commented on everyday situations, feelings, and emotions, usually in an easygoing or humorous way. Horace's general view of life was that it was short and uncertain, that death was inevitable, and that a person could only achieve immortality by creating or achieving something of lasting value. Therefore, it made sense to enjoy life and its pleasures, including love and wine, although not to gross and unseemly excess. His philosophy of living and enjoying one day at a time is evident in this excerpt from one of the poems collected in his masterpiece, the *Odes* (published 23–13 B.C.): "Happy the man, and happy he alone, he who can call today his own; he who, secure within, can say: 'Tomorrow do your worst, for I have lived today.'" (3.29.8)

Horace's other works, all of which have survived, include the *Epodes* (ca. 30 B.C.), *Satires* (ca. 30 B.C.), *Art of Poetry* (ca. 19 B.C.), and *Carmen Saeculare* (a long poem commissioned by Augustus for the Secular Games in 17 B.C.). These works, particularly the *Odes* and *Art of Poetry,* achieved widespread popularity and literary influence in Europe's Renaissance and again in the eighteenth century. **See** Maecenas, Gaius; **also** *Odes;* poetry (both Chapter 6).

Horatius the One-Eyed

(Publius Horatius Cocles) A legendary Roman hero, Horatius is said to have saved Rome from the invading Etruscans circa 508–504 B.C. In the patriotic story, which is likely fabricated or at least highly exaggerated, he single-handedly held the main bridge leading into the city, keeping the enemy army at bay until his companions finished demolishing the structure. One version of the tale says he then drowned, another that he swam to safety.

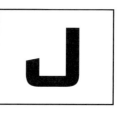

Jerome

(Eusebius Hieronymus, ca. A.D. 347–420) Later called one of the four great Latin "doctors" of the western Christian Church, he was an important late Roman Christian thinker and writer. Born in northern Italy and educated in Rome, in 374 he traveled to Antioch, where he learned Greek and studied Latin literature. Eventually, he adopted an ascetic lifestyle and settled permanently in Bethlehem (in Palestine), where he ran a monastery and devoted himself to scholarly studies. Deeply affected by the sacking of Rome in 410 by the Visigoths, he wrote, "My voice is stopped, and sobs cut off the words as I try to speak. Captive is the city which once took captive all the world." (*Letter 127*)

Jerome's major achievement was his translation of the Bible into Latin. Although other Latin versions already existed, they had been translated from the Greek version, the Septuagint; Jerome translated directly from the original Hebrew. His version eventually came to be accepted as the Vulgate, the standard Bible of the western church. His other works include *Concerning Famous Men,* a collection of biographies of 135 Christian writers, and the *Chronicle,* a historical work that modern historians find valuable in dating ancient events. **See** Vulgate (Chapter 3).

Jesus Christ

(ca. 4 B.C.–ca. A.D. 30–33) A Jewish preacher who grew up in Roman-controlled Palestine, his being and teachings became the basis for Christianity, which over time became Rome's official religion and eventually one of the world's great faiths. (His given name was Jesus; the name Christ came from the Greek word *Christos,* meaning Messiah, and was used by his followers only after his death.) Unfortunately, the amount of unbiased, reliable information about Jesus' life and teachings is meager. Most of what little is known about him comes from the four Gospels (Matthew, Mark, Luke, and John, the first four books of the New Testament). Because they are not direct eyewitness accounts, having been pieced together years later from anecdotes and sermons by people who had not known Jesus personally, their authenticity remains controversial among historians (although many Christians accept them as straightforward historical documents proving Jesus' divinity).

Nearly all scholars agree on at least one point, namely that Jesus was a real historical person. The consensus of present scholarship is that he was born about 4 B.C., in the small Palestinian village of Bethlehem, a few miles south of Jerusalem. According to Luke, Jesus' parents, Joseph and Mary, were residents of the town of Nazareth who traveled to Judaea to be counted in a Ro-

As a major religious figure, Jesus later exerted a profound influence on European art, including paintings like this one of his crucifixion.

man census and after Jesus' birth returned to their hometown. Jesus spent his childhood and young manhood in Nazareth. Evidently, his ministry began directly after an event that transformed his life—his baptism by John the Baptist, an itinerant Jewish preacher who advocated that the Jewish god's kingdom was imminent. John was executed by the authorities shortly afterward and Jesus himself went out and began preaching. Moving from village to village, mostly along the shores of the Sea of Galilee, he gathered several close followers, the original Twelve Apostles, and his sermons drew large crowds. Perhaps the most famous of the speeches attributed to him came to be called the Sermon on the Mount. Jesus rapidly earned a reputation throughout Galilee, not only for his sermons, for which he became known as a teacher, but also for healing the sick and performing miracles.

In time, the Jewish authorities arrested Jesus. The reasons for this are not clear and often debated. Some scholars feel that his suggestion that God's kingdom had already begun to arrive on earth, specifically through his own ministry and actions, made him appear subversive and potentially dangerous. Other scholars say that Jesus' ability to gather and appeal to large crowds made him seem a sort of rabble-rouser who posed a threat to law and order. Whatever the reasons, Jewish leaders handed Jesus over to the Roman governor, Pontius Pilate, who convicted him of sedition and ordered him to be crucified, a common mode of execution at the time. Jesus was crucified on a hill near Jerusalem and died after a brief period of suffering.

It was what happened after Jesus' death that determined that he would become the focus of a major religious movement. According to later Christian tradition as related in the Gospels, he was resurrected from the dead and admonished his apostles to preach repentance and the forgiveness of sins to all nations in his name. Accordingly, in the months and years that followed, his followers began to spread the word that he had been the Messiah, a superhuman figure that Jewish prophesy had told would come to earth to deliver the Jews from foreign domination. When later Christians, spearheaded by Paul of Tarsus, brought this message to the Gentiles (non-Jews), Christianity began to grow. **See** John the Baptist; Paul; **also** Christianity (Chapter 3).

John the Baptist

(before 4 B.C.–ca. A.D. 28) The roving preacher who Christian tradition holds baptized Jesus, John is mentioned in the Gospels as well as in the *Jewish Antiquities* of the ancient historian Josephus. Since John preached that God's kingdom (i.e., the ending of the present world and advent of a better one) was imminent, it is likely that he was an Essene, or at least a former Essene. (The Essenes were a radical sect of Jews who tended to live apart from other people in isolated communities. The fa-

mous Dead Sea Scrolls are likely writings produced by one such community.) The fact that John moved about the countryside interacting with people suggests that he had somehow broken with the more monastic Essenes. In any case, according to the Gospel of Mark: "John the baptizer appeared in the wilderness, preaching a baptism of repentance for the forgiveness of sins. . . . In those days Jesus came from Nazareth of Galilee and was baptized by John in the Jordan [River]." (Mark 1.4–9) Eventually, the authorities took note of John's activities. Not long after baptizing Jesus, he was arrested and executed by the local ruler, Herod Antipas, perhaps, as Josephus says, because Antipas feared that John might stir up public unrest or even an insurrection. **See** Jesus Christ.

Josephus, Flavius

(A.D. 37–ca. 94) A noted ancient Jewish historian who traveled to Rome as a young man. Returning to his native Judaea in 66, on the eve of the great Jewish rebellion against Rome, he tried to convince his countrymen that their cause was futile, but his warnings went unheeded. At the commencement of hostilities, he took charge of Galilee and defended the town of Jotapata, which fell in 67 after a fifty-day siege. Captured, Josephus returned to Rome. There, after managing to gain the favor of the emperor Vespasian, he deserted the Jewish cause, became a Roman citizen, received a house and a pension, and began writing his now famous detailed account of the rebellion—the *Jewish War,* composed in Aramaic and consisting of seven books. His other works, written in Greek, include the *Jewish Antiquities,* an ambitious history of the Jews from Adam to A.D. 66, and his *Vita* (*Life*), a rebuttal to the false charge that he himself had instigated the rebellion. Josephus was a great admirer of Rome and his works contain valuable descriptions of Roman customs, particularly military ones.

Jovian

(Flavius Jovinus, ca. A.D. 330–364) Emperor of Rome from 363 to 364, his best-known accomplishment was to reverse the propagan policies of his predecessor, Julian, who had attempted to slow or halt the growth of Christianity. Jovian restored the privileges of the church, whose acquisition of new converts, political influence, land, and wealth now resumed and greatly accelerated. The cause of his death is uncertain, but he may have been poisoned by the fumes given off by a charcoal-burning heater.

Jugurtha

For this Numidian prince who challenged Rome in the second century B.C., **see** the Jugurthine War (Chapter 7).

Julia

For this daughter of the emperor Augustus, **see** Augustus; Ovid.

Julia Domna

(d. after A.D. 217) The second wife of the emperor Septimius Severus and matriarch of the Severan dynasty, she was empress of Rome from 193 to 211. She was noted for her intelligence and interest in the arts and philosophy and is said to have invited numerous intellectuals to the court, including the scientist Galen. She was with her husband when he died in Britain in 211 and afterward attempted, unsuccessfully, to reconcile the differences between her two rival sons, Caracalla and Geta. The date of her death is unknown, as is its manner, which may have been either natural causes or suicide. **See** Caracalla; Severus, Septimius.

Julia Maesa

(d. A.D. 226) She was Julia Domna's sister and the grandmother of the emperors Elagabalus (by her daughter Julia Soaemius) and Severus Alexander (by her other daughter, Julia Mamaea). After Caracalla's death and the accession of the emperor Macrinus in 217, Julia Maesa organized a plot to destroy the new ruler and put Elagabalus on the throne. The conspiracy succeeded, after which Julia next groomed her other grandson, Severus Alexander, for the throne. When the latter became emperor after Elagabalus's murder in 222, she played a prominent role in his administration, influencing many of his decisions. **See** Elagabalus; Severus Alexander.

Julia Mamaea

(d. A.D. 235) Daughter of Julia Maesa and mother of the emperor Severus Alexander, she held the title of Augusta (empress or, as in her case, a major female figure in the royal family) from 222 to 235. At first, her influence was limited by the commanding presence of her mother, Julia Maesa; but when the latter died in 226, Julia Mamaea stepped forward to become nothing less than the Empire's virtual ruler, overseeing most of her son's activities and influencing his decisions. According to ancient accounts, she was so domineering and greedy for power and wealth that she eventually alienated the military, and a group of soldiers eventually assassinated her and her son, ending the Severan dynasty. **See** Julia Maesa; Severus Alexander.

Julian

(Flavius Claudius Julianus, the "Apostate," ca. A.D. 332–363) Emperor of Rome from 361 to 363, he was a distant relative of his predecessor, Constantius II, who had managed to survive a family purge. Unlike the prior few rulers, who were Christians, Julian was a pagan whose policies posed a potent threat to Christianity's continuing progress. For this reason, he earned the uncomplimentary nickname of the Apostate ("abandoner of the faith"). He revived animal sacrifices, abolished the Christian clergy's tax exemptions, and forbade

Christians from teaching rhetoric and grammar. Julian was an exceptionally intelligent, humane, and moral man, and for this reason he refused to initiate a violent persecution of the Christians. His contemporary, the great historian Ammianus Marcellinus, said of him: "Julian must be reckoned a man of heroic stature. . . . Philosophers tell us that there are four cardinal virtues: self-control, wisdom, justice, and courage; and, in addition to these, certain practical gifts: military skill, dignity, prosperity and generosity. All these Julian cultivated . . . with the utmost care." (*History* 25.4) If Julian had lived longer, he might have slowed or stopped the growth of Christianity. However, after ruling only eighteen months he died in 363 while campaigning against the Persians. He was the Empire's last pagan emperor.

Justin

(Marcus Junianus Justinus, second or third century A.D.) Almost nothing is known about this Roman historian, including the exact years he lived. He is noted for his epitome (brief summary) of the *Philippic Histories* of the first-century B.C. Roman historian Pompeius Trogus. Because Trogus's original work is lost, Justin's synopsis is a valuable source of information about the history of Macedonia and the other Hellenistic Greek kingdoms.

Justin Martyr

(ca. A.D. 100–165) A prominent Christian theologian and apologist, he was born and raised a pagan and discovered Christianity at about the age of thirty. Eventually, he opened a school for Christians in Rome. His *First Apology* (ca. 155), addressed to the emperor Antoninus Pius, and his *Second Apology* (ca. 161), addressed to the Senate, firmly defended Christian ideas and practices. The Roman authorities were not impressed, however; Justin and some of his followers were arrested and beheaded about 165.

Juvenal

(Decimus Junius Juvenalis, flourished early second century A.D.) Perhaps the greatest of the satirists produced by ancient Rome. Almost nothing certain is known about his life, except that he was born at Aquinum, on the Latium plain. His sixteen satires contain lines suggesting that he started out poor, managed to acquire a farm at Tivoli (near Rome), also had a house in Rome, and traveled to Egypt; however, some or all of these statements could well be fictitious, to suit the needs of his writing. The *Satires,* apparently composed between 127 and 110, contain much strong, bitter criticism and ridicule of a number of Roman customs and institutions and evoke a vivid, if not wholly realistic, picture of everyday life in his day. **See** satire (Chapter 6).

Lactantius

(Lucius Caecilius Firmianus, ca. A.D. 245–ca. 325) A noted Latin writer and Christian apologist, he was a native of North Africa. Eventually, he became famous enough for the emperor Diocletian to ask him to come to Nicomedia (in Asia Minor) and teach Latin rhetoric. Though it remains uncertain, it was probably in Nicomedia in the next few years that Lactantius became exposed to and converted to Christianity. Much later (perhaps in 317), the emperor Constantine hired him to tutor the royal prince. Of Lactantius's works, *On the Deaths of the Persecutors* (ca. 318) is valuable for its vivid descriptions of the Roman anti-Christian persecutions, particularly the great one initiated by Diocletian and Galerius, which the author witnessed firsthand. He also wrote *On God's Handiwork* (ca. 303), which tries to show that the human body is evidence of God's existence, and the *Divine Institutions* (ca. 305–313), which defends Christian ideas and practices.

Leo I

(ca. A.D. 401–474) Emperor of eastern Rome from 457 to 474, Leo was a capable administrator who set about ridding his court of the controlling influences of German-born generals and soldiers. While the Empire's western sphere was deteriorating under the onslaught of such influences, he built a strong base of support among the natives of Asia Minor, eventually befriending a local leader, Zeno, who became his son-in-law and heir. Leo's attempt to destroy the Vandals (based in North Africa), beginning in 468, failed; but he still managed to maintain his influence in the west, naming Anthemius to the western throne in 467 and Julius Nepos in 474. Two years later the western throne fell vacant, but Leo had helped to build a firm foundation for the survival of the eastern throne. **See** Zeno 2.

Lepidus, Marcus Aemilius

(d. ca. 13 B.C.) A Roman general and statesman best known for his role as one of the three members of the Second Triumvirate. This powerful political alliance, which also included Mark Antony and Octavian, was launched in 43 B.C. with bloody purges of their enemies. The three men proceeded to divide the Roman sphere among themselves, Lepidus's share consisting of Narbonese Gaul, parts of Spain, and North Africa. He already held the distinction of the office of *pon-*

tifex maximus (high priest). But his partners soon overshadowed him, to his increasing distress. When he finally turned on Octavian in 36 B.C., the younger man deposed him and put him under house arrest for the rest of his days. **See** Augustus.

Licinius, Valerius Licinianus

(d. A.D. 325) A coemperor with Constantine the Great, Licinius was born in the province of Upper Moesia sometime in the mid-to-late third century and worked his way up through the military ranks. In 308, the emperor Galerius chose him as a coemperor in the east. When Galerius died in 311, Licinius faced competition from Galerius's ambitious nephew, Maximinus Daia. The rivalry was short-lived, however, as Licinius soundly defeated the other man in a large-scale battle fought in 313. Shortly afterward, Licinius issued the famous Edict of Milan jointly in his own name and that of Constantine, who ruled in the west. The decree granted toleration to all Roman Christians. Though Licinius and Constantine started out as allies (with Licinius marrying Constantine's sister, Constantia), their relationship steadily deteriorated, and Constantine decisively defeated his rival in 324. Despite Constantia's pleas to spare her husband's life, Constantine executed Licinius the following year.

Livia

(58 B.C.–A.D. 29) One of the most powerful and respected women in Roman history, she was the wife of the first emperor, Augustus, and mother of the second, Tiberius. At first, she married Tiberius Claudius Nero, an opponent of Octavian (the future Augustus), and bore him two sons, Tiberius and Drusus the Elder. In 39 B.C., Octavian divorced his own wife and forced Nero to separate from Livia so that he, Octavian, could marry Livia. Utterly devoted to Octavian/Augustus, she represented his interests and those of the Roman state with un-

An idealized portrait of Augustus and his wife, Livia.

common dignity and tact, keeping a well-organized household and winning the admiration of the citizenry. When he died in A.D. 14 and Tiberius became emperor, Livia's abilities were so respected that she wielded authority not much inferior to her son's. Ancient historians, including Suetonius, say that she was often ruthless and suggest that she may have done away with rival family members to promote the careers of her sons and grandchildren, but these charges may have been rumors or exaggerations. When she died in 29 at the age of eighty-six, she was buried with full honors in Augustus's tomb; in 42, her grandson, the emperor Claudius, accorded her divine status. **See** Augustus; Tiberius.

Livius Andronicus, Lucius

(ca. 284–204 B.C.) Often referred to as the "father" of Roman literature, he was probably a Greek who was captured by the Romans when they sacked the city of Tarentum in 272 B.C. After becoming a tutor in a wealthy household, he earned his free-

dom and began to achieve his goal of introducing the Romans to the rich heritage of Greek literature. He translated Homer's *Odyssey* (a version that the later Roman poet Horace claimed to have memorized by heart) and wrote numerous tragedies and comedies for the stage, all based on Greek models. Only a few lines from these works have survived.

Livy

(Titus Livius) The outstanding prose writer of the Augustan Age of literature and one of the most popular of all Roman historians. Born in 59 B.C. in Patavium (now Padua), in northern Italy, he lived most of his life in Rome, where he witnessed firsthand the fall of the Republic and rise of Augustus and the Principate. At the urging of Augustus, who became his friend, he devoted much of his life to writing the massive and detailed *History of Rome from Its Foundation (Ab urbe condita libri)*, begun about 29 B.C. and subsequently published in installments. Livy died a famous and widely respected author in A.D. 17 in Patavium. **See** Augustan Age of literature; *History of Rome from Its Foundation* (both Chapter 6).

Lucretia

For this woman whose death was instrumental in the rebellion that ended the Roman Monarchy, **see** Brutus, Lucius Junius.

Lucretius

(Titus Lucretius Carus, ca. 99–ca. 55 B.C.) Almost nothing is known about the life of this Roman poet and philosopher of great stature. His only known work, *On the Nature of Things,* is a beautifully written work that extols the virtues of the Greek thinker Epicurus and his ideas. **See** *On the Nature of Things* (Chapter 6).

Lucullus, Lucius Licinius

(ca. 114–57 B.C.) A prominent Roman general, he was right-hand man to the dictator

Sulla. Lucullus served as governor of Africa in 77 B.C. and as consul in 74, when he engaged in a series of successful military campaigns against Mithridates, king of Pontus (in Asia Minor). Later at odds with the powerful figures Pompey and Caesar, Lucullus retired from politics in 59 B.C. and in his last two years indulged himself in good food, literature, and the arts.

Maecenas, Gaius

(d. 8 B.C.) One of the emperor Augustus's closest friends and the most famous literary patron of the Augustan Age, Maecenas was born into a well-to-do equestrian family. From 43 to 22 B.C., Maecenas served as Augustus's political and intellectual adviser, helping the younger man to deal with various Roman political factions and also to set up the Principate. After 22, however, the relationship cooled (presumably because of the execution, at Augustus's order, of Maecenas's brother-in-law on charges of treason). As a literary patron, Maecenas sponsored the prestigious circle of writers that included Virgil, Horace, and Propertius, among others. He suggested the subject of the renowned *Georgics* to Virgil and provided Horace with a lovely farm and villa in the countryside. In return, these writers lauded the imperial regime in their works. **See** Augustus; Horace; **also** Augustan Age of literature (Chapter 6).

Marcellus, Marcus Claudius

(d. 208 B.C.) An accomplished Roman general who earned fame for his exploits in the Second Punic War. In 211, he took the Greek city of Syracuse after a long and difficult siege (in which his army suffered many casualties at the hands of the brilliant Greek inventor Archimedes, who constructed frightening defensive weapons). The Roman people came to call Marcellus their "sword" because of his successes against the Carthaginians, while his colleague, Fabius Maximus (Rome's "shield") backed him up. **See** Fabius Maximus; **also** Punic Wars (Chapter 7).

Marcus Aurelius

(Marcus Aurelius Antoninus, A.D. 121–180) The last of the so-called five good emperors, he ruled the Roman Empire from 161 to 180. The son of a consul, M. Annius Verus, he received a sound education, studying under the great scholars M. Cornelius Fronto and Herodes Atticus. In 138, soon after the emperor Hadrian had adopted Antoninus Pius as his son and heir, Antoninus did the same for Marcus, thus ensuring a smooth line of succession to the throne. In 145, Marcus further sealed the bond by marrying Antoninus's daughter. When Antoninus died in 161, Marcus became emperor, sharing the throne with Lucius Verus, another of Antoninius's adopted sons, until Verus died in 169.

Marcus Aurelius's reign was marked mostly by tragic developments beyond his ability to foresee or prevent. In the 160s, a terrible plague swept through the realm, possibly killing millions. Then came encroaching barbarian tribes—the Marcomanni and others—along the Empire's northern borders; they crossed the Danube, attacked northern Italy, and threatened to march farther south. Responding to this threat, the emperor slowly but steadily pushed the invaders back until, by 179, he had almost completely eradicated the Marcomanni. His intention appears to have been to press on and subdue and Romanize the rest of northern Europe. If he had succeeded, Western history would have been very different. However, he fell ill and died in March 180; his son and heir,

Commodus, who lacked his vision (as well as his strong moral compass), failed to pursue his father's ambitious plans.

Known for his honesty and sense of justice, Marcus Aurelius was also noted for his intellectual capacity and pursuits. While fighting in the north, he composed his now famous *Meditations,* a work in twelve books, which was not published until after his death. In this touching and timeless glimpse into the mind of a truly good man, he expresses his Stoic beliefs about restraining the passions and emotions to achieve wisdom and happiness, and his desire to see an end to the injustices perpetrated by his fellow men and women. **See** Antoninus Pius; Commodus; **also** Marcomanni (Chapter 7).

Marius, Gaius

The most important military reformer of the late Republic, he was also the first Roman to demonstrate how a successful general could achieve political power by gaining the personal allegiance of his soldiers. In addition, he broke all precedents by winning the consulship seven times, five of these consecutively (107, 104–100, and 86 B.C.). Marius was born the son of a farmer in 157 B.C. at Arpinum (about sixty miles southeast of Rome). Little is known about his childhood except that he was poor and possessed courage, physical toughness, and great potential as a leader of men. As a young man he became a tribune of the people and in 115 B.C., at the age of forty-two, a praetor. That same year he married into a patrician family—the Caesars, of the Julii clan. Not yet born at this time was the nephew of his wife, Julia, Gaius Julius Caesar, who would later make his own mark on Roman history.

Not long after Marius's marriage, trouble erupted in the kingdom of Numidia in North Africa, and he made a name for himself as an army officer in what became known as the Jugurthine War. While this conflict was in progress, he began instituting military reforms, dropping all property qualifications and accepting volunteers from all classes (which not only greatly increased the number of potential recruits, but also produced a more permanent, professional force). Marius also supplied his troops with standard weapons and eventually arranged for his retired veterans to receive generous land allotments in northern Africa, southern Gaul, Sicily, and Greece. This made them fiercely loyal to him, as much or more so than to the state.

Marius's new and improved army proved itself in 105 B.C. when the Germanic Cimbri and Teutones began to overrun southern Gaul. In 102, he crushed the Teutones at Aquae Sextiae; the following year, he inflicted an even more shattering defeat on the Cimbri near Ferrara (in northern Italy). The successful campaign made him the hero of the hour and for many years he remained the most powerful and feared Roman general. But eventually his position was challenged by Sulla, who had in recent years attained much power and prestige of his own. In 87 B.C., while Sulla was campaigning in Asia Minor, Marius led his troops into Rome and murdered many of Sulla's aristocratic supporters. But less than a year later, Marius, now an old man, fell ill and died, leaving an ominous legacy. In the years that followed, the rule of the military strongmen, a phenomenon he had initiated, would begin to chip away in earnest at the Republic's increasingly shaky foundations. **See** Sulla, Lucius Cornelius; **also** Cimbri and Teutones; Jugurthine War (both Chapter 7).

Martial

(Marcus Valerius Martialis, ca. A.D. 40–ca. 103) A renowned Roman poet, he hailed from Spain and traveled to Rome in 64. Most of what little is known about his life comes from remarks in his own works. He claims to have begun as a poor man living in a third-floor apartment. But later, as people began to buy his books, he was able to afford a townhouse and also a cottage in the countryside a few miles south of the capital. Thirty-three poems survive from his *Book of Spectacles* (penned in 80 to commemorate the inauguration of the Colosseum). Martial's most important work, the *Epigrams,* in twelve books, began to appear in 86. All told, he produced over fifteen hundred epigrams, short poems each expressing a single idea, in which he described many common character types and social customs and situations of his day. Many of these are quite engaging and humorous, and some are obscene. His literary friends included Juvenal and Pliny the Younger, who called Martial talented, penetrating, witty, and sincere. **See** poetry (Chapter 6).

Masinissa

For this Numidian king who aided Rome against Carthage, **see** Punic Wars (Chapter 7).

Maxentius

For this fourth-century usurper of the Roman throne who fought the emperor Constantine, **see** Constantine I; **also** Tetrarchy (Chapter 4).

Maximinus I Thrax

(Gaius Julius Verius Maximinus, d. A.D. 238) Emperor of Rome from 235 to 238, he had the distinction of being physically the largest of all the emperors and became known for his tremendous strength and cruel nature. Born in Thrace (the origin of his nickname "Thrax"), he joined the army as a young man and because of his extraordinary stature quickly earned a position as bodyguard to the emperor Septimius Severus. Later, another Severan, Severus Alexander, gave Maximinus command of an army. But this proved a mistake, for these troops murdered the young emperor and proclaimed their leader his successor in 235. Maximinus proceeded to campaign against German border tribes and enjoyed

some success. But the news that other men had usurped the throne drew him to Rome, where, in 238, he was killed by his own soldiers, who had by this time become disenchanted with him. Besides his size, Maximinus's other distinction was that he was the first of the so-called soldier emperors to die by violent means in the turbulent period that is often called the "anarchy."

Messallina, Valeria

(d. A.D. 48) The third wife of the emperor Claudius, she was empress of Rome from 41 to 48. One of the most infamous women in history, she became known for her political intrigues and sexual and other excesses. Dominating court life, she influenced many of her husband's decisions, all the while silencing her political opponents and going through a veritable stable of lovers behind her husband's back. Thanks to a powerful courtier, Narcissus, Claudius eventually found out and assented to Messalina's execution. The shaken, saddened emperor vowed never to marry again, but did so the following year, to another disreputable character (Agrippina the Younger). **See** Claudius.

Milo, Titus Annius

(d. 48 B.C.) A noted Roman politician, he became a tribune of the people in 57 B.C. Contributing to an increasingly violent atmosphere, both in politics and the streets, he organized gangs of gladiators to attack the followers of his enemy, the equally unsavory Clodius. In 52 B.C., Milo succeeded in killing Clodius. For this, the popular general Pompey brought Milo to trial and the sentence was exile. Four years later, having failed to learn his lesson, Milo joined a rebellion against Julius Caesar and died fighting in southern Italy.

Mithridates VI Eupator

(d. 63 B.C.) King of Pontus (in northern Asia Minor) from 120 to 63 B.C., he proved to be one of Rome's most formidable enemies during the late Republic. At first, he shared the throne with his brother, but eventually Mithridates murdered this sibling, imprisoned his own mother, and married his own sister. Attempting to expand his power and rid Asia Minor of Roman influence, in 89 B.C. he launched the first of three so-called Mithridatic Wars. Ultimately, he was unable to overcome the Roman challenge and committed suicide by having a slave stab him. **See** Mithridatic Wars (Chapter 7).

Naevius, Gnaeus

(ca. 270–ca. 190 B.C.) A noted early Roman dramatist and epic poet, he fought in the First Punic War and soon afterward began producing his own plays. Although he copied many of his themes from Greek originals, Naevius was the first Roman to choose subjects from Roman history. Supposedly he and his plays, of which only scattered fragments survive, were outspoken, and eventually this got him into trouble when a noble Roman family felt slighted by one of his lines. Exiled, he moved to North Africa, where he composed an epic poem titled *Punic War,* only about sixty lines of which have survived. **See** poetry; theater and drama (both Chapter 6).

Namatianus, Rutilius Claudius

(late fourth and early fifth centuries A.D.) One of the last of the Roman Latin poets, he was the son of a Gallic imperial officer and grew up in Gaul. Between 412 and 414, he held high government posts under the emperor Honorius. Namatianus is best known for his elegiac poem *Voyage Home to Gaul,* a defense of paganism that contains numerous references to everyday life at the time. It also features a beautiful hymn of praise to "eternal" Rome and is therefore often called Rome's "swan song" (farewell performance).

Nepos, Cornelius

(ca. 100–ca. 25 B.C.) This noted Roman biographer and historian was a friend of the poet Catullus (who dedicated a book of poetry to him) and the great orator Cicero, and was particularly close to Cicero's letter-writing confidant, Atticus. Most of Nepos's works, including a universal history titled *Chronica* and a compilation of anecdotes, the *Exempla,* have not survived. He is best known for the one book that *has* survived—the *Lives of the Great Foreign Generals.* Its short biographies, including those of the Greeks Themistocles and Epaminondas and the Carthaginian Hannibal, were designed to illustrate their subjects' moral excellence and contain numerous historical inaccuracies and omissions. **See** prose writing (Chapter 6).

Nepos, Julius

(d. A.D. 480) It may be possible to argue on technical grounds that Nepos, rather than Romulus Augustulus, was actually the last official Roman emperor. As a young man, Nepos became related by marriage to Leo I, then emperor in the east. In 473, Leo helped him acquire the western throne and Nepos then gave the job of *magister militum* to Orestes, formerly a secretary to Attila the Hun. In 475, Orestes used his considerable power to oust Nepos and place his own son, Romulus Augustulus, on the throne. Nepos escaped to Dalmatia and, after the young new emperor was deposed the following year by the German Odoacer, appealed to Leo's successor, Zeno, for support to regain the throne. In Zeno's eyes, Nepos was still officially the western emperor and Odoacer seemed to agree in principle, although he delayed in allowing Nepos to return to the capital. This delay proved effective, for Nepos was assassinated in 480 by two members of his own staff. **See** Odoacer; Zeno 2.

Nero

The brutal reign of Rome's fifth emperor, the self-centered, cruel, and extravagant Nero, has come to symbolize the misuse of great power; numerous despicable acts, some of them factual, others exaggerated or fictitious, have been attributed to him. He was born in A.D. 37 in the small seaside town of Antium (about fifty miles south of Rome), the son of Agrippina the Younger, great-granddaughter of Augustus, and Gnaeus Domitius Ahenobarbus, an aristocrat with a reputation for shady dealings. In 49, Agrippina married the fourth emperor, Claudius, who the following year adopted the boy as his son. With her son now the heir apparent, in 54 the scheming and ambitious Agrippina had Claudius poisoned and the seventeen-year-old Nero ascended the throne as Nero Claudius Caesar Augustus.

At first, it appeared to all that Nero might become a responsible, constructive leader. The accounts of Suetonius, Tacitus, Dio Cassius, and other ancient historians all agree that in his first months in power he tried hard to be generous and enlightened. But it is unclear how much of this early good behavior stemmed from Nero's own character and how much from the influence of Seneca, the brilliant philosopher-writer who had been his tutor. Evidence suggests that Seneca made a concerted effort to guide and restrain the youth, who, at least privately, must already have revealed signs of a neurotic, cruel, and violent nature.

Unfortunately, Nero eventually revealed that darker nature and his reign grew increasingly more brutal and despotic.

Among the close relations he killed or had murdered were his stepbrother, his mother, his first wife (Octavia), and his second wife (Poppaea). He also illegally confiscated the properties of several wealthy men, all to help finance his own excessive luxuries. As his misdeeds multiplied, Nero came to ignore Seneca and other responsible advisers and from 62 on relied mainly on the advice of Ofonius Tigellinus, the ambitious commander of the Praetorian Guard, who encouraged his irresponsible and violent behavior.

Nero's greatest notoriety came in the wake of the terrible fire that devastated about two-thirds of the capital city in July 64. To his credit, he organized shelters for the homeless and launched ambitious rebuilding projects. But many Romans became convinced that he himself had purposely started the blaze, a charge that is almost certainly false. Their suspicions stemmed in part from his transformation of a large area destroyed by the fire into his own personal pleasure park and palace (the Golden House). Many Romans came

Nero was an egotist and tyrant who murdered his mother and wives and exploited his people until they turned on him.

to see this waste of valuable public space as just another of Nero's outrages and several highly placed individuals began to plot his assassination. To their regret, he discovered their schemes and responded by torturing, executing, or exiling hundreds of people. Among these unfortunates was Seneca, whom he ordered to commit suicide.

The decadent emperor's own days were numbered, however. Early in 68, Roman troops in various parts of the Empire began proclaiming their commanders emperor; soon afterward the Senate declared Nero an enemy of the people. Fleeing in disguise to a villa a few miles north of the city, the disgraced ruler took his own life when he realized that the soldiers hunting him were closing in. **See** Agrippina the Younger; Seneca the Younger.

Nerva, Marcus Cocceius

(ca. A.D. 30–98) First of the so-called five good emperors, he ruled Rome from 96 to 98. Nerva grew up in a noble household and as a young man, during Nero's reign, became a lawyer. Nero liked him, as did the emperor Vespasian, who made him coconsul in 71; in 90, Nerva shared another consulship, this time with Vespasian's son, Domitian. When Domitian was assassinated in 96, the conspirators and senators were happy to place Nerva on the throne. Although his short reign was marred by two rebellions, including one by the Praetorian Guard, he proved a just, kind, and popular ruler. Shortly before his death, he adopted Trajan, a provincial governor, as his son and heir, initiating the mode of succession that the next few emperors would use with highly positive results.

Numa Pompilius

(late eighth and early seventh centuries B.C.?) The legendary successor of Romulus and second king of Rome, tradition held that he reigned from about 717 to 673 B.C. The later Romans, including Livy in his monumental history, looked on this period as a sort of golden age in which many of their important religious and other institutions were established; however, it is likely that Numa was not a real person and that these institutions developed more gradually. **See** Monarchy (Chapter 4).

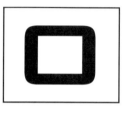

Octavia

(d. 11 B.C.) The sister of Octavian (later the emperor Augustus), she was related by blood or marriage to numerous other prominent Romans. First, her son from her first marriage, M. Claudius Marcellus, married Augustus's daughter, Julia. In 40 B.C., Octavia married Mark Antony to help seal the Treaty of Brundisium, and

In this modern etching, Augustus's sister, Octavia, faints at the beauty of the poet Virgil's verses.

though they were divorced eight years later, one of her daughters by him became the mother of the emperor Claudius and the other the grandmother of the emperor Nero. Octavia was known and widely respected for her loyalty and kindness; even though Antony abandoned her for Cleopatra, after the suicides of the infamous lovers Octavia raised their children as her own, as well as those born of Antony's other wife, Fulvia. **See** Antony, Mark; Augustus.

Octavian

For Julius Caesar's adopted son, who became the first Roman emperor, **see** his imperial name, Augustus.

Odaenath

For this third-century eastern king who seized some Roman territories, **see** Zenobia; **also** Palmyra (Chapter 2).

Odoacer

(d. A.D. 493) A German-born officer in the army of Orestes, the *magister militum* in 475, and the first barbarian king of Italy. In 476, after the government refused to award the German troops huge parcels of Italian land, they mutinied, proclaimed Odoacer their king, and moved on the capital, Ravenna. Orestes was killed and his son, Romulus Augustulus, was deposed, leaving the traditional throne vacant. Odoacer then appealed to the eastern emperor, Zeno, for recognition as *magister militum* of the west; but a former western emperor, Julius Nepos, challenged this claim. The point was moot, for Nepos was killed in 480 and Odoacer ruled what was left of the western Empire until he was ousted and killed by the Ostrogoths in 493.

Origen

(Origenes Adamantius, ca. A.D.185–ca. 254) One of the most prominent and influential Christian theologians and probably the first great scholar produced by the church, he was born in Alexandria and studied in a Christian school there. After being ordained a priest in 230, he opened a school of his own at Caesarea (in Asia Minor) and began writing. Perhaps his most famous work was the *Hexapla*, a version of the Old Testament divided into six parallel columns, one containing the original Hebrew and the others consisting of various Greek editions of the text. He also wrote a widely read apology, *Against Celsus*. In 250, during the emperor Decius's anti-Christian persecution, Origen was arrested and tortured, an experience that ruined his health, and he died a few years later. **See** Christianity (Chapter 3).

Otho

For this Roman general who took part in the famous power struggle in A.D. 69, **see** the victor of that conflict, Vespasian.

Ovid

(Publius Ovidius Naso) One of Rome's finest and most popular poets, Ovid was born in 43 B.C. Much younger than his celebrated contemporaries Virgil and Horace, he was never invited into Maecenas's literary circle. Ovid's mentor was another wealthy arts patron named Corvinus Messala. Although he utilized and excelled in a number of different poetic forms, including the love letter, Ovid is perhaps best known as a master of the love elegy. His love poems were generally witty and full of delicate, colorful description; but despite their beauty, many discussed private sexual matters in a manner too open and graphic for conservative Romans like Augustus, and this inevitably got the poet into trouble. The emperor was apparently disturbed by Ovid's first book of poems, the *Amores* (written ca. 20 B.C.), a bold and witty account of the author's love life with a married woman named Corinna. Ovid followed this with *The Art of Love* (ca. 1 B.C. and after), a charming, humorous, and sophisticated, but often sexually graphic, book of advice on the art of seduction, some of it addressed to men, the rest to women. Although the work convinced the prudish Augustus that Ovid had loose morals, the emperor tolerated the poet's audacity for a number of years.

But eventually the ax fell. For reasons that remain unclear (some rumors claim the poet was somehow involved with Augustus's daughter, Julia), in A.D. 8 Ovid was exiled to Tomis, a bleak frontier town on the shores of the Black Sea. He died there nine years later. His other works included a tragic play, *Medea,* now lost; some collections of letters; and one of his masterpieces, the *Metamorphoses,* a long narrative poem combining more than two hundred myths and legends. Ovid not only exerted a strong influence on later Roman writers, but became the most popular Latin poet of the European Renaissance and also influenced Shakespeare. **See** Augustan Age of literature; *Metamorphoses;* poetry (all Chapter 6).

Paul

(d. ca. A.D. 65–67) The person most responsible for bringing the Christian message to the Gentiles, a move that ensured the continuing growth of the faith, he was born Saul, in Tarsus (in southern Asia Minor), the son of a Jew of the tribe of Benjamin. Well educated as a young man, at first he opposed and persecuted the small Jewish sect whose members called themselves the people of "the Way" (before the term "Christian" had been coined). But after being converted, supposedly by a divine vision on the road to Damascus in about 36, he became a prominent member of the group.

Paul apparently came to believe that God had called him to a mission to bring word of Jesus' divinity to the Gentiles. Being Jews, the early Christians had been aiming their message at other Jews. But Paul noted that most Gentiles did not relish the idea of joining a Jewish sect that required them to circumcise themselves and follow strict Jewish dietary laws, and he saw the wisdom of dropping these requirements for Gentiles, reaching an agreement to that effect with church elders in Jerusalem in about 49. Thereafter, he and his associates journeyed far and wide, slowly but steadily gaining new converts. Circa 65, he was arrested by Roman authorities and sometime later beheaded during Nero's anti-Christian persecution. Several of Paul's letters, including those to the Romans, Corinthians, and Thessalonians, later became books in the Christian New Testament. **See** Jesus Christ; **also** Christianity (Chapter 3).

Paullus, Lucius Aemilius

(ca. 230–160 B.C.) A noted Roman general and statesman, he earned the nickname "Macedonius" after his victory over the Greeks at Pydna (in Macedonia) in 168 B.C. Among the spoils were the books belonging to the former Macedonian king, Perseus. Paullus brought these to Rome, creating that city's first large private library. **See** libraries (Chapter 6) **and** Macedonian Wars (Chapter 7).

Perseus Flaccus, Aulus

(A.D. 34–62) A prominent Roman satirist, he flourished mostly during the reign of Nero. Said to have been a modest and gentle individual, he refrained from public life and achieved a relatively small literary output, his main works being six satires that advocate Stoic principles, such as attaining virtue by pursuing a simple, studious life. Strongly influenced by the poet Horace, Perseus attained little fame until a colleague edited his works after his death.

Peter

(later Saint Peter, d. ca. A.D. 64) One of Jesus' original Twelve Apostles, according to the Gospels Peter was the "rock" on which Jesus intended his church to rise. Following Jesus' death, Peter emerged as the leading apostle and eventually journeyed to Rome to preach. There, he was arrested and crucified (upside down, at his own request, so as not to die exactly as Jesus had). His identification as the leading martyr and "bishop" of Rome steadily led to the supremacy of that city as the center of authority of the growing church. **See** Christianity (Chapter 7).

Petronius

(Titus Petronius Niger "Arbiter," d. A.D. 65) A noted Roman satirical writer and author of the famous *Satyricon,* he served as governor of Bithynia and later as a consul. Eventually, he became one of the emperor Nero's inner circle, supposedly as his "arbiter of good taste," from which the writer's nickname derived. In 65, Nero's crony Tigellinus falsely accused Petronius of involvement in an assassination plot and the writer committed suicide, but not before penning a letter telling Nero what he really thought of him. The *Satyricon* remains one of the most colorful and important surviving examples of Roman literature. **See** Nero; **also** *Satyricon* (Chapter 6).

Philip the Arab

(Marcus Julius Philippus, d. A.D. 249) One of the so-called soldier-emperors during the "anarchy" of the third century, he ruled Rome from 244 to 249. His nickname came from the fact that he was the son of an Arab chieftain who had become a Roman knight. After deposing Gordian and taking the throne, Philip made peace with Persia and then campaigned against the Germans in Dacia. His most notable endeavor was overseeing the huge celebration in 248 attending the one-thousandth anniversary of Rome's founding. The following year, Philip was challenged, defeated, and succeeded by one of his own generals, Decius.

Philip V

For this Greek king who opposed Rome in the second century B.C., **see** Flamininus, Titus Quinctius; Hannibal; **also** Battle of Cynoscephalae; Macedonian Wars (both Chapter 7).

Philo

(Philo Judaeus, or "Philo the Jew," ca. 30 B.C.–A.D. 45) Little is known about the life of this native of the Jewish community at Alexandria. He became very influential as a philosophical and religious writer who interpreted the Jewish Scriptures as allegorical rather than literal fact and explained Jewish philosophical ideas in terms of Greek philosophy. Later Christian writers, especially Clement and Origen, felt his influence. Among Philo's numerous surviving works are *Against Flaccus* and *Embassy to Gaius.*

Placidia, Galla

For the mother and royal regent of the fifth-century emperor Valentinian III, **see** Aëtius, Flavius; Valentinian III.

Plautius, Aulus

(early first century A.D.) The conqueror of Britain, he served as consul in 29 and then as governor of Pannonia. In 43, the emperor Claudius chose him to lead the invasion of Britain, which Julius Caesar had begun but not finished in the previous century. Plautius was successful, subduing much of the southern part of the island in the space of four years. **See** Claudius; **also** Britain (Chapter 2).

Plautus, Titus Maccius

(ca. 250–184 B.C.) One of the greatest Roman comic playwrights, he was supposedly of humble origin and got his start in the theater as a stage carpenter. Once he began writing, he proved adept at adopting the style, themes, and plots of the Greek New Comedy, using Menander, Philemon, and other Greeks as his models. But though he borrowed much, Plautus's presentation was often fresh, inventive, and more bawdy and overtly humorous than that of the Greeks. Of the 130 plays attributed to him by ancient sources, twenty survive. These include *The Pot of Gold,* about an old miser who fears someone will steal his treasure; *Milos Gloriosus* (or *The Braggart Warrior*), which shows a swaggering, womanizing soldier to be a fool; and *The Twin Menaechmi,* a tale of twins separated at birth and later reunited under confusing and hilarious circumstances. Other plays by Plautus are *Amphitryon, The Comedy of Asses,* and *The Haunted House.* He had a strong influence on early modern playwrights, including Shakespeare, who based his *Comedy of Errors* on *The Twin Menaechmi.* **See** theater and drama (Chapter 6).

Pliny the Elder

(Gaius Plinius Secundus, ca. A.D. 23–79) A distinguished Roman literary figure and encyclopedist, he was born at Comum (in northern Italy) into a well-to-do family and educated in Rome. As a young man he served in the army and later held several important government posts, including procurator (a civil administrator) in Gaul and Spain. In 79 the emperor Titus appointed him commander of the Roman fleet at Misenum.

Pliny was a classic workaholic. In addition to maintaining his many professional duties, he devoted almost every spare waking hour to acquiring new knowledge (even having servants read books to him while he ate, so as not to waste a moment), taking voluminous notes, and writing books covering a wide variety of subjects. Most of these are now lost, including those on oratory, grammar, history, and military tactics; but fortunately his masterwork, the *Natural History*, a huge collection of facts

A fanciful depiction of Pliny the Elder, one of the foremost encyclopedists of antiquity.

about nearly every aspect of the world he lived in, survives. Indeed, Pliny's insatiable curiosity about the natural world led to his untimely death. On August 24, 79, when Mount Vesuvius began erupting near the Bay of Naples, he rushed to the scene; as pumice stones and ash rained down around him, he stood fearlessly, dictating his observations to his secretary. Two days later, after the eruption had subsided, searchers found Pliny's body on an ash-covered beach, apparently the victim of deadly sulfuric fumes. **See** Vesuvius, Mount (Chapter 2); **also** *Natural History;* prose writing (both Chapter 6).

Pliny the Younger

(Gaius Plinius Caecilius Secundus, ca. A.D. 61–ca. 113) The nephew and adopted son of Pliny the Elder, the younger Pliny was a highly noted public servant, nobleman, and letter writer whose surviving correspondence provides much valuable information about life and some of the noted figures in his day. After receiving an excellent education, he became a high-profile lawyer, then served as praetor in 93 and consul in 100. In these years, he became friendly with the historians Tacitus and Suetonius, as well as the emperor Trajan, who appointed him governor of Bithynia, in Asia Minor. In their more than one hundred exchanges of letters, Pliny and Trajan addressed a wide variety of topics, including the treatment of slaves, criminals, and Christians, and this correspondence reveals a good deal about how a Roman province was administered. An extremely wealthy individual, Pliny owned estates in various parts of Italy and he describes them in detail in his letters. His letters also show that he was an honest, just man who treated his slaves with uncommon kindness. These clearly, often elegantly, written letters, many of which resemble essays, were published in ten books, nine by Pliny himself and the last posthumously. **See** Trajan; **also** prose writing (Chapter 6).

Plotinus

(ca. A.D. 205–270) The most prominent Greek philosopher of late antiquity, he taught at Rome and influenced a number of Greek and Roman thinkers, who admired him for his deep spirituality. He wrote many essays intended to be read by his students. One student, Porphyry, collected some of them in six books of nine essays each, the *Enneads* ("the nines") which were published in the fourth century. These works enunciate their author's Neoplatonic philosophy, which contends that on the highest level of existence is "the One," the force of supreme goodness; below that are the Mind and Soul; below them Nature, the motivating force of living things; and at reality's lowest level, material objects. According to Plotinus, humans have elements of Nature, Mind, and Soul within them and can strive—

through a life of righteousness, self-discipline, and meditation—to achieve mental and spiritual unity with these higher levels. Some Christian thinkers eventually absorbed aspects of this philosophy into their own worldview.

Plutarch

(Greek name: Plutarchos; Roman name: Lucius Mestrius Plutarchus, ca. A.D. 46–ca. 120) Born at Chaeronea (in central Greece), the Greek biographer, essayist, and moralist Plutarch proved to be one of the most widely read and best-loved writers in history. Active in local affairs in his native city as well as the priesthood of the shrine at Delphi, he also became a Roman citizen and resided for a time in Rome. He is most famous for his biographies of prominent Greek and Roman figures, collectively known as the *Parallel Lives*, fifty of which survive. Although he was not a historian by trade, Plutarch's sources included hundreds of ancient historical works that are now lost; therefore, for modern historians these colorfully written biographies constitute priceless mines of information about Greco-Roman history from about 600 to 200 B.C. His equally large output of commentary on literary, scientific, and moral issues was collected as the *Moralia* (*Moral Essays*). **See** *Parallel Lives* (Chapter 6).

Polybius

(ca. 200–ca. 117 B.C.) A Greek statesman and important historian, he was one of many Greek hostages taken to Rome after the Roman victory at Pydna in 168 B.C. There, he became the friend of the Roman general Scipio Aemilianus; when Scipio destroyed Carthage in 146, Polybius witnessed the event. Later, Polybius wrote a forty-volume history of Rome (the *Histories*) covering the period 264–146 B.C. Only the first five books survive complete, although numerous fragments of the others are extant. His writing style is not as lively and appealing as that of the earlier Greek historians Herodotus or Thucydides, but Polybius was a largely honest, thorough, and accurate historian, and his frequent analysis of historical methods advanced the art of historical writing. **See** *Histories* (Chapter 6).

Pompeius, Sextus

For this son of the great general Pompey and opponent of Octavian in one of the civil wars, **see** Agrippa, Marcus Vipsanius.

Pompey

(Gnaeus Pompeius Magnus, 106–48 B.C.) One of the greatest of all Roman statesmen and generals, he played a pivotal role in the turbulent last years of the Republic. His career began in the late 80s B.C. when he commanded and won some battles for Sulla. Subsequently, Sulla, by now dictator of Rome, granted him the honorary *cognomen* Magnus, meaning "great" or "distinguished." In 77 B.C., Pompey went to Spain to deal with the province's rebel governor, Quintus Sertorius. Returning to Italy in 71, Pompey was just in time to aid Marcus Crassus in putting down the slave revolt led by the infamous Spartacus, after which he and Crassus were elected the consuls for 70. Soon afterward came what were perhaps Pompey's greatest triumphs. First, in 67 he was given sweeping authority by the government to rid the sea lanes of pirates, who had been menacing shipping and coastal towns. He did so in just forty days, sinking some thirteen hundred pirate vessels and capturing four hundred more, all without the loss of a single Roman ship. This extraordinary feat made Pompey a national hero; yet he matched it in 66 by crushing the forces of Mithridates, king of Pontus (in Asia Minor), and creating the new provinces of Bithynia, Pontus, and Syria. On his return to Rome in 61 B.C., Pompey enjoyed the most

spectacular triumph staged in Rome up to that time.

Pompey seemed at the top of his form and the following year joined Crassus and Julius Caesar in forming what later came to be called the First Triumvirate. But soon his fortunes began a downward spiral. In 54 B.C., his wife, Julia (Caesar's daughter, whom Pompey had married a few years earlier), died. Then the Triumvirate steadily fell apart and relations between Pompey and Caesar deteriorated, until civil war erupted between the two men in 49. The following year, at Pharsalus (in Greece), Caesar defeated Pompey, who fled to Egypt. There, the local ruler, hoping to gain Caesar's favor, had Pompey murdered. **See** Caesar, Gaius Julius; Crassus, Marcus Licinius; Sertorius, Quintus; **also** piracy (Chapter 5); **and** Battle of Pharsalus; triumph (both Chapter 7).

Pontius Pilate

For this Roman governor who gave the order for Jesus' crucifixion, **see** Jesus Christ.

Poppaea, Sabina

(d. A.D. 65) The wife of Otho, governor of Spain (and emperor for a brief period in 69), and mistress to the emperor Nero. Supposedly it was at her urging that Nero killed his mother and first wife. In 62, Nero married Poppaea, who bore him a child who died in infancy; she was pregnant again in 65 when, in a fit of rage, he kicked her in the stomach, causing her death.

Probus, Marcus Aurelius

(ca. A.D. 232–282) Emperor of Rome from 276 to 282, he was one of the last of the so-called soldier-emperors and a strong ruler who helped the Empire recover from the afflictions of the third-century "anarchy." As a general under the emperor Aurelian, Probus achieved successes on the German frontier and then served as commander of Roman forces in

Syria and Egypt. After his troops proclaimed him emperor in 276, Probus distinguished himself by defeating the Vandals, crushing a number of illegal imperial claimants, and negotiating a truce with Persia. Though assassinated in 282, he had laid much of the groundwork for the sweeping reforms that Diocletian would soon initiate.

Propertius, Sextus

(ca. 50 B.C.–ca. A.D. 17) One of the leading Roman poets of the Augustan Age of literature, he studied law in Rome but then decided to become a poet instead. After some early success with a book of poems published circa 28 B.C., he joined the group of writers sponsored by the great literary patron Gaius Maecenas. Propertius's writing is passionate, sensitive, and sincere in tone and later influenced the style of Italian writers during and after the European Renaissance. His frequent preoccupation with death as a theme may have stemmed from his chronic poor health and untimely loss of family members and friends. His most famous work is perhaps the *Cynthia Monobiblos,* a collection of love poems to his mistress Cynthia (a pseudonym for a woman more likely named Hostia). **See** Augustan Age of literature; poetry (both Chapter 6).

Ptolemy

(Claudius Ptolemaeus, ca. A.D.100–ca. 178) The greatest geographer of ancient times, his *Guide to Geography* significantly shaped the worldview of early Europe. The treatise is divided into eight sections, the first of which discusses the principles of applying mathematics to geography and map making; the next six

The Greek scientist Ptolemy (second from right) receives a crown of laurel leaves to honor his scholarly achievements at the Museum.

books list the latitude and longitude of some eight thousand geographical locations; and the last book gives estimates for the longest day of the year in various latitudes and longitudes.

No less influential was Ptolemy's *Syntaxis* (*Mathematical Compilation*), later called the *Almagest.* This work gave the earth-centered cosmic model a workable and seemingly highly authoritative mathematical underpinning that guaranteed its universal acceptance until the sixteenth-century Polish astronomer Copernicus proved it wrong. Even then, the work's catalog of the latitudes and longitudes of 1,022 stars in forty-eight constellations continued as the standard reference work for sky maps in both the Western and Islamic worlds until the seventeenth century. Almost nothing of a definite nature is known about Ptolemy's personal life, other than that he was born in Egypt and lived and worked in Alexandria at that city's famous university, the Museum.

Ptolemy XII Auletes

(d. 51 B.C.) King of Egypt from 80 to 51 B.C. and father of the famous Cleopatra VII, he long sought recognition from powerful Romans, since his country was by this time little more than a Roman vassal state. In 59 B.C., the Senate gave him this recognition, thanks to the influence of Caesar and Pompey, who demanded a huge bribe in return. Ptolemy lost his throne to one of his daughters for a while until another powerful Roman helped him regain it in 55 B.C. But the Egyptian king died a sad, frustrated man in 51, leaving his throne to Cleopatra and the young Ptolemy XIII, a precarious political situation that would soon draw Caesar to Egypt and Cleopatra's bed. **See** Caesar, Gaius Julius; Cleopatra VII.

Ptolemy XIII

For this younger brother of the famous Cleopatra, queen of Egypt, **see** Cleopatra VII; Ptolemy XII Auletes.

Pulcheria, Aelia

For this sister and royal regent of the fifth-century emperor Theodosius II, **see** Theodosius II.

Pyrrhus

(319–272 B.C.) A second cousin of the Macedonian conqueror Alexander the Great, Pyrrhus was the most illustrious king of the Greek kingdom of Epirus and the first major Greek general to fight the Romans. As a boy, Pyrrhus was forced to flee Epirus. In young adulthood, he became friends with Egypt's Greek ruler, Ptolemy I, married his daughter, and with their help regained his throne. In 280 B.C., Pyrrhus answered a call for aid from the Greek city of Taras (Tarentum in Latin), in southern Italy, which was threatened by the Romans. There, he fought several battles against them. But though he was usually victorious, his losses were heavy, and he is famous for his remark, "One more victory like that over the Romans will destroy us completely!" (the source of the expression

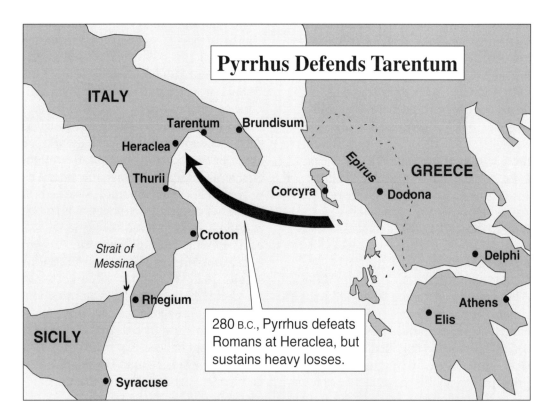

Pyrrhus Defends Tarentum

ITALY

Tarentum Brundisum

Heraclea

Thurii

Epirus GREECE

Corcyra Dodona

Croton

Strait of
Messina

Delphi

Rhegium

Athens

Elis

280 B.C., Pyrrhus defeats Romans at Heraclea, but sustains heavy losses.

SICILY

Syracuse

"Pyrrhic victory," meaning a very costly win). Deciding to cut his losses, Pyrrhus returned to Greece in 275 and soon afterward died prematurely in a street fight. **See** battlefield tactics (Chapter 7).

Quintilian

(Marcus Fabius Quintilianus, b. ca. A.D. 35) A native of Spain, he was a renowned Roman teacher of rhetoric who taught Pliny the Younger, among other notables. After serving as tutor to the great-nephews of the emperor Domitian, Quintilian retired and started writing. His *Decline of Oratory* is lost, but his most important work, *The Education of an Orator*, which describes the proper training of an orator from birth through manhood, has fortunately survived. After a complete copy was discovered in Switzerland in 1416, it exerted a powerful influence on several generations of educated Europeans. **See** rhetoric (Chapter 6).

Regulus, Marcus Atilius

(third century B.C.) A prominent Roman general during the First Punic War, he defeated the Carthaginian fleet at Cape Ecnomus, one of the largest sea battles in history. Circa 255 B.C., he led an army onto North African soil, but was defeated by a Greek mercenary general and taken prisoner. Supposedly Regulus was tortured to death, but some historians think this may have been Roman propaganda. **See** Punic Wars (Chapter 7).

Remus

For this brother of Rome's legendary founder, **see** Romulus.

Romulus

(eighth century B.C.?) The legendary founder and first king of Rome; according to later tales, he and his twin brother, Remus, were the grandchildren of the king of Alba Longa (in Latium). When they were infants, their great-uncle, who had usurped the throne, ordered them drowned in the Tiber; fortunately, however, the twins washed ashore, where a she-wolf fed them and some poor shepherds eventually took them in. When the brothers grew to manhood and learned their true identities, they returned to Alba, overthrew their great-uncle, and restored their grandfather to his throne. Then they set out to establish a new city of their own on the northern edge of the Latium plain. As it turned out, however, Romulus founded the city by himself, for he and Remus got into a petty squabble, fought, and Romulus slew his brother. Shortly after this tragedy, Romulus supposedly laid the new town's initial foundations. **See** Monarchy (Chapter 4) **and** *Aeneid* (Chapter 6).

Romulus Augustulus

(late fifth century A.D.) Generally viewed as the last emperor of the Roman Empire, he was the son of Orestes, the *magister militum* under the emperor Julius Nepos. The boy's name was Romulus Augustus, but he was given the nickname of Augustulus, which means "little Augustus." Soon after Orestes deposed Nepos in August 475, he placed the boy on the throne; but the following year the German officer Odoacer killed Orestes and removed Augustulus from the throne. Odoacer proved merciful, giving an estate and a pension to the boy, who lived on for an unknown number of years. **See** Nepos, Julius; Odoacer; **also** fall of Rome (Chapter 7).

Sallust

(Gaius Sallustius Crispus, 86–35 B.C.) A noted Roman historian, he was born to a plebeian family and served as a tribune of the plebs in 52 B.C. In 49, he served under Julius Caesar, commanding one of his legions. Later, Sallust served as praetor (47) and as governor of the new province of Numidia (46). But when, in the latter post, he was charged (though not convicted) of extortion, he retired to private life and devoted himself to writing. His *War* (or *Conspiracy*) *of Catiline* describes the events surrounding the failed coup led by the disgruntled nobleman Catiline in 63 B.C.; his *Jugurthine War* chronicles the conflict fought from 112 to 105 B.C. between Rome and Jugurtha, a Numidian king. Sallust's chief literary strengths were his attempts to explain the causes of the events he described and the vividness of his character sketches. His main weaknesses were his frequent chronological inaccuracies and an obvious bias against certain privileged upper-class individuals and families. **See** Catiline; **also** Jugurthine War (Chapter 7).

Salvian

(Salvianus, flourished fifth century A.D.) A late Roman Christian writer, he spent most of his adult life teaching in a monastery on an island off the coast of southern Gaul. His most important surviving work is *On the Governance of God,* in eight books, which sought to show that the troubles of the late Empire were part of God's retribution for human sins. In this regard, Salvian depicted the onrushing barbarians as a necessary cleansing element.

Sassanids

The term refers to a dynasty of Persian rulers who created a huge Near Eastern realm that rivaled and at times challenged that of Rome. The dynasty was established by Ardashir, the youngest son of a vassal lord of the Parthian Empire. In A.D. 224, Ardashir defeated the last Parthian (or Arsacid) ruler, Artabanus V, and soon afterward named himself "King of Kings" of a new imperial line. In 230, Ardashir attacked Roman Mesopotamia, and in 259, another Sassanid, Shapur I, defeated and captured the Roman emperor Valerian. In the 280s, after some setbacks, Sassanid Persia was forced to cede Mesopotamia and Armenia to the Romans. But in the 290s, the Sassanid ruler Narses invaded Syria and defeated the emperor Gallerius, and in the fourth century Shapur II forced on the Romans a treaty containing some humiliating terms. Thereafter, the two empires remained largely at peace. After the fall of western Rome, the eastern Roman rulers continued to have diplomatic relations with their Sassanid counterparts. Sassanid Persia prospered until 651, when it was overrun by Muslim armies. **See** Arsacids; Valerian.

Scaevola, Gaius Mucius

In Roman legend, he was a citizen who entered the camp of Lars Porsenna, the Etruscan king who was then besieging Rome, and tried but failed to kill Porsenna. Taken prisoner, Scaevola supposedly showed his defiance and bravery by thrusting his right hand into a fire; Porsenna was so impressed that he released the would-be assassin. (Appropriately, the *cognomen* Scaevola means "left-handed.")

Scipio, Publius Cornelius

(d. 211 B.C.) A noted Roman general of the Second Punic War, as consul in 218 B.C. he rushed an army to Gaul, hoping to stop Hannibal's advance. When he saw that he had arrived too late, Scipio sent his army to Spain under the command of his brother, Gnaeus, and returned to northern Italy, where he unsuccessfully engaged Hannibal at the Ticinus and Trebia Rivers. Later, in Spain, the Scipio brothers defeated a Carthaginian army and captured Saguntum, but they both met defeat and death soon afterward. **See** Punic Wars (Chapter 7).

Scipio, Publius Cornelius Aemilianus

(ca. 185–129 B.C.) A popular and capable Roman general and statesman, he was the second son of L. Aemilius Paullus, the victor of the Battle of Pydna. Adopted by the son of Scipio Africanus, Scipio Aemilianus fought in the Third Macedonian War and from 147 to 146 B.C. led Rome's forces against Carthage in the climax of the Third Punic War. After destroying Carthage, he received a magnificent triumph and the nickname "Africanus Minor" (to differentiate him from his adoptive grandfather, who was now called "Africanus Major"). Scipio Aemilianus was also known as a great orator, honest politician, and an avid patron of Greek and Roman literature. **See** Punic Wars (Chapter 7).

Scipio, Publius Cornelius "Africanus"

(236–183 B.C.) The eldest son of P. Cornelius Scipio and one of the greatest military leaders in Roman history. With the Second Punic War at its height, at the age of only twenty-five the younger Scipio secured command of Spain and by 206 B.C. had managed to drive the Carthaginians out of that region. Elected consul in 205, he soon crossed over into Africa, and in 202 scored a tremendous victory by defeating the great Hannibal at Zama and bringing the war to a close. For this feat, he received the title "Africanus." So great was his prestige in the following few years that he was elected both consul again and censor and also served as head of the Senate. In 190 B.C., Scipio and his brother Lucius led an army against the Seleucid ruler Antiochus III, whom Lucius defeated at Magnesia (in Asia Minor). But when they returned to Rome, they became the victims of vicious and unfair political attacks spearheaded by Cato the Elder, who accused them of various kinds of misconduct. Embittered, Scipio went into retirement and eventually died of illness. **See** Hannibal; **also** Battle of Zama; Punic Wars (both Chapter 7).

Sejanus

For this notorious henchman of the second emperor, Tiberius, **see** Tiberius; Agrippina the Elder.

Seneca the Younger

(Lucius Annaeus Seneca; ca. A.D. 5–65) A talented poet, playwright, and Stoic philosopher, Seneca also tutored and advised the infamous emperor Nero. Born in Spain, Seneca traveled to Rome as a young man and studied rhetoric and philosophy. After gaining a reputation as an orator, in 41 he was exiled to Corsica by the emperor Claudius, probably at the request of the scheming Messalina; but Agrippina the Younger brought him back in 49 to tutor her son Nero. When Nero ascended the throne in 54, Seneca became one of his chief advisers, which contributed to the relative stability of the early part of the reign. But as Nero sank into tyranny, even the humane Seneca could no longer control him. In 65 the emperor accused him, probably falsely, of taking part in a major conspiracy against the throne, and Seneca was forced to commit suicide.

A prodigious writer, Seneca produced works on natural history, geography, ethics, and a number of other subjects, as well as poetry, plays, and many letters. Of those that survive, among the most important are the *Dialogues,* including *On the Constancy of the Wise Man,* which maintains that a truly wise man is immune from insults and suffering; *On the Tranquility of the Soul,* which deals with attaining peace of mind; and *On Leisure,* describing the benefits of relaxation and philosophic speculation. His moral essays include *On Clemency,* in which he stresses that a ruler must be merciful. Most of his letters also deal with moral and philosophical themes, such as the nature of goodness and death. Seneca's *Natural Questions* is a collection of observations of natural phenomena, which he tries to reconcile with the Stoic worldview. More important from a literary standpoint are his nine tragedies, based on Greek models and written for recitation in upper-class gatherings; they include *Medea, The Trojan Women,* and *Oedipus.* **See** Nero; **also** theater and drama (Chapter 6).

Sertorius, Quintus

(early first century B.C.) A prominent Roman military leader, he began as a supporter of Marius, but came to oppose Marius's large-scale political purges. Sertorius served as praetor in 83 B.C., then became governor of Spain. Soon he led a major rebellion against Rome and scored a number of successes against Roman generals, including Pompey, before being murdered by one of his own officers in the late 70s B.C. **See** Pompey.

Servius Tullius

(sixth century B.C.?) The sixth of the legendary kings of early Rome, he supposedly reigned from 578 to 535 B.C. He may have been a real person, although some of the stories attributed to him and his rule, such as his miraculous birth to the god Vulcan and a slave girl, are obviously mythical. According to traditional tales, the son of his predecessor eventually murdered him and became the last king, Tarquinius Superbus. **See** Monarchy (Chapter 4).

Severus, Septimius

(Lucius Septimius Severus, A.D. 145–211) As Roman emperor from 193 to 211, he was a strong general and ruler who founded the Severan dynasty, whose members ruled Rome from 193 to 235. Born at Lepcis Magna (in North Africa), of parents from prominent equestrian families, he rose to high government posts as a young man. These included quaestor, tribune of the people, and praetor. In 184 he became governor of one of the Gallic provinces and in 191 of

Upper Pannonia, where he still resided when the emperor Commodus's death ignited a contest for the throne. Severus was proclaimed emperor by his troops and marched them to Rome; but other strong leaders, including Pescennius Niger, claimed the purple, and he had to defeat them before his position was completely secure. Severus accomplished this task by 196. From 197 to 199, he fought and defeated the Parthians and founded the province of Mesopotamia. In 208, he and his eldest son Caracalla invaded Caledonia (Scotland), which turned out to be an indecisive operation; three years later, in the British town of York, Severus died. It is said that on his deathbed he told his sons to enrich and appease the soldiers at the expense of everyone else.

Severus Alexander, Marcus Aurelius

(A.D. 208–235) Emperor of Rome from 222 to 235, he was the son of Julia Mamaea and cousin of the eccentric emperor Elagabalus. Thanks to the influence of their grandmother, Julia Maesa, Elagabalus adopted the other youth and made him Caesar and heir to the throne. However, Severus Alexander soon proved more popular with the Senate and Praetorian Guard, and Elagabalus's jealousy and attempts to remove his cousin brought about the latter's assassination. Severus Alexander's policies as emperor were largely engineered by his grandmother at first, and after her death by his mother. His most positive achievement was a successful campaign against Sassanid Persia in 232. Three years later, while attempting to negotiate with a German tribe, the young emperor and his mother were murdered by their own soldiers and Macrinus took the throne, initiating the age of the "soldier emperors." **See** Elagabalus; Julia Maesa; Julia Mamaea.

Shapur I

For this Persian ruler who captured the Roman emperor Valerian in the third century, **see** Sassanids.

lowers died in the final battle; while the six thousand surviving slaves were crucified along the road to Rome as a warning to others who might contemplate rebelling. Spartacus's heroic, tragic story is the subject of a popular modern novel by Howard Fast and a spectacular 1960 film produced by and starring Kirk Douglas. **See** slaves and slavery (Chapter 5).

Statius, Publius Papinius

(ca. A.D. 45–ca. 96) The son of a teacher and poet, Statius was a Roman poet whose talent gained him the patronage and friendship of the emperor Domitian. Statius's best-known works were the *Thebaid* (published ca. 91), an epic poem about the quarrel between the sons of the legendary Greek figure Oedipus, and the *Silvae,* a collection of thirty-two short poems (published in installments beginning in 91). The last poem of the *Silvae* is a hauntingly beautiful expression of his grief over the death of his adopted son.

Stilicho, Flavius

(d. A.D. 408) The son of a Vandal cavalry officer and a Roman woman, he was one of the most powerful political figures of the Later Empire. About 384, he married the emperor Theodosius's niece and received the rank of count (*comes*). After Stilicho distinguished himself as a military leader, Theodosius promoted him to the top military post in the western Empire—*magister militum*—and also made him guardian of his son, Honorius. On Theodosius's death in 395, Stilicho proclaimed himself guardian of Honorius's brother, Arcadius (who ruled in the east), and attempted to consolidate his own power throughout the Empire. But he was repeatedly thwarted by invading Visigoths, revolts by Roman generals and usurpers, and the jealousy and hatred of important members of the western and eastern courts. Finally, when Arcadius died in 408, Stilicho was accused of trying to put his own son on the eastern throne and Honorius had him arrested and executed. **See** Honorius.

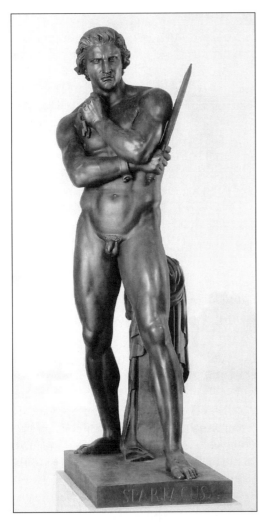

This bronze statue of the rebellious slave Spartacus was created by French sculptor Denis Foyatier in 1847.

Spartacus

(early first century B.C.) A Thracian slave who led the last and most famous of Rome's large slave rebellions. The revolt began when a group of slaves at a gladiator school in Capua escaped and began plundering the surrounding countryside. They freed many slaves in central Italy, trained them to fight, and defeated several small Roman armies sent against them. The government eventually appointed the wealthy aristocrat Marcus Crassus to quell the uprising, and in 71 B.C. he defeated the slaves in Lucania (in southern Italy). Spartacus and most of his fol-

Strabo

(ca. 64 B.C.–ca. A.D. 25) A Greek traveler and geographer, he was born in Amasia (in northern Asia Minor) and moved to Rome in 44 B.C. to further his education. From there, he traveled widely throughout the Mediterranean world and took notes on the histories, economies, inhabitants, animals, and plants of the locales he visited. This information became the basis for his monumental *Geography* in seventeen books (completed ca. 7 B.C.), which survives and provides modern scholars with much valuable information about the Roman world of his day. Strabo also composed an important historical treatise in forty-seven books, the *Historical Sketches,* which has not survived.

Suetonius

(Gaius Suetonius Tranquillus, ca. A.D. 69–ca. 130) A noted Roman biographer and historian, he was born in North Africa and studied law in Rome, after which he served on Pliny the Elder's staff in Bithynia (ca. 110–112). On returning to Rome, Suetonius acquired the prestigious position of director of the imperial libraries under the emperor Trajan. Next came the important job of secretary of correspondence under Hadrian. But after the mid–120s, nothing more is known about the historian's life. Suetonius's fame rests principally on his collection of imperial biographies, *The Twelve Caesars.* His *On Famous Men,* containing brief biographies of Virgil, Horace, and other Roman writers and grammarians, survives in part; but his *Roman Masters and Customs, Roman Festivals, Greek Games,* and other works are unfortunately lost. **See** prose writing; *The Twelve Caesars* (both Chapter 6).

Sulla, Lucius Cornelius

(ca. 138–78 B.C.) A prominent Roman general, he led the aristocratic faction against Marius's popular faction in the

Sulla, an aristocrat and conservative politician, wanted wealthy patricians to control the Senate and other institutions.

civil unrest of the 80s B.C. Born into a patrician family, Sulla made a name for himself in the Jugurthine War and the Social War. Elected consul in 88 B.C., he was passed over for the command of Roman forces that were leaving to deal with Mithridates of Pontus, who was causing trouble for Rome in Asia Minor. In response, Sulla marched his army into Rome and took the city by force, the first time in Roman history a consul had done so. He then headed for Asia Minor, where he defeated Mithridates. Returning in 83 B.C., Sulla fought the popular faction again and once more took the city by force; he then acquired the office of dictator and conducted a bloody purge of his political enemies. After instituting some administrative reforms, he retired to private life in 79 B.C. and died the following year. **See** Marius, Gaius; **also** Jugurthine War (Chapter 7).

Symmachus, Quintus Aurelius

(ca. A.D. 340–ca. 402) A Roman aristocrat and senator noted for his expert oratory and especially for his vigorous defense of paganism. After the Christian bishop Ambrose convinced the emperor Gratian to remove the Altar of Victory from the Senate (in 382), in 384 Symmachus addressed a letter to the young emperor Valentinian II calling for restoration of the shrine and also for mutual tolerance between pagans and Christians. Ambrose rebutted the plea and the shrine was never restored. Symmachus left behind more than nine hundred letters, which his son published after his death. **See** Ambrose; **also** hunting (Chapter 5).

Tacitus, Publius Cornelius

(ca. A.D. 56–ca. 120?) Relatively little is known about the life of Tacitus, one of the greatest historians of antiquity and arguably Rome's most distinguished historian. Possibly born in Gaul, he served as quaestor in 81, praetor in 88, and governor of the province of Asia in 112–113; he also married the daughter of Gnaeus Julius Agricola (A.D. 40–93), a noted general and governor of Britain. Tacitus's first two published works came in 98. One, the *Agricola,* praises and describes the career of his father-in-law and also recounts the trials that honorable men like Agricola and Tacitus himself had been forced to endure under the recent tyranny of the emperor Domitian. The other work, the *Germania,* gives a vivid description of the Germanic tribes then living beyond the Rhine and Danube Rivers. Tacitus's greatest works were the *Annals* and *Histories,* covering the reigns of the early emperors. **See** *Annals/Histories;* prose writing (both Chapter 6).

Tarquinius Superbus

(sixth century B.C.) Also known as "Tarquin the Proud," he was the last king of Rome, supposedly ruling from 534 to 509 B.C. Although he was likely a real person, many of the stories later attributed to him are probably fictitious or at least exaggerated. In general, it would probably be fairly accurate to say, as the Augustan historian Livy does, that Tarquin was a tyrannical but constructive ruler who erected the first version of the Temple of Jupiter on the Capitoline hill. Shortly after the Roman fathers deposed him, they established the Republic (ca. 509 B.C.). **See** Rome (Chapter 2); **also** Monarchy (Chapter 4).

Terence

(Publius Terentius Afer, d. ca. 159 B.C.) Little for certain is known about the life of this important Roman comedic playwright, except that he was apparently born a slave at Carthage, brought to Rome as a young man, and there freed. He molded his writing style on Greek New Comedy, especially the works of Menander, following the originals more closely than his immediate Roman predecessor in the genre, Plautus. Terence's dialogue is more natural than Plautus's and his humor on the whole more sophisticated. The six surviving plays of Terence are *The Girl from Andros, The Mother-in-Law, Self-Tormentor, The Eunuch, The Brothers,* and *Phormio.* **See** Plautus, Titus Maccius; **also** prose writing; theater and drama (both Chapter 6).

Tertullian

(Quintus Septimius Florens Tertullianus, ca. A.D. 160–ca. 230) A noted Roman Christian writer and apologist, he was born at Carthage of pagan parents and received a thorough education that included rhetoric, philosophy, and law. Sometime before 197, he converted to Christianity and soon began writing religious works in Latin, some of which defended the faith by refuting the anti-Christian charges of pagan critics. The most famous of these was his *Apology* (ca. 197).

It advocated that Christians should resist contamination by "immoral" pagan ideas and practices and also be willing to martyr themselves for their faith. "The blood of the martyrs is the seed of the Church," he supposedly declared. Tertullian is often referred to as the "father of Latin theology." **See** Christianity (Chapter 3).

Theodosius I

(A.D. 347–395) Often referred to as Theodosius "the Great," he was emperor of eastern Rome from 379 to 392 and of both east and west from 392 to 395. Born in Spain, he entered the army and served on the staff of his father, a prominent general. In 378, following the disastrous Roman defeat at Adrianople, the emperor Gratian gave Theodosius charge of an army on the Danube frontier, where the latter conducted successful campaigns against the Goths. As a reward, Gratian made him emperor of the east in January 379. By 382, Theodosius had concluded that it was necessary to negotiate with the Goths and he allowed them to settle in Thrace in return for the service of their warriors in the Roman army.

Later, in 387, a general named Magnus invaded Italy, posing a threat to the western emperor, Valentinian II; Theodosius came to the rescue, defeating Magnus, and later defeated another western imperial claimant (Eugenius, supported by his *magister militum,* Arbogast) in a huge battle in 394. Theodosius is also known for his antipagan policies. Under the influence of the bishop Ambrose, in the early 390s he closed the pagan temples, destroying some and converting many others to Christian churches or museums. The young sons of Theodosius, Honorius and Arcadius, succeeded him on his death in 395.

Theodosius II

(A.D. 401–450) His reign as emperor of eastern Rome from 408 to 450 was the longest in Roman imperial history. The son of the emperor Arcadius and grandson of Theodosius the Great, the younger Theodosius ascended the throne at the age of seven, so that the government was in the hands of his regent, Anthemius, for several years. Anthemius was a constructive administrator who strengthened Constantinople's defenses. But his influence was terminated in 414 when Theodosius's sister, Aelia Pulcheria, assumed the duties of regent. A devout Christian, she supervised the young emperor's education and imparted to him a love of literature, religion, and philosophy. These intellectual interests culminated in a massive and historically important collection of Roman laws, the Theodosian Code, completed in 438. By contrast, Theodosius's efforts in foreign affairs had mixed results. On the one hand, he concluded a lasting peace with Sassanid Persia in 422, contributing to the stability of the Roman east in succeeding decades; on the other, his generals were not very successful against the Huns, who were terrorizing the Danube frontier. Theodosius died after falling from his horse in 450. **See** laws (Chapter 4).

Tiberius

(Tiberius Claudius Nero, 42 B.C.–A.D. 37) The Roman Empire's second emperor, he reigned from A.D. 14 to 37. The eldest son of Augustus's wife Livia and her former husband, Tiberius Claudius Nero, Tiberius received a first-rate education and early won Augustus's trust. The latter charged him with numerous important military missions, including campaigns in the east and Germany, and eventually adopted him as his son and heir in A.D. 4. More Germanic campaigns followed for Tiberius, including his stabilization of the Rhine frontier after Varus's disastrous defeat in the Teutoburg Forest (in 9). In 14, when Augustus died, Tiberius succeeded him.

As emperor, Tiberius at first ruled moderately and largely carried on the policies of his illustrious predecessor. He administered the provinces efficiently and the army remained disciplined and loyal under his watch; also, he managed the economy well, increasing the size of the imperial treasury some twenty-seven-fold. Also like Augustus, Tiberius preferred to live quietly and modestly and disliked the insincere flattery so often aimed at him. But despite his abilities and good intent, the new emperor became increasingly unpopular with the Senate and the citizenry, partly because he eliminated the popular assemblies and many other outward republican trappings, and also because he did not spend much money on public entertainment.

More serious, however, was Tiberius's increasing personal unhappiness and bitterness, coupled with his choice of Lucius Aelius Sejanus, the prefect of the Praetorian Guard, as his close aide. As the emperor steadily withdrew from public life, Sejanus, a grasping, coldhearted individual, eventually came to run the government almost entirely on his own, maintaining what was in effect a reign of terror. In 31, while at his villa on the island of Capri, where he had long remained in seclusion, Tiberius discovered that he was to become Sejanus's next victim; he promptly arrested and executed Sejanus. When he died a lonely, hated old man in 37, Tiberius had no living sons; he was succeeded by Augustus's great-grandson, Gaius Caesar (Caligula). **See** Augustus.

Tibullus, Albius

(ca. 55–19 B.C.) A popular Roman poet during the Augustan Age, he was a member of the circle of writers surrounding the noted literary patron Messala Corvinus and also a friend of both Horace and Ovid. Tibullus wrote two books of elegies, the first containing five poems celebrating his love for one Delia (whose real name was Plania). In the second book, three of the poems mention his strong feelings for another woman, whom he calls Nemesis. Besides romantic love, his favorite theme was the virtue of life in the countryside. **See** Augustan Age of literature; poetry (both Chapter 6).

Tigellinus

For this unscrupulous assistant to the corrupt first-century emperor Nero, **see** Nero.

Titus

(Titus Flavius Vespasianus) The elder son of the emperor Vespasian, Titus was born in A.D. 39. He accompanied his father to Judaea in the late 60s to put down a Jewish rebellion and ended up finishing the job after Vespasian returned to Rome to claim the throne. Titus's capture of Jerusalem (in 70) was later commemorated by the Arch of Titus, built by his brother Domitian. Like his father, Titus proved to be a remarkably fair, honest, and efficient ruler, who took a keen interest in his subjects. He would often have friendly conversations with the poorest and humblest of them at the public games or in the bathhouses, happily listened to their grievances, and did them favors.

Titus's short reign of just over twenty-six months (from 79 to 81) was marked by several noteworthy events, including the inauguration of the new Flavian amphitheater (later called the Colosseum); the great eruption of Mount Vesuvius in Campania (August 24, 79), which destroyed the towns of Pompeii and Herculaneum; a terrible fire that swept through Rome (80), destroying the Temple of Jupiter on the Capitoline hill; and the onset of a plague (the identity of which remains unknown) that killed many people in the capital. Titus responded quickly and generously to the three disasters, showing, as the historian Suetonius put it, "far more than an emperor's concern. It resembled the deep love of a father for his children, which he conveyed . . . by helping the victims to the utmost extent of his purse." (Titus 11.8, in *The Twelve Caesars*) It is no wonder that the Roman people expressed genuine sadness at this ruler's untimely death, apparently of a fever, in September 81. **See** Vespasian; **also** theaters and amphitheaters (Chapter 6) **and** Judaea (Chapter 7).

Trajan

(Marcus Ulpius Trajanus, A.D. 53–117) The second of the so-called five good emperors, he ruled the Empire from 98 to 117. Hailing from Spain, he was the first emperor born outside of Italy. After a successful military career as a young man, he won the admiration of the emperor Nerva, who adopted him as his son and

heir in 97. Ascending the throne the following year, Trajan quickly demonstrated that he was an able, thoughtful ruler; he showed courtesy to the Senate, increased state funds for poor children, initiated a huge program of public building, and ran the Empire's finances in a sound, honest manner. He also expanded the realm, conquering Dacia (101–106) and making it a province and invading the Parthian Empire (114–116) and thereby securing Armenia and Mesopotamia. Under his rule, the Empire reached its largest extent—about 3.5 million square miles. Trajan is also known for his hefty correspondence with his friend Pliny the Younger when the latter was governor of Bithynia (mentioning among other things a lenient imperial policy regarding Christians), and for the tall, sculpture-covered column the emperor raised in Rome, a monument that still stands as testimony

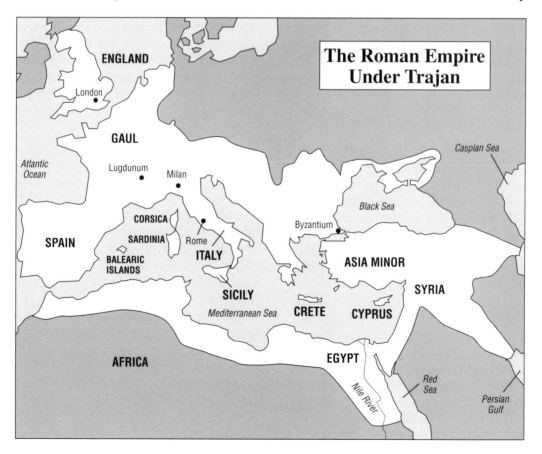

to his enlightened reign. **See** Hadrian; Pliny the Younger.

Trebonius, Gaius

(d. 43 B.C.) A noted public figure during the final years of the Republic, he supported the aristocratic faction and the members of the First Triumvirate (Caesar, Pompey, and Crassus). As tribune of the people in 55 B.C., Trebonius pushed through a law that helped Pompey's and Crassus's careers. Then he served under Caesar in Gaul and during the civil war that Caesar fought with Pompey. Caesar rewarded him by securing him the consulship in 45; but the following year Trebonius turned on his mentor, joining the assassination plot against him. The betrayal did not go unpunished, for in 43 B.C. another of Caesar's former officers, Dolabella, stabbed Trebonius to death in his bed.

Trogus, Pompeius

For this first-century B.C. Roman historian, **see** Justin.

Ulpian

(Domitius Ulpianus, d. A.D. 228) The prefect of the Praetorian Guard under the emperor Severus Alexander and a noted jurist. Ulpian apparently did most of his writing between 211 and 217, during the reign of Caracalla, a vast output of nearly three hundred books. Mostly compilations of prior laws and legal writings, along with commentary, they were consulted heavily by the men who produced the great law code of the sixth-century Roman/Byzantine emperor, Justinian. **See** *Corpus Juris Civilis;* jurists (both Chapter 4).

Valens, Flavius Julius

(ca. A.D. 328–378) From 364 to 378, he was emperor of eastern Rome. Serving in various posts under the emperors Julian and Jovian, he became a tribune under and eventually coemperor with his brother, Valentinian I, who ruled in the west. In his short reign, Valens variously fought the Goths, Persians, and an imperial usurper. But he is best known for his horrendous defeat at Adrianople in 378, one of the worst military disasters in Roman history, in which he met his death. **See** Valentinian I; **also** Battle of Adrianople (Chapter 7).

Valentinian I

(Flavius Valentinianus, A.D. 321–375) As ruler of western Rome from 364 to 375, he proved a generally capable and well-meaning, if somewhat unpopular and not always successful, ruler. Rising through the army ranks as a young man, he served with distinction under the emperors Constantius II, Julian, and Jovian, and with the support of the troops succeeded Jovian as emperor in 364. Almost immediately, Valentinian named his brother Valens as emperor of the east, then launched a series of military campaigns on the Rhine frontier and in Britain. The German borders did not remain quiet, however, and Valentinian had to return later to repel more barbarian incursions. In 375, while receiving the delegation of a German tribe, he became so enraged at their disrespect for his office that he burst a blood vessel and died.

Valentinian II

(Flavius Valentinianus, A.D. 371–392) Emperor of western Rome from 375 to 392, this son of the emperor Valentinian I was a weak, ineffectual ruler like many of those who followed him on the Roman throne. At first, his half-brother, Gratian, with whom he ruled jointly, made all the important decisions; later, after Gratian's death in 383, Theodosius I allowed Valentinian to remain on the throne but controlled him either directly or through powerful ministers.

Valentinian III

(Flavius Placidus, ca. A.D. 419–455) The western Roman ruler from 425 to 455, he was the last comparatively stable emperor of the western Empire. Son of the emperor Constantius III, he fled to the eastern court in 423 after quarreling with the western emperor Honorius; but when Honorius died soon afterward, Valentinian returned to Italy and ascended the throne. At first, his mother, Galla Placidia, acting as regent, controlled Valentinian, until Flavius Aëtius, the *magister militum,* superceded her authority in 433. For several years Aëtius more or less ran the government, but eventual conspiracies against him broke his hold on Valentinian, who personally executed the general in 454. The following year, the emperor was himself assassinated by the members of a palace conspiracy. **See** Aëtius, Flavius; Honorius.

Valerian

(Publius Licinius Valerianus, d. A.D. 260) One of the soldier emperors during the "anarchy," he ruled from 253 to 260. Little is known about his early life, but he definitely served under the emperor Decius, with whom he shared a distinct dislike for Christians. By 253 Valerian was in command of the troops along the Rhine and that year they proclaimed him emperor. Soon, he was on the throne in Rome with his son, Gallienus, at his side as coemperor. On the way to fight the Goths, Valerian heard that the Persians were on the rampage in the east; he hurried there but was defeated by the Sassanid ruler Shapur I, who captured and executed him. Reportedly, the unfortunate Roman leader was stuffed and put on display in a Persian temple.

Varro, Marcus Terentius

(116–27 B.C.) One of the greatest and most versatile of all Roman thinkers and writers, Varro received an excellent education in Rome and went on to become an officer under Pompey the Great, first against pirates in Spain, and later, in 49 B.C., against Julius Caesar. Caesar later pardoned Varro, however, making him Rome's chief librarian. In 43 B.C., shortly after Caesar's death, Mark Antony condemned Varro, who managed to escape; but after Octavian (later Augustus) defeated Antony in 31 B.C., Varro returned to Rome and spent the rest of his days studying and writing. He produced a vast output of works on a wide variety of topics, including agriculture, law, history, grammar, music, medicine, education, and philosophy. In all, he may have written more than six hundred books. Unfortunately, only sections of two have survived—*On Farming* and *On the Latin Language* (books 5–10 of which are dedicated to the orator Cicero). One of the greatest and most influential of Varro's lost works was the *Human and Divine Antiquities,* an encyclopedia of Roman history and religion.

Varus, Publius Quinctilius

(d. A.D. 9) One of the more famous Roman generals, primarily because he was in command during one of the most crippling military defeats in Roman history. Born into a noble family, Varus married the emperor Augustus's great-niece and shortly afterward (A.D. 6) became governor of the province of Syria. In 9, the emperor sent him to Germany, expecting Varus to begin a general and peaceful Romanization of the region. However, Varus's treatment of the natives was apparently tactless and abusive. And later that year, a German force ambushed his army in the Teutoburg Forest (near the Rhine River), wiping it out almost to the last man. **See** Battle of the Teutoburg Forest (Chapter 7).

Vegetius

(Flavius Vegetius Renatus, late fourth century A.D.) A Roman civil servant, and perhaps a Christian, he is noted for his military handbook, *The Art of War.* Written at a time when the Roman army had begun to decline in quality, the work calls for bringing back traditional training methods and discipline. It must be consulted with care, because in discussing the army of his own day Vegetius drew mainly on old sources describing the Roman military in prior ages.

Vercingetorix

(d. 46 B.C.) The chief of the Gallic tribe of the Averni and Julius Caesar's most able and feared opponent during the Roman conquest of Gaul in the 50s B.C. Defeated at the siege of Alesia (in 52 B.C.), Vercingetorix was taken prisoner, paraded in Caesar's victory triumph in Rome (in 46 B.C.), and subsequently murdered in a Roman dungeon. The modern French (whose nation encompasses what was once Roman Gaul) recognize the Averni chief as one of their national heroes. **See** Averni; siege of Alesia (both Chapter 7).

Vespasian

(Titus Flavius Vespasianus, A.D. 9–79) The founder of the Flavian dynasty of Roman emperors, Vespasian came from a middle-class family of soldiers and civil servants. As a tax collector in the Roman province of Asia, his father had earned a reputation as an honest and hardworking man, and Vespasian displayed these same qualities as a professional soldier. He rose through the ranks through talent alone and eventually attained the rank of general, serving with distinction in Britain and Africa.

In 68, when Vespasian was crushing a rebellion of the Jews in the province of Judaea, news came that the unpopular, despotic emperor, Nero, had committed suicide and that the Roman troops in Spain had declared their general, Galba, as emperor. In the months that followed, there was a crisis the likes of which Rome had not faced since the bloody civil wars in the final years of the Republic. Galba was old and feeble, and after becoming emperor he made the mistake of refusing to pay the imperial bodyguards the bonuses he had promised them. So they promptly murdered him. In the power struggle that ensued, two other powerful generals, Otho and Vitellius, declared themselves emperor and Vespasian allowed his own troops to proclaim him emperor too. Because four men in all claimed the imperial office in little more than a year, A.D. 69 thereafter became known as "the year of the four emperors." Vitellius managed to defeat Otho. But then Vespasian's forces marched on Rome and crushed those of Vitellius, whom Vespasian's soldiers dragged into the Forum, murdered, and threw into the Tiber. That left Vespasian firmly in power.

Vespasian showed the same qualities as emperor that he had as a soldier. On ascending the throne, he immediately established good relations with the senators and other aristocrats. They saw that he was a tolerant, frugal, and efficient bureaucrat interested only in restoring good government to Rome, and they were impressed with his strict economic policies, which steadily replenished a state treasury that had been drained by Nero's excesses. Indeed, the main theme of Vespasian's reign was the creation of a new Rome, one of which all Romans could be proud. To symbolize this goal, the coins he struck bore the motto *Roma resurgens,* meaning "Rome reborn." Vespasian also became one of Rome's more notable emperor-builders, restoring the temple of Jupiter Capitolinus (which had been destroyed during the brief civil war) and initiating work on the large amphitheater that later became known as the Colosseum. Just, practical, and good-natured, in 79 Vespasian became ill and died at the age of seventy, leaving his son, Titus, to succeed him. **See** Domitian; Titus; **also** theaters and amphitheaters (Chapter 6); **and** Judaea (Chapter 7).

Virgil (or Vergil)

(Publius Vergilius Maro) Perhaps the greatest and certainly the most popular and influential literary figure of Rome's Augustan Age of literature, Virgil was born in 70 B.C. on a farm in northern Italy. Like most rural Romans, he came to love the land and the virtues of agricultural life, which later became major themes in his works. Shortly after the Battle of Philippi in 42 B.C., Virgil met the literary patron Maecenas, and through him, the young Octavian (the future Augustus). The poet soon made his name with the *Eclogues,* a collection of short poems about country life, and then worked for seven years on another set of pastoral verses, the *Georgics,* finished just in time for Octavian's triumphant return to Rome in 29 B.C. Thereafter, until his death ten years later, Virgil was the most respected and imitated writer in the known world.

Virgil had many literary talents but his greatest was his ability to capture a vision of and make people feel genuine nostalgia for the "good old days." As historian John B. Firth puts it: "The great secret of the power which he wielded over his contemporaries and over the ages which were to follow lies not so much in . . . his moral earnestness and in the spirit of humanity . . . which permeates his work. . . . Deep religion and intense burning patriotism—in these lie the secret of Virgil's influence. . . . He looked back with regret to the bygone days when men lived simpler lives, and not only feared, but

walked with, the gods." (*Augustus Caesar,* pp. 208–209).

Virgil's talent for dramatizing the heroic characters and events of past ages reached its zenith in his masterpiece, the epic poem the *Aeneid.* This definitive version of the old Roman legend of the Trojan prince Aeneas's founding of the Roman race became Rome's national patriotic epic. This is not surprising, for in it Virgil put into stirring words and verses the Romans' deep pride in their past and their belief that they had a superior destiny. **See** Aeneas; Maecenas, Gaius; **also** *Aeneid;* Augustan Age of literature; poetry (all Chapter 6).

Vitellius

For this Roman general who took part in the power struggle of A.D. 69, **see** the winner of that struggle, Vespasian.

Vitruvius

(Marcus Vitruvius Pollio) Little is known about the life of Vitruvius beyond that he served in the military under Julius Caesar and was a practicing Roman architect and engineer from about 46 to 30 B.C. Vitruvius was apparently already an old man by the late 20s B.C., when he penned the ten books composing his great treatise— *On Architecture,* which he dedicated to the emperor Augustus. **See** building materials and techniques; *On Architecture;* orders, architectural (all Chapter 6).

Zeno 1.

(ca. 333–262 B.C.) About 300 B.C., the Greek intellectual Zeno (or Zenon) of Citium (on the island of Cyprus), founded the Stoic philosophical school, which would subsequently have a profound influence on Roman thought. Zeno moved to Athens circa 313–311 and studied at Plato's Academy; but soon he underwent radical changes in thinking and began lecturing in the Athenian Agora in a building called the Stoa Poikile ("Painted Stoa"), from which the movement drew its name. He became so respected that when he died Athens honored him with a public funeral. **See** Stoicism (Chapter 6).

Zeno 2.

(Tarasicodissa, d. A.D. 491) Emperor of eastern Rome from 474 to 475 and again from 476 to 491, he was at first Tarasicodissa, a powerful chieftain of Isauria, a wild region of central Asia Minor. The eastern emperor Leo I recognized his considerable talents, took him and his formidable warriors into the imperial service, and changed his name to Zeno. After marrying Leo's daughter (ca. 470), Zeno was involved in various military campaigns and became consul, *magister militum* of the east, and finally, at Leo's death in 474, emperor. In 475, Leo's widow, Verina, engineered a successful coup and Zeno fled back to Isauria; but the following year, after the people of Constantinople rose up against the conspirators, Zeno returned and regained the throne. An important moment in his reign was his demand that the German Odoacer recognize Julius Nepos as emperor of the west, an action Odoacer agreed to but on which he never followed through. **See** Leo I; Odoacer.

Zenobia

(mid–third century A.D.) Queen of the prosperous city of Palmyra (in Syria), she became famous for her audacity in standing up to Rome. The Palmyrene king, Odaenath, at first allied himself with the Romans, but soon afterward claimed ownership of many

Zenobia, queen of the Near Eastern city-state of Palmyra, sits on her throne, flanked by an attendant.

of the Near Eastern territories they deemed vital to their own empire. When he died, circa 267, his widow, Zenobia, invaded and annexed Egypt and other neighboring lands. Politically savvy as well as brave, she managed to hold out against the Romans for more than five years until the emperor Aurelian defeated her (in 271) and dismantled her short-lived empire. She suffered the indignity of marching in chains in his victory parade; but she had the last laugh, for he died soon afterward and she went on to make a new life for herself in Italy. There, near the capital, she lived out the rest of her days in a luxurious villa, granted to her partly out of respect for her beauty, intelligence, and many talents, which rivaled those of the most educated Roman men. **See** Aurelian; **also** Palmyra (Chapter 2).

CHAPTER 2

IMPORTANT GEOGRAPHICAL PLACES

Achaea

The ancient name for the northern reaches of the Peloponnesus, the large peninsula that makes up the southern third of Greece. In 146 B.C. it became part of the Roman province of Macedonia. Later, in 27 B.C., the Romans turned most of central and southern Greece into a new province called Achaea.

Actium

A sandy peninsula on Greece's western coast, Actium bordered the strait that joins the sea to the Ambracian Gulf. Colonists from Corinth settled the area in the sixth century B.C. In 31 B.C., Mark Antony, then at war with Octavian, established his camp at Actium, which soon gave its name to the great naval battle his and Octavian's forces fought in the nearby waters. **See** Battle of Actium (Chapter 7).

Adrianople

(or Hadrianopolis) This city in Thrace (a region of northern Greece) was originally called Uscudama; but about A.D. 125 the Roman emperor Hadrian renamed it Hadri-

anopolis, after himself. Two famous battles were fought there, the first being the victory of Constantine I over Licinius in 324, which gave Constantine control over both the eastern and western parts of the Empire. The second was the defeat of the eastern emperor Valens by the Visigoths in 378, a decisive event in the decline of the Roman army and ultimately the Empire itself. **See** Valens, Flavius Julius (Chapter 1); **also** Battle of Adrianople; fall of Rome (both Chapter 7).

Adriatic Sea

The large waterway separating the Italian peninsula from the Balkans; its southern reaches were sometimes called the Ionian Sea. The Adriatic was known for its dangerous storms, which often sank warships and merchant vessels alike.

Aetna, Mount

(also Etna) A large volcano (just shy of eleven thousand feet) situated in northeastern Sicily. According to early tradition, it was the location of the forge operated by the god Vulcan. Numerous eruptions were recorded in classical times, including one in 479 B.C., which the Greek playwright Aeschylus described. An anonymous first-century A.D. poem, the *Aetna,* describes the volcano's outbursts and attempts to explain their cause. And the Greek geographer Strabo writes that lookout points and huts with sleeping accommodations were established along its slopes for use by mountain-climbing enthusiasts.

Aetolia

An ancient name for a region of western Greece lying north of the Gulf of Corinth. In the fourth century B.C., several Aetolian towns formed an alliance—the Aetolian League—which expanded its influence over much of central Greece in the following century. In the Second Macedonian War (200–197 B.C.), the Aetolians supported Rome against Macedonia's King Philip V; but soon afterward they turned against the Romans, who responded by ending Aetolia's independence. The region became part of the Roman province of Achaea in 27 B.C.

Africa

This Roman province was first created after Rome's defeat of Carthage in the Third Punic War (mid–second century B.C.). At first it consisted of about five thousand square miles of territory in what is now northern Tunisia. In 46 B.C., Julius Caesar added the North African kingdom of Numidia to the province, which later Roman leaders split into several smaller ones. The area became known for its vast grain fields and also as the birthplace of several important Christian leaders, including Tertullian and Augustine. Carthage, rebuilt as a Roman colony, was the largest and most important of the province's cities, but Africa had many other thriving towns, including Utica and Hippo (where Augustine served as bishop), situated west of Carthage, and Oea and Lepcis Magna (hometown of the emperor Septimius Severus), located east of Carthage.

Alba Longa

For this town in eastern Italy, **see** Latium; **also** Latin League (Chapter 7).

Alesia

For this town in Gaul, **see** siege of Alesia (Chapter 7).

Alexandria

Located on Egypt's northern coast near the Nile River's western mouth, Alexandria was one of the great cities of the ancient world and in the early Empire second in importance only to Rome. The Greek conqueror Alexander the Great established Alexandria in 331 B.C., naming it after himself. After his death (in 323 B.C.), one of his leading generals, Ptolemy, took control of Egypt, founded the Greek Ptolemaic dynasty, and transferred the country's seat of government from Memphis to Alexandria. Thereafter the city grew rapidly, achieving a population of perhaps five hundred thousand, tremendous commercial importance, and great wealth by about 200 B.C. It also became famous for its prestigious university, the Museum, and the largest library in the known world. After the Roman emperor Augustus defeated the last Ptolemaic ruler, Cleopatra VII, in 30 B.C., he annexed Egypt as a province of the Roman Empire and Alexandria became the provincial capital. **See** Cleopatra VII (Chapter 1).

Alps

A massive mountain range lying above the northern reaches of the Italian peninsula, the Alps long constituted a formidable barrier against invaders from the north. This made the famous crossing of the Alps by the Carthaginian general Hannibal and his army in 218 B.C. (during the Second Punic War) both unexpected by and damaging to the Romans. Julius Caesar's conquest of Gaul in the 50s B.C. stimulated the opening of new routes and construction of roads through the Alps, in time making them more a gateway than a barrier between Italy and northern and western Europe. **See** Hannibal (Chapter 1).

Antioch

Founded circa 300 B.C. by Greek conqueror Alexander the Great's general Seleucus (and named after Seleucus's father, Antiochus), this city became a great commercial and cultural center. Located on the left bank of the Orontes River in northern Syria, it served as a capital of the Seleucid Empire for some two centuries. During the years that Rome dominated the Mediterranean world, the city retained its preeminence in the east until the mid–fourth century, when Constantinople (on the Bosporus) began to eclipse it. Much of Antioch was destroyed by invading Persians in 538.

Apennine Mountains
A series of mountain chains running for about 870 miles north-to-south through the Italian "boot," the Apennines reach their highest point at Monte Corno, which rises to 9,560 feet in the central chain. The northern Apennines had many hardwood forests, while the slopes of the southern peaks favored olive and grape cultivation. The Apennines were long inhabited by rugged hill tribes, perhaps the most famous and formidable being the Samnites. By the early third century B.C., Rome had subdued all of these peoples and extended its influence over the whole Apennine region.

Aquileia
A strategically important city in northeastern Italy, near the head of the Adriatic Sea, it was long a commercial connection between Italy and the Danubian lands to the north. Aquileia was badly sacked by a Roman army in A.D. 238 during a period of severe political and civil strife. The city managed to recover, regaining prosperity and attaining a population of nearly one hundred thousand. But it was totally destroyed in 452 by the army of Asian conqueror Attila the Hun; the Aquileian survivors subsequently fled to some nearby lagoons, where they established a settlement that eventually grew into the renowned city of Venice.

Arausio
For this town in Gaul, **see** Gaul.

Arles
For this town in Gaul, **see** Gaul.

Asia Minor
(or Anatolia) This large peninsula, today occupied by the nation of Turkey, is bordered in the north by the Black Sea, the west by the Aegean Sea, and the south by the Mediterranean Sea. In Rome's early republican years, before its expansion into the east, parts of Asia Minor were settled or conquered by a number of peoples, including Greeks and Persians. In the second century B.C., the Romans made inroads into the area by defeating the Seleucid ruler Antiochus III at Magnesia (near the Aegean coast) and eventually they came to dominate most of it. During the Empire, Asia Minor was divided into several provinces, including Lydia, Asia, Cappadocia, Bithynia, Galatia, and Pontus. Populous, prosperous, and well traveled, the peninsula was strategically important as a corridor to Armenia and the Parthian and Persian realms, with which Rome was frequently at odds.

Athens
Long the cultural center of the Greek world, Athens, located on the Attic peninsula in eastern Greece, was absorbed into the Roman realm along with the rest of mainland Greece in the second century B.C. (becoming part of the province of Achaea). Without the political importance it had held in prior centuries, the city remained an important center of learning, famous for its philosophical schools. Athens rebelled in 86 B.C. but suffered punishment after the Roman dictator Sulla recaptured it. Thereafter, it struggled economically and had to rely on wealthy individuals to finance most new public buildings. One such mentor, Herodes Atticus (ca. A.D. 104–178), used a large part of his huge personal fortune to beautify the city, and the emperor Hadrian, an enthusiastic lover of Greek culture, completed the

The Temple of Hephaestos, in Athens's Agora. The city's architectural wonders continued to draw tourists during Roman imperial times.

Temple of Olympian Zeus and erected a library there. In 267, a Germanic tribe descended through Greece and sacked Athens, badly damaging it. In the early sixth century the eastern emperor Justinian I closed the city's philosophical schools, removing its last claim to fame.

Augusta Treverorum

(or Trier) Located on the Moselle River in what is now western Germany, it began as Treves, the capital of the Treviri, a Gallic tribe that furnished Julius Caesar with cavalry recruits during his conquests in the 50s B.C. In 16 B.C., Augustus reestablished it as a Roman city—Augusta Treverorum—and it became a prosperous center known for its fabrics, pottery, and native sculpture. Later, in Diocletian's reign, the city became the administrative capital of one of his tetrarchs, Constantius. He and his famous son, Constantine, built a palace, a basilica, and lavish public baths there. Circa 406, the Vandals sacked and burned Trier, which subsequently continued to deteriorate as other Germanic tribes occupied it in their turn.

Beneventum

A city of southern Italy, situated about forty miles northeast of Naples, it became a Roman colony in 268 B.C. An important communications center and military base on the Via Appia (the major road from Rome to the coastal city of Brundisium), Beneventum remained loyal to Rome during the Second Punic War (218–201 B.C.) and Social War (90–87 B.C.). The city's most famous structure was a magnificent triumphal arch erected by the emperor Trajan in the second century A.D.

Bithynia

Located in northwestern Asia Minor near the Bosporus at a crucial junction between Europe and Asia, the kingdom of Bithynia became a Roman province in 74 B.C. when its ruler left it to Rome in his will. About ten years later, the province was expanded to include the neighboring region of Pontus. The area long enjoyed marked prosperity, thanks to its exploitation of abundant local supplies of timber and iron, as well as lucrative east-west trade routes that passed through it. Nicomedia, the provincial capital, became for a time (during Diocletian's reign) the eastern seat of Roman imperial power. Another Bithynian city, Nicaea, often vied with Nicomedia for prestige and was the site of the famous religious meeting (the Council of Nicaea) held by Constantine I in 325.

Black Sea

The large body of water lying north of Asia Minor, the Greeks and Romans accessed the Black Sea via the Bosporus strait. The Romans, who called the sea the Pontus Euxinus ("hospitable sea"), exercised considerable influence in its waters and over the kingdoms that lined its northern shores. These kingdoms supplied the Roman provinces of northern Asia Minor with grain and engaged in vigorous trade in wine, fabrics, and other products. Beginning in the mid–third century A.D., Rome steadily lost its influence in the region to the Goths and other "barbarian" peoples.

Bosporus

For this waterway on the Black Sea's southern rim, **see** Black Sea; Constantinople.

Britain

The Greeks and Romans knew about the existence of the British Isles as early as the fourth century B.C.; by the second century B.C., Mediterranean traders were regularly visiting Britain to acquire tin, for which it had become famous. In 55 B.C. and again the following year, Julius Caesar invaded southern Britain as part of his Gallic conquests. But though he succeeded in crossing the Thames River and forcing Cassivellaunus, king of the most powerful tribe in the region, to pay him tribute, Caesar soon withdrew to Gaul and never returned; nearly a century passed before the Romans mounted another major expedition to Britain. In A.D. 43, in Claudius's reign, a force of forty thousand troops commanded by a skilled general, Aulus Plautius, captured Camulodunum (modern Colchester) and transformed the island's southern reaches into the province of Britannia. In the following few years, Plautius, now governor, made further conquests, as did his successor, Ostorius Scapula, who advanced into Wales.

In 60, the Iceni tribe, led by its warrior-princess Boudicca, initiated a large-scale rebellion of the southern tribes, but despite some initial serious losses, the Romans successfully crushed the rebels. Soon afterward, the provincial capital was transferred to Londinium (London). Subsequently, Gnaeus Julius Agricola, governor from circa 77–84, made inroads into Caledonia (Scotland); he also proved once and for all that Britain is an island by ordering ships to sail around its northern coast. A few years later, however, the Romans pulled back from Caledonia and established a frontier on its southern edge, along which the emperor Hadrian built his famous defensive wall in the early second century. In the early 180s, northern tribesmen swept southward over the wall and inflicted considerable damage to Roman settlements, until they were driven back in 184.

In the early third century, the Romans divided Britain into two provinces—Upper Britain, with its capital at Eboracum (York), and Lower Britain, with its capital at Londinium. Though most of the century witnessed peace and prosperity in these provinces, trouble erupted circa 287 when Carausius, commander of the provincial fleet, defied the central government by declaring himself "emperor" of Britain. In 294, however, one of his officers, Allectus, killed him and seized power. Order was finally restored after 296, the year that Constantius (one of Diocletian's tetrarchs) invaded the island and defeated Allectus. For a few decades, Roman Britain enjoyed prosperity once again; but as the fourth century wore on, tribal peoples, including the Picts in the north and Saxon raiders in the south, increasingly overran the provinces. Despite a more or less successful restoration of law and order by the emperor Valentinian I in the 360s, his successors repeatedly withdrew troops from Britain to deal with serious barbarian threats to Gaul and Italy; by the early fifth century, the island had largely been abandoned to the natives.

Brundisium

An important port city located on Italy's southeastern coast, by the second century B.C. it had become a frequent jumping-off point for military expeditions and travelers heading for Greece and the east. In 40 B.C., Octavian and Antony made a treaty in the city, which accordingly became known as the Treaty of Brundisium. One of the most famous satires of the Augustan poet Horace describes an uncomfortable journey he and some friends took from Rome to Brundisium on the renowned Appian Way, which connected the two cities.

A section of Hadrian's Wall snakes its way through the northern British countryside. The barrier was designed to keep local tribesmen out of Roman territory.

Byzantium

For this important town on the Bosporus, **see** Constantinople.

Campania

The territory of western Italy lying south of the Latium plain between the coast and the Apennine Mountains, Campania was extremely fertile and lush thanks to its rich volcanic soil. Its chief towns were Capua, Cumae, Neapolis (Naples), Pompeii, and Herculaneum. Because of its picturesque beauty, the area became a popular retreat for Roman nobles, who built numerous villas there.

Campus Martius

Meaning "Field of Mars" (from an altar of Mars erected there), this large, flat, open area situated between Rome's Capitoline, Quirinal, and Pincian hills was long used as a military exercise ground. But during the late Republic and on into the Empire, numerous temples and altars were erected there, as well as the city's first amphitheater (of Taurus), Marcus Agrippa's baths, the Pantheon, the Theater of Marcellus, and Augustus's Ara Pacis (Altar of Peace). Agrippa's and Augustus's mausoleums also rose there.

Camulodunum

For this important town in Britain, **see** Britain.

Cannae

A small town located in the region of Apulia, in southeastern Italy, it was the site of Rome's worst military defeat on land—the battle fought there in 216 B.C. in which the Carthaginian leader Hannibal cleverly out- maneuvered and crushed an army led by the consuls Paullus and Varro. **See** Hannibal (Chapter 1); **also** Battle of Cannae; Punic Wars (both Chapter 7).

Capitoline

For this hill in Rome, **see** seven hills of Rome.

Cappadocia

A region of eastern Asia Minor that eventually became a Roman province, it was a geographically rugged, largely culturally backward frontier area that bordered the empires of Rome's enemies, the Parthians and later the Sassanian Persians. Long ruled by kings, in the 180s B.C. Cappadocia came under the influence of the Romans, who installed a series of client rulers there. In A.D. 17, Rome annexed it as a province; thereafter, various emperors merged it with other provinces or split it up as the changing political situation dictated.

Capri

A small (about four square miles), mountainous island located in the Gulf of Cumae (Bay of Naples), it became one of Augustus's favorite vacation spots. Later, in A.D. 27, his successor, Tiberius, settled on Capri, more or less isolating himself for the last ten years of his reign. Subsequently, the island became a place of exile for several Roman notables.

Capua

The principal city of the region of Campania (in western Italy), Capua was located sixteen miles inland from Neapolis (Naples). Originally an Etruscan town, Capua came under Roman domination in the late fourth century B.C. and, thanks to its metalworking and other local industries, soon became one of Italy's wealthiest and most important cities. In 216 B.C., after Hannibal defeated the Romans at Cannae, the city switched to the Carthaginian side in the Second Punic War; but the Romans recaptured it in 211 B.C. and punished it by beheading its leaders, exiling most of the rest of the populace, and resettling it with new colonists. During the Empire, Capua remained one of Rome's most prominent and prosperous cities, until it was sacked by the Vandals in A.D. 456.

Carthage

One of the major cities, and for a time nations, of the ancient world, Carthage was located on a peninsula projecting into the Mediterranean Sea at the tip of what is now Tunisia, in North Africa. It was founded by traders from the Phoenician city of Tyre perhaps in the ninth century B.C., although scholars have proposed earlier or later dates. Some time in the 600s B.C., Carthage became independent of Tyre and rapidly began expanding its power, wealth, and influence in the western Mediterranean sphere. It came to control the major sea routes in that region as well as most of the islands (including Corsica and Sardinia) and parts of Spain. But the Carthaginians managed to gain only partial control of Sicily, where they long competed with Greek cities on the island. Carthage's interests in the Sicilian region also brought it into conflict with the Romans, resulting in the three bloody Punic Wars (spanning the period from 264 to 146 B.C.), all of which the Carthaginians lost. At the conclusion of the third war, the Romans destroyed Carthage and turned the heart of its North African territory into the province of Africa.

In the late first century B.C., Julius Caesar and Augustus spearheaded the successful attempt to create a Roman colony on Carthage's site. The new city grew quickly and by the second century A.D. had become a major metropolis, with a population of perhaps three hundred thousand and a reputation as an educational and cultural center. The birthplace of Tertullian and other important church figures, it also became a focus of much Christian activity. The city fell to the Vandals in 439 and for more than a century afterward was the capital of a North African Vandal state. **See** Hannibal (Chapter 1); **also** Punic Wars (Chapter 7).

Cilicia

This region of southeastern Asia Minor became a Roman province in the first century B.C. Rich in timber, vines, olives, and dates, as well as harbors and coves to anchor ships, the area had earlier come under the influence of the Persians and Greeks; by the early first century B.C. it was a haven for pirates who raided Mediterranean commerce. Shortly after the Roman general Pompey the Great ended the pirate menace (in the 60s B.C.), the Romans expanded the province of Cilicia inland to the border of Phrygia. Three centuries later, under Diocletian and Constantine, the province was divided into three smaller ones. Its main city was Tarsus, on the Cydnus River. **See** Tarsus; **also** piracy (Chapter 5).

Cisalpine Gaul

For this region of northern Italy, **see** Gaul.

Colonia Agrippina

For this town in Germany, **see** Germany.

Constantinople

A major Roman city on the northern coast of the Propontis (Sea of Marmara), it guarded the lower end of the strategic Bosporus strait, through which the vital trade route between the Mediterranean and Black Seas passed. Originally it was a Greek city named Byzantium, founded in the seventh century B.C. by settlers from Megara (located west of Athens on the Greek mainland). Byzantium grew prosperous from its rich local fisheries and its exploitation of the lucrative grain trade from the Black Sea. Over the centuries, though enjoying periods of independence, the city fell under the control or influence of many states, including Persia, Sparta, Athens, Macedonia (after a famous siege by King Philip II in 339 B.C.), and finally the Romans.

When the Romans created their province of Bithynia-Pontus in the first century B.C., Byzantium, though theoretically still free, became a part of the Roman world and subject to Roman needs and demands. During a round of civil strife in the late second century A.D., the city was besieged and destroyed by the emperor Septimius Severus; however, he recognized its strategic importance and soon rebuilt it, larger than before. Later, Constantine I also appreciated the value of the city's location; after a major restoration project (including the importation of magnificent works of art from many other parts of the Empire), in 330 he inaugurated it as the realm's eastern capital, renaming it Constantinople, the "City of Constantine." This hastened the division of the Roman world into two separate spheres, a process initiated by the emperor's immediate predecessors. Constantinople survived the fall of the western Empire and remained the capital of the eastern Empire, which thereafter mutated into the Byzantine Empire. In 1453, the Ottoman Turks besieged and captured the city. Today called Istanbul, it remains one of the world's great metropolises. **See** Constantine I (Chapter 1).

Corinth

Originally an important Greek city located near the strategic Isthmus of Corinth, the narrow land strip that separates the Peloponnesus from the rest of mainland Greece, it was long a major commercial and cultural center. In 146 B.C., during Rome's conquest of Greece, a Roman general utterly destroyed the city as an object lesson to any who might contemplate defying Rome. In the following century, however, in a project initiated by Julius Caesar shortly before his death, Corinth

was rebuilt as a Roman colony and eventually became the capital of the province of Achaea. About the year A.D. 268, a group of invading Goths partially destroyed the city; in the next few centuries, more barbarian attacks, along with severe earthquakes, completed its eradication.

Corsica

A large island lying north of Sardinia, it was at first fought over by Etruscans, Greeks, and Carthaginians, the latter gaining control of it by the close of the fourth century B.C.; but after its defeat of Carthage in the First Punic War, Rome annexed Corsica (in 227 B.C.), making it part of the province of Sardinia. Corsica's main product was wax, although it also produced cattle, building stone, and timber. Eventually, the island, whose interior remained largely a wilderness, became a popular spot for Roman nobles to exile their political enemies.

Cumae

A town on the coast of Campania (in southwestern Italy), just north of the upper rim of the Gulf of Cumae (Bay of Naples). Cumae was settled by Greeks in the eighth century B.C. and later became famous for the Cumaean Sibyl, an oracle who delivered prophesies. In the 420s B.C., Italian tribes captured the town, and in 338 B.C. the Romans took charge of it. After Cumae received a new harbor (ca. 36 B.C.), its population grew and it remained prosperous in succeeding centuries. **See** Sibyl (Chapter 3).

Cyrenaica

(also Cyrene) The region of North Africa lying to the west of Egypt, its coastal portion became known as Pentapolis because five Greek cities were established there in the seventh and sixth centuries B.C. The area was part of Alexander the Great's realm (in the 320s B.C.) and later was dominated by Egypt's Ptolemaic rulers before one of them willed it to Rome in 96 B.C. It became a province about twenty years later. After a rocky start caused by conflicts with local nomadic tribes and some administrative corruption, Cyrenaica prospered until A.D. 115, when a rebellion of the local Jews caused widespread damage to property and agriculture. The recovery was uneven and slow and the region never regained its former level of prosperity.

Dacia

This large, rugged, mountainous region was located north of the Danube River in what is now eastern Hungary. Settled in the seventh or sixth century B.C. by people from northern Thrace, its tribal culture supported itself through pastoralism (animal raising) and exploiting the iron, gold, and silver plentiful in the Carpathian Mountains. The Dacians frequently raided the nearby Roman border provinces of Moesia and Pannonia and remained an irritation to these areas, as well as to Roman rulers, until the emperor Trajan conquered Dacia in the early second century A.D. He made the region a province of the Empire; then his successor, Hadrian, divided it in two, creating Upper Dacia and Lower Dacia (and later divided Upper Dacia into two provinces, making three in all). Under Roman rule, however, most Dacians stubbornly held onto their culture and resisted assimilation. They must have been elated when, in 271, the emperor Aurelian, worried that the region could not be adequately defended against barbarian tribes beyond its borders, abandoned the Dacian provinces. This move ominously foreshadowed Rome's larger territorial losses to the northern tribes in the succeeding two centuries.

Dalmatia

For this Balkan region bordering the Adriatic Sea, **see** Illyricum.

Danube River

One of the major rivers of Europe and the Roman Empire, it was long recognized as the northern border of the Roman realm. For this reason, in the Empire's last four centuries the long Danube frontier was the scene of almost relentless wars, Roman wall- and fort-building, and barbarian incursions. The Romans gave the river's upper section, running from its source in western Germany to Vienna, the name Danubius. They called its lower course, running from Vienna to the Black Sea, the Ister.

Dyrrachium

A prominent city located on the eastern coast of the Adriatic Sea, it was originally a Greek city called Epidamnus. It came under Rome's influence about 229 B.C., after which it became the principal base for Roman armies embarking on campaigns into the Balkan Peninsula.

Egypt

For over two thousand years, Egypt, located in Africa's northeast corner, had been a powerful kingdom. All of its major cities were located in the thin strip of fertile territory bordering the mighty Nile River, which flows into the Mediterranean Sea. Dynasties of local kings (the pharaohs) long ruled Egypt until the first of several foreign powers, Persia, held control of the country from the late sixth to late fourth centuries B.C.

Then, in 332 B.C., the Greek conqueror Alexander the Great expelled the Persians, shortly after which he died, and one of his generals, Ptolemy, took the Egyptian throne and established a Greek dynasty. During Ptolemaic rule, which lasted for the next two and a half centuries, Egypt grew progressively weaker, and in the early first century B.C. it fell increasingly under Roman domination. After Ptolemy XII Auletes died in 51 B.C., a power struggle ensued between his heirs, Ptolemy XIII and Cleopatra VII. With the aid of Julius Caesar, who had recently defeated his chief rival, Pompey, Cleopatra secured the Egyptian throne, which she held until she and another powerful Roman ally (and lover), Mark Antony, were defeated at Actium in 31 B.C. The victor of the battle, Octavian, saw the tremendous potential benefits of Rome's total control of Egypt's abundant wealth and grain; he promptly annexed the country outright, making it a Roman province under his direct control.

Thereafter, Egypt remained one of Rome's most valuable assets, although from time to time it proved fertile ground for would-be usurpers to raise money and troops to challenge the throne. As it had been under the Greeks, Alexandria remained a great center of scientific and other learning, as well as a crucial commercial center for the eastern portions of the realm. In the Empire's last two centuries, Egypt was subdivided into six small provinces—Aegyptus, Jovia, Augustamnica, Arcadia, Upper Thebaid, and Lower Thebaid. **See** Alexandria; **also** Cleopatra VII; Ptolemy XII (both Chapter 1).

Ephesus
One of the major Greek cities on the western coast of Asia Minor, it was briefly part of Alexander's empire and later came under the sway of Pergamum. In 133 B.C., Pergamum's ruler, Attalus III, willed his kingdom to Rome; thereafter, Ephesus became the principal urban center of the Roman province of Asia. The city was known for its thriving markets and also for its splendid temple of the goddess Artemis (the Roman Diana).

Etruria
(present-day Tuscany) The homeland of the Etruscans, Etruria was a fertile, picturesque Italian region located immediately north of Rome and the Tiber River. Before Rome absorbed it, largely in the late fourth century B.C., the region was divided into several independent Etruscan city-states, among them Clusium, Tarquinii, and Veii. **See** Etruscans (Chapter 7).

Euphrates River
For this important Near Eastern river, **see** Mesopotamia.

Galatia
This large region of central Asia Minor became a Roman protectorate in 85 B.C. and a province in 25 B.C. In the next few decades, Rome established several colonies there; by the early 50s A.D., Christian communities had taken root, as evidenced by Paul's well-known Epistle to the Galatians. Among the important commodities Galatia produced were wool and red dye.

Gaul
The name "Gauls" originally referred to tribal Celtic peoples who migrated across the Alps into northern Italy beginning about 400 B.C. Subsequently, because so many Gauls settled in northern Italy's Po Valley, that region became known as Cisalpine Gaul (Gallia Cisalpina). A fertile region, it enjoyed prosperity while it became increasingly Romanized.

The Romans came to call the more remote lands northwest of the Alps (what are now France and Belgium) Transalpine Gaul (Gallia Transalpina). Long inhabited by Celtic peoples, who built villages and hilltop fortresses (*oppida*) there, it remained largely beyond Roman influence until 121 B.C. In that year, Rome seized a large piece of territory lying just north of what is now France's Mediterranean coast; this became the province of Narbonese Gaul (or the Narbonensis), with its capital of Narbo (about twelve miles from the sea). Between 58 and 51 B.C., Julius Caesar invaded the lands lying to the west and north of the Narbonese in his famous Gallic campaigns and brought all of Transalpine Gaul under Roman control in short order. His adopted son, Augustus, divided the conquered region into three provinces—Belgica, Lugdunensis, and Aquitania. (These were further subdivided in the Later Empire.)

Thereafter, Transalpine Gaul, which became steadily Romanized, grew into one of the Roman Empire's major breadbaskets, producing large amounts of grain and other crops. Besides Narbo, its major cities, which featured paved roads, aqueducts, baths, amphitheaters, and other as-

pects of urban Roman civilization, included Lugdunum (Lyons), on the upper reaches of the Rhone River; Augusta Treverorum (Trier), in the north, near the Moselle River; Arles, in the Narbonese, about forty-five miles from the Mediterranean coast; Arausio (Orange), near the Rhone (where the Romans were defeated by the Cimbri tribe in 106 B.C.); and Massilia, an important trading center on the Mediterranean coast. Several of these and other Gallic towns became important producers of fine pottery that made its way to all parts of the Empire. **See** Augusta Treverorum; Massilia; **also** Caesar, Gaius Julius (Chapter 1); **and** Celts; Cimbri and Teutones (Chapter 7).

Germany

(Germania) The name the Romans gave to the heavily forested lands of northeastern Europe, mostly lying east of the Rhine River and north of the Danube River. The various tribes and peoples of this region, who had separate names and identities (Cimbri, Suebi, Marcomanni, Goths, Franks, and many others), were collectively called Germans, and also often

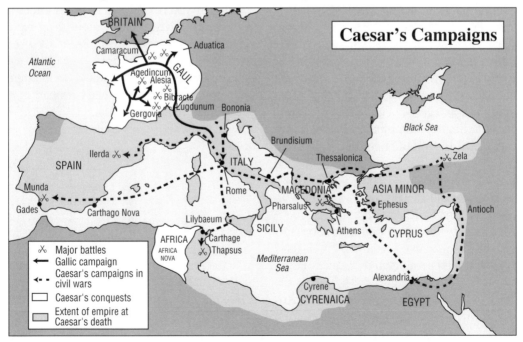

"barbarians." In his *Germania,* written in 98 B.C., the Roman historian Tacitus gives a now famous description of the Germans, whom the Romans long looked on as uncultured backwoods types. "Their physical characteristics," he writes, "are always the same: fierce-looking blue eyes, reddish hair and big frames." About their formidable warriors, Tacitus adds:

> Only a few use swords or lances. The spears that they carry—*framaea* is the native word—have short and narrow heads, but are so sharp and easy to handle that the same weapon serves, as needed, for close or distant fighting. The [barbarian] horseman asks no more than his shield and spear. . . . They are either naked or only lightly clad in their cloaks. . . . Few have breastplates; only here and there will you see a helmet of metal or hide. (*Germania* 4–6)

In the late first century B.C. and early first century A.D., Augustus's generals made inroads into Germany and he at first contemplated absorbing the area and Romanizing its peoples. However, the embarrassing and costly defeat of his general, Varus, in the Teutoburg Forest in A.D. 9 caused him to abandon the project; he and most of his successors subsequently recognized the Danube as the northernmost Roman border. One of the most important Roman commercial and military centers along that border was Colonia Agrippina (later Cologne), established on the south (left) bank of the Rhine in 38 B.C. Rome's failure to subdue and absorb Germany had serious repercussions during the Empire's later years. Indeed, it proved a fatal error, for it was from this region that tribal peoples descended on the Roman border provinces in the late second and mid–third centuries, and then again on a much larger scale in the fourth and fifth centuries, bringing about the dissolution of the Roman realm. **See** Rome; **also** Augustus; Varus, Publius Quinctilius (both Chapter 1);

also Battle of the Teutoburg Forest; fall of Rome; names of individual German tribes (all Chapter 7).

Herculaneum
A Roman town located on the lower slope of Mount Vesuvius, not far from Pompeii. Oscans, Etruscans, and Samnites successively occupied the site until it came under Roman domination in the late fourth century B.C. According to the Greek geographer Strabo, the town was a favorite resort of well-to-do Romans, and a number of fine villas were built in the area. Herculaneum was badly damaged by an earthquake in A.D. 62 and, like Pompeii, was buried by Vesuvius's great eruption of A.D. 79. After its rediscovery in the eighteenth century, Herculaneum became one of the most important archaeological sites in the world, as its excavated buildings and artifacts came to reveal much about ancient Roman life. Recent excavations there have yielded a number of skeletons, analysis of which has taught modern researchers a great deal about the physiology of average Romans in the era of the early Empire. **See** Vesuvius, Mount; Pompeii.

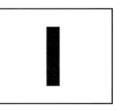

Illyricum
(Illyria) The northwestern portion of the Balkan Peninsula, Illyricum bordered the eastern shore of the Adriatic Sea. Origi-

nally, the area was inhabited by a rustic Indo-European people, the Illyrians, who established a kingdom there in the early third century B.C. In the late third and early second centuries B.C., the Romans conquered Illyria and it became the province of Illyricum about 118 B.C. From here various Roman generals launched military campaigns into Greece and Asia Minor. In the early first century A.D., the province was subdivided into two smaller provinces, Dalmatia in the north and Pannonia in the south. At Split (or Spalato), near Dalmatia's coast, the emperor Diocletian built an enormous palace (in the late third century) and retired (in 305). During Diocletian's reign, the region of Illyricum became a diocese containing seven even smaller provinces. **See** palaces (Chapter 6).

Jerusalem

For this important city in Roman Judaea (in Palestine), **see** Judaea; **also** Judaism (Chapter 3); **and** siege of Jerusalem (Chapter 7).

Judaea

The general name for the southern portion of Palestine, site of the ancient Jewish kingdom of Judah, and also for the Roman province in the area. The Persians occupied Judaea from 538 to 332 B.C., after which Alexander the Great and then his successors, the Ptolemies and Seleucids, ruled it until a prominent Jewish family, the Maccabees, gained a measure of local autonomy in the mid–second century B.C.

Rome's domination of the region began in 63 B.C. when Pompey the Great captured the capital, Jerusalem, site of the sacred temple originally erected by the biblical King Solomon. From the early 30s B.C. on, Judaea was a vassal state of Rome, ruled by a local client king, Herod. On his death in 4 B.C., Rome divided the area between his three sons. But this proved unworkable, so in A.D. 6 Roman leaders turned it into a province. It was one of the governors of this province, Pontius Pilate, who tried and crucified Jesus Christ, circa 30–33.

From 66 to 73, the Jews, who deeply resented the Roman occupation, launched a full-scale rebellion, which the future emperors Vespasian and Titus put down with brutal force; Titus almost completely destroyed Jerusalem, which was slowly rebuilt. Two more Jewish insurrections, in 115–117 and 132–135, were also unsuccessful, resulting in the displacement of many Jews to other parts of the Mediterranean world. From 135 on, the region came to be called Syria-Paletina. **See** Herod the Great; Jesus Christ; Titus; Vespasian (all Chapter 1); **also** Christianity; Judaism (both Chapter 3); **and** siege of Jerusalem; siege of Masada (both Chapter 7).

Latium

This region and well-watered rolling plain of western Italy bordered the Tyrrhenian Sea in the west, the Apennine Mountains in the east, the Tiber River in the north, and the volcanic region of Campania in the south. According to Roman tradition, one of Latium's earliest and chief towns, Alba Longa, was the parent city of Rome, for it was here that the legendary Romulus and Remus got their start. What is more certain is that the original Latin tribes who settled the area formed a religious confederation and later some kind of political alliance (the Latin League) to fend off incursions by the Etruscans and eventually the Romans. By 338, Rome had reduced all of Latium to subject status. In the centuries that followed, when Latium was firmly a part of the Roman heartland, most of the original Latin towns in the region fell into ruin and local agriculture was replaced by pasturage. **See** Romulus (Chapter 1); **also** *Aeneid* (Chapter 6); **and** Latin League (Chapter 7).

Lepcis Magna
For this prominent city in North Africa, **see** Africa.

Londinium
For this important town, the future British city of London, **see** Britain.

Lugdunum
For this town in Gaul, **see** Gaul.

Lusitania
A region of the Iberian Peninsula now more or less occupied by the nation of Portugal, it was early inhabited by a tribal people (perhaps of Celtic origin), the Lusitani. The Romans began to absorb Lusitania in the years following the Second Punic War, but it did not become a province until Augustus made it one about 25 B.C. The area was known for its copper mines, abundant wheat fields, and numerous horse farms. **See** Spain.

Macedonian Kingdom
Originally, Macedonia was a kingdom of northern Greece that in the fourth century B.C. rose to power and prominence under King Philip II, father of Alexander the Great. After Alexander's successors fought over his empire, in the early 270s B.C. Antigonus Gonatas (grandson of Alexander's general Antigonus) estab-

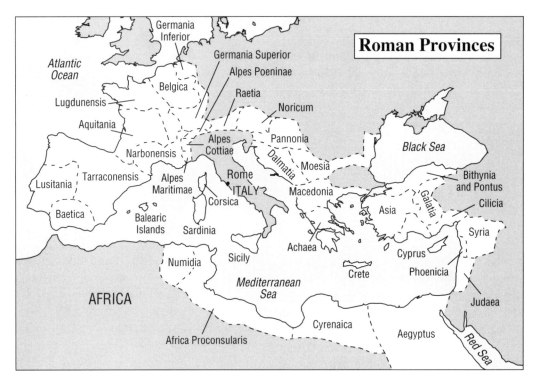

lished the Antigonid dynasty and his new kingdom of Macedonia vied with other Hellenistic realms for control of the eastern Mediterranean sphere for the next century. During the Second Punic War, Macedonia's King Philip V allied himself with Rome's enemy, Carthage; the Romans punished him by attacking and defeating him in the Second Macedonian War (200–197 B.C.). After winning another war against Macedonia (172–168 B.C.), the Romans ended the Antigonid line and in 146 B.C. made the area a province. (Most of southern Greece did not become a province until Augustus's time.) **See** Macedonian Wars (Chapter 7).

Magna Graecia

("Greater Greece") The collective term for the Greek cities (among them Taras, Sybaris, and Elea) that sprang up in southern Italy in the eighth through the sixth centuries B.C. The region was long prosperous and all of its major cities developed a high level of culture. But they failed to unite and one by one fell under Roman influence in the early third century B.C.

Masada

For this Jewish hilltop fortress captured by the Romans in the first century, **see** siege of Masada (Chapter 7).

Massilia

(also Massalia) The site of the modern French city of Marseilles, it was a port city on Gaul's southern coast, founded about 600 B.C. by colonists from the Greek city of Phocaea. The Greeks traded with the native Gauls, receiving tin and grain in exchange for Greek wine and luxury goods. In the sixth century B.C. the city became a Roman ally. It retained its independence after the establishment of the Roman province of Narbonese in the second century B.C., but was captured in 49 B.C. by Julius Caesar during his civil war with Pompey and thereafter largely absorbed by Rome.

Mauretania

A large territory and long a kingdom of northwestern Africa, bordered by Numidia in the east and the Mediterranean Sea in the north, it at first fought with but then became an ally of Carthage. Later, from 108 to 105 B.C., the Mauretanian king sided with Rome against the Numidian upstart Jugurtha. In the first century B.C., the local rulers became involved in the power struggles among Caesar, Antony, Octavian, and other prominent Romans; and in 33 B.C. Octavian annexed the region and established several military colonies there. Not until the 40s A.D., however, did the emperor Claudius officially convert Mauretania into two provinces—Tingitana and Caesariensis. The region, known for its purple dye, timber, and accomplished cavalry, was overrun by the Vandals in the fifth century.

Mediolanum

The site of the modern city of Milan, it was a Gallic city of northern Italy that came under permanent Roman control in 194 B.C. In time it became the principal city of the region; an important junction of the trade routes running into Gaul, the Alps, and Illyricum; a crucial focal point of the Empire's northern defenses; and in the Later Empire an imperial capital. It was here that Constantine I and Licinius met in A.D. 313, soon after which they issued the famous Edict of Milan, granting toleration to Roman Christians. The city was also a tempting target for invaders from central Europe; Attila the Hun sacked it in 452.

Mesopotamia

Traditionally the name for the region lying between the Tigris and Euphrates Rivers in what is now Iraq, it was part of the Persian Empire before Alexander the Great conquered it, after which it became part of the Greek Seleucid Kingdom. About 140 B.C., the Parthians overran Mesopotamia. The Romans subsequently fought the Parthians for control of the area and in A.D. 115, the emperor Trajan made its northwestern portion the Roman province of Mesopotamia. His successor, Hadrian, gave it up, but later the emperors Marcus Aurelius and Septimius Severus fought to regain it. The Romans continued to contest the region after the Sassanian Persians eclipsed the Parthians in the third century. After the emperor Galerius defeated the Persians in 298, Rome established two provinces—Mesopotamia and Osrhoena—there. Over the century that followed, however, the Persians steadily regained control over much of Mesopotamia.

Misenum

A promontory made up of three ancient volcanic craters, Misenum was located on the northern edge of the Gulf of Cumae (Bay of Naples), in southwestern Italy. Its fine pair of harbors became the main base of the Roman fleet under Augustus and a port town soon grew up nearby. A number of Roman notables kept villas and other residences in the area, including the famed writer Pliny the Elder, who in A.D. 79 paid the ultimate price when he saw the eruption of Mount Vesuvius in the distance and hurried across the bay to observe it at close range.

Moesia

A region lying north of Macedonia and Thrace, it was conquered by Rome in the first century B.C. and at first made a part of the province of Macedonia. Moesia became a province in its own right about A.D. 15 under the emperor Tiberius, and later, in 86, the emperor Domitian split it into two provinces—Upper and Lower Moesia. Further, more complicated reorganization of the area occurred in the late third century under the emperor Diocletian.

Narbo

For this first prominent Roman city in Gaul, **see** Gaul.

Narbonese Gaul

For this first of Rome's Gallic provinces, **see** Gaul.

Nicaea

For this important city in northwestern Asia Minor, **see** Bithynia; **also** Constantine I (Chapter 1); **and** Christianity (Chapter 3).

Nicomedia

For this prominent city in Asia Minor that long served as Rome's eastern capital, **see** Bithynia; **also** Diocletian (Chapter 1).

Nile River

For this famous Egyptian river, **see** Egypt.

Noricum

A Celtic kingdom and later a Roman province located south of the Danube River in what is now Austria, it came largely under Roman control in the late first century B.C. The emperor Claudius officially made it a province in the 40s A.D., with its capital at Virunum. The area was overrun by German tribes in the second century, but Marcus Aurelius recovered it; in the fourth century it was divided into Noricum Ripense and Noricum Mediterraneum. Subsequently, more German incursions, including those by the Ostrogoths, Visogoths, and Alamanni, wrested the region from Roman control by the 470s and 480s.

Numidia

A kingdom of North Africa, Numidia later became a Roman province. Located west of

Carthage and encompassing most of what is now Algeria, it was ruled by the powerful king Masinissa in the late third and early second centuries B.C. Masinissa allied himself with Rome against Carthage in the Second and Third Punic Wars. After his death, his sons divided the kingdom; but his grandson, Jugurtha, reunited it and launched an unsuccessful war against Rome. Numidia became a Roman province in the first century B.C. (with the Roman historian Sallust as its first governor). In time, Roman military colonies were established in the area, which also became important for its agriculture and connection to the north African slave trade. Rome eventually lost most of Numidia to the Vandals in the fifth century (except for its southern portions, which fell to desert tribesmen). **See** Jugurthine War; Punic Wars (both Chapter 7).

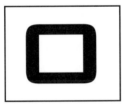

Olympus, Mount
At 9,570 feet, Mount Olympus, located in northeastern Greece, is the tallest mountain in that land. In early tradition, it was thought to be the home of the principal Greek gods (who became prototypes for several major Roman gods). The Greeks and Romans often referred to these deities as the Olympians, after the name of the mountain.

Ostia
Rome's port city, it was located at the mouth of the Tiber River on the coast of Latium about sixteen miles from Rome. According to tradition, King Ancus Marcius established Ostia in the seventh century B.C., but modern scholars think this more

likely occurred in the following century. The city long regulated trade, collected customs dues, and stored foodstuffs, particularly grain, for shipment upriver to Rome. In the first century A.D. Ostia underwent major renovations and its population increased considerably, necessitating the construction of extra housing, which mostly took the form of large apartment blocks, some of which were excavated in the twentieth century. The city declined in the fifth century, partly because of attacks by the Visigoths and other marauders and also due to the steady buildup of silt in its harbors.

Palatine
For this hill in Rome, **see** seven hills of Rome.

Palmyra
Located in a large oasis in the Syrian desert, this city rose to prominence in the third century B.C. thanks to prosperity gained via a major trade route running

The snow-capped peaks of the Mount Olympus range are visible in this photo taken from the south.

through the region. In the early first century A.D., Palmyra was incorporated into the Roman province of Syria and thereafter acted as an important element in Rome's defenses against the Parthians and Sassanian Persians. The city's moment in the sun occurred in the third century when a local Arab prince, Odaenath, led its forces in a defeat of the Persians on Rome's behalf; then his wife, Zenobia, challenged Rome by attempting to create an independent Palmyrene empire. **See** Zenobia (Chapter 1).

Pannonia

For this Roman province located in what is now eastern Austria, **see** Illyricum.

Parthia

For this Near Eastern realm that frequently opposed Rome, **see** Arsacids (Chapter 1).

Patavium

The site of the modern city of Padua, in northeastern Italy, established according to legend by a Trojan warrior named Antenor in the dim past. But the actual founders were probably the region's local residents. Patavium was noteworthy for the major roads, including the Via Annia, which passed through it, and also for its fine wool and wine.

Pergamum

(also Pergamon) An important Greek city and kingdom in northwestern Asia Minor, it rose to prominence in the third century B.C. under the Hellenistic ruling dynasty of the Attalids. The last of these rulers, Attalus III Philometor (reigned 138–133 B.C.), left the kingdom to the Romans in his will and they promptly converted it into their province of Asia. Pergamum was noted for its sanctuary and hospital of Asclepius, Greek god of healing (where the emperor Caracalla is said to have come for a cure), as well as its huge library (second in size only to the one in Alexandria) and magnificent public buildings.

Pharsalus

For this Greek town where Caesar defeated Pompey, **see** Battle of Pharsalus (Chapter 7).

Philippi

Located in eastern Macedonia about nine miles from the Aegean coast, this Greek city (named after Macedonia's King Philip II) was important for its strategic location on the land route from the Adriatic Sea to Byzantium (later Constantinople) and also for its access to nearby gold mines. Philippi was also noted as the site of the great battle (actually two battles) fought in 42 B.C., in which Antony and Octavian defeated the ringleaders of the conspiracy against Caesar, and for the visit made to the city in A.D. 49 by the Christian apostle Paul, which resulted in the Letter to the Philippians, later incorporated into the New Testament. **See** Battle of Philippi (Chapter 7).

Po Valley

The large, fertile region of northern Italy encompassing the watershed of the Po (or Padus) River and its tributaries; it came to be called Cisalpine Gaul. **See** Gaul.

Pompeii

This famous Roman city is located near the Bay of Naples and about five miles from Mount Vesuvius. From about 420 B.C., the Samnites controlled it until the Third Samnite War (298–290 B.C.), when it came under Roman influence. In A.D. 62, the city, whose population was then about twenty thousand, was severely damaged by an earthquake, and Vesuvius's great eruption of 79 finished it off. Buried for almost two millennia, Pompeii was rediscovered in the eighteenth century and became one of the most famous and valuable archaeological sites in the world, mainly because most of its contents were unusually well preserved by the volcanic materials that encased them. **See** Herculaneum; Vesuvius, Mount; **also** mosaics; painting (both Chapter 6).

The calcified bodies of some of Pompeii's residents, killed during Vesuvius's A.D. 79 eruption, still lie as modern scholars found them.

Pontus

A region, a kingdom, and later a Roman province located in northern Asia Minor, it first rose to prominence under King Mithridates I in about 300 B.C. The later members of his dynasty continued to expand its influence until Mithridates VI tried to do so at the expense of the Romans, who fought him in a series of wars and eventually defeated him and turned the area into the province of Bithynia-and-Pontus (in the 60s B.C.). It was reannexed and renamed several times in ensuing years, until the emperor Diocletian made it two provinces—Pontus Polemoniacus and Diospontus—in the late third century. **See** Mithridates VI (Chapter 1); **also** Mithridatic Wars (Chapter 7).

Ptolemaic Kingdom

Encompassing Egypt and at times parts of Palestine, it was established by Alexander the Great's general Ptolemy, who called himself King Ptolemy I and founded the Ptolemaic dynasty. The kingdom prospered as one of the three major Hellenistic Greek realms until Cleopatra VII, last of the Ptolemies, was defeated at Actium and committed suicide in 31–30 B.C. **See** Egypt; **also** Cleopatra VII; Ptolemy XII Auletes (both Chapter 1).

Puteoli

A city on the coast of southwestern Italy, along the Gulf of Cumae (Bay of Naples), Puteoli became an important trading center by the beginning of the second century B.C. Grain from Egypt and luxury goods from other parts of the Mediterranean flowed into its port and from there to Rome and inland sites. Puteoli was also important for its local deposits of volcanic clay, called *pulvis Puteolanus,* which became a key ingredient of one of the greatest of Roman inventions—concrete. **See** building materials and techniques (Chapter 6).

Pydna

For this Greek city, site of several important ancient battles, **see** Battle of Pydna (Chapter 7).

Ravenna

Located in northeastern Italy near the Adriatic coast, it was originally inhabited by the Etruscans and later by invading Gauls. Once Ravenna came under Roman control, it became a naval base (under Augustus), a ship-building and trading center, and an exporter of linen, wine, timber, and fish. The city's importance increased dramatically in 404, when the western emperor Honorius, convinced that the complex of lagoons surrounding it would provide formidable defenses, made it his capital. Here the last Roman emperor was deposed by the German Odoacer in 476.

Rhegium

A city of southern Italy, Greek colonists built it along the Strait of Messina, across from the island of Sicily, perhaps in the eighth century B.C. A Roman garrison occupied Rhegium circa 282 B.C., and during the Punic Wars it was a crucial departure point for armies crossing into Sicily. The city was also the site of one of Rome's major coin mints.

Rhine River

This major waterway marked the traditional boundary between Roman territory and Germania (Germany), where "barbarian" tribes held sway. Julius Caesar built his now famous wooden bridge over the river in the 50s B.C. to intimidate the natives. Thereafter, various Roman rulers made short-lived attempts to extend Rome's reach beyond the Rhine, none of which amounted to anything. **See** Germany.

Rhodes

A Greek island near the southwestern coast of Asia Minor, it was a powerful, prosperous city-state during the Hellenistic era (323–30 B.C.). In 305–304 B.C., it became famous for withstanding the siege of the Greek warlord Demetrius. Later, during the Second Macedonian War (200–197 B.C.), it supported Rome against Macedonia's King Philip V; but when the city backed Pompey in his civil war against Caesar in the 40s B.C., Caesar sacked its main town. This was subsequently rebuilt and Rhodes remained a prominent Greco-Roman maritime center throughout the remainder of antiquity.

Rome

Located on a bend in the Tiber River a few miles inland from the western Italian coast, Rome became both one of the great cities of the ancient world and the center of a mighty realm also often referred to as Rome. According to tradition, the city of Rome was founded in the eighth century B.C. by the legendary hero Romulus; based on calculations made by the noted first-century B.C. scholar M. Terentius Varro, 753 B.C. became the most widely accepted founding date. Modern scholars believe that early Roman culture did not appear suddenly but rather developed slowly over the course of many centuries. Archaeology has revealed that the group of Latin-speaking tribes to which the Romans belonged lived in Italy long before the eighth century B.C. Moreover, there was likely no single, purposeful founding of Rome; rather, the city's site was long occupied by primitive villages, which gradually came together to form one town. In the 1930s the remains of the bases of some primitive huts were discovered on Rome's Palatine hill and tentatively dated to the eighth century B.C. Both the site and period are the same as those identified in the chief myth of Romulus. Also, in 1988 excavators found the remains of a fortification wall, also dating from the eighth century B.C., on the edge of the Palatine hill. However, the fact that the huts and wall date from the eighth century B.C. is far from definitive proof that Rome was established at that time. Archaeologists have determined beyond a doubt that the Palatine and some of the other nearby Roman hills were inhabited long before, at least by 1000 B.C. and likely a good deal earlier.

These early inhabitants of Rome may have been native to central Italy, an offshoot of what historians term the "Apennine culture," a Bronze Age society that practiced inhumation (burial of the dead). Another possibility is that the Latin-speaking tribes who gave rise to the Romans migrated into Italy sometime in the second millennium. The traditional view was that they came in waves across the Alps; however, studies of the distribution of early Italian languages have led some scholars to conclude that at least some early migrants moved southwestward through the Balkans and crossed the Adriatic Sea into eastern Italy.

Wherever the original inhabitants of the area came from, it appears that the separate villages on the seven hills coalesced into a single town and became a city-state in the late eighth century B.C. at the earliest and more credibly in the early-to-mid–seventh century B.C. It is probably the distant but imperishable memory of this event that the later Romans identified with the founding by Romulus. At this time and for a long time afterward Rome remained a small, unimposing place with dirty, unpaved streets lined with timber huts with thatched roofs. The few larger buildings—temples and communal meeting places—

were smaller than later versions and also constructed of wood. Most traces of these early structures were erased over the centuries that followed as larger, more durable buildings were erected in their places. For several centuries, most Romans did not live in this urban center, but dwelled instead in simple huts in the surrounding countryside, hardy shepherds and farmers living a rustic, uncultured existence.

At first, the small Roman city-state was ruled by kings. The exact length of the monarchial period, as well as the number of kings and the lengths of their reigns, is unknown. According to later tradition, there were seven kings, beginning with Romulus, who supposedly reigned from 753 to 717 B.C. During the Monarchy, the Romans were frequently in conflict with their immediate neighbors and Roman territory steadily expanded outward, especially into the Latium plain in the south. The Romans were also periodically at war with the Etruscans, who lived directly north of Rome. Nevertheless, Etruscan culture impressed and influenced the Romans, who borrowed from it various artistic, architectural, religious, legal, and political concepts. During this period, partly in imitation of Etruscan cities, Rome began its transformation from a crude, ramshackle town to one with stone sewers, a paved forum (main square), and some stone public buildings.

About the year 509 B.C., the leading Roman fathers, making up the noble patrician class, threw out their king and established the Roman Republic. The Roman people came to view this representative system of government with great pride and patriotism, which helped fuel new and greater stages of Roman expansion. Roman armies captured the main Etruscan stronghold of Veii about 396 B.C. and in the decades that followed many other towns and peoples of central Italy became incorporated into the growing Roman sphere. By the early third century B.C., with Rome's defeat of the Samnites, a powerful hill people, Roman territory had expanded to cover some fifty thousand square miles, well more than a hundred times its original size.

The conquest of central Italy did not satisfy the Romans' growing appetite for territory and power. In the late 280s B.C. they turned on the numerous Greek cities that had sprung up across southern Italy in the preceding few centuries and in the space of only two decades absorbed them, becoming the undisputed masters of all Italy south of the Po Valley. Next, Rome cast its gaze beyond the shores of Italy and onto neighboring Mediterranean coasts. The empire of Carthage fell to Roman steel after the three devastating Punic Wars, fought between 264 and 146 B.C. As prizes, Rome gained the large and fertile island of Sicily, at the foot of the Italian boot, other western Mediterranean islands, Spain, and much of North Africa.

Rome had originally been strictly a land power; however, out of necessity during the Punic conflicts it built a powerful navy. Soon after obliterating Carthage, it unleashed its formidable combined land and

naval forces on the Greek kingdoms clustered in the Mediterranean's eastern sphere, including Macedonia, Seleucia, and Egypt. By the end of the second century B.C., the Mediterranean had become, in effect, a Roman lake.

But Rome's phenomenal success had come at a price. By the dawn of the first century B.C., ominous cracks had appeared in the Republic's structure. First, in their rise to Mediterranean mastery the Romans had found it increasingly difficult to administer so many diverse lands and peoples with a governmental system that had been designed to rule a single people inhabiting a small city-state. Also, conquest and rule required large, well-disciplined armies and able generals, both of which Rome had in abundance. But, unwisely, the state ahdered to a policy of not rewarding its soldiers with pensions and land when they retired. Meeting this need, the wealthiest and most powerful generals began using their influence to secure such benefits for their men. Consequently, the troops began to show more allegiance to their generals than to the state.

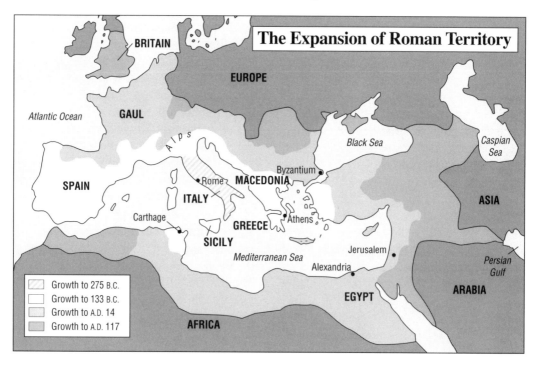

The Expansion of Roman Territory

BRITAIN
EUROPE
Atlantic Ocean
GAUL
Alps
Black Sea
Caspian Sea
Byzantium
Rome MACEDONIA
SPAIN
ITALY
ASIA
Carthage
Athens
GREECE
SICILY
Jerusalem
Mediterranean Sea
Persian Gulf
Alexandria
ARABIA
EGYPT
AFRICA

Growth to 275 B.C.
Growth to 133 B.C.
Growth to A.D. 14
Growth to A.D. 117

The "private ends" of these generals increasingly consisted of amassing great political power and challenging the government's authority. Among the most successful were Sulla, the first Roman consul to seize the capital by force; Pompey, who won lasting fame after ridding the Mediterranean of pirates; Caesar, who conquered the wild lands of Gaul and met a violent end at the hands of senatorial assassins in 44 B.C.; and Antony, Caesar's protégé, famous for his love affair and alliance with Egypt's Queen Cleopatra. These and other contenders for state power met head-on in a series of horrendously destructive civil wars that killed hundreds of thousands of people and brought the Republic and its ideals of representative government crashing down. Cicero, the last great republican champion, quite literally lost his head, the victim of Antony's henchmen.

From this long and destructive orgy of personal ambition and civil strife, one man finally emerged victorious—Octavian, Caesar's adopted son. Soon after the defeat of his last rivals, Antony and Cleopatra, in a large naval battle near the Greek town of Actium in 31 B.C., the Senate, now virtually powerless, conferred on Octavian the title of Augustus, "the exalted one." Though quite prudently he never personally used the title of emperor, he became in fact the first ruler of a new, more autocratic Roman state, the Roman Empire.

During Augustus's reign, Rome, long a dingy, graceless, and unattractive city, at last became the grand metropolis of polished marble that awed the world in the centuries that followed. He built a new forum, with a temple of the war god Mars at its center, as well as theaters and other structures, including the crowning artistic masterpiece of his reign, the Ara Pacis (Altar of Peace), completed in 9 B.C. An equally impressive Augustan achievement was the fine flowering of literature in this period, highlighted by the works of such great writers as the historian Livy and the poets Virgil, Horace, and Ovid.

For the most part, Augustus's immediate successors maintained the peace his reign had initiated. During the Roman Empire's first two centuries, the Mediterranean world that it controlled and administered enjoyed a degree of peace and prosperity it had never known and would not know again for almost two thousand years. This extraordinary era later became known as the *Pax Romana,* or "Roman peace." During this era Roman civilization attained its greatest size, grandeur, and political influence. Under the emperor Trajan (reigned A.D. 98–117), the realm stretched from the Atlantic Ocean in the west to the Persian Gulf in the east, and from North Africa in the south to central Britain in the north, a colossal political unit encompassing some 3.5 million square miles and more than 100 million people.

The first obvious signs that the Empire faced serious problems occurred in the late second and early third centuries, marking the transition from the *Pax Romana* to what historians often call "the anarchy." In the turbulent mid–third century, Rome experienced a severe crisis in which its political and economic stability was shattered. On one hand, it faced external threats, including violations of the northern borders by Germanic tribes and full-scale war with the formidable Sassanian Persian Empire on its eastern border. Among Rome's internal problems in this period were poor leadership, a breakdown of military discipline and efficiency, disruption of trade, a decline in farming, and a severe devaluation of money. On the political front, between 235 and 284 more than fifty rulers claimed the throne, only half of whom were legally recognized, and all but one died by assassination or other violent means. A sign of the insecurity of the times and the vulnerability of the capital city was the perceived need to build miles-long defensive fortifications (Aurelian's Wall) around Rome itself.

Though disunity and chaos appeared to spell the end of the old Roman world, beginning in the year 268 a series of strong military leaders took control of the Roman state and in one of the most remarkable reversals in history the stubborn and resilient Romans were able to regain the initiative, pushing back the Germans and defeating illegal imperial claimants in various parts of the realm. Then in 284 the remarkably capable Diocletian assumed the throne. He completely reorganized the Roman state, creating what modern historians often refer to as the Later Empire. First, he transformed the imperial government and court into an "eastern" style monarchy similar in many ways to that in Persia; then he divided the leadership, creating a four-man ruling partnership (the Tetrarchy). He also drastically overhauled the Roman economy, ordering that nearly all workers remain in their present professions for life. Though certainly more orderly than the Roman realm that had recently almost collapsed, the new one was, overall, a less prosperous, less optimistic, and more regimented place in which to live.

One of the major developments of the Later Empire was the ascendancy and triumph of Christianity, whose members had suffered from numerous persecutions since the late first century. Diocletian and his coemperor Galerius were the last emperors to stage a large-scale Christian persecution; subsequently the emperor Constantine I (reigned 307–337) granted the sect tolerance and himself converted to it, lending it credibility and prestige. Thereafter, the Christians gained an increasingly firm foothold in the government, achieving a controlling influence over its political and religious apparatus by the 390s.

Meanwhile, in the decades following Constantine's death, pressure from the barbarian tribes on the northern borders was increasing. In about 370, the Huns, a fierce nomadic people from central Asia, swept into eastern Europe, driving the Goths and other Germanic peoples into the Roman border provinces. The Huns' advance set in motion the greatest migrations of peoples in history, as the Goths, Vandals, Franks, Angles, Saxons, and many other tribes spread over Europe in search of new lands. These invasions constitute a major cause of the Empire's ensuing shrinkage and demise. Not only was the Roman army increasingly less effective in stopping the intruders, but the government periodically and unwisely struck deals with them. This process, in which various tribes were given pieces of Roman territory, steadily reduced the size of the realm and the authority of the central government. In 410, one barbarian group, the Visigoths, sacked the city of Rome, an event that sent shock waves through the Mediterranean world by showing that the Roman heartland was dangerously vulnerable to attack. Sure enough, in 455 Rome suffered the indignity of a second capture, this time by the Vandals.

The western Empire was now a shrunken ghost of the mighty state of the *Pax Romana.* (The eastern portion of the realm, ruled from its capital of Constantinople, remained stronger and more intact; eventually it would evolve into the Greek-speaking Byzantine Empire.) The last few western emperors, all of them weak and ineffectual rulers, reigned over a pitiful realm consisting only of the Italian peninsula and portions of a few nearby provinces. Even these lands were not safe or secure, partly because barbarian claims on Roman territory continued, and also because what was left of the once powerful Roman army was fast disintegrating. On September 4, 476, a German-born Roman general named Odoacer led a contingent of troops into Ravenna (at the time the capital of the western Empire) and without striking a blow de-

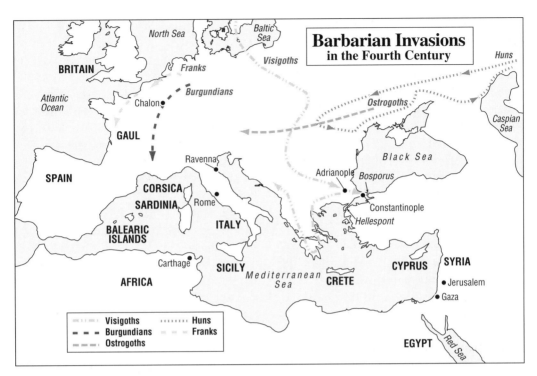

Barbarian Invasions in the Fourth Century

posed the young emperor, Romulus Augustulus. No emperor took the boy's place; and the western imperial government, which had been barely functioning for decades, now simply ceased to exist. Though the city of Rome still stood and life for its residents went on as before for a while under German-born rulers, the vast Mediterranean dominion that the Romans had once conquered with such boldness and vigor had slipped quietly into the realm of legend. **See** Augustus; Romulus (both Chapter 1); Christianity (Chapter 3); Empire, Roman; Monarchy; Republic, Roman; Senate (all Chapter 4); Augustan Age of literature (Chapter 6); fall of Rome; Punic Wars (both Chapter 7).

Rubicon River

A stream flowing through northeastern Italy, in republican times it denoted the boundary between Italy proper and Cisalpine Gaul. It became famous after Julius Caesar crossed it with his army in 49 B.C., thereby initiating a civil war with his enemy, Pompey. **See** Caesar, Gaius Julius (Chapter 1).

Saguntum

This city on Spain's eastern coast became an ally of Rome in the third century B.C. during the era when the Carthaginians were attempting to develop a power base there. In 218 B.C., after Hannibal captured the city following an eight-month siege, Rome declared war, initiating the second of its three great conflicts with Carthage. Much later, during the Empire, Saguntum was a prosperous Roman town known for its grain, pottery, and a distinctive type of fig. **See** Hannibal (Chapter 1); **and** Punic Wars (Chapter 7).

Sardinia

Lying west of the Italian peninsula, Sardinia is the second-largest island in the Mediterranean Sea. Rich in copper and other metals, it was long an important stop in the sea's trade routes, and the Phoenicians, Carthaginians, and Greeks all established settlements or trading posts there. In the 220s B.C., the Romans took over the island and made it a province, which thereafter supplied Rome with grain as well as copper, iron, and silver. During the Empire, Roman leaders also used the island as a place to exile their political enemies. In A.D. 429, Sardinia fell under the control of the Vandals as they crossed from southern Europe to North Africa.

Seleucid Kingdom

One of the three major Greek Hellenistic kingdoms, it was established by Seleucus, one of the chief successors of Alexander the Great. Encompassing much of the Near East, including the old Persian heartland, Mesopotamia, and parts of Asia Minor, it faced Rome in the early second century B.C. after the Romans had defeated Macedonia's Philip V. In 190 B.C., the Seleucid monarch Antiochus III was defeated by a Roman army at Magnesia; in the decades that followed most of the kingdom fell to the Parthians, who subsequently became one of Rome's principal enemies in the region. **See** Arsacids (Chapter 1); **and** Battle of Magnesia (Chapter 7).

seven hills of Rome

This series of low hills on which the city of Rome grew included the Palatine (located just south of the Campus Martius), where several emperors built their palaces; the Capitoline (actually two hills with a depression between), on which rose several versions of the Temple of Jupiter, heart of the Roman state religion; the Quirinal (beside the Campus Martius), where Diocletian and Constantine built large-scale baths; the Caelian (in the southeast), site of a number of military camps; the Aventine (in the south), mostly a residential area featuring apartment blocks and townhouses; the Viminal (near the Quirinal), where the urban cohorts and

Praetorian Guard were based; and the Esquiline (beside the Viminal), which featured extensive gardens, as well as the baths of Titus and Trajan.

Rome's streets and buildings also filled the shallow valleys between these hills, of course. The valley lying between the Caelian, Palatine, and Esquiline hills, for example, became the site of many splendid public buildings, including the Colosseum. Filling the valley between the Esquiline, Quirinal, and Viminal hills was a district called the Subura, heavily crowded with stores, barbershops, and often slum residences. The city eventually grew to include outlying areas beyond these seven hills and their interconnecting valleys, mostly on and around the Pincian hills (in the north); the Janiculum, a hill lying across the Tiber from the main part of the city; and the Vatican hill, also across the Tiber, where Constantine erected St. Peter's Basilica.

Sicily

A large island (covering 9,830 square miles) lying off the southwestern coast of Italy and separated from it by the narrow Strait of Messina, Sicily was one of Rome's most important territories. The island's eastern section was heavily colonized by Greeks beginning in the eighth century B.C., the most important Greek city being Syracuse. Meanwhile, the Phoenicians (a maritime people from the Palestinian coast) settled in the island's eastern section, which eventually came under the control of Carthage (which began as a Phoenician outpost).

The island, and especially its surrounding waters, became a heated battleground between the Romans and Carthaginians during the First Punic War (264–241 B.C.); at the conclusion of the conflict, Rome gained control of most of the island, with the major exception of the city-state of Syracuse. This fell to the Romans during the Second Punic War (218–201 B.C.). Sicily subsequently became an important source of grain and other foodstuffs for Italy. It was also the site of two major slave rebellions, in 135–132 and 104–100 B.C. In the fifth century A.D., the Vandals invaded the island and subsequently, after Rome's fall, other barbarian groups controlled it. **See** Syracuse; **also** slaves and slavery (Chapter 5); **and** Punic Wars (Chapter 7).

Spain

(Hispania) In Roman times, it encompassed the whole Iberian Peninsula (today comprising Spain and Portugal). Native Iberians, along with Celts from the north, first settled the region in the Stone Age and Bronze Age, followed by Greeks in the eighth and seventh centuries B.C., and finally by Carthaginians in the third century B.C. The latter, led by Hamilcar Barca, attempted to build a minor empire there, establishing Carthago Nova (New Carthage) in 228 B.C. But the Carthaginians soon clashed with the Romans, who by 206 B.C. had taken control of much of the area.

In the century that followed, Rome completed its conquest of the natives and established two provinces, Nearer Spain and Farther Spain. Augustus subsequently redrew the region's boundaries, making three provinces—Citerior (later Tarraconensis, in the north), Baetica (east-central and south), and Lusitania (west). Over the centuries, Spain produced many important Roman figures, among them the emperor Trajan and the writers Seneca the Younger, Martial, and Quintilian; it also proved to be a hotbed and haven of rebels and political usurpers, including Sertorius, who challenged Sulla and Pompey. In the Later Empire, the Vandals, Alans, Suebi, and other barbarian tribes invaded Roman Spain and some settled permanently there. **See** Lusitania; **also** Sertorius, Quintus (Chapter 1).

Split

For this important Roman city in Illyricum in which the emperor Diocletian erected a large palace, **see** Illyricum.

Syracuse

Located in eastern Sicily, it was originally a Greek city, whose king, Hiero, allied himself to Rome near the beginning of the First Punic War (264–241 B.C.). However, his grandson chose to support the Carthaginians against the Romans in the Second Punic War (218–201 B.C.), and the Romans, led by M. Claudius Marcellus, laid siege to the city in 213–211 B.C. Despite a spectacular defense engineered by its native son, the brilliant inventor Archimedes, Marcellus captured Syracuse, which subsequently became the capital of the Roman province of Sicily. **See** Sicily; **also** Marcellus, Marcus Claudius (Chapter 1); **and** Punic Wars (Chapter 7).

Syria

In ancient times, this region roughly encompassed the fertile lands bordered by the eastern Mediterranean coast in the west, Palestine in the south, the Arabian desert in the southeast, and Mesopotamia in the east. The Persians held it until Alexander the Great incorporated it into his empire in 332 B.C. Following his death, the area was divided between the Greek Seleucid and Ptolemaic kingdoms, until the Seleucids managed to take over the Ptolemies' share circa 200 B.C. But the Seleucid hold on Syria steadily weakened as Rome slowly absorbed the region, much of which became a Roman province in 63 B.C., through the efforts of Pompey.

In the years that followed, Syria prospered, attaining a large population; its cities, led by Antioch, one of the major metropolises of the Roman world, were cosmopolitan and highly cultured. In the third century, Syria was the scene of much political and military drama, as the Sassanid Persians invaded and the Romans, as well as the leaders of the city of Palmyra, wrestled for control. In the early Later Empire, with order restored, Roman leaders subdivided Syria into five provinces. **See** Antioch; Palmyra.

Tarentum

Originally a Greek city called Taras, Tarentum was established in the late eighth century B.C. on a peninsula along Italy's southern coast (on the so-called instep of the Italian "boot"). In 282 B.C., the Tarantines fell into a dispute with Rome, in which they sank several Roman ships; fearing an attack by the Roman land army, they called on the Greek king Pyrrhus to defend them. He scored a few narrow victories over Roman forces but was unable to make decisive headway and eventually withdrew, leaving Taras with no choice but surrender to Rome. Afterward, as Tarentum, it slowly became Romanized (though it retained much of its Greek character). By the late first century B.C. the poet Horace described it as a nice quiet place for the tired professional man to take a vacation. **See** Pyrrhus (Chapter 1).

Tarsus

(or Tarsos) The principal city of Cilicia (in southern Asia Minor), built on the banks of the Cydnus River, it had a measure of local autonomy under the Persians. Alexander the Great seized it in 333 B.C. and built a coin mint there. After his demise, the Greek Seleucids and Ptolemies contested its control until powerful Romans, including Pompey, Caesar, and Antony occupied it at various times. Antony made it one of his headquarters and it was there, in 41 B.C., that he summoned

Cleopatra, who made the famous and spectacular entrance described by Plutarch:

> She came sailing up the river Cydnus in a barge with a stern of gold, its purple sails billowing in the wind, while her rowers caressed the water with oars of silver which dipped in time to the music of the flute. . . . Cleopatra herself reclined beneath a canopy of cloth of gold, dressed in the character of Venus . . . [while] boys costumed as Cupids cooled her with fans. (*Life of Antony* 26)

Later, during the Empire, Tarsus's mint continued to operate, turning out coins for numerous emperors. **See** Cilicia; **also** Cleopatra VII; Antony, Mark (both Chapter 1).

Teutoberg Forest

For this place in Germany where a Roman army was annihilated during Augustus's reign, **see** Germany; **also** Varus (Chapter 1); **and** Battle of the Teutoburg Forest (Chapter 7).

Thessalonica

(also Thessaloniki or Salonica) The largest city of Macedonia (northern Greece), it

A later European painting depicts Cleopatra's barge (shown as a Dutch ship) docked at Tarsus.

was established by Cassander, one of the successors of Alexander the Great, in 316 B.C. After reducing the city by siege in the 160s B.C., the Romans made it the capital of their province of Macedonia-Achaea. The Christian apostle Paul visited Thessalonica about A.D. 50 (and again in 56), and wrote the Letter to the Thessalonians, which later became part of the New Testament. During the Later Empire, the city was an imperial capital and the site of an important coin mint. Eventually, after the fall of western Rome, it survived and prospered as one of the leading cities of the Byzantine Empire.

Thrace

The territory lying directly north of the Aegean Sea (originally thought of as extending all the way to the Danube River), it was long inhabited by native Thracians, whom the powerful city-states of the southern Greek mainland looked on as culturally backward and warlike. The city-states intermittently colonized the area until Macedonia's Philip II directly annexed it in the 340s B.C. After the death of Philip's son, Alexander the Great, in 323 B.C., one of Alexander's successors, Lysimachus, took over and ruled Thrace; but another Macedonian, Philip V, later made it part of his own realm. It was the defeat and dissolution of the Macedonian Kingdom by the Romans (in 168 B.C.) that began Rome's influence in and domination of the region. Thrace officially became a Roman province under the emperor Claudius in the 40s A.D. The area was known for its gold mines and agricultural products, and also as the birthplace of Spartacus, the gladiator who led the largest slave rebellion in Roman history.

Tiber River

At roughly 250 miles in length, the Tiber is the longest river on the Italian peninsula. It is most famous for its proximity to the city of Rome, which grew up along a bend of the waterway located about 16 miles from the sea. The Tiber's southern reaches traditionally marked the boundary between Etruria (land of the Etruscans) and the Latium plain. The river was navigable for most of the year up to Narnia, about 80 miles north of Rome.

Tigris River

For this important Near Eastern river, **see** Mesopotamia.

Tivoli

(or Tibur) Located about eighteen miles northeast of Rome, Tivoli was a town nestled along the Anio River. Early a member of the Latin League, it fought against the Romans until losing much of its surrounding territory to them by 338 B.C. Thereafter, Tivoli was noted for its fine building stone (travertine) and its fruit orchards, although its main claim to fame was a series of luxurious villas, one used by Augustus and another that housed the defeated Palmyrene queen Zenobia. The most splendid of all was that of the emperor Hadrian, built in the 120s and 130s A.D., which included a palace, long roofed walkways, gardens, bathhouses, and replicas of famous buildings from around the Mediterranean world. **See** Hadrian (Chapter 1); **and** palaces (Chapter 6).

Transalpine Gaul

For this region now encompassed by France, **see** Gaul.

Trasimene, Lake

The largest lake on the Italian peninsula, it covers an area of some forty-nine square miles. It was most famous as the site of a stunning victory by Hannibal over the Romans in 217 B.C., at the opening of the Second Punic War. **See** Battle of Lake Trasimene; Punic Wars (both Chapter 7).

Veii

An important Etruscan city-state located in southeastern Etruria not far north of Rome. Circa 750–700 B.C., a group of villages in the area coalesced into the city of Veii, which in the next two centuries became wealthy and influential. However, increasing rivalry with Rome caused tensions and finally war between the two city-states. After a long siege, Veii fell to the Romans in 396 B.C. Later, the emperor Augustus established a colony on its ruins. **See** Etruscans (Chapter 7).

Vesuvius, Mount

A famous volcano located near the Gulf of Cumae (Bay of Naples), Vesuvius lies on Italy's western coast. Because it had not erupted in human memory, the Romans assumed it was harmless,but the huge eruption of August 24, A.D. 79, proved them wrong. The disaster buried the nearby towns of Pompeii and Herculaneum in ash and mud, encasing them until their rediscovery in modern times. The noted Roman naturalist Pliny the Elder died while attempting to study the eruption up close. **See**

A modern reconstruction of the Etruscan citadel of Veii, as it may have appeared in the fourth or fifth century B.C.

Herculaneum; Pompeii; **also** Pliny the Elder (Chapter 1).

Zama

For this site in North Africa where the Romans finally defeated Hannibal, **see** Hannibal; Scipio, Publius Cornelius "Africanus" (both Chapter 1); **and** Battle of Zama (Chapter 7).

CHAPTER 3

GODS AND RELIGION

Aesculapius

The Roman name for the Greek healing god Asclepius, he was the son of Apollo, another deity who healed, and Coronis, a mortal woman. Shrines to Asclepius/Aesculapius existed throughout the Mediterranean world; the Romans built their most famous one, adjoined by a clinic where sick people could rest and recover, on an island in the Tiber River. His festival was celebrated on January 1. **See** medicine (Chapter 5).

afterlife

From about the third century B.C. on, the Romans shared the same general ideas about the afterlife with the Greeks, whose views on the subject varied considerably, as is the case in most modern societies. Some people held that the soul continues to exist after death, while others thought that it floats away into the sky, as advocated by the Greek philosopher Plato in his treatise *Phaedo*. The Epicureans preached that the soul is made up of atoms, which dissipate and vanish after death, while the Stoics advanced no single, dogmatic belief

about the soul's fate. There was also widespread disagreement over where the soul resides, if it does indeed survive after death; whether a dead person can perceive the living; and if the dead receive either rewards or punishments in the afterlife.

The most common traditional folk beliefs, derived originally from the epic poems of the Greek poet Homer, held that both good and bad souls descended into the underworld (Hades). There, according to one view, wrongdoers suffered various punishments in a ghastly place called Tartarus; while more virtuous people, particularly renowned heroes, lived on in abodes of eternal happiness. However, it is questionable whether such beliefs were still common in Rome's mid-to-late republican and imperial eras. Evidence shows that many people believed, for instance, that the soul lived on inside a dead person's grave marker or in the tomb itself; for this reason it was common practice to bring gifts to the tomb, pour sacrificial wine on it (or into it through pipes), and/or perform periodic celebrations at the gravesite to appease the dead. Also, in the apparent belief that the dead could rise up and haunt the living, some people decapitated the bodies or placed large stones over the coffins.

The mystery religions, including Christianity, were notable for advancing the notion of a happy afterlife (heaven, in the

Christian version), which increasingly appealed to confused, fearful, and downtrodden people. In the Later Empire, after Christianity's triumph, the Christian concepts of heaven and eventually hell (as advocated by Augustine and other Christian writers) became common across Europe. **See** burial customs (Chapter 5).

Apollo

God of healing, oracles and prophecy, and music and poetry, he was introduced to the Romans through contacts with the Etruscans, north of Rome, and the Greek settlements of southern Italy. His chief symbol was the laurel tree. The emperor Augustus, who adopted Apollo as his patron deity, held that the god had helped ensure the Roman victory at Actium in 31 B.C. and showed his gratitude by erecting a small but impressive temple to him on the Palatine hill.

Arianism

A widely popular Christian sect that arose in the early third century, mainstream bishops viewed it as a threat to the church and it became known as the Arian heresy, after Arius, a priest of Alexandria, Egypt. Essentially, the Arians held that, though Jesus had existed since before time began, he had been created by God the Father and was therefore not fully divine.

The idea that Jesus was inferior to God provoked such heated debate among church leaders that Constantine himself intervened, calling a great council in 325 at Nicaea, which more than two hundred bishops attended. (This was the first of seven Ecumenical Councils held by the early church, the last also taking place in Nicaea in 787.) Constantine himself sided with the majority against the Arians. He appears to have suggested that the church adopt the concept of *homoousios,* "of the same substance," essentially meaning that Christ and God were one and the same. With this imperial support, the anti-Arians prevailed and formulated a creed designed to clarify the "proper" way of viewing God and Christ; with a few later additions it became known as the Nicene Creed, the most universally accepted statement of Christian belief for many centuries to come.

But though cursed by many, Arianism was far from dead. Constantine's son, Constantius II, was an Arian who encouraged the spread of Arian views. During his reign, Arian Christian missionaries converted many of the Goths, a Germanic tribe living mainly north of the Danube River; the result was that millions of Arian Christians did not embrace the Nicene version of Christianity until early medieval times. **See** Christianity.

Arval priests

For these priests who sought protection for farmers and their fields, **see** priests.

astrology

The belief that the stars, planets, and other heavenly bodies influence earthly life and events began in ancient Mesopotamia, eventually spread to Greece, and by the second century B.C. had reached Rome, where it became quite popular. It was generally thought that celestial influences were one of several manifestations of divine power and intervention; that is, that the will of the gods could be discerned, at least to some extent, in the stars. Astrological pamphlets and charts began to circulate widely in the late Republic, and in imperial times most Romans accepted the basic tenets of the belief. Augustus, the poets Ovid and Propertius, and the architect Vitruvius, for instance, were all believers, and a number of Roman emperors consulted astrologers to aid in their decision making. Still, some Romans, including the great orator Cicero, were skeptical. In the Later Empire, the Christian writer Augustine declared that astrology was invalid, and the government banned it, though many people continued to believe in and practice it.

Atargatis

(or Dea Syria, "the Syrian Goddess") A deity who originated in Syria and southern Asia Minor, her main temple was at Hierapolis. Her worship spread throughout the Near East and Greece beginning in the second century B.C., but was apparently not as widespread in the western parts of the Roman realm. A colorful and humorous description of a band of Atargatis's wandering priests taking part in a bizarre public display of self-humiliation appears in Apuleius's novel *The Golden Ass*.

augurs

A college (organization) of priests who performed augury (also called auspices), a form of divination in which they read, or interpreted, divine signs that supposedly appeared in the flight patterns and other behaviors of birds. The object was to ascertain whether a proposed course of action by the state, a military general, or other group or individual was approved by the gods. Augurs, who were generally elected from the aristocracy and served for life, followed strict rules and procedures and underwent extensive training. **See** divination, priests.

auspices

For this search for divine signs in the behavior of birds, **see** augurs.

Bacchanalia

For this fertility celebration, **see** Bacchus.

Bacchus

The Latin/Roman version of the Greek fertility god Dionysus, who was also the god of wine and ecstasy. According to the Ro-

man historian Livy, his rites, known as the Bacchanalia (or the Bacchic Mysteries, or the *orgia*), originally included drunken orgies and other acts generally viewed as socially unacceptable or immoral. Consequently, in 186 B.C. the Senate banned the Bacchanalia from Italy, although scattered examples of it occurred in later times.

Bellona

Originally called Duellona, she was the goddess of war, sometimes viewed by the Romans as the sister of Mars, the war god. The Romans built a temple for her in the Campus Martius and held a festival for her on June 3.

Bona Dea

A fertility goddess, she was worshiped almost exclusively by women. Bona Dea, whom the Romans sometimes identified with another fertility deity, Fauna, had a festival celebrated annually on December 3.

Capitoline Triad

For this group of three prominent gods, **see** their names—Juno, Jupiter, and Minerva.

Castor and Pollux

(together known as the Dioscuri) Characters derived from Greek mythology, they were the semidivine twin sons of a mortal woman, Leda, and the brothers of Helen of Troy. (They are also routinely identified with the constellation Gemini, the Twins.) The Romans worshiped them from early times, erecting temples that usually bore the name of the dominant brother, Castor. The Dioscuri were particularly popular among Roman equites, who regarded them as their patron deities. **See** equites (Chapter 5).

Ceres

A very ancient Italian goddess, she personified nature's yearly renewal and regeneration. Her popular festival, the Cerialia, was held from April 12 to 19. People often offered sacrifices to her after a funeral to purify the house of the deceased.

Christianity

Now the world's largest faith, with dozens of denominations totaling almost 2 billion members in all, Christianity came into being in Roman-controlled Palestine in the first century A.D.; by a century or so after Rome's fall (in the late fifth century), it had risen to become the dominant faith of Europe in the early Middle Ages.

The social, political, and religious setting of the faith's birth consisted of a mixture of Greco-Roman and Jewish influences. The Romans gained control of Palestine in the first century B.C. and annexed its southern section, Judaea (site of the ancient Jewish kingdom of Judah), in A.D. 6. Many diverse faiths and philosophical schools flourished in the Roman world at the time, with which Christianity had to compete and some of which influenced it to some degree. Among the most popular of these faiths were Rome's traditional state religion (with its pantheon headed by Jupiter) and several eastern "mystery" cults imported into the Roman world during the last two centuries B.C. (including those of Cybele, Mithras, and Isis).

Much more influential on Christianity's inception and development was the faith from which it sprang—Judaism. The monotheistic Jews had always seen themselves as set apart from other people, both spiritually and culturally, and the Christians inherited this feeling of special exclusivity. Moreover, the two faiths shared the same ethical tradition, which emphasized the stability of family life, chastity, and helping the poor and sick. The Christians also shared with the Jews the Old Testament (or Scriptures).

Christianity and Judaism began to separate in the first century A.D. in the decades immediately following the death of the figure who became the inspiration for the Christian faith—Jesus Christ. After his crucifixion (about A.D. 30–33), at the orders of the Roman prefect Pontius Pilate, some of his followers claimed that Jesus had risen from the dead, and they began to spread the word that he had been the Messiah and Son of God. Their message was at first directed strictly to Jews, for they still considered themselves Jews and followed Jewish customs, such as circumcision and strict dietary laws. For a while, the new community, calling itself the people of "the Way," was persecuted by most other Jews. About the year 36, however, a Jew named Saul of Tarsus, who became known as Paul, converted to "the Way." He embarked on a mission to bring word of Jesus' divinity to the Gentiles (non-Jews), which opened up whole new vistas for attracting converts. For a while, the Jewish members of the community, which by now called itself Christian, flourished alongside the Gentiles, until the former were largely wiped out during the sack of Jerusalem by the Romans in 70.

Having largely separated from Judaism proper, while retaining many Jewish customs, beliefs, and writings, the Gentile Christian community began to expand across the Mediterranean world. After Paul and the last few original apostles passed away, new generations of missionary leaders took their places. In the first century or so of expansion, they sought not only to win over new members, but also to maintain harmony and set standards of worship among the many far-flung Christian communities. Church fathers also stressed the importance of a hierarchy of authority within church organization. In addition to having elders (presbyters), each community came to have a strong overall leader, the bishop (from the Greek word *episkopos,* meaning "overseer").

In the mid-to-late second century, some of the better-educated church leaders became known as apologists; Justin Martyr, Tertullian, and Origen were among the most influential. They wrote long, persuasive tracts explaining Christian beliefs and calling for toleration and recognition for Christians within Roman society, which was still predominantly pagan. This was necessary because the Roman government persecuted Christians from the late first to early fourth centuries. Due to a number of misunderstandings about Christian beliefs and practices, and also because they refused to take part in emperor worship (which was seen as a potential threat to public order), Christians were viewed by many as antisocial or even criminal. The worst of the persecutions was the one instigated by the emperors Diocletian and Galerius in 303, when the government ordered the closing of all Christian churches, the surrender and burning of holy books, and the banning of Christian religious meetings. There was much bloodshed and misery, mainly in the eastern half of the Empire.

Soon, however, the Christians came under the protective wing of the emperor Constantine I, who at first saw the Christian god as a manifestation of his own favorite god, the Unconquered Sun. In 312, Constantine defeated one of his rivals using a Christian symbol as a battle emblem. Convinced that the Christian god had ensured his victory, he was now willing and eager to reward both that deity and its followers. During his ensuing reign, therefore, Christianity underwent a relatively sudden transition from a minor, misunderstood, often persecuted faith to a widely tolerated, legally sanctioned, and rapidly growing one. Official toleration came in 313 with the so-called Edict of Milan. Constantine's support for the Christians remained steadfast in the later years of his reign and he converted to the faith on his deathbed.

Thanks in large degree to Constantine's pro-Christian policies, after his death Christianity underwent spectacular growth, gaining political as well as spiritual authority. His three sons—Constantine II, Constantius II, and Constans—were all pious and committed Christians. Paganism found itself increasingly under attack by zealous Christian bishops, including Ambrose of Milan, the most prominent and influential among them. Ambrose convinced the emperor Gratian to confiscate the funds of the state priesthood and to remove the time-honored statue of the goddess Victory from Rome's Senate House. Also influenced by Ambrose, the emperor Theodosius I abolished all pagan sacrifices and cults and officially closed all pagan temples in the early 390s. Although the number of pagans in the Empire remained large, Christian leaders had by this time managed to achieve a controlling influence over the political and religious apparatus of the Roman state.

At the same time, Christian leaders, thinkers, and writers continued to carry the Christian revolution into Roman social and personal life. The church labeled such pastimes as gambling, gladiatorial combats,

Roman soldiers break up a Christian religious ceremony in Rome's underground catacombs.

horse racing, and mixed public bathing as sinful. Female virginity became a treasured virtue; and sex, outside of married couples attempting to create children, was increasingly frowned on. Christian social morality was further reinforced by theologians of the late fourth and early fifth centuries, the most prominent among them Augustine of Hippo. He penned his monumental *City of God* as a rebuttal to the pagan argument that Rome's sacking by the Visigoths in 410 was a punishment sent by the pagan gods for their abandonment by the Christians. Under the influence of Augustine and others like him, intense guilt and the fear of going to hell began to replace public shame as conditioners of moral behavior.

Meanwhile, a growing number of Christians became hermits and monks, adopting lifestyles of social isolation, extreme self-discipline, and self-denial. This marked the beginning of the monastic movement that would later become a major and accepted feature of medieval Christian life. Only a generation after Augustine's death, the western Empire collapsed, but the church survived and set about converting those "barbarians" who had not already accepted Christian beliefs. Born in Rome's cultural and religious melting pot, Christianity soon became the spiritual guide for all of Europe. **See** Arianism; Donatism; Judaism; worship; **also** Ambrose; Augustine; Constantine I; Jesus Christ; Paul; Tertullian (all Chapter 1).

Consus

An ancient deity associated with grain and the granary. His festivals, the Consualia, took place on August 21 and December 15, at which times a special underground altar and barn located under the Circus Maximus in Rome were temporarily uncovered.

Council of Nicaea

For this famous first meeting of most of the Christian bishops in the Roman world, **see** Arianism.

cult

The general worship of a god, goddess, or hero, including all of the beliefs, rites, and ceremonies attending that worship. Thus, the cult of Isis was the religious worship of that goddess. The word *cult* comes from the Latin word *cultus,* meaning "cultivation" or "care," for it was a cornerstone of Greek and Roman religion that the favor of the gods had to be regularly cultivated and perpetuated through sacrifice and other forms of worship. **See** worship.

Cupid

The son of the deities Venus and Vulcan, Cupid was the young male god of love. He was often portrayed in art with wings and a quiver of arrows, and also appeared as a symbol of life after death on coffins. He plays a leading role in the myth of Cupid and Psyche, as told in the Latin novel *The Golden Ass* by Apuleius.

curses

Generally speaking, curses were requests made of the gods to punish wrongdoers or personal enemies. The usual procedure was to inscribe a curse tablet (*defixio*) with the name of the enemy and the punishment desired, and then to bury it, place it in a tomb, or throw it down a well. Another kind of curse consisted of a magic charm (*devotio*), often a wax image of a person; piercing the image with sharp objects was thought to inflict pain or even death. **See** magic.

Cybele

(the "Great Mother") A goddess who originated in Phrygia (in west-central Asia Minor), she was a fertility deity who, it was thought, could also cure (or inflict) disease and protect people in wartime. Her male consort, Attis, was later worshiped along with her. Known to the Greeks by the fifth century B.C., the Romans began worshiping her in 204 B.C., near the close of the Second Punic War. At this time, a Roman ambassador journeyed to Phrygia and brought her sacred black stone (supposedly a meteorite) back to Rome, where a few years later it was installed in a temple built to her on the Palatine hill. During the early Empire, Cybele's festival, the Megalesia, celebrated from April 4 to 10, became popular throughout the realm.

devotio

One type of *devotio* was a magic charm (see curses). Another type consisted of a ritual in which a military general "devoted" (i.e., sacrificed or martyred) himself to gain victory. The original example was set by the consul Publius Decius Mus, who in a battle in 340 B.C. supposedly devoted himself by calling on the gods to witness his sacrifice and then charged into the enemy ranks to his death. The Romans won the battle.

Diana

At first an Italian goddess of forests and wild nature, she eventually came to be identified with the Greek deity Artemis and thereafter took on her image as goddess of hunting and the moon and protector of women. The *Hymn to Diana,* by the poet Catullus, effectively describes her various roles. An early temple to Diana was raised on Rome's Aventine hill; her festival was held on August 13.

Dioscuri

For these twin sons of Leda, **see** Castor and Pollux.

Dis

(also Dis Pater, Hades, Orcus, and Pluto) The god of death, he ruled the underworld with his wife, Proserpina. To invoke Dis, one pounded on the earth; his worship included the sacrifice of black sheep, with the person performing the act averting his or her eyes. The Romans erected few temples or altars to this deity, who was widely seen as a dark and fearsome force. **See** Proserpina.

divination

The art of observing and reading divine and supernatural signs or omens to predict the future. Most of what is known about ancient divination comes from Cicero's *On Divination.* There were many different kinds, which fell into two general categories—natural divination, which included dreams and spoken prophecy; and artificial divination, including observations of natural phenomena, animals, objects, and seemingly random events.

Regarding natural divination, most Romans readily accepted that events that occurred in dreams could be interpreted for divine signs, either by the dreamer him- or herself, or by a professional diviner. The noted physician Galen, for example, supposedly entered the field of medicine because of something his father observed in a dream. Also, by sleeping in a temple of the healing god Aesculapius, a sick person would, hopefully, receive advice, via a dream, on the best cure, a practice known as "incubation."

The other kind of natural divination, spoken prophesy, involved oracles—people who were supposedly mediums between the gods and humans, and whose words were carefully studied for their divine meanings and implications. (Their shrines and prophecies were also called oracles.) The most famous oracle in the Greco-Roman world was the priestess of the Temple of Apollo at Delphi (in central Greece). Italy had no oracular shrines of this magnitude; however, the Sibylline Books were seen as a collection of oracles and the Romans consulted these in times of crisis.

One of the most important forms of artificial divination was augury, the observation of birds' behavior. Searching for divine signs in the entrails of sacrificial animals, carried out by diviners called haruspices, was also widely practiced, as was observing unusual plant growth; involuntary human movements, such as sneezing; weather phenomena, especially thunder and lightning; and patterns in dice throwing or drawing lots. In most cases, each new generation accepted the forms of divination already known, but was skepti-

cal of new forms. A few Romans, most notably the Christians, rejected most forms of divination outright; in A.D. 391 the Roman government, by then controlled by Christians, banned divination (although many pagans continued to practice it privately). **See** augurs; haruspices; Sibyl.

Donatism

An early Christian sect, it drew many adherents; however, mainstream bishops looked on it as heresy. The dispute arose in 313, when Donatus, bishop of Numidia, appealed to the emperor Constantine to deny a priest named Caecilian the right to become a bishop. The Donatists, as they came to be called, argued that church officials who had handed over the Scriptures to the Romans during Diocletian's persecution (303–311) were impure and immoral. Since the cleric who was to consecrate Caecilian a bishop was one of these "betrayers of the faith," the ceremony would be invalid. In general, the Donatists maintained that the church's recent show of undue leniency to these "traitors" was a symptom of its increasing moral laxity. In response, the influential bishop of Rome denounced the Donatists, as did most other bishops; Constantine took the same position, ordering in 316 that Donatists be expelled from their churches. This did not end the controversy, however; Donatists, including a particularly violent subgroup, the "circumcellions," continued to flourish on the fringes of the faith until the seventh century.

A priest examines a bird, hoping to divine some sign from the gods. Various kinds of divination were widely practiced in the Roman world.

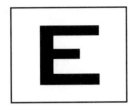

Edict of Milan

For this famous fourth-century decree that granted the Christians toleration, **see** Christianity; **also** Licinius, Valerius Licinianus (Chapter 1), **and** Mediolanum (Chapter 2).

Eleusinian Mysteries

Originating in pre-Roman Greece, this sacred religious cult and festival (which took place in September) was dedicated to Demeter, the Greek goddess who oversaw agriculture. The cult, which required new members to undergo a secret initiation, remained popular and active among many Greeks and Romans throughout the late Republic and Empire, until the emperor Theodosius I suppressed it in A.D. 393.

Membership in the Mysteries was open to all, male or female, free or slave. New initiates first purified themselves by bathing in the sea, then sacrificed a young pig. After that they joined the other members in a great procession in which the "sacred objects" (stored in the Eleusinion, a temple near the foot of the Acropolis in Athens) were carried to Demeter's sanctuary at Eleusis, several miles to the northwest. The nature of these objects was as secret as the initiation itself. The festival's climax occurred in the sanctuary's initiation hall (*telesterion*), where apparently a cult leader revealed the sacred objects. The next day the initiates fasted; eventually they broke this fast by drinking a special concoction of barley water.

emperor worship

The imperial cult, in which the Roman emperors were worshipped like gods, began under Augustus and his successor, Tiberius.

They recognized that such a practice might be frowned on in Italy and other parts of the west, but the peoples of the east had long been used to this practice. In Egypt, for example, Augustus was seen as the natural successor to the semidivine Egyptian pharaohs and worshiped literally as a god. And in many other parts of the east, people hailed him as their savior and prayed and sacrificed to his image. Some of these groups went further and began worshiping his family line, which promised to produce his successors. Augustus not only tolerated such cults, but for political reasons actually encouraged them, reasoning that they would bind the Empire's eastern inhabitants more closely to him, and through him to the Roman state.

Despite Augustus's initial misgivings, it was perhaps inevitable that the concept of the imperial cult would eventually spread to Italy and Rome, even though the Romans themselves had no native tradition of a divine ruler. The initial Roman worship of Augustus began in a relatively subtle way when he was proclaimed *pontifex maximus* (high priest) in 12 B.C. According to custom, the pontiff's home was public and sacred ground, and the spirits that attended that home (see *numina*) were revered in the state religion by all Romans. From that time on, people began worshiping the spirits (*lares*) of Augustus's family home. They also worshiped his *genius* (guardian spirit). This spirit now ensured the continuity of the entire Roman people, who, because he was both political and religious head of state, constituted his larger family. The worship of Augustus's *lares* and *genius* spread quickly throughout Italy and then to western provinces such as Spain and Gaul. Special temples for the *genius,* called *Augustea,* were erected and the imperial cult became a regular concern of local communities. The refusal to take part in emperor worship became one of the black marks against the Christians and a cause of their persecution.

Fates

These three goddesses probably originated as protectors of the birth process, but they came to be seen as somehow guiding people's destinies. Usually pictured in art and literature as women spinning or weaving, the Greeks called them Klotho, Lachesis, and Atropos; the Romans knew them as Nona, Decuma, and Morta, collectively called the Parcae. Some people thought that their fateful spinning led up to and halted at the moment of birth; others held that the spinning continued throughout life until the thread ran out.

Faunus

(or Pan) In early Italy he was a pastoral deity who protected hunters and oversaw agriculture. It was also thought that he revealed the future in people's dreams and through oracles (divine speech) delivered in sacred groves. As Greek influence on Rome increased, he became identified with the Greek pastoral god Pan. It also became common to picture multiples of him—Fauni (fauns), which were identified with the Greek satyrs, who were half-man and half-goat.

feriae

For these Roman religious celebrations, **see** festivals.

festivals

The Romans celebrated many religious festivals (*feriae*) to honor and make private and public sacrifice to the gods. The belief was that failing to celebrate a festival or to do so in an incorrect or improper manner might provoke the anger of the god or gods involved. Nevertheless, as is

true today, only some of the populace took an active part in the festivals, while the rest just enjoyed the holiday. In the public festivals (*feriae publicae*), priests conducted rituals outside the temples while an assembly of citizens watched; usually feasting and merriment followed, for religious and secular activities were mixed on most such occasions. Another kind of celebration with a religious element was the staging of public games (*ludi*), almost always held in honor of a god or gods. These were technically not *feriae,* but most people observed them in the same manner as festivals.

Some festivals were observed all across the Roman realm, a prominent example being the Saturnalia, celebrated from December 17 to 23. It originated as an observance of the winter solstice and honored Saturn, the god of sowing seeds. Traditional elements included suspension of all business activities, sacrifices to the god, feasts, wearing formal clothes, gift giving, exchanging goodwill sentiments, and lighting candles; also, in many homes masters and slaves changed places for a day, the masters serving the slaves. (After Christianity's rise, that faith converted the Saturnalia to Christmas, substituting Christ for Saturn; but most of the old customs were retained. The Christians converted other old Roman festivals as well, among them the Lupercalia, which became the Feast of the Purification of the Virgin Mary.) By contrast, other Roman festivals honored local gods and were therefore geographically more limited in scope.

Following are just a few of the other popular Roman festivals, including some *ludi.* The Compitalia (the date varied but was most often January 3–5) observed the end of the agricultural year; people erected shrines at crossroads, placing plows and dolls (one for each person in the household) there. The Lupercalia (February 15) celebrated and promoted fertility; priests sacrificed goats in the Lupercal, a cave on the Palatine hill, and smeared two teams of young men with the sacrificial blood; the teams then raced through the streets, striking passersby with strips of goatskin, supposedly to make them fertile. The Megalisia (April 4–10) celebrated the eastern goddess Cybele after she was imported into Rome in the late Republic; games (*ludi Megalensis*) were held in her honor. The Floralia (April 28–May 3) was the spring and flower festival of the goddess Flora; in imperial times, six days of games (*ludi Florales*) were held. The Vestalia (June 9) honored the goddess Vesta; married women went to her temple and offered her gifts and food. The *ludi Apollinares* (July 6–13) were games honoring Apollo; by the early Empire, they had lost most of their sacred character and were viewed mainly as an excuse to have a good time. The *ludi Romani* (September 5–19), honoring Jupiter, also lost much of its original religious significance over time; traditionally a cow was sacrificed, then all of the Roman magistrates had a feast in the god's temple. **See** names of specific gods, especially Fortuna and Mars.

fetiales

For these priests who dealt with foreign treaties, **see** priests.

flamines

For these religious leaders, each of whom served a different god, **see** priests.

Flora

An Italian goddess of the spring season and the flowers that accompany it, she had a temple (erected in 238 B.C.) near the Circus Maximus. From April 28 to May 3, the Romans celebrated her festival, the Floralia, which involved considerable merriment, some of it on the vulgar side.

Fortuna

(or Fors Fortuna) Originally a fertility goddess, she came to be identified with the Greek Tyche, deity of chance or luck. Her festival, held on June 24, was extremely popular. Large numbers of people rowed or walked to her principle shrine (which included an oracle), located about a mile downstream from Rome; after watching the ceremonies they held picnics and feasts.

Furies

(*furiae* or *dirae*) Frightening female spirits who avenged crimes, most often murder, by hunting down and punishing the guilty. They were originally Greek figures (the Erinyes, who were transformed into the kindly Eumenides in Aeschylus's trilogy of plays, the *Oresteia*); but through contact with Greek culture, the Romans came to recognize them, too.

genius

For this spirit thought to inhabit the body of the father of a family, **see** *numina*.

Gnosticism

Derived from the Greek word *gnosis,* meaning "knowledge," this religious movement had both pagan and Christian adherents (the Christian ones rising to prominence in the second century A.D.). They held that there was an all-powerful but distant and unknowable god, who gave rise to a lesser, imperfect god; it was the latter who created the earth, which was likewise imperfect. According to this view, some humans possessed a divine spark—part of the perfect god—and might be reunited with that deity after death. Opinions differed on whether the perfect god had sent a redeemer to bring *gnosis,* "true knowledge of God," to individual humans. Gnostic Christians thought Jesus was that redeemer or the first of several redeemers. As might be expected, the mainstream church vehemently rejected Gnosticism.

Hades
For this god of the underworld, **see** Dis.

haruspices
Special priests who practiced artificial divination, the interpretation of the will of the gods and future events, by observing the entrails (*exta*) of sacrificial animals. The general view was that the shape of an animal's liver could reveal how a god or gods felt about the government's policies or upcoming plans. Spots or other markings on the liver or another organ might also be significant. In addition, haruspices examined and interpreted prodigies, unusual or monstrous births and growths, believing that these also carried divine signs. **See** divination.

Hercules
The Roman equivalent of the Greek hero Heracles. (Some Romans also identified him with the Phoenician god Melqart.) His cult may have been the earliest foreign one imported into Italy by the Greeks who settled in the southern third of the peninsula. The Romans worshiped him both as a victory deity and a protector of commercial activity, erecting an altar, the Ara Maxima, to him in Rome's cattle market. In his epic poem, the *Aeneid,* Virgil tells how Hercules slew the fire-breathing monster Cacus, who had stolen some of the hero's cattle.

Isis
This mother, fertility, and marriage goddess originated in Egypt as the sister and wife of the god Osiris (whom the Romans came to call Serapis) and the mother of the god Horus (the Roman Harpocrates). The Hellenistic Greeks identified her with Aphrodite, goddess of love. When she was imported into Rome during the late Republic, she was viewed as a kind and compassionate mother figure, sometimes pictured in art holding or nursing her son

The great Hercules (called Heracles by the Greeks), depicted in this statue created in the late medieval period, was one of Rome's favorite heroes.

(which influenced later portrayals of the Virgin Mary and baby Jesus), and her cult became widely popular. The rituals and beliefs of Isis's cult, which were similar to those of the mystery religions, included initiation, baptism, and the promise of eternal salvation.

Janus

The god of beginnings, as well as of gates and doorways; his familiar symbol was a head with two faces looking in opposite directions. The Romans named the first month in their calendar (January) after him. A very ancient god, he once may have been as important as Jupiter. And he came to have various manifestations, such as Janus Patulcius, who opened doors; Janus Clusivus, who closed doors; and Janus the Father, a creator deity. His temple, in the Roman Forum, was small but important; its doors were left open during wartime and closed in times of peace.

Jews

For this ancient people who occupied Palestine and came under Roman control in the first century B.C., **see** Christianity, Judaism; **also** Judaea (Chapter 2).

Judaism

The religion of the Jews, it was one of several important faiths practiced in the eastern Roman sphere (and eventually throughout the Empire), and also the direct precursor and mother faith of Christianity. The Jews were not only monotheistic, a rarity in ancient times before the rise of Christianity, but also extremely exclusive, allowing only the worship of their own god. The Christians inherited this attitude of exclusivity, which many Roman pagans viewed as a form of religious intolerance, and it contributed to the persecution of both Jews and Christians.

The Jews saw (and still see) their god as the one and only creator of the world and the dispenser of moral law, as described in their sacred writings, particularly the Scriptures, or Old Testament (which became part of the Christian Bible). Their fierce religious and nationalistic spirit brought them into serious conflicts with a number of peoples who conquered and tried to suppress or absorb them. Centuries of foreign oppression led to Jewish beliefs in a messiah, a superhuman or divine figure who would someday come to earth to deliver them. (The Christian sect of Judaism, of course, came to see Jesus Christ as the Messiah, while other Jews held that the deliverer would come later.) The Jews, most of whom at first lived in Rome's province of Judaea (in Palestine), were often at odds with the Roman government, until their general dispersal throughout the known world (the Diaspora), which followed their rebellions of the first and second centuries A.D. **See** Christianity; **also** Jesus Christ (Chapter 1); **and** Judaea (Chapter 2).

Juno

(or Iuno) Originally she was a prominent Italian goddess; a protector of women and the sanctity of marriage; and the wife of Jupiter, the chief god. Thanks to contact with Greek culture, she became identified with the Greek goddess Hera, wife of Zeus, Jupiter's Greek equivalent. Juno had several manifestations, among them Juno Lucina, who oversaw childbirth; Juno Regina, who was part of the Capitoline Triad (worshiped on Rome's Capitoline hill), which also included Jupiter and Minerva; Juno Caprotina, a fertility goddess; Juno Sispes, a protector of the state; and Juno Sororia, who protected girls during puberty. All of these and other sides of Juno's character had festivals celebrated at various times of the year. Besides the temple on the Capitoline, shrines to Juno were built on the Aventine hill and in the Campus Martius, both in Rome, as well as in other cities.

Jupiter

The supreme god of the Roman state pantheon, he was originally an Italian sky god thought to cause rain and lightning and to oversee agriculture. During the Roman Monarchy, there developed the cult of Jupiter *Optimus Maximus* (the "best and greatest" of all Jupiters), part of the Capitoline Triad, a group that included two other prominent deities, Juno and Minerva. (The principle temple to Jupiter and the Triad was located on Rome's Capitoline hill, where generals deposited the spoils of war and the Senate held its first meeting each year.) The equivalent of the Greek god Zeus, Jupiter's chief symbols were the thunderbolt and the eagle. Besides *Optimus Maximus,* he had a number of different manifestations, among them *Divis pater* (Father of Heaven), *Fugurator* (Sender of Lightning), *Invictus* (Invincible), *Latialis* (Leader of the Latin Feast), *Prodigalialis* (Sender of Omens), and *Triumphator* (Victor). Each had its special characteristics, cult following, and temples.

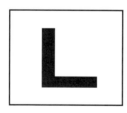

lares

For these spirits thought to keep the home safe, **see** *numina.*

libations

For these sacrifices involving liquids, **see** worship.

magic

Roman religion was heavily laced with superstition, and the line between religious ritual (in which people requested that the gods bring about certain events) and magic (in which people themselves tried to make events happen through spells and other rituals) was often blurred. Astrology, divination, curses, and other practices common in the Roman world all possessed aspects of magic; people sometimes utilized spells, amulets, charms, dolls, and chanted words and phrases to bring about specific outcomes, such as a personal victory, the acquisition of wealth, or the downfall of an enemy.

One form of magic, sympathetic magic (*simila similibus*) employed symbolic ritual, such as beating on a shield in a certain way to bring rain, or burning a wax doll representing an enemy. Another form, contagious magic (*pars pro toto*), involved the use of the intended victim's hair, clothing, or other personal possessions. People generally made a distinction between "good" magic and "evil" magic. But the evil variety blackened magic's reputation so that, although many people secretly practiced magic, Roman leaders and writers frequently denounced it. The great encyclopedist Pliny the Elder dismissed it as fraudulent, and laws were eventually passed that carried stiff fines for people whose magic was thought to have harmed someone. **See** astrology, curses, divination.

manes

For these spirits of deceased ancestors, **see** *numina.*

Mars

Originally an Italian god of agriculture, Mars protected farmers' fields and boundaries. But in time he came to be identified with Ares, the Greek god of war, and as Mars Ultor (Mars the Avenger), war became his principle domain, although he continued to oversee agriculture as Mars the Father. The Romans came to see him as second in importance only to Jupiter. March, originally the first month in the Roman year (because it witnessed the annual rebirth of agriculture), was named after him (as was the great parade ground in Rome, the Campus Martius, or "Field of Mars"). Several religious festivals to honor him were held in that month, including one that began on March 1 and lasted for over three weeks, featuring parades, dancing, hymn singing, and feasts; the Equirria, held on March 14, which featured horse races in the Campus Martius; and the Greater Quinquatrus, from March 19 to 23, on the last day of which Rome's sacred war trumpets (*tubae*) were purified. Mars's most important altar stood, appropriately, in the Campus Martius, and he had numerous temples, including one erected by Augustus in the main Forum and one on the Appian Way outside the city.

Mercury

The Roman messenger god and deity of trade and commercial success, he was frequently depicted holding a herald's staff with snakes coiled around it and wearing a winged hat and sandals. Particularly popular in Gaul and Britain, Mercury was venerated as the inventor of the various creative arts. His festival was celebrated on May 15.

messiah

For this superhuman figure the Jews predicted would come to earth to save them from persecution, **see** Judaism; **also** Jesus Christ (Chapter 1).

Minerva

An Italian goddess of crafts and trade guilds, she was one of the three deities in the Capitoline Triad (along with Jupiter and Juno). Eventually she came to be associated with the Greek goddess Athena in her role as Athena Promachos, the "warrior champion." In time Minerva, in this guise, was honored at the Greater Quinquatras festival in March, along with the war god Mars. She had a temple on the Aventine hill and a shrine on the Caelian hill.

Mithras

This ancient Indo-Iranian (later Persian) god of light and truth was imported into Rome in the late first century B.C. and his cult, seen as an eastern mystery religion, became very widespread. Worship of Mithras was restricted to men and was particularly popular among merchants and soldiers. According to Mithraism, Mithras

A modern drawing shows the messenger god Mercury with his traditional symbols—a herald's staff and winged cap and sandals.

supported another god, Ahura-Mazda, in the eternal battle between light (goodness) and darkness (evil); Ahura-Mazda sent Mithras to earth to kill a sacred bull and from that animal's blood sprang all living things. The beliefs and rituals of Mithraism involved the miraculous birth of a baby, baptism, a sacred meal of bread and wine, the promise of resurrection after death, and other elements in common with other eastern-derived religions, including Christianity. His temples were built underground because his killing of the sacred bull was thought to have taken place in a cave.

monasticism

For this religious movement in which people showed their faith in God by going into seclusion, **see** Christianity; **also** Benedict (Chapter 1).

Neptune

A very ancient Italian god of water; under later Greek influence he came to be identified with the Greek god Poseidon, lord of the sea. Because Poseidon was strongly associated with horses, Neptune was sometimes identified with the Roman god Consus, who was also associated with horses. Neptune's festival, the Neptunalia, was held on July 23.

Nicene Creed

For this statement of belief in God formulated in the fourth century, **see** Arianism.

numina

A group of spirits the Romans worshiped from their dimly remembered tribal days. The *numina* were thought to reside in everything in the natural world, including inanimate objects like rocks and trees, a belief system now called animism. Some of these minor deities regularly watched over and presumably even directed many aspects of people's daily activities, professions, ceremonies, and personal pursuits. Eventually, a number of these ancient spirits developed into full-fledged gods with human images (the more familiar deities of the national pantheon); yet even then, many of the more formless *numina* continued to be worshiped throughout the Republic and Empire.

The Romans usually divided the *numina* into convenient groups. Household spirits included the *penates,* who protected the family food storage; notable family events often began with a prayer to them and it was customary to throw a morsel of food on the hearth fire as an offering to them. The *lares* kept the home safe and also guarded streets and crossroads. They were worshiped, usually at the family hearth, at specific times of the month. There were also *lares* who protected a neighborhood (*lares compitales*) and a whole city (*lares publici*), the latter having a temple of their own in Rome.

Another category of *numina,* the *manes,* were spirits of deceased ancestors, who watched over various family members; busts of these ancestors (*imagines*) were often set up in the house to keep their memory alive. (A more hostile version of the *manes,* the *lemures,* were thought to haunt the household on certain days in May, during the Lemuria, a festival designed to appease and drive away these spirits.) The Romans also recognized a special type of guardian spirit known as the *genius.* They believed that each family was protected by its unique *genius,* who inhabited the body of the living paterfamilias (father) and secured the continuity of the family line by passing from father to son on the father's death. The materfamilias's (mother's) *genius,* who passed from her body to that of her daughter, was called the Juno.

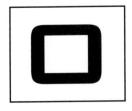

Ops

The Roman goddess of abundance, she was normally seen as the consort of the agricultural god Saturn. Her festivals were the Opiconsivia, celebrated on August 25, and Opalia, held on December 19.

oracles

For these priestesses thought to be mediums between humans and the gods, **see** divination.

Orphism

A minor mystery cult derived from an earlier Greek version, it gained some Roman adherents during the early Empire. Its beliefs and rituals revolved around the mythical Greek character Orpheus, the poet who attempted but failed to rescue his beloved, Eurydice, from the underworld and was later torn to pieces. Orpheus's guilt over his failure was a central tenet of the faith; the secret rites of Orphism supposedly freed worshipers from their collective or individual guilt and improved their chances for a happy afterlife. Not much is known about the cult, outside of references in ancient poems attributed to Orpheus; it may not have been a well-organized spiritual movement like the cults of Isis and Cybele.

Pales

A Roman deity of sheep and shepherds, corresponding somewhat to the Greek god Pan,

Pales was described as male by some Roman writers and as female by others. Pales' festival, coinciding with Rome's traditional birthday, was the Parilia, held on April 21. On that day, people cleaned their sheep pens, decorated them with green plants, and purified them with smoke from burning sulfur.

penates

For these spirits thought to guard a family's food storage, **see** *numina.*

pietas

In a loose sense, *pietas* corresponds with the modern concept of piety—duty and devotion to God, family, and friends—except that the Romans gave it a wider meaning and took it much more seriously. Roman *pietas* involved the maintenance of good relations not only with the gods and family, but also with one's ancestors, fellow citizens, and the institutions and traditions of the state. A lack of *pietas* was thought to be potentially harmful for both individuals and the community because it might incur the wrath of the gods.

Pluto

For this god of the underworld, **see** Dis.

pontifex maximus

For this chief priest of the Roman state, **see** priests.

Portunus

The god thought to protect harbors, although he appears to have originated as a protector of doors. His festival, the Portunalia, was held on August 17, and he was usually depicted in art holding a key in his hand. In his epic poem, the *Aeneid,* Virgil has Portunus bestow extra advantage to one of the vessels in a boat race.

prayer

For this age-old communication between humans and the gods, **see** worship.

priests

Rome's state religion had no full-time, professional priests in the sense of a modern priest who devotes his life to guiding his congregation. Most Roman priests were men of high social status who received training in religious matters and then executed their religious duties on a part-time basis. Exceptions were those who headed the staffs of temples (*sacerdotes*), who were full-time officials paid by the state; but their job was to maintain the temple and its sanctuary (surrounding sacred grounds), not to guide people in spiritual matters. The staffs working under these priests included security people, clerks, assistants to help in the rituals (somewhat like modern altar boys), and slaves to do menial jobs.

The various kinds of priests were organized into groups called "colleges," some of which were more prestigious than others. There were also some priestesses, usually in the cults of foreign female deities such as Isis, although the state religion had an important group of female priests, the Vestal Virgins, who tended the sacred fire on the state hearth. In general, public priests and priestesses fulfilled the same function as the paterfamilias at home, but on a larger scale. At the family altar, the father led private rituals to maintain favorable relations with the gods; the public priests officiated in ceremonies at large outdoor altars hoping to appease the gods on behalf of the state and the people as a whole.

The highest priests of Rome's state religion were the *pontifices,* or pontiffs, who belonged to the most important priestly college, the *collegium pontificum.* Originally, probably three such priests served jointly, but by the late Republic that number had increased to sixteen. Their duties were to determine the dates of religious festivals, to decide on which days it was all right for people to conduct legal business, to keep records of major events (*Annales Maximi*), and in general to keep the state religion running smoothly. The most important and prestigious among them was the *pontifex maximus,* Rome's chief priest; after Julius Caesar and Augustus held this post, it became traditional for each Roman emperor to do so (until Christian bishops convinced Gratian to eliminate it in the 380s A.D.). A more specialized high priest was the *rex sacrorum,* "king of the sacred objects." For tradition's sake (since maintaining tradition was extremely important to the Romans), he performed certain public sacrifices once performed by the Roman kings before they were eliminated in the late sixth century B.C.

Among the other groups of priests were the augurs and haruspices, who performed divination, interpreting divine signs by observing the behavior of birds or the entrails of sacrificial animals. The *flamines,* who were members of the *collegium pontificum* along with the pontiffs, were priests assigned to serve particular gods. From the early Republic on, a *flamen* served each of the following gods: Ceres, Falacer, Flora, Furrina, Jupiter, Mars, Palatua, Pomona, Portunus, Quirinus, Volturnus, and Vulcan. The major *flamines,* those serving Jupiter, Mars, and Quirinus, were patricians, while the others were plebeians. Another group of priests, the *fetiales,* chosen from aristocratic families, were involved in rituals attending foreign relations, such as making treaties and declaring war. War could not be officially declared, for example, until one of them hurled a spear into enemy territory (or into an area representing such territory inside the temple of the war goddess Bellona). The oldest priestly college in Rome was that of the arval priests (*fratres arvales*), who offered public sacrifices to maintain the fertility of farmers' fields. And still another group of priests, the *epulones* ("feast organizers"), saw to the banquets given during the most important state religious festivals. **See** augurs; haruspices; Regia; temples; Vestal Virgins; worship.

Proserpina

The goddess of the underworld, who ruled with her husband, Dis. Apparently she was early identified with the Greek Persephone, a daughter of the gods Zeus and Demeter, whom Hades (the Greek version of Dis) kidnapped and took down into the lower depths. Eventually, she was allowed to spend six months of each year aboveground before returning to the underworld for the other six. Persephone/Proserpina came to symbolize not only death (as Hades/Dis did), but also the germination of seeds, since these are first placed underground before they can give birth to new life that rises into the light. **See** Dis.

Regia

Originally a royal palace that tradition said was built by one of Rome's legendary kings. During the Republic, this structure, which stood at the base of the Palatine hill near the main Forum, and which was rebuilt several times over the years, became the official headquarters of the *pontifex maximus,* chief priest of the Roman state. **See** priests.

sacrifice

For this age-old process of making offerings to the gods, **see** worship.

Saturn

The original functions of this very ancient Italian god are somewhat obscure. He may have been the overseer of seed sowing or a bringer of blight, or both. In any case, the Romans came to see him as an agricultural god who symbolized the legendary golden age of the past (before the advent of the later, progressively inferior ages of silver, bronze, and iron). His festival, the Saturnalia, beginning on December 17, was one of the most important of the year. Saturn's temple, at the foot of the Capitoline hill, served as Rome's treasury and also housed the tablets bearing the state's law codes. **See** festivals.

Saturnalia

For this popular Roman religious celebration held in December, **see** festivals.

Serapis

The founder of Egypt's Greek Ptolemaic dynasty, Ptolemy I (reigned 323–283 B.C.), introduced this new god, essentially a version of the traditional Egyptian god Osiris, who both ruled the kingdom of dead and symbolized fertility and new life. Ptolemy's goal in promoting the worship of Serapis was to provide a deity that would appeal to both his Egyptian and Greek subjects. So the god took on some roles usually associated with Greek gods, such as healer (the role of Asclepius). Ptolemy III (reigned 246–221 B.C.) erected a large temple of Serapis—the Serapeum—in Alexandria. And in the late Republic and early Empire, the god's cult spread to the Roman world. Serapis was also seen as a sky god, so the Romans sometimes identified him with Jupiter. **See** Isis.

Sibyl

The name meant a priestess who was thought to have prophetic powers; there were various Sibyls in various times and places, many of whom had individual names. Their prophecies were supposedly delivered when they were possessed by the god Apollo, in a manner similar to Greek oracles, who also spoke for Apollo while in trances. People wrote down what Sibyls said when in this state and later collected these writings. The most famous example, the Sibylline Books, consisted of the prophecies of the most important of all Roman Sibyls—the one who resided at Cumae, in Italy's Campania. According to the poet Virgil, it was she who took Aeneas into the underworld and showed him Rome's glorious future. Another legend told how she offered Rome's last king, Tarquinius Superbus, nine books of her prophecy for a high price; after he continually refused the deal, she burned six of the books, but he finally gave in and bought the last three (at the original price!).

This was supposedly the origin of the Sibylline Books, which the later Romans consulted from time to time, partly for guidance in making future plans and policies. They also consulted them to find out how to appease angry gods who had, it was thought, caused disasters such as earthquakes and plagues. The books were stored in a chest in a chamber beneath Jupiter's temple on the Capitoline hill in Rome. Presumably they were lost when the temple was destroyed in the fifth century A.D. Many early Christians came to view the Sibyls as equivalent to Old Testament prophets and portrayed them that way in Christian art and literature. **See** divination.

Sibylline Books

For these special, closely guarded collections of ancient prophecies, **see** Sibyl.

Silvanus

In the Roman sphere, he was the god of uncultivated or wild lands and was sometimes identified with the Greek god Pan. As Rome conquered and absorbed various European regions, local peoples came to associate Silvanus with their own gods; for example, in southern Gaul, he was identified with a Celtic hammer god. Romans planning to cut down trees in the forest often sacrificed to Silvanus first to gain his favor.

Sol Invictus

This Syrian god, whose name meant "the unconquered sun," became popular in Rome and other parts of the western Empire in the third century A.D., thanks to the encouragement of the emperor Aurelian. He hoped that the god's cult would help to unify Roman pagans everywhere, and the god did indeed become widely popular. He was the favorite of the young Constantine, who for a long time associated him with the Christian god. Sol Invictus's birthday—December 25, roughly coinciding with the winter solstice and Saturnalia festival—was faithfully observed by millions. (Unable to stop this observance, the Christians simply incorporated it into their own religion, making it Jesus' birthday.) **See** Constantine I (Chapter 1).

temples

Roman pagan temples were long referred to as *aedes*. Such a structure was erected in a *templum*, an area that had been consecrated as sacred. In time the term *templum*, or temple, was extended to the building, too. Rome's earliest temples were likely made of wood, but by the fourth century B.C. stone was regularly employed. The architectural style was for the most part borrowed from the Etruscans and especially the Greeks. Typically it employed a rectangular building surrounded by a colonnade (row of columns), the front and back columns supporting triangular gables called pediments. A wide staircase led up to the front door and some temples had back staircases as well. By the late Republic, most Roman temples utilized Greek Corinthian columns (having tops decorated with ornate stone leaves, as opposed to simpler Doric and Ionic columns). During the Empire, when Rome's influence spread into Gaul, Germany, and Britain, some of the temples in these areas had a Romano-Celtic style (probably consisting of a small, fairly spare rectangular structure with a pitched roof and a roofed porch running around the perimeter).

Whether in the Greek or Romano-Celtic style, a Roman temple featured a central room (the *cella*), which contained the cult image—a statue, often larger than life-size, of the god it was built to honor. In many temples, a back room served as a storehouse for the valuable offerings made by worshipers. As in the case of Greek temples, no major worship took place inside the structure (as it does in Christian churches), since it was believed that the god occasionally occupied it and wanted his or her privacy. Instead, sacrifices took place at an altar or altars constructed outside, most often on or near the front steps. Sometimes the state paid for temple construction; it was also fairly common for victorious generals to provide the money out of their war spoils. The most prodigious known temple builder was Augustus, who bragged in his *Res gestae* that he had erected twelve temples and restored eighty-two more. **See** worship; **also** building materials and techniques (Chapter 6).

This reconstruction of a Roman temple shows some of the standard features of Greco-Roman architecture, including a colonnade and a pediment containing sculptures.

of the Greeks, the Romans came to associate her with the Greek love goddess, Aphrodite. Venus had a temple on the Capitoline hill as well as at other locations in the region of Rome. She was often pictured as the escort of the war god Mars and her symbols were roses, doves, and dolphins.

Vesta

The Roman goddess of the hearth, she was widely worshiped in Roman homes, as well as by the state. In her temple in the Roman Forum, a sacred fire was constantly maintained by priestesses (the Vestal Virgins) and restarted each year on March 1 (considered New Year's Day). In Vesta's public festival, the Vestalia, celebrated on June 9, women marched barefoot carrying food offerings for her. **See** Vestal Virgins.

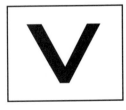

Venus

Originally she was an obscure Italian goddess, perhaps having something to do with vegetable gardens. But under the influence

Vestal Virgins

At first two, then four, and eventually six priestesses of Rome's state religion, their main duties were to watch over the sacred fire on the state hearth in the Temple of Vesta (in Rome) and to care for certain sacred objects. They also made a special salt cake used in various religious festivals. They were chosen by the *pontifex maximus* from a pool of aristocratic (patrician) girls age six to ten; once accepted, they had to serve for at least thirty years. Many ended up serving for life. Maintained at state expense, they lived in a house called the Hall of Vesta, located near the main Forum, and wore plain white linen dresses. The white emphasized their purity, for they had to remain virgins throughout their service. Any of their number who was found guilty of being unchaste was buried alive and her lover was beaten to death. The Vestal Virgins had the power to grant a reprieve to a criminal if they met him on his way to his execution, and anyone standing among them was immune from attack. **See** priests, Vesta.

votive offerings

For these sacrifices made to fulfill a vow, **see** worship.

vows

For these promises to give the gods gifts, **see** worship.

Vulcan

(or Vulcanus) An early Roman fire god, he became identified with the Greek Hephaestos, god of the forge. In the capacity of a smelter of metals, he was called Vulcan Mulciber, and he was often seen as a more destructive counterpart of Vesta, who represented a more positive force of fire. Vulcan was often pictured living and working beneath volcanoes, assisted by giants called Cyclopes. His most famous shrines were in Rome's main Forum, at the base of the Capitoline hill, and at the

port city of Ostia. His festivals were held on May 23 and August 23.

Vulgate

Latin for "common text," the word most often refers to the Latin version of the Christian Bible that came to be the standard in western Europe in medieval times. The noted late Roman Christian scholar Jerome translated it from the original Hebrew, with the exception of a few of its books, which either he translated from a Greek version or were translated by others. The first complete collection of all of these pieces in a single book appeared in the sixth century, and the oldest surviving manuscript of the Vulgate is the *Codex Amiatinus,* dating from about A.D. 700. **See** Jerome (Chapter 1).

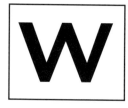

worship

Religious worship was not only one of the traditional pillars of Roman community life, it also provided guidance and comfort for the individual in his or her everyday life. The relationship that developed between a person and the gods took the form of a sacred contract. It was thought that if a person observed the proper rituals—consisting mainly of sacrifice and prayer—the god being worshiped would react favorably; if the person failed in his or her religious duty, the god would become angry and perhaps exact punishment. The Latin expression coined to describe this relationship was *"do ut des,"* meaning "I, the mortal, give to you, the god, so that you may give back to me."

Among the common rituals of Roman worship, sacrifice was perhaps of prime importance because offering the gods material gifts was seen as the most promising way of gaining their favor. One very common kind of sacrifice involved the fulfillment of a vow. Either a person privately vowed or the state publicly vowed to give a god a gift, if and when the god granted the request of the person or the state. Such vows were often recorded in writing. If the god did not deliver, there was no obligation to go through with the sacrifice. Sacrifices made in fulfillment of vows were known as votive offerings or ex-votos; they ranged from lavish gifts, such as monuments, statues, and entire altars, to modest ones, such as figurines, coins, and bronze, silver, or gold plaques (called votive plaques) that bore written dedications to and sometimes artistic representations of the god. Most often these offerings were deposited in temples, but they were sometimes placed in sacred springs or deep pits. Other motives for sacrifice included obeying a request supposedly made by a god in a dream, appeasing a god when consulting his oracle, seeking the favor of a god or gods, and celebrating an anniversary or a special event.

Sometimes plants were sacrificed. And some rituals involved liquid sacrifices, called libations, which most commonly consisted of pouring wine, honey, or milk on the ground or over an altar. But the most popular form of sacrifice involved the killing and eating of animals such as oxen, goats, sheep, and pigs. Male animals were offered to male deities and female animals to female deities. Usually, someone led the "victim" of an intended sacrifice to an altar and, after sprinkling salt, wine, flour, or a sacred cake over the beast's head, a priest slit its throat, cut it up, and then threw the bones and fat into the altar fire for the god to consume (via the smoke that rose into the sky). The rest of the animal was cooked and eaten by the worshipers. During the sacrifice, the priest kept his head covered with his toga and musicians played, both with the intent of avoiding the sights or sounds of bad omens; if such an omen did appear, the entire ritual had to be repeated. Indeed, it was important to get all the steps of the ritual right, for if any single detail was wrong, it was believed that the god would refuse the sacrifice.

The use of strict formulas and procedures was also important in the other major ritual—prayer. There were traditionally accepted forms of addressing a god and making requests of it, and if the person praying made a mistake, he or she had to start over. The most common stance taken during prayer was to stand upright, turn the face toward heaven, and raise the arms upward with the palms also turned upward. (Roman Christians prayed this way too, but kept their arms horizon-

Roman worshipers prepare to sacrifice some bulls.

tal to distinguish themselves from pagans.)

As to the content of prayers, the Romans prayed for many of the same things people pray for today—good health, peace, personal prosperity or gain, and so forth. The first-century A.D. humorist Perseus made the point that when praying aloud in front of others, people usually asked for socially acceptable things such as a sound mind or good credit. In private, however, says Perseus, someone might express the hope that one's uncle would drop dead, or that one might get rich quick. The satirist Juvenal offered this penetrating and moving observation that will likely hold true for as long as the human race survives:

Few people in the world know what constitutes real happiness. Most pray for blessings that bring about their ruin. The usual ambitions are eloquence, physical strength, wealth, political power, military glory, beauty. . . . [However] wealth causes many to be strangled or poisoned. . . . Political power causes envy and headlong ruin. . . . Many pray for a long life, but old age is filled with unhappiness of all kinds—physical ugliness . . . deafness . . . paralysis, senility, the deaths of all one's relatives. . . . What is there left to pray for in order to achieve happiness? A sound mind in a sound body; courage not to fear death; ability to endure hardship; and, above all, virtue. (*Tenth Satire*)

CHAPTER 4
GOVERNMENT AND LAW

aedile

This important Roman republican official was in charge of maintaining and repairing public structures (including temples, aqueducts, and roads); overseeing public markets (particularly the integrity of weights and measures); and public games and festivals (until Augustus's time, when the praetors took over this duty). There were originally two aediles, both plebeians elected to one-year terms by the *comitia tributa.* Beginning in 367 B.C., two more aediles (called curule aediles) were annually elected by the patricians. The office gave ambitious politicians the chance to gain considerable popularity with voters, especially through the staging of lavish public games.

assemblies

The Roman Republic had four popular (or people's) assemblies, in which citizens could vote on legislation and elect various public officials. Most of these bodies had no say in shaping the political bills that came to them. They simply voted yea or nay on each piece of legislation, doing so aloud until se-

cret ballots began in 139 B.C. But though no formal discussion was allowed, in practice informal discussions (*contiones*) sometimes occurred prior to voting.

All four assemblies met outdoors at a *comitium,* or "place of assembly"; consequently, three of the four bodies acquired names containing the plural of the word *comitia.* The *comitia curiata,* about which relatively little is known, was the earliest assembly. Its structure was derived from the division of the Roman citizenry into thirty wards (*curiae*), ten from each of the state's original three tribes. Over time, this assembly became increasingly less important; by the late Republic it met only for ceremonial purposes.

The *comitia centuriata,* or centuriate assembly, developed out of and eventually assumed the functions of the *comitia curiata.* The centuriate assembly met in the Campus Martius (Rome's military parade ground) and was divided into voting blocks or units called centuries. A voter's age and the value of his property determined which century he belonged to; the poor tended to have fewer centuries and therefore fewer votes and less influence than the well-to-do in this body. The centuriate assembly voted on declaring war or making peace and elected Rome's high officials, including the consuls.

The *comitia tributa,* or tribal assembly, met in Rome's main Forum and its membership was divided among thirty-five tribes. It elected minor public officials and served as a court of appeal for people condemned to death. The tribal assembly also voted on political bills put before it by public officials.

The last of the four assemblies, the *concilium plebis,* also met in the Forum. This body was the only one of the four whose membership was restricted to plebeians and it was appropriately presided over by the tribunes of the people. It could formulate resolutions (*plebiscita*), which after 287 B.C. became binding on both patricians and plebeians, constituting a sort of balance or check on the huge power of the aristocratic Senate. This assembly also elected the tribunes and plebeian aediles. Although the four assemblies continued to exist after the fall of the Republic, this was largely a concession to tradition, and under the emperors they lost their former authority and importance and remained largely ceremonial in nature. **See** Senate.

censor

During the Republic, two censors (*censores*) were elected every five years by the centuriate assembly. The duties of these very powerful and prestigious officials were to conduct a census of property owners and their holdings; to make and maintain lists of all citizens; to oversee public morality; to prepare lists of proposed senators and to remove corrupt senators; to supervise the leasing of public land; to decide on new public construction projects; and to award contracts for such projects. In the early Empire, the emperors assumed most of the powers of the censors, who ceased to be of importance.

census

As early as the sixth century B.C., during the Roman Monarchy, a census of the people was taken every five years to aid the state in levying taxes and organizing the army. During the Republic, censuses were conducted less regularly, but they became regular again in imperial times. Although there were no more censuses in Italy after the late first century A.D. (because the area was no longer directly taxed), the provinces continued to conduct them, for tax purposes, at first every five years and eventually every twelve or fourteen years. The process was said to be unusually efficient in the province of Egypt.

citizenship

Roman citizenship was highly coveted throughout most of Rome's history because a citizen enjoyed social and legal rights, privileges, and a range of freedoms that noncitizens did not. Among these were the political rights to vote, hold public office, and sue someone in court; *commercium,* the right to engage in personal business affairs and transactions, which might bring prosperity to oneself and one's family; and *conubium,* the right to be legally married under Roman law, which ensured that one's children would be legitimate, would inherit one's property, and would themselves be citizens.

In the Republic, all free men and women born of Roman families were technically citizens (*cives*), although at first only men who could afford to own weapons—that is, those eligible for military service—could attend meetings of the citizen assemblies or hold public office. Because women were never accorded such political rights, they were always second-class citizens. Foreigners living in Roman territory (*peregrini*) were not citizens, and of course neither were slaves. So Rome's body of active, fully privileged citizens was at first relatively small. Over the course of the centuries, however, that body steadily grew as citizenship and/or political rights were extended to various groups. For example, Rome frequently called on allies and other noncitizens to fight in the Roman army, and when these men completed military service, they received citizenship as a reward; moreover, because they now acquired *conubium,* they could legalize their marriages, which meant that their children would be citizens, too. The state also periodically granted citizenship to individuals in return for various outstanding accomplishments or services, or for other reasons.

Eventually, the demand for Roman citizenship by the noncitizen residents of Italy became so great that a war (the Social War) erupted in the early first century B.C. The result was that all free-born Italians became citizens. Provincials (people born in the provinces) remained noncitizens, except for those born of citizens or who had citizenship conferred on them for one reason or another. This state of affairs finally changed in A.D. 212 when the emperor Caracalla extended citizenship to all free-born residents of the Empire. **See** assemblies; Empire, Roman; Republic, Roman; **also** Caracalla (Chapter 1); Rome (Chapter 2); family (Chapter 5); **and** Social War (Chapter 7).

colonies

Throughout the years of the Republic and well into the Empire, Rome established various colonies (*coloniae*), at first usually on state-owned land and for strategic or defensive purposes. For example, the earliest colonies formed a defensive perimeter to protect the city of Rome from Italian hill tribes and other potentially hostile neighbors. The Latin colonies established by Rome before and after 338 B.C. (when Rome gained control over many of its Latin neighbors) were populated either by Roman citizens (which helped to relieve population pressure in Rome itself) or by Latin allies. The Latins possessed most of

the rights of Roman citizens (the main exception being the right to vote) and they contributed recruits for the Roman army. Either way, the result was the steady Romanization of increasingly larger surrounding territories, because the colonies were modeled on Rome; that is, they employed Roman language, institutions, and customs. In late republican and early imperial times, most new colonies were founded outside Italy with the purpose of providing land for army veterans. Both Julius Caesar and his adopted son, Augustus, established numerous such colonies. It also became common during the Empire to award the title of "colony" to an already existing provincial town in order to raise its status.

comitia centuriata

For this Roman assembly that met in the Campus Martius, **see** assemblies.

consilium plebis

For this Roman assembly whose membership was restricted to plebs, **see** assemblies.

consul

In 509 B.C., when the Roman fathers set up the Republic, they faced the problem of selecting a high state official to fulfill the duties of the kings they had recently eliminated, without giving that person absolute kingly powers. Their solution was the introduction of two annually elected magistrates who would serve jointly—the consuls (originally called praetors). Because their terms of service were so short and because one consul had to share power with the other (and could counterbalance the other's authority), it was very difficult for consuls to abuse their powers seriously. The Senate nominated the new consul candidates, who were then elected by the *comitia centuriata.* Their duties were to lead the army (each commanding equal manpower, at first two legions), to act as overall administers of the state, and to carry out the Senate's policies, especially in foreign affairs. At first, only patricians could run for the office of consul, but in 367 B.C. the privilege was extended to plebeians. The consuls' names came to denote the year, so that the year now referred to as 59 B.C. was then called "the year of Caesar and Bibulus" (Bibulus being the man who shared the consulship with Julius Caesar in that year).

In the first century B.C., during the turbulent events that brought the Republic to its knees, the office of consul was changed, distorted, and often tarnished, as powerful generals, such as Sulla, Pompey, and Caesar held the real power most of the time, even when they were not serving as consuls. Then, with the rise of the emperors shortly afterward, the consulship, along with other republican institutions, lost most of its power and influence; from then on the emperors largely chose who became consul. Still, thanks to Augustus, who wanted to wrap his new autocratic system inside a republican façade, the consuls remained prestigious. The emperors and their relatives often served in the office; and the consuls had some glamorous duties, including supervising certain criminal trials and presiding over some of Rome's public games and religious festivals.

Corpus Juris Civilis

("Complete Civil Law") A huge collection of laws and legal commentary compiled at the order of the eastern Roman (or Byzantine) emperor Justinian I (reigned A.D. 527–565). Assisted by a noted jurist, Tribonian, and a large clerical staff, Justinian drew on nearly two thousand legal works, including the Theodosian Code, compiled during the preceding century. The *Corpus* became the blueprint for the legal systems of the European kingdoms and nations that grew on the wreckage of the Roman Empire. **See** laws.

courts

Roman law courts took several forms, depending on the era and the kind of case being tried. During the Monarchy, the kings could apparently oversee trials and pass judgment. In the early to mid-Republic, the Senate inherited this right to hear cases and mete out justice. Also in this period, public criminal courts (*quaestiones perpetuae*), equipped with juries, were introduced and these significantly increased in number in the first century B.C. The jurors (*judices*) typically numbered 50 to 75 and were presided over by a praetor, who announced the verdict and decided the punishment, if any. A special civil court at Rome—the *centumviri* ("hundred men") heard cases involving property claims and inheritance. (There were actually 105 jurors in this court during the Republic, a number that increased to 180 during the Empire.) It must be emphasized that the jurors in these courts were usually members of the upper classes and heard mostly cases arising in those classes. The system of justice for the lower classes is somewhat unclear, but it was probably handled mainly by junior magistrates (*tresviri capitales*), who had the job of rounding up criminals and seeing that punishments were meted out. In the provinces there were no standing courts with juries, so the governors were in charge of justice; they often traveled around their provinces to hear and judge criminal cases.

In many court cases, a person bringing charges had to summon the accused person to appear, which sometimes required the use of force. In some cases the plaintiff conducted the prosecution himself, but often he called on a lawyer (*advocatus*) to speak for him. Such lawyers were unpaid (as were the jurors and praetors) and received instead tremendous prestige in the community, as well as various political and other favors and the chance for political advancement. Although trials took place in a number of different forums, it became most common to hold them in large meeting halls called basilicas. There, the lawyers presented their cases, using their oratorical skills to sway jurors and impress the spectators. Sometimes, those who could afford to do so hired professional applauders (*laudiceni*) to cheer on their lawyers.

During the Empire, the criminal and civil courts went on much as before, but they followed some new rules of procedure introduced by Augustus, the first emperor. Also, new courts arose, including the hearing of important cases by the emperors themselves and also by the consuls (who no longer held important political authority). The Senate became a special court that heard cases involving treason and political corruption, while ordinary criminals came to be tried and punished by the urban Prefect of the City (*praefectus urbi*), who was in charge of maintaining order in the capital. Outside of Rome, the praetorian prefect, commander of the Praetorian Guard, administered such common justice. (These prefects apparently came to replace the republican junior magistrates.) **See** crime and punishment; laws; praetor; Prefect of the City.

crime and punishment

Punishment varied widely according to factors such as the nature and severity of the crime, and, eventually, the social status of the offender. The Romans recognized two kinds of crime—private and public. Private crimes, including failing to fulfill a contract or pay a debt, fraud, minor theft, and assault, were viewed as minor offenses and usually punished by monetary fines or by forcing the convicted person to compensate his victim. Public crimes included treason, certain forms of murder, and extortion by public officials. Treason and murder normally carried death sentences, especially during the Empire, when capital punishment was more common.

The most prevalent forms of execution were beheading with a sword (used mainly for soldiers), crucifixion, exposure to wild animals or trained gladiators, burning alive, and drowning. However, depending on mitigating circumstances and the discretion of judges, many other kinds of punishment might be imposed for these and other public crimes. Beatings, partial or total confiscation of property, exile, and condemnation to gladiatorial schools or mines or quarries were also fairly common. Imprisonment was not used as a form of punishment; rather, prisons served mainly to detain suspects during trials or convicted persons awaiting execution.

During the Republic, all Roman citizens were theoretically equal in the eyes of the law and subject to the same punishments for the same crimes. In the Empire, beginning in the second and third centuries A.D., however, a distinction arose between two legal classes of citizens—the *honestiores* ("the more honorable and respectable") and the *humiliores* ("the lowly or insignificant"). The *honestiores* included patricians, equites, soldiers, municipal office holders, and the families of these people; the *humiliores* included everyone else, the bulk of the populace. The *humiliores* almost always received more severe punishments for the same crimes. Whereas they might be sentenced to death, the mines, or the arena for a certain offense, for instance, *honestiores* convicted of the same crime would likely be allowed to go into voluntary exile (*exsilium*). Such exile might be temporary or permanent; the latter was accompanied by loss of property and citizenship. **See** courts.

cursus honorum

("course of honors") A sequence or series of prestigious public offices that a young Roman man of substance was expected to follow in a successful political career during republican times. The custom grew during the first centuries of the Republic and was fixed by law in 180 B.C. (although on occasion people did not follow it exactly). The usual sequence began with service in the army. Then came the office of quaestor, followed by aedile (which was optional), praetor, consul, and finally censor. Most commonly, each term of service was separated by an interval of two years. These offices, except that of quaestor, were said to be "curule" magistracies because those holding them were entitled to use a special "chair of state" (the *sella curulis*). The first man in a family to attain a curule magistracy, particularly the consulship, was given the prestigious title of *novus homo,* or "new man."

decemviri

The original *decemviri,* or "ten men," composed a committee that was given political power in 450 B.C. and accomplished the important task of compiling the famous law code known as the Twelve Tables. Later groups of *decemviri* were appointed by the praetors and censors to important administrative tasks such as acting as judges in disputes over social status and gathering and recording information about property ownership and inheritance.

dictator

An important public office during the Republic, the dictatorship was conceived as a way to help the state survive a national emergency. During such an emergency, the consuls, on the recommendation of the Senate, appointed a dictator, who held supreme military and judicial authority for a period of six months, after which time he was expected to step down. The dictator's second in command was the master of the horse (*magister equitum*). One of the most

famous and effective dictators was Quintus Fabius Maximus, "the Delayer," who was instrumental in Rome's deliverance from Hannibal in the Second Punic War. In the political turmoil of the first century B.C., the office of dictator was abused, and it was abolished altogether after Julius Caesar's assassination in 44 B.C.

Dominate

The general name given to the Later Empire and its government, in which the emperor was addressed as *Dominus* ("Lord") and the pretense that Rome was governed to some degree by the old republican institutions was finally dropped. The Dominate began during the reign of Diocletian, who came to power in 284 and in a sense reinvented the Empire and imperial court, modeling the latter on those of eastern monarchies such as Persia. **See** Principate.

emperor

The supreme political, judicial, and religious leader of the Roman Empire, the position was created by Augustus, although he never actually used the term to describe himself, preferring instead the term *princeps,* meaning "first citizen." The term *emperor* seems to have developed from *imperator*, which originally meant "supreme commander" and was given to a general by his troops following a victory. After he had secured power after the last of the civil wars, Augustus received this title on a permanent basis and all of his successors bore it as well.

Although the Senate and many other republican institutions remained in place throughout the years of the Empire, that realm operated largely according to the

This famous statue of Augustus, the first Roman emperor, was discovered at Prima Porta, near Rome.

whims of the emperor. Still, these now largely powerless old republican institutions, along with the Roman legal system, constituted the foundation on which the emperors based their own authority. Thus, an emperor, though very powerful, could not seriously abuse his authority for long, for to do so meant going against centuries of cherished tradition and also a huge body of accepted laws. In theory, the people were willing to accept his authority as long as he lived up to his own responsibilities as the state's best possible citizen (*optimus princeps*). These responsibilities included showing piousness in the service of the gods, justice in dealings with the people, strength in the face of the enemy (and mercy after a victory), and temperance in everyday life. Accordingly, most of the few emperors who did lapse into tyranny—notorious

characters like Caligula, Nero, Domitian, and Commodus—provoked public outrage, had short reigns, and met violent ends.

Empire, Roman

The Roman realm that existed from the accession of Augustus in 27 B.C., following the collapse of the Roman Republic, until the emperor Romulus Augustulus was deposed in A.D. 476. The term *Empire* also refers to this roughly five-hundred-year-long time period. At its height in the second century A.D., the Empire encompassed about 3.5 million square miles and 100 million people. Its government was mainly autocratic in nature, as a succession of emperors, supported by the army, held most of the power. **See** Dominate; emperor; Principate; provincial government; Senate; taxation; **also** Augustus and other named individual emperors (all Chapter 1). For an overview of the Empire's history, **see** Rome (Chapter 2).

fasces

For this symbol of Roman power, **see** lictors.

fasti

This term had various meanings, the earliest being inscribed lists that served as calendars. The most famous were the *fasti consulares,* lists of the consuls serving from year to year, the years being named after these men. Such lists have survived for many of the years from 509 B.C. until the early sixth century A.D., although those dating from before 300 B.C. are considered unreliable. There were also *fasti* that listed priests and triumphs. In addition, the term *fasti* was used to describe certain days in the calendar drawn up by Rome's chief priests. *Dies fasti* were days on which it was permitted to transact business, while *dies nefasti* were days when, for religious reasons, businesses were closed.

governors
For these administrators of Rome's provinces, **see** provincial government.

imperium
Meaning "power to command," it was originally the supreme authority vested in Rome's kings. This authority, to command in war and execute the law (including the death penalty), passed on to certain officials in the Republic, including the consuls, military tribunes holding consular powers, praetors, dictators, masters of the horse, and provincial governors. Over time, it became clear that the one-year term limits on consuls and praetors were sometimes inconvenient because a commander leading a military campaign had to possess the *imperium;* if the campaign lasted more than a year, he would, by law, have to step down and allow a new commander to take over. The solution was for the Senate to extend the *imperium* by investing a former consul with the rank of proconsul, meaning "in place of the consul." He could then continue to hold *imperium* and conduct his

campaign indefinitely. Proconsuls and propraetors ("in place of the praetor"), who often ended up serving as governors and judges in the provinces, were part of a system of public offices called the promagistracy.

jurists
Legal experts who sometimes advised lawyers, judges, and eventually emperors on matters pertaining to the vast body of Roman law. Jurists, who were generally viewed as prestigious scholars, not only interpreted the law, but also helped collect, codify, and comment on the major collections of Roman law, including the Theodosian Code and *Corpus Juris Civilis.* Among the most famous of Roman jurists were Gaius (second century A.D.), Ulpian (third century A.D.), and Tribonian (sixth century A.D.).

laws
Law was one of the pillars on which Roman civilization rested. Throughout most of Roman history, the common masses had little real say in government; it was of more concern to them that they received fair treatment under the majestic protective umbrella of Roman law. The great body of that law was also the main structural link between the Republic and Empire, preserving the best of the political and legal tradition of Rome's past, while continually

growing and adapting to the needs and demands of changing times. Roman law also survived the fall of the Empire; many of its principles and statutes became the basis for later European legal systems.

Above all, Roman law was based on common sense and practical ideas. What seemed obvious to the Romans (and still does to us) was that written laws should reflect naturally existing principles of justice that apply to all citizens within a state. Their first application of this and other rational legal concepts occurred in about 450 B.C., when they wrote down their first set of laws (*leges*) in the famous Twelve Tables. Though most of these statutes have disappeared, some of their substance survives in references and quotations in later works. Like many other laws that followed, they emphasized individual citizens' rights and especially rights pertaining to the ownership of property. Later laws, which were developed and altered as social conditions warranted, dealt with inheritance, women's rights, money matters, masters versus slaves, and many other issues, including moral behavior. But all of them, down to the Empire's last years, continued to use the original laws in the Twelve Tables as precedents.

Over the centuries, the sources and interpreters of Roman law were many and varied. In the early Republic, an assembly, the *comitia centuriata,* passed laws, which were named after the leaders who proposed them. After 287 B.C., when the resolutions (*plebiscita*) of another assembly, the *concilium plebis,* became binding on all Romans, this body came to introduce most new laws. However, certain important decrees of the Senate (*senatus consulta*) had the force of law (if voted on by the tribunes), as did decrees issued by officials holding the *imperium* ("power to command"). In addition, judges and jurists often wrote down their interpretations of various laws in documents called edicts (*edicti*), which became part of the growing

corpus of legal matter that new generations of legislators, lawyers, judges, and jurists drew on in administering the law and creating new legislation. Provincial governors also issued legal edicts, and because they took local customs into account in doing so, laws could differ considerably from one province to another.

During the Empire, the assemblies at first continued to pass laws, but mostly they simply rubber-stamped legal decrees and edicts issued by the emperors. By the end of the first century A.D., the assemblies had ceased their activities and the emperors and the Senate (through its decrees), both acting on the advice of jurists, were the only major sources of new legislation. The emperors also significantly reduced the authority of judges to interpret laws. In addition, the Empire witnessed several attempts to compile and codify the huge, diverse, and still growing body of Roman law. In the second century, for example, the emperor Hadrian ordered that all of the provincial edicts be collected and standardized. And in the fifth century, the eastern emperor Theodosius II, in cooperation with the western emperor Valentinian III, codified all the laws that had been passed since Constantine I (early fourth century). This so-called Theodosian Code (*Codex Theodosianus*), completed in 438, consisted of sixteen books of laws, decrees, and legal commentary; it became a major basis for the even larger law codification completed by the emperor Justinian in the century that followed. **See** *Corpus Juris Civilis;* crime and punishment; jurists.

lictors

During the Republic, lictors were special attendants who walked in front of magistrates who held *imperium,* such as consuls and dictators. Twelve lictors (*lictores*) preceded a consul, six a praetor (when commanding an army), and twenty-four a dictator. Over his left

shoulder, each lictor carried the *fasces.*
Consisting of a double-headed ax surrounded by a bundle of rods, the *fasces*
originally symbolized the power of kings
and other high leaders to punish and inflict the death penalty; but over time they
became more general symbols of magistrates' authority. (In the 1930s, the Italian
Fascist Party took its name from the Italian equivalent, *fascio,* and used the *fasces*
as its symbol.) **See** *imperium.*

maiestas

A term used to denote treason against the
state, and especially against the person of
the emperor, it was invoked most often in
the first century A.D. The original Roman
term for treason, always a very serious offense punishable by death, was *perduellio.*
In the late first century B.C., while he was
reorganizing the Roman state, Augustus
created a treason law known as the *Lex Julia maiestas,* which expanded the definition of treason to include not only conspiracies against his life, but also slander
against him, adultery with a member of his
family, and disrespect for the government.
Though the law was not seriously abused
during Augustus's reign, his successor,
Tiberius, used it to justify the reign of terror instigated by his strong-arm man, Sejanus. Tacitus's *Annals* contains numerous
anecdotes about an imperial network of in-
formers who provided evidence, much of
it of a questionable nature, of treasonous
activity by members of the nobility. Of
Tiberius's immediate successors, the
despots Nero and Domitian were the only
ones who invoked the *maiestas* law with
any frequency; it was little used after the
first century.

Monarchy

The Roman government and state, ruled
by kings, directly preceding the foundation
of the Republic. The exact length of the
monarchial period (also referred to as the
Monarchy), as well as the number of kings
and the lengths of their reigns, is unknown. According to later tradition, there
were seven kings, beginning with Romulus, who supposedly reigned from 753 to
717 B.C. He was then succeeded by Numa
Pompilius, Tullus Hostilius, Ancus Marcius, Tarquinius Priscus, Servius Tullius,
and Tarquinius Superbus (or "Tarquin the
Proud"). Some of these rulers, especially
the first three, were likely legendary rather
than real persons, although the last four
may well have been real. In any case, recent scholarship suggests that the period of
the Monarchy was shorter than tradition
held. Also, there may well have been more
than seven kings, some of whose identities
and deeds merged with those of the traditional seven in historical accounts fashioned centuries later.

The way these rulers were chosen and
how much power and authority they held
is uncertain. But traditional accounts
recorded by Livy and other later writers
suggest that some kind of election was
held, in which selected male citizens,
probably those who could afford to bear
weapons, met periodically in an assembly
and either chose or ratified nominees.
More importantly, those chosen had to be
ratified by the heads of the leading families (the Roman "fathers," or *patres*).

Not much is known for sure about
Rome's history during the Monarchy. What
is certain is that the Romans were frequently
in conflict with their immediate neighbors
and that Roman territory steadily expanded,
especially into the Latium plain in the south.
For instance, heroic myths, some of which
may be exaggerated versions of real events,
tell of Rome's takeover of Alba Longa, the
region in which the legendary Aeneas had
supposedly settled centuries before. In one

of the most famous tales, attributed to the reign of Tullus Hostilius (673–642 B.C.), the Romans and Albans were at war. But they wanted to conserve their manpower to fight their common enemy, the Etruscans. So the two sides each chose three champions who would fight to decide the war's outcome. Though two of the three Romans, members of a noble family, the Horatii, were killed, the third was ultimately victorious.

The Monarchy finally came to an end circa 509 B.C. According to Livy, when King Tarquin the Proud was away from the city, the Roman fathers, meeting as the Senate, declared his rule null and void; soon afterward they set up a new government based on republican ideals. **See** Aeneas; Brutus, Lucius Junius; Romulus (all Chapter 1); **also** Rome (Chapter 2); **and** Etruscans (Chapter 7).

novus homo
For this Latin term meaning "new man," **see** *cursus honorum.*

Optimates
("the best class") Made up of aristocrats and members of the upper classes, this political party or group was formed in response to the emergence of the people's party—the Populares—in the late 130s B.C. The Optimates, who were more conservative as well as more numerous than the Populares, worked to maintain the power and influence of the senatorial class during the turbulent political times of the late Republic. **See** Populares.

plebiscita
For these resolutions passed by Rome's assemblies, **see** assemblies.

Populares
("on the people's side") A political party or group that emerged in the late 130s B.C. under the inspiration of the social reforms and violent death of Tiberius Sempronius Gracchus, the Populares worked with the aid of and for the good of the common people. The party challenged the political dominance of the senatorial and upper classes, which responded by forming an opposing party, the Optimates. The two factions remained at odds in the Republic's last decades. **See** Optimates; **also** Gracchus, Tiberius Sempronius (Chapter 1).

praetor
During the early Republic, two praetors at first assumed the military and political powers of the kings, but they were soon renamed consuls and from midrepublican times onward the praetors no longer held military command and acted mainly as supreme judges in charge of the courts. The *praetor urbanus* ("city praetor") handled cases that involved Roman citizens; the *praetor peregrinus* (added in 241 B.C.) dealt with cases involving foreigners. As the realm expanded and the justice system with it, their number steadily increased, until by around 80 B.C. there were eight praetors. They were elected to one-year terms by the *comitia centuriata*. **See** consul.

Prefect of the City

(*praefectus urbi,* or urban prefect) The chief administrator of the city of Rome during the Empire. In the Monarchy and Republic, the prefects were assistants to the kings and consuls and held limited powers. But in shaping his new Roman order in the late first century B.C., Augustus greatly expanded the powers and duties of the office, giving the Prefect of the City authority to run the day-to-day business of the capital on a permanent basis; to try legal cases in Rome and within a one-hundred-mile radius of it; and to command the urban cohorts (which acted as Rome's police force). In the mid–fourth century, a second *praefectus urbi* assumed similar duties in Constantinople. **See** crime and punishment; **also** urban cohorts (Chapter 7).

princeps

For this Latin term meaning "first citizen," **see** emperor.

Principate

A general term used to denote the Empire and its rule by the emperors from the reign of Augustus to that of Diocletian, when the Dominate began. The term *Principate* derives from *princeps,* a title assumed by Augustus and used by him and his successors to support the impression that they were governing through the authority of the old republican institutions. **See** Dominate; emperor.

proconsul

For this title of some provincial governors, **see** *imperium;* provincial government.

procurator

A public official during the Empire who operated under the direct authority of the emperor, fulfilling various important tasks. Most commonly a procurator acted as governor of a Roman territory or minor province, a famous example being Pontius Pilate, who administered Judaea from A.D.

26 to 36. A procurator was in charge of all finances in such an area, the equivalent of a quaestor in a senatorial province. In said senatorial provinces, procurators usually managed imperial estates or helped the quaestors with tax collection. Most procurators were equites, although occasionally a freedman was raised to the office. **See** provincial government.

provincial government

In republican days, provinces were administered by governors appointed by the Senate and granted complete authority over tax collection, justice, and maintaining law and order. To facilitate the latter, a governor could raise and command troops; therefore, he possessed the *imperium* ("power to command"), although it was valid only in his own province. A governor was assisted by a quaestor (financial official) and a staff of formal advisers (*legati*) and informal advisers (*amici,* or "friends"). It was common for a consul or praetor to become a provincial governor (with the title of proconsul) at the end of his consulship or praetorship.

In the early Empire (or Principate), provinces were either public (or senatorial) or imperial. Public provinces were still run by governors with the title of proconsul appointed by the Senate, usually for one-year terms; they continued to receive the aid of quaestors and *legati.* The imperial provinces, by contrast, were under the direct authority of the emperor, following the precedent of Augustus's direct rule of Egypt after his defeat of Cleopatra VII. The emperor appointed governors to manage his provinces; usually they were ex-consuls or ex-praetors, although some, in minor provinces, were prefects and procurators. Most commonly, these officials, who served in effect as an emperor's *legati,* since he was technically the governor of these provinces, were equites with some kind of military background. A famous example is Pliny the Younger, who as an ex-consul was appointed by the emperor Trajan in A.D. 110 to run the province of Bithynia. (Their correspondence, which has survived, provides valuable information about how such provinces were administered.)

In the Later Empire (or Dominate), the number of provinces increased significantly as Diocletian and his successors redrew the imperial map; so the number of governors also increased. Governors had various titles, including *corrector* ("reformer") and *praeses* ("guardian"), and most were still equites, although fewer and fewer had military backgrounds. Diocletian's provincial reforms also included the creation of dioceses, administrative units consisting of two or more provinces run by officials called vicars (*vicarii*), who reported to the Praetorian prefect (who in turn reported to the emperor).

On the local level, various public officials who were subordinate to the governors of the provinces had a considerable degree of autonomy until the Later Empire, when their importance steadily diminished. Towns and cities were run by magistrates and town councils, whose titles and duties differed somewhat according to their region. In the eastern part of the realm, where the old Greek Hellenistic kingdoms had once held sway, the local magistrates were called archons and a town council was a *boule* (both Greek terms). In the western Roman sphere, the Italian system of local administration prevailed. The chief magistrates were the *duumviri* (or *duoviri*), two of whom often ruled jointly, as consuls did; they were assisted by aediles (in charge of public works) and quaestors (in charge of finances). These officials were popularly elected, although they had to own a certain amount of property to qualify. Local governments also had town councils, whose members, called *curiales* or *decuriones,* were local representatives of Rome's main government. They were usually well-to-do landowners who had to serve on the councils whether they liked it or not and also had to pass their positions on to their sons. Because they came to be in charge of tax collection, they were very unpopular with people of all social classes. In the Later Empire, when such service became unbearable, many of these local councilors fled or found other ways

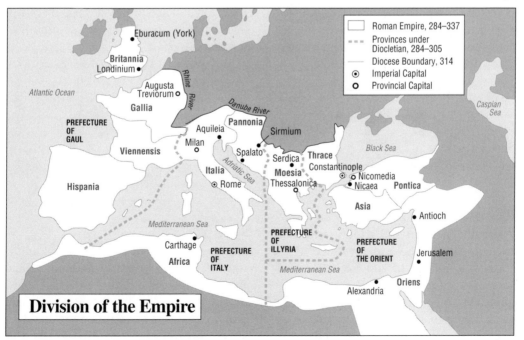

Division of the Empire

to avoid service, contributing to the steady economic deterioration of the provinces. **See** taxation.

publicani
For these widely detested tax collectors, **see** taxation.

quaestor
In both the Republic and Empire, the quaestors (*quaestores*) were public officials who handled financial affairs. In the earliest days of the Republic, they were assistants to the consuls. But not long after 450 B.C., two were elected annually by the *comitia tributa* to administer the treasury and act as paymasters for the army. As the Roman realm expanded, more quaestors were added to manage the finances of the provinces. Quaestors were also elected on the local level to handle the finances of cities and towns. The office of quaestor was part of the *cursus honorum;* thus, a man could not become a senator without having first served as quaestor.

Republic, Roman
The Roman realm and government that existed from the fall of the Monarchy, in about 509 B.C., to the acquisition of total power by Octavian in 30 B.C. (or to his acquisition of the title of Augustus in 27 B.C.). The term *Republic* also refers to this roughly five-hundred-year-long period.

The Republic was largely run by representatives of the people, although only free adult males, a minority of the population, could vote or hold public office. Some of these male citizens met periodically in the Roman assemblies, where they voted on new laws and also annually elected magistrates, including the consuls, praetors, censors, quaestors, and aediles. Another legislative body, the Senate, the most prestigious governmental body, held considerable influence over the assemblies and magistrates and much indirect power as a result, so the republican state was actually an oligarchy (a government run by a select group) rather than a true democracy.

Still, in an age when kings and other absolute monarchs ruled almost everywhere else in the known world, the Roman Republic was indeed a progressive and enlightened political entity. Though most Romans did not have a say in state policy, many had a measurable voice in choosing leaders and making laws. These laws often offered an umbrella of protection for members of all classes against the arbitrary abuses of potentially corrupt leaders, at least until the first century B.C., when political turmoil and civil war brought about the Republic's collapse. **See** assemblies; Senate; individual listings for republican offices. For an overview of the history of the Republic, **see** Rome (Chapter 2).

Senate
The chief legislative body of the Republic and a repository of tradition and great prestige throughout both the Republic and Empire. Originally, the Senate was the advisory council to the Roman kings. After the creation of the Republic, circa 509

B.C., it served, in theory, the same function for Rome's elected magistrates. However, it was at first composed exclusively of patricians (landed aristocrats), who held their positions for life; patricians came not only to dictate most of the policies of the consuls, but also, through the use of wealth and high position, indirectly to influence the way the members of the assemblies voted. Thus, except under extreme circumstances, the Senate held the real power in the Republic, especially in its last two centuries.

A man was eligible to join the Senate after he had served in his first magistracy, which was usually the first office in the *cursus honorum,* that of quaestor. So the body became in essence a group of ex-magistrates. In midrepublican times, the qualification of belonging to the patrician class was dropped and plebeians were allowed to join, although they remained in the minority. At first there were one hundred senators, but over the centuries this number increased to three hundred, then six hundred (by 80 B.C.), and finally nine hundred (in the 40s B.C.). Senators received no pay, but this posed no hardship because virtually all were rich property owners. A senator could be removed only for committing some serious offense against the state, in which case the censors, who kept the lists of senators, replaced him. Meetings of the Senate could be held on any of the grounds within the capital that had been consecrated by Rome's chief priests, but most often the senators met in the Senate House (*Curia Hostilia*), situated in the northwest corner of the main Forum.

As the de facto chief organ of the government, the Senate wielded power in a number of ways. In addition to its indirect influence on the magistrates and assemblies, it prepared the legislation that the assemblies voted on; issued decrees (*decreta* or *senatus consulta*) that could be legally binding (if voted on by the tri-bunes); appointed governors and other officials to the provinces; conducted foreign relations; and had significant administrative authority over state finances and religious practices. The Senate also wielded the *senatus consultum ultimum* ("final resolution of the Senate"), a decree it could issue to the consuls during a serious national emergency. Under its authorization, the consuls could suspend the people's right of legal appeal and use any force necessary to protect the state. It was used only on occasion, one of the most famous examples occurring in 63 B.C. when Catiline and his fellow conspirators planned to kill the consuls and seize control of the government.

During the first century B.C., the Senate's authority was increasingly challenged by powerful generals, who ran roughshod over the traditional republican institutions. And following Octavian's seizure of absolute power following his victory at Actium (31 B.C.), the senators had no choice but to support his sweeping reforms, which rapidly transformed the dead Republic into what became known as the Roman Empire. Octavian, renamed Augustus, reduced the number of senators to six hundred and introduced a property qualification (a million *sesterces*) for entry. In the years that followed, the Senate's authority continued to decrease and the only significant powers it retained were control over some of the provinces, administration of the state treasury, the right to issue decrees, and authority to conduct high-profile trials, including those involving treason. Nevertheless, the body remained a symbol of Roman tradition and membership brought a person much prestige and moral authority. When Constantine I inaugurated Constantinople in 330 A.D., he set up the eastern version of the Senate, which a generation later gained equality with the one in Rome. The western Senate survived the ouster of the last emperor in

476; but over the next century, this most potent symbol of ancient Roman government slowly faded into obscurity. **See** consul; laws; Republic, Roman; **also** Rome (Chapter 2).

senatus consultum ultimum

For this emergency decree passed occasionally by the Senate, **see** Senate.

SPQR

The symbol of the Republic; regularly displayed on documents and monuments, it stood for *Senatus Populusque Romanus,* "the Senate and People of Rome." For the sake of tradition and continuity, Augustus and his successors retained it as the official mark of the Empire.

taxation

In the early Republic, Roman citizens paid no regular taxes, except during times of emergency, when the government levied a special tax on land and property—the *tributum.* This tax was eliminated in 167 B.C., mainly because of the revenue that was pouring into the state treasury from Rome's conquests in the eastern Mediterranean. The exception was in such conquered territories, where noncitizens had to pay *tributum* of a fixed amount annually. Whatever tax collection system already existed in a conquered land remained in place as long as it continued to operate efficiently. In the late Republic, Roman citizens did have to pay some indirect taxes, which took the form of a 5 percent charge on the freeing of a slave and harbor charges levied on shipping.

At the start of the Empire, Augustus reformed the tax system. He ordered a census in each province to determine the number of taxable persons; those eligible had to pay a direct land tax (*tributum solis*), while those who did not own land paid a poll tax (*tributum capitis*). Rome and Italy remained exempt from direct taxation, as did Roman citizens in many other parts of the realm. However, Augustus and his immediate successors added some new indirect taxes, among them a 5 percent charge on inheritances, a 4 percent charge on the sale of a slave, and a 1 percent charge on auction sales.

The situation changed again in A.D. 212 when the emperor Caracalla granted citizenship to all adult residents of the Empire. All citizens were now subject to paying the *tributum,* except in Italy, which was still exempt. That exception was eliminated in the late third century A.D., as Diocletian's social and economic reforms came into effect. By that time, money had lost much of its value, so in many places people were allowed to pay their taxes in kind (that is, in the form of goods such as food, wine, and clothes, most of which were used by the army).

Tax collection during the Empire was overseen by procurators in senatorial provinces and by quaestors in imperial provinces. Both sometimes contracted professional tax collectors, known as publicans (*publicani*), many of whom turned out to be corrupt and raised the ire of the populace. In the Later Empire, more and more of the burden of collecting taxes fell on local councilmen (*curiales* or *decuriones*), who, like other tax collectors, were widely detested. These unfortunate individuals were not only obligated to fulfill this duty but had to pay any shortfalls in collection from their own pockets, the penalty for failing to do so being torture or even death. **See** provincial government.

Tetrarchy

The four-man ruling coalition created by Diocletian in A.D. 293, it consisted of two men ruling in the west and two in the east. As the reigning Augustus, or senior emperor, Diocletian had earlier made Maximian his Caesar, or junior emperor. In forming the first Tetrarchy, Diocletian (based in the east) raised Maximian (based in the west) to the rank of Augustus (although Diocletian retained seniority and greater authority) and appointed a new Caesar to each Augustus. Diocletian's Caesar was Galerius, while Constantius I Chlorus (father of Constantine the Great) was Caesar to Maximian.

On Diocletian's retirement in 305 (at which time he forced Maximian to retire too), Galerius and Constantius became the Augusti of a second Tetrarchy. Flavius Valerius Severus became Constantius's Caesar in the west, while Maximinus Daia became Galerius's Caesar in the east. The following year, Constantius died in Britain, which raised Severus to the rank of Augustus in his place; but the Tetrarchy soon fell apart, as Constantine, Maxentius (son of the former Augustus, Maximian), and the others challenged one another for supremacy. The resulting civil discords ended in 312 with Constantine's victory over Maxentius at Rome's Milvian Bridge. **See** Constantine I; Diocletian; Galerius (all Chapter 1); **also** Rome (Chapter 2).

Theodosian Code
For this massive collection of laws compiled in the fifth century, **see** laws.

tribune, plebeian
(*tribuni plebis,* or tribune of the people) In the Republic, the plebeian tribunes were public officials of plebeian birth who were elected annually by the people's assembly, the *concilium plebis.* When they were introduced in the early fifth century B.C., two served together, but by the middle of that century their number had increased to ten. Representatives of the common people, they held authority known as the tribunician power (*tribunicia potestas*), which entitled them to veto

The members of the Tetrarchy ("rule of four") created by the emperor Diocletian hug one another in this famous sculpture now on display in Venice.

any political legislation or plan within the city of Rome, including the election of magistrates and decrees of the Senate (with the exception of the directives of dictators). This often served to balance or check the otherwise overbearing authority of the senators, consuls, and other members of the aristocratic and privileged elite.

By the early 40s B.C., Julius Caesar had managed to usurp most of the powers of the tribunes; this became the precedent followed by his adopted son, Augustus, who permanently transferred the *tribunicia potestas* to himself and his successors (based on his promise to protect and defend the Roman people as a whole, just as the tribunes had protected the plebeians). The tribunate continued into the Empire. However, the tribunes now held mainly ceremonial power, and their office became a mandatory prerequisite for plebeians aspiring to join the Senate.

Twelve Tables

For this collection of laws, Rome's first, **see** laws.

veto

For this power of a plebeian official to block a proposed law, **see** tribune, plebeian.

vicar

For this administrator of a diocese in the Later Empire, **see** provincial government.

CHAPTER 5
SOCIAL AND ECONOMIC CUSTOMS AND INSTITUTIONS

adoption

Adoption in the modern sense—that is, childless couples taking legal charge of abandoned children—was rare in ancient Roman society. Most Roman adoption (*adoptio*) involved the extension of legal power and protection by the paterfamilias (male head) of a family over the son (or on rare occasions the daughter) of another man. The person being adopted, often a teenager or adult, automatically lost any rights he or she had in the old family. Many men who initiated the procedure of adoption did so because they did not have sons of their own and wanted to ensure the survival of the family name and property. Adoption for political reasons—to increase the prestige of the adoptee or to form a familial alliance—was also common. An adoptee normally took his new father's three names, adding his own *nomen* modified by the suffix *-anus.* Among the most famous examples of adoption were Julius Caesar's adoption of his great-nephew Octavian (later Augustus, the first emperor), Trajan's adoption of Hadrian as his son and heir, and Hadrian's like treatment of Antoninus Pius. **See** family; names.

ager publicus

For this term meaning "public land," **see** farming.

amphorae

Large pottery jars used to transport liquids such as wine and olive oil (and occasionally solid foods such as olives, dates, and nuts). They were widely used by the Greeks, whose word for such a jar, *amphoreus,* was adopted by the Romans as amphora. There were at least forty different types and styles of amphorae, but most can be generally described as standing three to four feet high, having a capacity of from six to twenty gallons, being wide in the middle and tapering to a narrow mouth, and having two vertical handles near that mouth. The inside of such a vessel was often coated with rosin (a residue from the distillation of resin from pine trees) or some other material to make it watertight, and the mouth was sealed by a stopper made of cork or fired clay. Many, if not most, amphorae were stamped or painted with inscriptions, often including the names of the owners of the estates where they were made or the merchants who transported them; the origin of the contents; the weight of said contents; and shipping information.

These Roman amphorae, standing about three feet high, are displayed at the British Museum in London.

On merchant ships, the jars were stacked, either upright or on their sides, in several layers. Archaeological evidence from the examination of shipwrecks off the coasts of France and Italy indicate that some of the larger ships carried several thousand amphorae at a time. In fact, olive oil amphorae were as common as milk and fruit juice containers are today, a fact graphically illustrated by an ancient rubbish heap discovered in Rome. Composed solely of discarded oil amphorae, archaeologists estimate that the mound is 3,000 feet in circumference and 140 feet high, and contains the remains of over 40 million jugs! **See** trade.

athletic games

The Romans made a distinction between Greek-style athletic contests, which emphasized original Olympic events such as running, jumping, discus throwing, and wrestling, and their own more violent pub-lic contests, including gladiatorial combat, wild animal fights, and large-scale chariot races. Except for boxing and chariot racing, most Romans had little interest in Greek athletics and much preferred their own spectacle sports.

The general Roman disdain for Greek sports began in the 190s B.C., when the Romans started to overrun the Greek-controlled eastern Mediterranean sphere and had their first major exposure to Greek athletics. The Greek games were held at the local level throughout the Greek world, as well as at a number of large international festivals, the most famous held every four years at Olympia, in southern Greece. Greeks of all social classes took part and customarily trained and competed in the nude. Upper-class Romans consistently rejected Greek-style games as effeminate (unmanly) and morally decadent. The prominent first-century B.C. orator Cicero expressed this typical Roman view when he quoted with approval the words of an earlier Roman writer: "To strip in public is the beginning of evil-doing" (*Tusculan Disputations* 4.33.70). Attempting to explain such apparent prudishness, the Greek biographer and moralist Plutarch wrote:

> The Romans considered nothing to be the cause of the Greeks' enslavement and degeneracy as much as the gymnasia and palaestras [wrestling facilities], which gave rise to much time-wasting and laziness in the cities . . . and the ruination of the youths' bodies through sleep, strolls, exercises, and precise diets, because of which they stopped practicing with weaponry and were happy to be called nimble and wrestlers and handsome instead of hoplites [warriors] and good horsemen. (*Moral Essays* 274d)

Perhaps the most important difference between Greek and Roman sports, however, centered on the issue of citizen participation. The vast majority of Romans greatly enjoyed watching large-scale, violent games, which they viewed as a form of entertainment; but for a Roman citizen actually to participate in such public spectacles was viewed as improper, undignified, and socially unacceptable. This view was completely contrary to that of Greek society, which encouraged and glorified athletic participation by citizens. One reason for this Roman view was undoubtedly pride. The Romans were, for much of their history, a conservative, austere people who took special pride in their military prowess and considered losing in battle the ultimate disgrace. Simply put, for most Romans defeat in an athletic competition was too much like defeat in war.

Despite such attitudes, Roman dislike of Greek games softened somewhat in the early Empire, as a few of the emperors instituted their own versions of Olympic competitions. The first emperor, Augustus, for example, founded the Actian Games to celebrate his victory in the battle of Actium in 31 B.C.; Nero, the egotistical fifth emperor, established the "Neronian" games in Rome in the 60s A.D.; and circa A.D. 132, the emperor Hadrian, an avid admirer of Greek culture, attempted to replace the games held at Olympia with a new festival in Athens (a move that failed when most Greek athletes, out of reverence for tradition, refused to attend). During these years, some Roman citizens began attending such athletic games along with Greeks. Yet most leading Romans continued to promote the puritanical idea that such attendance was a symptom of society's moral decay. Tacitus summarized this view in his commentary on Nero's games: "Traditional morals, already gradually deteriorating, have been utterly ruined by this imported laxity! . . . Foreign influences demoralize our young men into shirkers, gymnasts, and perverts. . . . It only remains to strip and fight in boxing-gloves instead of joining the army" (*Annals*

14.17–18). **See** public games; **also** theaters and amphitheaters (Chapter 6).

aureus

For this valuable Roman gold coin, **see** money.

bakers and bakeries

For these producers of bread and pastries, **see** farming.

banking

Banks and bankers were integral to Rome's economy. In most cases, Roman bankers, called *argentarii* (singular, *argentarius*), were either money changers who exchanged the various kinds of Roman coins for foreign currencies (or vice versa) or private businessmen, most of them equites or freedmen (since patricians generally considered dealing with money to be beneath their dignity) who lent people money. In the late Republic and early Empire, the most prevalent range of interest rates for such loans was 6 to 10 percent in Italy and the more economically stable provinces. In outlying provinces, where making loans was riskier, the rates could be much higher. (It was common for provincials to borrow money to pay their taxes, from which Roman citizens were long exempt; such borrowers frequently ran up large debts that they could not fully repay.) Bankers also provided other important services, such as taking money and other valuables on deposit; buying, selling, and managing land and buildings; and collecting outstanding debts for someone else. Agents for these bankers typically ran money-changing tables (*mensa publica*) in forums, marketplaces, and other central public areas. **See** money; trade.

baths, public

Perhaps the most common of Roman leisure pastimes, one enjoyed by Romans of nearly all walks of life from the first century B.C. on, was a visit to the public bath (*thermarum;* plural, *thermae*). Before that time, private and public baths were called *balineae.* They were typically small rooms with single bathtubs that had to be filled and emptied by hand; for a hot bath, water had to be warmed in a kettle over a fire. The first public bathhouses, privately run establishments that appeared in Rome in the second century B.C., offered such simple bathing facilities.

With the invention of the hypocaust (a system that used hot air from a furnace to warm large volumes of water) in the first century B.C., larger-scale bathhouses equipped with more complex facilities rapidly spread across the Roman world. By the era of Augustus's reign, the capital city already boasted more than 170 private *thermae,* and in the first century A.D. various emperors began building large public versions. They became so important an institution that most people attended them daily or at least a few times a week instead of bathing at home. Even the poor could afford to go often, since the entrance fee for adults was minimal—a *quadrans,* perhaps equivalent to about a quarter of a penny today. Children were admitted free. Most bathhouses either offered separate facilities for women or staggered their hours so that men and women attended at different times.

The larger *thermae* were huge, beautifully decorated buildings with complex and ingenious hot and cold water systems within a series of separate but connected rooms. A room for undressing and dressing, called the *apodyterium,* was equipped with benches and often cubicles to store bathers' clothes; many patrons then entered a warm room without a bath, the *tepidarium,* where they remained until they started perspiring; next came the *caldarium,* a hot room with a pool of hot water;

then the *frigidarium,* a cold room with a pool of cold water. Many baths included an *unctorium,* where bathers rubbed themselves with oil, then scraped it off with strigils, scrapers made of wood, bone, or metal. Many bathhouses had in addition a swimming pool (*natatio*) and a saunalike dry room (*laconicum*).

The *thermae* were much more than places where Romans perspired, washed, and swam, however. They were also social centers, where people gathered to exchange news, exercise, play games, conduct business, and engage in quiet reading and study. In addition to its extensive bathing facilities, a large public bath featured massage parlors and hair salons; indoor and outdoor exercise rooms and gyms, where people played handball and *harpastum* (a rough-and-tumble ball game similar to rugby), lifted weights, and wrestled; snack bars and gift shops; gardens for strolling and leisure conversation; and libraries and reading rooms. Combining many features of modern malls and social clubs, the *thermae* were places where people could enjoy themselves for a pleasant hour or an entire day.

It is no wonder, then, that public bathhouses became increasingly numerous and remained widely popular during the Empire. In A.D. 20, the first large state-run public baths opened; by the year 284 there were eleven such large-scale facilities, along with about one thousand smaller privately owned baths, in the city of Rome alone. Among the largest and most splendid of the eleven public bathhouses was that erected by the emperor Caracalla between A.D. 212 and 216 (although parts of the complex were completed by the last member of his dynasty, Severus Alexander). The total complex measured 1,107 by 1,104 feet and was surrounded by majestic column-lined porches. The immense atrium, or front hall, featured an elevated gallery supported by eight columns, each of them five feet in diameter and forty-

Extensive sections of the Roman baths at Bath, England, pictured here, are remarkably well-preserved.

eight feet high. The main *caldarium* alone was 165 feet across and had seven heated pools. The complex also included two gyms, several libraries and reading rooms, beautiful sculptured gardens, and a cellar honeycombed with over three miles of heating and ventilation tunnels. Other notable public baths in Rome were those of Agrippa, Nero, Titus, Trajan, Diocletian, and Constantine. **See** heating and lighting.

"bread and circuses"

For this governmental policy of appeasing the Roman masses, **see** public games.

bronze

For this common metal, an alloy of copper and tin, **see** metalworking; money.

burial customs

Roman funeral and burial practices varied considerably from era to era. The members of the so-called Apennine culture,

which existed in central Italy in the Bronze Age (until about 1200 B.C.), early forebears of the Romans, practiced inhumation (burial of the dead). In the centuries that followed, by contrast, cremation (burning the dead and collecting their ashes) was the prevalent method. In the Monarchy and early Republic both inhumation and cremation were practiced, though inhumation appears to have been the preferred choice. Then cremation once more became dominant in the late Republic and remained so until the mid–third century A.D., when inhumation again became more prevalent. (Inhumation became especially widespread in the fourth and fifth centuries because Christians, who made up an increasing percentage of the population in this period, strongly objected to cremation.) It must be emphasized that throughout Roman history both methods of body disposal were employed, regardless of which was more popular at a given time.

The choice of one of these two methods dictated specific funeral customs, which might also vary according to people's economic circumstances. In the case of cremation, bodies were burned on pyres (piles of branches, or wooden or stone platforms covered by branches), most often set up in cemeteries. (Personal belongings and gifts brought by mourners were sometimes burned along with the body.) Cremation of rich or famous persons occasionally took place in public squares or other public spaces; for instance, Augustus was cremated in a huge public ceremony in Rome's Campus Martius. After the cremation was complete, poorer folk collected the ashes and bones and placed them in cloth bags or urns; well-to-do persons more often utilized stone chests or richly decorated gold boxes. Some families kept such urns, chests, or boxes in their homes, as is customary today, while others chose to store them in underground vaults called *columbarii,* in cemeteries, which they periodically visited to pay their respects.

In the case of inhumation, the vast majority of poor people using this method ended up in mass graves, the sites of which were often forgotten over time. Their funerals were likely simple affairs attended mainly by family members and a few friends, and the bodies were protected only by a shroud, a sack, or perhaps some broken pottery or roof tiles. Some less-well-off people belonged to funeral clubs (*collegia funeraticia*) that helped pay burial expenses. Families that could afford more elaborate funerals placed their dead in coffins (sarcophagi) made of wood, lead, or stone, sometimes decorated with sculpted reliefs or precious stones. In such a funeral, the mourners, sometimes including women paid to take part, marched in a solemn procession through the city streets, carrying the deceased on an open bier. They might stop for a while in a public square to perform a ceremony called *laudatio,* in which someone delivered a funeral oration (*laudatio funebris*). Well-to-do families might also hire groups of musicians and/or dancers to accompany the procession. In addition, during the Republic and early Empire, members of some prominent families wore masks (*imagines,* made of wax or other materials) of the dead person's ancestors; these masked mourners rode in chariots.

The funeral procession eventually entered a cemetery, which was almost always outside a city's walls. This was so that the living could avoid religious "pollution," which was thought to result from contact with dead bodies; accordingly, all of those involved in a funeral had to be "purified" through certain religious rituals afterward. The cemeteries containing tombs and grave markers were most often located along the roadsides outside towns and cities, sometimes giving the impression of rows of miniature buildings. Those who could afford it placed their dead in stone tombs or under large tombstones, both of which might bear carved or painted images of the deceased and dedicatory inscriptions (words and phrases meant to honor the dead person's memory). Grave goods, traditionally thought to be useful to the deceased in the afterlife, were often placed inside tombs or coffins (as well as burned with the body during cremation). Such goods commonly included food and drink, as well as clothes, shoes, jewelry, and other personal items. (The exception was Christian burials, which did not commonly feature grave goods.) At the gravesite, mourners might partake in various religious rituals, depending on the particular beliefs of the family, and a feast in honor of the deceased. Sometimes the mourners returned nine days later and had another feast, and similar rituals would be repeated during the Parentalia (February 13–21), a religious festival that honored dead parents, and other festivals.

calendar

Unfortunately, the Romans did not have one, standard system for reckoning the passage of the years, which often makes it difficult for modern scholars to calculate exact dates in their history. Beginning with the founding of the Republic in 509 B.C., they dated years according to the names of the two consuls serving annually. But this cumbersome system required a great deal of memorization and was largely impractical for everyday use. In the Empire, a system of reckoning years by the reigns of the emperors was sometimes employed.

Also, in the first century B.C. the noted scholar Publius Terentius Varro devised a system based on the best guess of the scholars of his era for the date of Rome's establishment. This system dated events "from Rome's founding" (*ab urbe condita,* abbreviated AUC). (The system more familiar today, which employs the labels B.C., meaning "before Christ," and A.D., or *anno Domini,* meaning "the year of the Lord," was introduced by Christian scholars in the sixth century A.D. These scholars calculated that Christ had been born in the year delineated by Varro as 754 AUC and labeled it A.D. 1 in their new chronology. There was no year 0 in their system; therefore, Rome was founded 753 years before the year 1, or 753 B.C.)

Before and after Varro's time, other dating systems were used in various regions of the Roman realm, most of these based on traditional local calendars. Still another system, used in the Empire's last two centuries, reckoned the years according to cycles of taxation, which were at first five years in length and later fifteen.

Regarding the reckoning of months and days within each year, the Romans originally employed an agricultural calendar with ten months, nine months of roughly the same length and a longer tenth month, lasting from December to March, when farmers did little or no work. Sometime in the sixth century B.C., they switched to a lunar calendar (based on the cycles of the moon) with twelve months, March being the first month of the year. January became the first month in 153 B.C. The names and lengths of these Roman months have largely survived to the present, including *Januarius* (January), *Februarius* (February), *Martius* (March), *Aprilis* (April), *Maius* (May), *Junius* (June), *Quinctilis* (renamed *Julius* to honor Julius Caesar in 44 B.C.; the modern July), *Sextilis* (renamed *Augustus* to honor Augustus in 8 B.C.; the modern August), *September* (September), *October* (October), *November* (November), and *December* (December).

Because the lunar cycle did not exactly match the solar cycle (earth's movement around the sun once each year), accumulating error had to be corrected on a periodic basis. This was the job of Rome's chief priests, the pontiffs, who added a few extra (intercalary) days every other year. But over the years, they fell behind, and by the mid–first century B.C. the lunar calendar was three months ahead of the solar one. To correct this problem, Julius Caesar ordered that the year 46 B.C. be extended to 445 days, and that beginning on January 1, 45 B.C., a year would comprise 365 days, with additional leap-years that added an extra day every three years (later changed to four). This so-called Julian calendar is, with some minor changes instituted by Pope Gregory XIII in 1582, the one in use in the Western world today.

The Roman days of the month were not numbered sequentially, as is the case today. Rather, a given day was said to be a certain number of days before one of three special named days—the Kalends, the first day of the month; the Nones, the fifth or seventh day of the month (depending on the length of that month); and the Ides, the thirteenth or fifteenth day of the month. In this system, for example, June 3 was designated as "the third day before the Nones of June"; June 10 was "the fourth day before the Ides of June"; and June 25 was "the seventh day before the Kalends of July." See *fasti* (Chapter 4).

chariot races
For this highly popular form of entertainment, **see** public games.

children
For the social status, homelife, and schooling of young Romans, **see** education; family.

clan
For this extended kinship group consisting of several families, **see** *gens;* marriage; names.

clients
For these people who did favors for and also received favors in return from their social betters, **see** patronage.

clothing
Roman clothing was of two basic kinds— "outdoor wear" (sometimes worn indoors), which was draped around the body and frequently displayed social distinctions; and "indoor garments" (sometimes worn outdoors), which were worn underneath outdoor clothes and usually consisted of individual pieces stitched together. Regarding the importance of the right outdoor wear, Roman citizens, city dwellers in particular, were ever conscious of their social status and concerned about their appearance in public. Proper and becoming clothes, hairstyles, makeup, and jewelry were a must for members of the upper classes, as well as for those of lesser means trying to get ahead or make a favorable impression. For example, clients, no matter how poor, always made

sure to be well dressed and neatly groomed when visiting their patrons, even if doing so meant going into debt. Juvenal joked in one of his satires about people in Rome dressing above their means and how many seemed to live in a state of "showy poverty." And the humorist Martial described a wealthy dinner host who was so clothes-conscious that he changed his outfit eleven times during a single banquet.

The most important and fashionable article of outdoor clothing for men was the toga, the garment that most clearly identified a person as a citizen. (In fact, in early republican times, only citizens were allowed to wear it, a restriction that was later relaxed.) It consisted of an oblong piece of cloth, about nineteen feet long, wrapped around the body to create various folds and drapes. It is interesting to note that throughout Rome's history many people complained about wearing the toga because it was impractical, not warm enough in winter, and too warm in summer, restricted body movements, and left only one arm free (the other had to support the garment's main drape). But reverence for tradition won out, and the toga, which symbolized the peaceful citizen (as opposed to the soldier in his armor) remained the outdoor garment of choice for many Romans throughout the Republic and Empire. Different kinds of togas denoted social or political rank or status. An average citizen wore the plain off-white or brown *toga alba* (pure white being reserved for political candidates to make them stand out in a crowd); senators and other high officials the *toga praetexta,* which featured a purple border (purple being the traditional color of royalty in ancient times); a triumphing general the all-purple, gold-trimmed *toga picta*; and mourners attending a funeral the black *toga pulla.* In the early Republic, women also wore the toga for formal wear; but over time they adopted instead an outer cloak called the *palla,* which could be draped in many ways, including over the head, and came in numerous colors.

The most common indoor, or casual, garment was the simple tunic (worn both indoors and outdoors, depending on the occasion or one's social status), which was often worn under the toga. The tunic was made from two rectangular pieces of cloth stitched up the sides, with holes cut for the head and arms. Men and women alike wore it knee-length; many women wore an ankle-length dress, the *stola,* over it. Rich women wore *stolae* of silk or other fine fabric, while ordinary women settled for linen or wool. For undergarments, men wore a wool or linen loincloth held in place by a belt. (The custom was to cinch one's belt tight, for a loose belt or no belt at all was seen as a sign of indecency or moral laxity.) Women also wore loincloths, and also cloth bras and corsets, under their outer clothes.

In addition to these basic types of clothes, people of both genders and all ages also wore cloaks, capes, scarves, hoods, headbands, and hats when fashion or the weather dictated. Decorative fastening pins called *fibulae* held cloaks, scarves, togas, and other garments in place at the shoulder. In some rural areas, due to various foreign influences, men wore trousers, though mainly in informal settings. And in extremely casual surroundings, such as at the public baths or the beach, men might strip down to their loincloths, while some women wore bikinis almost exactly like those in use today. For footwear, the sandal (*crepida*), which came in a wide variety of shapes and styles, was popular in the warm Mediterranean climate; however, canvas and leather shoes and boots were quite common. Soldiers' and farmworkers' boots often featured soles studded with nails for better traction. **See** grooming.

coinage
For a description of the main kinds of Roman coins, **see** money.

cooking
For the methods the Romans used to prepare food, **see** food and drink.

cosmetics
A Roman woman's application of makeup was part of her grooming routine. **See** grooming.

cremation
For this process of burning dead bodies, **see** burial customs.

denarius
For this common Roman coin, **see** money.

divorce
As in modern society, many Roman marriages ended in divorce (*divortium*). In the first few centuries of the Republic, divorce was fairly rare and always initiated by the husband. Adultery (*adulterium*) was a common reason cited; but later, when women were allowed to initiate divorce, they could not cite adultery as a cause because society viewed it as a given that men could have sexual relations with mistresses, prostitutes, and slaves without fear of social stigma or recrimination.

By the late Republic and early Empire, more liberal social attitudes and the enhanced status and rights of women had made divorce, initiated both by women and men, quite common and also devoid of social stigma. Moreover, no reasons for the breakup had to be given. The woman had the right to have her dowry returned, although in most cases the man retained custody of the children, if any. It appears that divorce became particularly common among the upper classes. Some modern scholars suggest that as many as one-sixth of upper-class unions ended in divorce after less than ten years. In an era in which it was not unusual for a woman, particularly an upper-class one, to marry three or more times, the witty Seneca quipped, "No woman need blush to break off her marriage since the most illustrious ladies have adopted the practice of reckoning the year . . . by [the names of] their husbands. They divorce in order to re-marry. They marry in order to divorce" (*De Beneficiis* 3.16.2). **See** family; marriage.

dowry

For this money or property a woman brought to her marriage, **see** marriage.

education

Those young Romans fortunate enough to receive a formal education were able to unlock the door to the special skills of reading and writing, which for a man might lead to improved social status and financial condition, or perhaps a literary reputation. In the early Republic, education was less formal and consisted mainly of fathers teaching their sons to use weapons, read, or both. From the third century B.C. on, however, a more formal educational system developed. Young boys and girls (age seven to eleven) from families who could afford to do so attended a *ludus,* a private elementary school, which was supported by their parents rather than the state. (Children from most poor families were not able to attend school and usually remained illiterate; in fact, throughout Rome's history a majority of Romans were either partially or completely illiterate.) At a typical elementary school, which consisted of a single rented room, often in the rear of a shop, the teacher (*magister* or *litterator*), taught basic Latin reading and writing skills, and also some simple arithmetic, to about twelve students at a time.

At about the age of eleven, girls usually left school. Some continued their education at home, receiving instruction from

A Roman teacher (center) instructs two male students. Young men of means often prepared for the two most prestigious professions, politics and the law.

their parents or private tutors, but most began preparing for marriage, which most often occurred when they were about fourteen or fifteen. Boys, on the other hand, went on to secondary school. There, under a teacher called a *grammaticus* (who was usually much better educated than an elementary-level instructor), they studied such subjects as geometry, geography, history, and music, and also learned to read and write Greek, since Greek civilization had such a profound influence on all aspects of Roman life. The primary function of secondary school, however, was to prepare young men for the study of rhetoric, the art of persuasive speech and public oratory. This skill was considered absolutely essential for the educated man, especially if he expected to go into law or politics, the two most prestigious professions.

equites

(or equestrians, or knights) They originated as the cavalrymen of the Roman Monarchy. Only well-to-do persons could afford to maintain and train horses, so the equites slowly emerged as a wealthy social class that came to be known as the equestrian order (*ordo equester*). By the mid-Republic, most equites had become businessmen and their opportunities increased significantly after 218 B.C., the year that senators were prohibited from taking part in commercial activities. Banking, tax collection, trade, mine and quarry operation, road building, and army equipment supply were typical fields the equites exploited. Beginning in the second century B.C., they were allowed to join the Senate if the minimum value of their property was four hundred thousand *sesterces,* and many equites came to have social status and influence equal to senators. Also like senators, during the early Empire the equites lost most of their political clout but retained their social importance and influence. By the fourth century, however, the equestrian order had blended into the privileged classes and ceased to be a distinct social group.

exposure

An ancient custom practiced by many ancient societies, exposure consisted of leaving an unwanted newborn infant outside to die. By his power of *patria potestas,* the male head of a family had the right to condemn a baby to this fate, as well as to sell it or have it killed outright (deformed infants were usually drowned, for instance). The reasons for exposure varied, but poverty, the perceived need to limit the number of one's heirs, and the desire to have a son rather than a daughter were perhaps the most common. Regarding the latter, some evidence suggests that female infants were exposed more often than male ones, though this remains inconclusive. Because babies were exposed in public places, childless couples and others sometimes rescued and raised them, so that not all of those exposed died, and foundlings and their subsequent lives and adventures are a frequent theme employed by Plautus and other playwrights. (Some of those babies who were rescued were raised as slaves and later sold.) Thanks to rising demands by Christian leaders, exposure was outlawed in A.D. 374, although some people simply ignored this prohibition. **See** family.

family

The most basic and time-honored Roman social unit was the family (*familia,* or "household"). Most Roman families appear to have been nuclear, consisting of father, mother, and their children and slaves (although some families may have been extended to include grandparents, uncles, aunts, cousins, and/or in-laws). The head of the family was the paterfamilias (plural, patresfamilias), usually the oldest father present. By ancient tradition, he held power and authority known as *patria potestas* over all other members of the household, including of course any slaves or hired workers who lived with the family. This power gave him the right to control all property earned or acquired by these dependents, to regulate and punish them, and even to decide whether a newborn infant should be reared or exposed (left outside to die).

At least these were the powers that early custom and law allowed the paterfamilias. In actual practice, most family heads were not merciless tyrants and cases of fathers throwing their wives or children out or killing them were relatively rare and occurred mostly in Rome's earlier centuries. Over time, new laws set certain restrictions on the *patria potestas;* in any case, calls from a father's relatives, friends, and peers for him to act reasonably tended to restrain him from unusually cruel behavior. According to custom, he was obliged to convene a council of relatives and friends when he was considering punishing his children severely, and in such cases he usually abided by the council's verdict.

By tradition, the materfamilias, the paterfamilias's wife or mother, was also subject to the absolute authority of the male head of household. Though Roman women were considered citizens, like women in other ancient societies they did not enjoy the same rights as male citizens. They could not vote or hold public office, for example (although they could become public priestesses). In the early years of the Republic, Roman men treated their women largely as inferiors, mainly because men saw themselves as more intelligent and competent. As Cicero, writing in the more enlightened and less chauvin-

istic first century B.C., described it: "Our ancestors established the rule that all women, because of their weakness of intellect, should be under the power of guardians." (*For Murena* 12.27) These guardians (*tutelae*) were always men, who controlled the property of their wives, mothers, and daughters and barred them from voting, holding public office, or initiating divorce proceedings.

By Cicero's time, the lot of Roman women had improved considerably and continued to improve in the first two centuries of the Empire. Though they still had no political rights, many women gained the rights to inherit and control their own property, to file for divorce at will, and in most (though certainly not all) households became more men's partners than their servants.

The high degree of love and respect that at least some men came to feel for their wives is illustrated in a letter penned by Pliny the Younger to his wife, Calpurnia, while she was away: "It is incredible how I miss you; such is the tenderness of my affection for you, and so unaccustomed are we to a separation! I lie awake the greatest part of the night in conjuring up your image, and by day . . . my feet carry me of their own accord to your apartment, at those hours I used to visit you; but not finding you there, I return with as much sorrow and disappointment as an excluded lover." (*Letters* 7.5)

Upper-class Roman women, like Calpurnia (about whom we know the most, since the bulk of the surviving evidence is about them rather than poorer women), regularly attended parties and public functions with their husbands and enjoyed a degree of freedom unprecedented in the ancient world. A few women even ventured into roles and occupations usually filled only by men; cases of female doctors, writers, business owners, and even gladiators have been documented.

The children raised by the paterfamilias

and materfamilias were usually born at home with the aid of a midwife (*obstetrix*) and one or more female relatives. The most common custom was for the mother to deliver the child while sitting in an upright position in a special birthing chair. After nine days had passed, a naming ceremony (*lustratio*) took place (assuming, of course, that the father had made the decision to rear the child). Wet nurses were then frequently employed, even among the poorer classes. According to law, children belonged to the father, so mothers did not usually gain custody of them after a divorce. (Illegitimate children could and did take their mother's name, but they had no legal rights.)

Roman children played with many kinds of toys familar to modern children, including dolls (and dollhouses with miniature furniture), tops, hoops, miniature wagons and chariots (the equivalent of today's toy cars and trucks), swings, seesaws, and marbles. Free children often played with the children of the household slaves, and it was not uncommon for the paterfamilias and his wife to form close attachments to these young slaves, as well as to their parents. Long relationships involving mutual love and respect sometimes led to the manumission (freeing) of family slaves. **See** adoption; divorce; education; exposure; marriage; slaves and slavery.

farming

Because Rome had originally begun as a farming society and agriculture remained always the main basis of its economy, urban and rural Romans alike had a strong emotional attachment to country life. As noted scholar Garry Wills memorably puts it, "Romans always had a sharp nostalgia for the fields. Even their worst poets surpass themselves when a landscape is to be described. And all of them associated morality with simplicity, simplicity with the countryside. The city was foul, the country pure" (*Roman Culture*, p. 24). Indeed, Virgil and other Augustan poets captured the perceived virtues of pastoral life in many of their works. "Happy old man!" Virgil wrote. "These lands will still be yours. . . . Here, amid familiar streams . . . you shall court the cooling shade. . . . Under the towering rock, the woodsman's song shall fill the air" (*First Eclogue* 46–56). However, such idyllic views of the fields were largely those of the members of upper classes who did not have to work in them. The harsher reality was that the vast majority of rural people were poor farmers whose lives consisted mainly of long hours, weeks, and years of back-breaking toil for which material rewards were few and meager.

With the help of his wife, children, and sometimes a slave or hired hand if he could afford one, the average farmer grew grains, such as emmer wheat, to make flour for bread, one of the staple foods. Autumn was planting season. Using a crude plow (of wood, sometimes equipped with an iron blade) pulled by an ox, one person broke up the earth, while a second tossed the seeds by hand from a bag hung around the neck. Cultivation and weeding were accomplished mainly by hand, using wooden hoes and spades (the edges of which were sometimes sheathed by metal for better efficiency and durability). Harvest time was April or May, when the workers cut the grain using hooks and sickles having wooden handles and iron blades. (In Gaul and some other areas, a harvesting machine, the *vallus*, consisting of a row of blades mounted on wheels pushed along by a donkey or mule, came into use.) The most common method of threshing the harvested grain (separating it from the stalks and chaff) was to spread it on a stone floor and have donkeys, horses, or other animals trample it. Finally, workers threw the threshed grain into the air (a process called winnowing); the excess chaff blew away and the heavier grain fell back to be collected.

Usually, a farmer sold whatever grain his family did not eat to a *pistor*, a combination of miller and baker who lived in a nearby town. The baker crushed the grain using a millstone, fashioned it into dough, and then baked it in a brick oven heated by charcoal. Archaeologists have excavated many bakeries (*pistrinae*) at Pompeii, which may have had more than thirty such facilities in all. In one, the bakery of Modestus, they found eighty-one loaves of bread still sitting in the oven where the bakers left them when they fled the eruption of Vesuvius in A.D. 79 (the disaster that buried the town with a layer of ash and pumice, which preserved the bakeries and other buildings). Pompeii's bakers had their various specialties; one even made his own brand of dog biscuits from the grain he bought from neighboring farms.

Grains were not the only output of such farms. Farmers also grew vegetables and fruits, including carrots, radishes, cabbage, beans, beets, lentils, peas, onions, grapes, plums, pears, and apricots. These and other crops grew well in the coastal lowlands of Italy and several of Rome's provinces, which benefited from the pleasant Mediterranean climate, consisting of short, mild winters followed by long, hot, and sunny springs and summers. The climate and soil were particularly favorable for growing olives, a crop second in importance only to wheat. Some olives were eaten. Most, however, were pressed to produce olive oil, which the Romans and other peoples used in cooking, as a body lotion, to make perfumes, and as fuel for oil lamps.

Farmers also raised livestock, including goats, chicken, geese, ducks, sheep, and pigs. They slaughtered some of these to eat themselves and sold the surplus. By the mid-Republic, cattle and sheep raising had become important farming industries on a par with grain production in Italy. In many areas, such grazing animals pastured on cleared hillsides in summer and were

This modern representation of a Roman bakery is based on the well-preserved ruins of bakeries in the town of Pompeii.

moved to lowland pastures in fall and winter. Pigs often foraged in mountain forests. An important by-product of raising livestock was the manure these animals produced, which farmers used to enrich their fields. (Residues from olive pressing and wine making were substituted in those regions where manure was scarce.)

Regarding land use, in general the coastal regions of Italy were dedicated to growing grains, fruits, and vegetables (and for animal pasturage), although grain production declined in these areas during the Empire. Olives and grapevines grew on the slopes of the Apennines and nuts in highly elevated forests. The same pattern of land use prevailed in most other parts of Rome's Mediterranean/European realm, with minor local variations. Gaul, Britain, and the northern provinces grew few or no olives, for example; the area now occupied by Lebanon specialized in growing cedar trees (the wood of which was widely valued); and Egypt and other parts of the east grew not only grain, but also the reeds that produced papyrus parchment.

Other patterns and aspects of land use—ownership and the nature of the workforce—changed over the centuries. In the first few centuries of the Republic, many small farmers owned their own land, a typical holding consisting of two to five acres. The image of the honest, frugal, hardworking, self-sufficient small farmer, exemplified by the legendary Cincinnatus, became a model for the good Roman citizen.

Disputes between such small farmers (who were mostly plebs) and the government increased as Rome extended its control over the whole Italian peninsula. Farms and other real estate confiscated from enemies or rebels became public lands (ager publicus) administered by the state. In the last two republican centuries, the state leased huge amounts of this public land to patricians and other wealthy individuals, who turned their shares into large-scale farming estates (latifundia).

Typically encompassing thousands of acres, these estates, utilizing the cheap labor of many slaves, cornered the agricultural market by the early years of the Empire. (They were typically run by hired managers [bailiffs], since most of the owners were absentee landlords who spent much of their time in the city.) There were latifundia in the provinces, too, but they were usually not as large as those in Italy.

In the Empire, the emperor was the largest landowner/farmer of all because he owned numerous imperial estates throughout the realm. As might be expected, increasing numbers of small farmers found it impossible to compete with the large estates, went out of business, and migrated to Rome and other cities in search of work. Many others became poor tenant farmers who worked small portions of the latifundia in exchange for a share of the harvest. Most of what is known about Roman farming comes from treatises on the subject by Cato the Elder, Varro, and Columella.

food and drink

The kinds of food the Romans ate depended on their economic situation and the local customs of the regions in which they lived. Overall, though, the most common diet across the Roman realm, especially in early times, was fairly simple and plain, consisting of bread and porridge made from grains, a few fruits and vegetables, olive oil and wine, and on occasion, for those who could afford it, fish, fowl, pork, and beef. The exception, of course, was the array of richer, more exotic foods consumed by wealthier members of the upper classes, mainly from the first century B.C. on, and particularly at their dinner parties, which could be fairly frequent.

In private houses (domus) and villas, food preparation took place in the kitchen, as it does today. Most cooking was done over an open hearth or brazier, which was equipped with a metal grill or metal stands to hold the pots, pans, and kettles (made of pottery or bronze) and/or a chain above the fire to hang them on. Smoke from the fire escaped through a hole in the roof or a wall. In early republican centuries, bread was baked at home in small brick ovens shaped like domes. But after public bakery shops became common in the second century B.C., more and more city dwellers bought their bread from a baker (*pistor*), while the majority of country folk continued the custom of home baking. In the Empire, many city dwellers lived in tenement apartments that lacked kitchen facilities. They variously cooked on portable grills set up in outside courtyards or at communal hearths somewhere in the tenement block; bought their bread from *pistores;* and ate out at inexpensive snack bars (*thermopolii*).

Meals for the average family began with breakfast (*ientaculum*), although some Romans skipped it. A light meal, it normally consisted of bread or wheat biscuits, either dipped in wine or covered with honey, sometimes along with a little cheese or some olives and/or raisins. In early Roman times, the main meal of the day—dinner (*cena*)—was eaten in the afternoon. However, over time this custom changed, as dinner became an early evening meal and a light lunch, called *prandium,* was added in the late morning or early afternoon. Lunch fare varied, consisting of cold foods such as bread, salads, fruits, and leftovers from yesterday's main meal.

In those households that could afford it, that main meal, the *cena,* was served in three courses, collectively called *ab ovo usque ad malla* ("from the egg to the apples"). The first course, *gustatio* or *pro-mulsis*, featured appetizers such as salads, mushrooms and other raw vegetables, oysters, eggs, and sardines; the second and main course, *prima mensa,* featured cooked vegetables and meats (such as fish, poultry, lamb, wild boar, and pork, the Romans' favorite meat); and the third course, *secunda mensa,* was the dessert, typically consisting of fruit, nuts, and honey cakes and other pastries. It must be emphasized that the majority of Romans and provincials were poor or of minimal means and could not often afford to eat such varied three-course dinners; they enjoyed this sort of fare, if at all, only on holidays, birthdays, and other special occasions. The satirist Juvenal claimed that he rarely ate so well: Even when invited to dinner at a rich man's house, he was served cheap fare while his host kept the best foods for himself, a common custom.

According to Juvenal, one of the dishes his wealthy host consumed was lobster. Some of the many other exotic delicacies served at upper-class banquets included pheasant, ostrich, peacocks and peacock brains, flamingo tongues, and fish livers. The well-to-do and literate could consult cookbooks that suggested imaginative ways of preparing expensive and exotic foods as well as more ordinary fare. A surviving Roman cookbook dating from perhaps the late fourth century A.D. includes, for example, recipes for preparing peacock, ostrich, and pig. One of the simpler recipes is for boiled ham with dried figs and bay leaves. When the ham was almost completely cooked, the chef removed the skin, made little cuts in the meat, and filled these with honey. Then the ham received a coating of a paste made from flour and oil and went back into the oven for a while. Fruit, honey cakes, and cooled wine stirred with spices rounded out the meal.

Speaking of spices, the Romans used several kinds, along with herbs, many of them imported from the far-flung reaches of their realm and some from as far away as India and China. Pliny the Elder provided a long discussion of the origins and characteristics of herbs and spices in his encyclopedic first-century A.D. work, the *Natural History*. Among the many examples he describes are salt, pepper, ginger, cinnamon, balsam, sweet marjoram, myrrh, cassia, frankincense, rue, mint, and parsley.

As custom demanded, banquet guests recline on comfortable couches while slaves scurry to serve them.

bowl called a *crater,* from which they ladled it into goblets; drinking undiluted wine was seen as undignified or even uncivilized. (Drinking milk was also viewed as uncivilized.) Sweetening wine with honey produced a popular drink called *mulsum,* and poor people often drank *posca,* a mixture of water and a low-quality, vinegarlike wine. Beer, an alternative to wine, was popular mainly in the northern provinces.

Regarding dining habits and manners, most Romans sat upright on chairs, stools, and benches to eat their meals as people do today. The exception was at dinner parties, particularly those of the rich, which became common beginning in the late Republic, where the diners reclined on couches. At formal banquets, guests were assigned to such couches according to their social status, those of higher status having the privilege of sitting closer to the host or guest of honor. Most foods were eaten with the fingers (meats and other items having been precut or sliced in the kitchen), although spoons were employed for soup, pudding, and eggs. Dinner guests typically brought their own napkins, in which they might later wrap up their leftovers (the Roman equivalent of a "doggie bag"). In one of his epigrams, Martial humorously described a fellow who shamelessly took home the scraps of other diners as well. And the poet Catullus wrote about someone who filched others' napkins: "While we are relaxed and inattentive, telling jokes and drinking, you are stealing our

Some of these herbs were used to make tangy sauces, one of the most popular being a salty fish sauce called *garum.* (By contrast, *defrutum* was a sweet sauce made by boiling fruit juice until it thickened.)

The main drink for poor and rich people alike was wine, which in wealthy homes was chilled with ice. (Donkey trains shipped ice in from the nearest mountains and people stored it in underground pits until they were ready to use it.) Almost all Romans mixed their wine with water in a large napkins. Do you think this is cute? Well, you're wrong, you ill-mannered fool. It's an ugly and quite vulgar type of behavior" (*Poems* 12). In many homes, and in all wealthy ones, slaves served most or all the courses of a dinner or banquet and cleaned up the mess afterward. **See** farming; houses; slaves and slavery; trade.

freedmen

Manumission, the freeing of slaves, was an important aspect not only of the slavery institution, but also of everyday Roman life, for emancipated slaves occupied numerous crucial social and economic positions. A slave granted liberty (*libertas*) appropriately became known as a freedman (*libertus*) or freedwoman (*liberta;* in English, the term *freedmen* often denotes both men and women). These terms were used in reference to an ex-slave as an individual, while the terms *libertinus* and *libertina* described them more generally as members of a social class. Thus, Tiro, the famous orator Cicero's former slave, could be described either specifically as Cicero's illustrious *libertus*, or more generally as a Roman *libertinus.*

Freedmen had existed in Roman society since early republican times. But their numbers and social prominence were relatively insignificant until masters began freeing some of the masses of slaves taken as war captives in the third and second centuries B.C. After that, *libertini* could be found in nearly every social and occupational niche, often taking jobs freeborn Romans did not want and routinely working alongside both slaves and the freeborn. Manumission became an important means of upward social mobility for slaves, but only up to a point, for most freeborn Romans refused to accept ex-slaves as complete equals, no matter how talented, loyal, or honest they might be.

A Roman slave might achieve freedom in a number of ways, a common one being to buy it with his or her *peculium* (money given to the slave by the master). The price a slave had to pay for manumission no doubt varied widely, but it is likely that the master wanted back at least the amount he had originally paid for the slave. Or the price of freedom might be met by other means than money, as in the case of some masters who manumitted female slaves who had produced a certain number of children (who were automatically the slaves of those masters). Another common way slaves gained their freedom was when kind masters granted it as a reward for years of loyalty and good service. Mutual affection and even genuine feelings of brotherly or fatherly love might also be involved, as in the case of Cicero and Tiro. Other masters manumitted slaves in open recognition of their obvious intellectual and literary talents, for at least a few Romans were genuinely ashamed to keep in servitude people culturally superior to themselves. A slave also became free when his master adopted him.

The standard formal procedure for manumission was for the master and slave to stand before a public magistrate; the master held the slave's head and said words to the effect of "I desire this man (or woman) to be free," then removed his hands, symbolically "letting go" of his legal grasp over the slave; after which, the magistrate touched the slave with his rod (*vindicta*). The freedman then donned the *pilleus,* a felt cap symbolizing his freedom. But perhaps more common were informal methods of manumission. For instance, a master could write a letter declaring his slave free. Or a master could announce a slave's emancipation in front of friends who acted as witnesses (a method called *inter amicos,* literally "among friends").

All of these forms of manumission occurred when the master was still living. On the other hand, a number of masters provided in their wills that when they died some or all of their slaves would become free, a process known as *manumissio testamento.* The motives for choosing this method were sometimes selfish. By announcing beforehand his intentions, a master might hope to instill gratitude in his slaves, who would, presumably, then give him more faithful service in his remaining years. The novelist Petronius poked fun at this common ploy in his *Satyricon* by having the pretentious character Trimalchio (himself a wealthy freedman) announce that he has made such a will. Still, at least some masters chose *manumissio testamento* out of the heartfelt belief that it was the right and generous thing to do for slaves who had given them so many years of hard work and devoted service.

Whether a slave received freedom via the master's will or by some other method, he or she could look forward to some of the benefits enjoyed by freeborn Romans. However, *libertini* did face certain restrictions that made them less free and of a distinctly lower status than the freeborn. First, a freedman was still bound to the former master under the rules of patronage (the master becoming the patron and the freedman the client). One of these rules obligated the freedman to perform certain services (*operae*) for his or her patron for a specified number of days each year. Also, a freedman could not sue his former master; a freedman who attacked and injured a patron might be sentenced to work in the mines; and for committing adultery with the patron's wife, the sentence could be death. Moreover, freedmen had to accept other social restrictions. They could not become senators, hold public office, join the state priesthood, or serve as legionary soldiers or Praetorian guards. And freedmen often had to endure all manner of social inequities, such as sitting in lower seats and eating inferior food at upper-class dinner parties.

The career avenues open to freedmen included managers in the trades and industries, financial dealers, doctors, architects, scholars, teachers, scribes, and secretaries. (Some, especially natives of Greece and Greek-speaking lands, had already been well educated before being enslaved through capture or sale. In many other cases, masters systematically educated household slaves from childhood with the express idea of turning them into tutors, scholars, and secretaries.) Many freedmen, both male and female, also worked alongside slaves and lower-class freeborn Romans in less prestigious professions, such as laborer, gladiator, actor, singer, dancer, and musician. In addition, freedwomen performed as spinners, weavers, and bakery workers, although a few held more responsible or influential positions, such as landlady, moneylender, or shopkeeper.

Public freedmen, especially in the civil services, were frequently the most visible and influential of their class. While they were excluded from holding public office, positions on the staffs of public officials were wide open to them. Once again, education was an important factor, for such jobs usually required reading, writing, and financial skills, as well as knowledge of Greek, all of which *libertini* possessed more often than humble freeborn Romans. Thus, it was not unusual for a freedman on an emperor's or governor's staff to wield considerably more influence and authority than most freeborn civil servants.

Overall, freedmen often imparted much valuable knowledge and culture to their patrons and to society as a whole. These realities show that men and women who had once been slaves played an integral role in Roman life; and that Rome owed a good deal of its success to their contributions. **See** names; patronage; slaves and slavery; trade.

fullers and fulling

After cloth had been woven, it remained unfinished; finishing it—by cleansing, thickening, and dyeing it—was the job of fullers, whose shops could be found in every town. (Thirty-nine sites used by fullers have been excavated at Pompeii, a town with a population of only about twenty thousand.) Typically, the fuller stood holding the cloth in a large vat filled with "fuller's earth," an absorbent clay mixed with ash and urine. He worked the cloth into the fuller's earth, kneading it vigorously. Afterward, he combed the cloth to raise its nap, sometimes bleached it with sulfur fumes, and in some cases dyed it by placing it in a kettle of boiling water and adding the desired colored dye. **See** clothes; spinning and weaving.

funerals

Funerals in Rome were part of a complex collection of beliefs, customs, and rituals surrounding the treatment of the dead. **See** burial customs.

gambling

The Romans had a passion for gambling no less fervent than that of today's lottery players, football bettors, and blackjack devotees. Roman gambling was so prevalent in republican times that laws were passed against it; the penalty for engaging in betting (*sponsiones*), for example, was a fine amounting to four times the value of the stakes. In the Empire, the emperors maintained these prohibitions. However, there were exceptions and loopholes; gambling appears to have been acceptable during the popular Saturnalia festival in December, for instance, and betting on public games such as chariot races and gladiatorial combats was allowed. In any case, laws against gambling were difficult to enforce and likely only rarely invoked. Throughout most of Rome's history, but especially during the Empire, huge amounts of money were wagered on horse and chariot races, dice games, and numerous other games. "When was gambling more frantic than it is today?" Juvenal asked at the beginning of the second century. "Is it not plain lunacy to lose ten thousand on the turn of the dice, yet not have a shirt to give your shivering slave?" (*First Satire* 87–93)

Besides betting on sporting events, the most popular games of chance involved coins, dice (*tesserae*), pebbles, pieces of bone, and other tokens. One common game was "heads or tails" (*capita et navia*), which, like it does today, involved making guesses about the outcomes of coin tosses. In "odd or even" (*par impar*) a player hid some pebbles, nuts, or other tokens in his hand and his opponent had to guess how many he held. A variation of odd or even was *micatio* (still played as *morra* in southern Italy); two players repeatedly raised random numbers of fingers and simultaneously guessed how many until one guessed right and won the wager.

Also extremely popular was knuckle-bones (*tali*), also still played today in many countries. The *tali* were small goat or sheep bones or bronze, ivory, or stone replicas that a player threw (four at a time) into the air and tried to catch on the back of his hand. The number of tokens that landed and also their position determined the score. Roman dice, made of ivory, wood, or stone, were almost exactly like modern dice and were usually thrown three at a time (three sixes being the highest score possible). Dice were also involved in *duodecim scripta,* a game similar to modern backgammon. Another popular pastime that Romans wagered on, *latrunculi,* was a complex war game resembling modern chess. Apparently it was exempt from the antigaming prohibitions because it involved strategy and skill rather than mere chance.

gens

A Roman's *nomen,* usually the second of his three names, denoted his *gens* (plural, *gentes*), or clan. Therefore, Gaius Julius Caesar was a member of the clan of the Julii. Theoretically, a clan was a large social group made up of all the households (*familia*) claiming descent from one common, noble ancestor. The *gentes* were probably originally the handful of aristocratic families whose patresfamilias were the fathers (*patres*) who had formed the advisory board (*senatus,* the forerunner of the Senate) of the Roman kings. By midrepublican times, thanks to increasing social mobility and constant mingling of families through intermarriage, clans had lost much of their social importance. Still, many Romans continued to recognize their clan heritage through their names; clans often held pieces of property common to all of their members; and some clans (or at least representatives from them) met on special occasions, for instance to perform traditional religious rights. **See** family; names.

gladiators

For these popular but low-class public fighters, **see** public games.

glass

Jars, cups, bottles, and other glass vessels had been made in Mesopotamia at least since the mid–second millennium, and by the time Rome was founded, a glass industry existed in northern Syria as well. After Alexander the Great established Alexandria in the 330s B.C., glassmaking skills spread there from Syria and the city soon became the principal center of production for the Mediterranean sphere, including Rome. Subsequently, the industry spread to Rome itself, as well as to the Italian cities of Puteoli and Aquileia, and during the Empire to most of Rome's provinces.

Glass items were at first very expensive because the techniques of making them were at first painstaking and time-consuming. One common method, for ex-

ample, was to form molten (hot liquid) glass around a core of mud or some other material; when the glass cooled, the core was carefully removed. Consistency of shape and thickness were difficult to achieve. In the first century B.C., however, a revolution occurred when someone (probably a Syrian glassmaker) invented the technique of glassblowing. Glass jars, bottles, bowls, perfume flasks, and so forth could now be made faster, larger, and cheaper, and by the first century A.D. glass vessels were common items in Roman homes. Particularly popular in that century was colored glass, made by deliberately adding certain impurities to the molten glass (cobalt for a deep blue color, copper for greenish blues and reds, manganese for pinks and purples.) By the end of the first century, however, clear glass became more popular. At the same time, the techniques of glass cutting and engraving spread far and wide, producing some exquisite artistic effects on glass vessels.

Also in the first century A.D., the Romans invented window glass, which they crafted by casting molten glass on a flat wooden mold. But window glass was fragile and difficult to transport safely, so it re-

These exquisite vases of colored glass, in the British Museum, are some of the many surviving examples of Roman expertise in glassmaking.

mained expensive and never came into general use. (Some rich people used sheets of glass not only for windows but also to enclose alcoves or garden greenhouses, a use that is quite common today.)

grave goods

For these items placed in graves or tombs along with the bodies, **see** burial customs.

grooming

As many people do today, the Romans considered good grooming an essential habit. The term *grooming* is here used to describe the general culture (*cultus*) of the body, including such elements as proper clothes, bathing, hair and beard styles, cosmetics, and perfumes. For the most part, preoccupation with such body culture was a phenomenon of city and town life; country farmers and peasants tended to be more unkempt and less style-conscious (though they seem to have washed regularly). Some of the differences between the urban and rural spheres became clear when country folk visited the city, immediately seeming out of place and sometimes even ridiculous to city dwellers. Describing one such rustic visitor, the poet Horace quipped: "He might awake a smile because his hair is cut in country style, his toga doesn't fit right, and his loose shoe will hardly stay on his foot" (*Odes* 1.3.3).

In general, most Romans, including country folk, bathed, or at least washed, on a regular daily basis, in large degree because washing was an important element of many religious rituals, symbolizing purification. All religious sanctuaries had tubs of water, or even small bathhouses, at their gates for the use of worshipers. And cleanliness was seen as important even when worshiping at the family altar.

For men, the main element of body *cultus,* besides clothes and bathing, was the proper trimming of the hair and beard. Most Roman men apparently wore beards and long hair in the early Republic. In the late Republic and early Empire, however, they maintained short hair and the clean-shaven look (although many men did not shave every day, a few days' growth being acceptable). Shaving, whether at the hands of a barber or oneself, was an unpleasant experience because the Romans did not use soap to soften the whiskers; they used only water, so scratches and cuts were common.

Speaking of the barber (*tonsor*), his profession became so important in the late Republic and early Empire that many wealthy households kept one or more *tonsores* in their permanent employ. The majority of men, who could not afford this luxury, went to their local barbershop (*tonstrina*), of which there were many in Rome and other cities. Such shops served both grooming and social functions, since the patrons exchanged news and gossip and even conducted business while waiting for a trim. They sat on benches and could check their appearance in mirrors on the walls when the barber was finished. Some barbers came to specialize in the use of curling irons that gave a few very fashion-conscious men sculptured, "foofed" hairdos, which the poet Martial saw as overdone in young men and downright ridiculous in older men trying to look young. "Will you please," he begged of one of the latter, "confess yourself old, so as after all to appear so? Nothing is more unsightly than a bald head with dressed hair" (*Epigrams* 10.83). During the reign of the emperor Hadrian (early second century A.D.), beards came back in style, although most men still kept their hair short.

Roman women were even more obsessed with grooming than men. In the early Republic women usually wore their long hair up in buns; but later, as they became more socially liberated, they adopted a wide range of styles, including curled and foofed hairdos not unlike those popular with some men. Also, both women and men in the Empire sometimes wore wigs made from hair taken from slaves or war captives. (Blond hair from German prisoners became very popular.)

Roman women also wore what most people today would consider a great deal of makeup. They used a chalklike powder or sometimes white lead to make their complexions pale, which was considered stylish, painted their lips and cheeks red, and lined their eyes and eyebrows with black *stibium,* powdered antimony mixed with water. Martial poked fun at one woman's painted, artificial look, saying, "Your hair [a wig] is at the hairdresser's; you . . . sleep tucked away in a hundred cosmetics boxes . . . [and] wink at men under an eyebrow which you took out of a drawer" (*Epigrams* 9.37). Indeed, the makeup table of a typical middle-class or wealthy woman was crammed with razors, brushes, hairnets, wigs, and jars of creams, pastes, oils, colored dyes, and perfumes. (Both men and women used perfume to cover body odor, in the same way that people use deodorants today; the Romans also sometimes added a bit of perfume to their wine to sweeten the breath.) In addition, some women carried a "pocket set," or portable grooming kit, usually on a ring attached to their belts when away from home. A typical set contained tweezers, a nail cleaner, an ear cleaner similar to a modern Q-tip, a toothpick, as well as a small mirror and various other makeup items. **See** baths, public; clothing.

guilds

Many of the male workers of the various Roman trades and industries, as well as members of some religious groups, often banded together in local guilds or associations known as *collegia,* or "colleges." These were not trade unions or mutual aid societies; nor did they train apprentices, as did the guilds that developed in medieval times. A Roman guild was instead a free, private association, the members of which

had in common a specific trade or the worship of a certain god. Almost every city and town had one or more guilds. One town, for instance, had an association of weavers and a guild of people who worshiped Hercules. The members of each guild generally lived in the town (or nearby villages and farms) and knew one another.

Roman guilds were essentially clubs that afforded low-income men the opportunity to meet and socialize away from the company of women. The clubs charged dues, which were used to pay for members-only banquets. In the case of funeral guilds (*collegia funeraticia*), the dues also provided needy members with the money to pay for funerals for their loved ones or themselves. Slaves often joined the *collegia* to make sure that they would receive a decent burial when they died.

heating and lighting

For heat, most Roman *insulae* (apartment houses), *domus* (townhouses), and villas utilized portable braziers (open metal containers in which charcoal was burned). Some extra warmth also radiated from the kitchen hearth (if any). A few well-to-do homes, most notably *domus* and villas in regions that grew cold in the winter (as well as bathhouses and sections of palaces), had a more complex heating system known as a hypocaust, probably invented by businessman Gaius Sergius Orata circa 100 B.C. In the most common version of the system, the house was built over a shallow cellar and supported by brick or concrete piers (*pilae*) two to three feet high. Brick channels connected the cellar to a furnace located away from the house. Warm air circulated from the furnace through the channels and gently heated the ground floor, which was made of concrete, a material that retained heat well. In some more elaborate versions, warm air also circulated into hollow spaces in some of the walls. The main reason that the use of the hypocaust, a fairly effective ancient version of central heating, was not more widespread was the considerable cost of construction, fuel, operation, and maintenance (the latter two accomplished by slaves).

For light, people used wax or tallow candles (*candelae*), torches (*faces*), and lamps (*lucernae*). In early Roman times, candles, resting in candleholders (*candelabrae*) were the chief indoor lighting; while torches, made from dry wood soaked in oil or smeared with pitch, were used outside to light walkways and streets. From the late Republic on, lamps that burned olive oil, melted grease, or fish oil came mostly to replace candles. They were usually made of pottery, but bronze, lead, glass, gold, silver, and even stone versions were also used. Such lamps came in many forms, some fashioned to rest on tables, others to hang from the ceiling, and still others to sit atop tall bronze stands (still called *candelabrae,* even though the candles had been replaced). Most Roman lamps were beautifully crafted, even the cheapest versions often displaying graceful proportions. **See** houses.

houses

The size, style, and features of Roman homes varied considerably according to the wealth and social status of the owners or renters. Most farmers, whether independent or tenant, were poor and lived in humble dwellings with few comforts. Their poor counterparts in the cities usually dwelled in crowded rented apartments in apartment blocks (*insulae*) that were usually (though certainly not always) also spare of comforts and conveniences. By contrast, the well-to-do resided both in their often spacious and well-decorated urban townhouses (*domus*) and the comfortable country villas (*villae*) they escaped to from time to time. Because of the stark differences between rich and poor homes, their occupants' cooking, eating, and sanitary habits often varied considerably.

Poor farmhouses were the typical abode of a large proportion of the population of the ancient Mediterranean world. Such dwellings were usually small one-, two-, or three-room cottages or shacks built of stone, wood, or thatch. Most had dirt floors, little furniture, and relied on a central hearth for heating and cooking. The incomes of farm families varied, of course, and a few small farmers were better off than others, so at least some farmhouses were likely larger and more comfortable.

However, a country house that was sufficiently large and comfortable (often beautifully decorated with fine furniture and paintings, sculptures, mosaics, and other artistic touches) was no longer a mere farmhouse. It was a villa, a kind of dwelling that did not become common until the early Empire, and then mainly in the realm's western sphere. In addition to its comfortable and/or elegant interior spaces, a villa also typically had well-tended gardens, often featuring fountains and statues. It was also frequently the headquarters of a farming estate that was almost completely self-sufficient (having its own mill, bakery, olive presses, barns, chicken coops, beehives, bathhouse, hypocausts, and so on). Farming villas were of various styles, the most common being the "peristyle" villa, which was built around an inner courtyard or garden and surrounded by a colonnaded (column-lined) porch.

Also following the peristyle model to one degree or another were many of the wealthy seaside villas (*villae maritimae*), which were not usually part of farm complexes. Most often they were used as retreats by rich Romans, sometimes including the emperors themselves. The famous letter writer Pliny the Younger had such a villa about seventeen miles from Rome on the coast near Ostia, a home he described in a letter to a friend as "large enough for my needs, but not expensive to maintain" (*Letters* 2.17). This and other such remarks suggest that his was a rather modest villa for a wealthy Roman notable. Yet in the same letter he went on to describe his foyer, four dining rooms, two drawing rooms, parlor, library, at least five bedrooms, four bathing rooms, servants' quarters, an adjoining cottage with study and bedroom, a wide terrace with gardens, and a tennis court!

Moreover, Pliny's was not the only fine residence in what was clearly a fashionable resort area. He mentioned another villa located between his house and the nearest village. And his breathtaking view of the shoreline took in other, even larger villas belonging to members of the privileged classes. "The whole coast is beautifully diversified," he added, "by the adjoining or detached villas that spread along it, which whether you are traveling along the sea or the shore, give the visual effect of a series of little towns" (*Letters* 2.17).

Pliny's pleasant seaside retreat represented a world of comfort and solitude that most city dwellers could only dream about and envy. In early Roman times, most of the inhabitants of cities lived in small houses and shacks similar to farmhouses. But that changed as the cities grew. By the late Republic, the majority of Rome's inhabitants lived in

apartments in tenement blocks, an arrangement that continued to the end of the Empire. (A surviving fourth-century A.D. public record lists 46,602 *insulae* in Rome, compared with only 1,797 private *domus*.) However, a few residents of *insulae* were well-to-do. They lived in larger, more costly ground-floor apartments, which were made of stone and therefore sturdier and safer than the upper floors, which were often constructed of wood and mud brick.

The front side of a typical *insula* was perhaps 250 to 350 feet wide and housed rows of small shops, taverns, and snack bars on its ground floor (in addition to a few large apartments). Each of the upper floors probably had about five to ten individual one- or two-room apartments, called *cenaculae*. Most *insulae* were at least three to five stories high. The poet Martial lived for a while on the third floor of one near the Quirinal hill and mentioned neighbors who had to climb far more stairs than he did. Some evidence suggests that tenement blocks rising six and seven stories were not uncommon.

*This reconstruction of a street scene in ancient Rome features several run-down apartment blocks (*insulae*), where most urban Romans lived.*

And the tallest of all, the famous Insula of Felicula, erected perhaps in the second century A.D., was very likely ten or more stories high, making it the skyscraper of its day.

Not surprisingly, lacking the steel skeletons used in constructing large buildings today, the most massive *insulae* carried too large a load and sometimes collapsed suddenly, killing and injuring hundreds of residents. "What countryman ever bargained . . . for his house collapsing about his ears?" complained the satirist Juvenal. "Here we live in a city shored up, for the most part, with cheap stays and props. Our landlords paper over the big cracks in the ramshackle construction, reassuring the tenants they can sleep secure, when all the time the building is poised like a house of cards [ready to collapse]" (*Third Satire* 190–99). Because the tenants used oil lamps or candles for lighting and wood-burning braziers for heat, fires were always a deadly hazard. Juvenal asserted that "fires and midnight panics are not . . . uncommon events. By the time the smoke's got up to your third-floor apartment . . . your heroic downstairs neighbor is roaring for water and moving his belongings to safety. If the alarm goes off at ground level, the last to fry will be the attic tenant, way up among the nesting pigeons with nothing but [roofing] tiles between himself and the weather" (*Third Satire* 200–206). (Hoping to reduce the danger of such disasters, Augustus introduced a regulation limiting the height of *insulae* to about fifty-eight feet; one of his successors, Nero, imposed a set of fire safety regulations. The ultimate effectiveness of these measures is unknown.)

The dangers of fire and collapse were not the only drawbacks of living in *insulae*. They had no running water, so residents had to fetch their water from public fountains and carry it up several flights of stairs. And few rooms had toilets with drainage pipes leading to the public sewers, forcing the majority of the residents to use public latrines (*foricae*), available on the ground floors of most tenement blocks. These had rows of toilets without dividers or privacy; those who preferred the privacy of home eliminated their wastes into chamber pots (*lasani*). They then emptied these into vats under stairwells or, if the neighbors objected to this practice, dumped them into the streets. Juvenal complained about the dangers of these foul missiles (as well as roofing tiles and flower pots) falling on passersby, joking, "You may well be deemed a fool . . . if you go out to dinner without having made your will" (*Third Satire* 273–75). Another drawback of *insulae* was that most of the apartments lacked the luxury of kitchens. A majority of the urban poor variously used communal cooking facilities located somewhere in their block; or took food that had to be cooked to a local baker (*pistor*), who for a fee tossed it into his oven; or ate cold foods; or ate out at the snack bars (*thermopolii*) found on nearly every block.

Since very few of the poorly built *insulae* have survived intact, little is known about how their apartments were subdivided and their rooms laid out. By contrast, many well-preserved *domus* have been excavated, revealing much about how more well-to-do urban Romans lived. Although these comfortable townhouses varied in size and exact layout, most had the same basic features, often borrowed from earlier Etruscan and Greek models. Roman versions frequently featured a front room or large foyer, called the atrium, where the paterfamilias visited with his clients in the morning and received his dinner guests at night. (The term *atrium* is derived from the Latin word *ater,* meaning "black," a reference to the fact that in Rome's earliest years the atrium was the main living room of a house. The walls of that room were invariably blackened by smoke from the hearth.) The atrium was usually decorated elegantly with ornamented columns, expensive statues, tiled mosaics, and wall paintings. Light entered from a central opening in the roof, the *compluvium,* directly below which rested the *impluvium,* a wide basin that captured and held rainwater. Roman atriums also frequently featured an alcove that held the *lararium,* a small shrine to the family gods and spirits, where members of the household regularly prayed. Sometimes near this altar was a cupboard in which the family kept its *imago,* a lifelike mask of an illustrious ancestor, often complete with wax skin and a wig. Families with many prominent forebears had several such cupboards.

Corridors led away from the atrium to various other rooms. (In two-story *domus*, stairs led upward to another corridor lined with rooms. Stairs might also lead downward, for a few townhouses apparently had cellars.) Among these rooms were several bedrooms (*cubiculi*), including one or two used for servants' quarters; the *tablinum,* a study or storeroom for family records used mainly by the paterfamilias; the kitchen; the dining room (*triclinium*), of which there were sometimes two or three; in some houses a library; often a small bathroom equipped with a toilet that piped wastes into the city sewers (but sometimes without a tub, since most Romans visited the public baths daily); and a walled garden called the *peristylium* (from which the modern word *peristyle* is derived).

The pleasant peristyle was perhaps the most popular part of a Roman home and some families set up their altars and *imago* cupboards there rather than in the atrium. Peristyles were favorite spots in which to relax and enjoy a small slice of nature in the form of the family gardens. The degree to which Romans loved their often elaborate and manicured home gardens is evident in a poem in which Martial brags about the gardens at his home in Spain, to which he re-

turned after living for thirty-five years in Rome: "This latticed shade of vine, my conduits [water pipes] and cascade [artificial waterfall], my roses . . . my vegetables . . . my private tank where tame eels swim, my dovecote [pigeon house] just as white and trim as its own inmates—everything in the small realm in which I'm king was given me by my patroness ͺand friend, Marcella (whom heaven bless)" (*Epigrams* 12.31).

While the atrium and peristyle of a *domus* served mainly ceremonial and recreational functions, the bedrooms, kitchen, and dining room catered to more practical needs. As for their furnishings, most bedrooms and sitting rooms had very little furniture by modern standards (emphasizing instead fine statues, paintings, and mosaics), which gave these chambers an open, airy, and elegant look. The most versatile piece of furniture was the *lectus,* a couch with a padded seat, arm- or headrests, and often pillows and a wooden back, used for sitting, for reclining to eat, and also for sleeping. People also employed various tables, chairs, stools (some of them portable), cupboards, shelves, and storage chests as need and want dictated. In the Empire, sideboards (hutches), in which valuable items were displayed, were introduced, as were bureaus with drawers. The typical kitchen had one or more fairly large tables for food preparation, as well as shelves, cupboards, and storage bins in which amphorae containing wine and olive oil and other containers were stacked. **See** family; farming; food and drink; heating and lighting; snack bars; **also** building materials and techniques; mosaics; painting; sculpture (all Chapter 6).

hunting

In ancient times, hunting was both a means of securing food and a sport. Many country people of poor or average means hunted small game to provide meat for their families. Although a few probably hunted animals for sport, that pastime was normally associated with aristocrats and other well-to-do individuals who could afford horses, hounds, teams of servants to carry supplies and dead game, and so forth.

Indeed, wealthy Romans likely periodically invited friends to their country estates to spend a few days taking part in well-organized hunting parties. Sometimes the hunters pursued their prey on horseback, other times on foot, using nets, nooses, spears, and bows and arrows. In still other instances, there was no actual pursuit; instead the hunters (if those that used this method can legitimately be called that) waited in what they hoped was a strategic spot while servants with dogs drove the animals into nets. Having trapped the animals, the hunters dispatched them using spears and other weapons. Pliny the Younger disapproved of this approach, thinking it dishonest and unsporting, and praised his friend, the emperor Trajan, for tracking his prey through the wilderness like a "real man."

Almost any animal was fair game for Roman hunters, although the most common prey included wild boars, bears, foxes, deer, rabbits, and birds, including geese, ducks, and in some regions pheasants. (Bird hunting is referred to as fowling.) A few ancient writers described or offered advice about hunting specific species. "In hunting the swift race of hares," wrote the early-third-century A.D. poet Oppian (whose real name and place of birth are still disputed by scholars), "the hunter should run ahead and turn them aside from any height of land or rock, and with his craft of hunting should drive them downhill. For when the hares see the men and dogs, they dash uphill, since they know that their front legs are shorter than their rear ones. Therefore hares do well on hills, but a man on horseback has trouble" (*On Hunting* 4.425–432).

Hunting expeditions of the upper-class elite became especially popular in the fourth century A.D., an era in which a small number of Roman notables amassed truly enormous fortunes. One of these men, the Roman politician and orator Quintus Aurelius Symmachus, who owned nineteen houses and estates scattered throughout Italy, told a young friend:

> I am delighted that your hunting has been so successful, that you can honor the gods and gratify your friends—the gods by nailing up antlers of stags and fangs of wild boars on the walls of their temples, your friends by sending them presents of game. . . . This is the right occupation for men of your age. Young men should relax from their studies not in dicing, playing ball, or trundling a hoop, but in exhausting spirited activity and in the enjoyment of exercising courage in a way that can do no harm. I shall encourage my boy to hunt as soon as he is old enough. (*Letters* 5.68)

hypocaust

For this system that heated the floors and walls of bathhouses and some well-to-do homes, **see** heating and lighting.

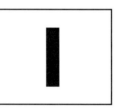

industry

As applied to life in the ancient world, the term *industry* refers to growing, gathering, or manufacturing basic commodities and materials. **See** farming; freedmen; fullers and fulling; glass; metalworking; mining; money; quarrying; slaves and slavery; spinning and weaving; trade; **also** building materials and techniques; pottery (both Chapter 6).

inhumation

For this process of burying the remains of the dead, **see** burial customs.

insulae

For these large apartment blocks found in cities, **see** houses.

iron

The strongest metal known to the Romans. **See** metalworking.

jewelry

Both Roman men and women wore jewelry, the main kind for men being rings. They were usually made of iron (although some men came to wear gold rings) and used for imprinting one's seal in wax. Good taste dictated wearing only one ring at a time, but a few more ostentatious fellows wore several, in extreme cases one or more on each finger. Roman women apparently had a passionate fondness for jewelry of all types. In the early Republic, their use of jewelry was more modest, partly because social customs tended to be more conservative and austere; also, precious metals and gems were less common and only upper-class women were allowed to wear gold rings. In later republican times, however, when Rome absorbed the Greek east, more liberal attitudes and styles and the ready availability of precious metals and gems made the wearing of a wide range of jewelry a must for the fashionable Roman woman.

Then, as now, the most common types of jewelry included gold chains, bracelets, and anklets; strings of pearls; gold or silver rings inset with precious gem; earrings of gold, silver, bronze, pearl, and emerald; and decorative hair pins, brooches (*fibulae*), medallions, and cameos (made by carving a face or other subject in relief on the surface of a gem or small stone). The richest women owned priceless collections of jewelry; according to the encyclopedist Pliny the Elder, for example, Lollia Paulina, the emperor Caligula's wife, had a single set of pearls and emeralds (consisting of a necklace, ring, crown, and earrings) worth 40 million *sesterces,* a huge sum. People also commonly dedicated valuable jewelry items to goddesses and adorned their statues with them. By contrast, as still happens today, poorer women had to content themselves largely with jewelry made of nonprecious metals and fake gems fashioned of colored glass. **See** clothing; grooming.

A gold necklace, bracelet (left), and armband, all found in the ruins of Pompeii, illustrate the considerable skills of Roman jewelers.

knights

For these well-to-do, upper-class businessmen, **see** equites.

latifundia

For these large farming estates, **see** farming.

livestock

As is done today, raising animals took place on farms. **See** farming.

ludi

For these popular public games, **see** public games; **also** festivals (Chapter 3).

maps

The Romans used maps, usually created by surveyors, during the Republic, though not much is known about them. Maps were a good deal more common in the Empire, when geographical knowledge was more extensive. There were various names for maps, including *formae, descriptio* (a world map), *itinerarium pictum* (a trip itinerary decorated with pictures), and *mappa* ("cloth," used in late Roman times). Cartography (map making) thrived in the second century A.D., especially among Greek scientists working in Alexandria and elsewhere. The outstanding example was Ptolemy, whose *Geography* remained in use in medieval and early modern times. Ptolemy's geographical information, which was often considerably inaccurate, did not list roads, since his work was not meant as a travelers' aid.

Many such aids did exist, however, since people who traveled the Roman roads, especially those going long distances, needed to know not only these distances but also the locations of thousands of inns, guesthouses, and other facilities. They bought pamphletlike road books called *itineraria* (from which the modern word *itinerary* derives). Each of these road books listed the towns, inns, stables, major sites, and other notable places along a given road or route. A few such road books have survived. One, created in the early fourth century, when Christianity was rising to prominence in the Roman Empire, was apparently intended for use by religious pilgrims; it shows the route from Burdigala (modern Bordeaux), in Gaul, to Jerusalem, in Palestine (the Holy Land). The portion of the itinerary within Gaul itself lists roads totaling about 370 miles and shows thirty posting stations and eleven inns. Also listed are numerous short unspecified detours along the way, which may have been to visit local chapels or the guesthouses of fellow Christians.

Also available were road maps that were quite similar in some ways to modern road guides. One of these has survived in a fashion. A medieval copy of an ancient Roman map, this priceless relic, called the Peutinger Table, was discovered in Germany in the late fifteenth century and now rests in the Library of Vienna, in Austria. The map, measuring thirteen inches wide by twenty-two feet long, shows the Roman Empire broken into its constituent lands and the road systems within each (as well as several lands lying beyond the Empire to the east). The names of towns and cities are shown, as are numbers indicating the distances between them in Roman miles. The map has, in addition, little symbols representing inns, posting stations, and other stopping places, categorized by the extent and quality of the facilities offered, just as in modern guides. One symbol, for example, is a picture of a four-sided building with a courtyard in the middle; apparently it stands for an inn with excellent facilities. A symbol showing a house with a twin-peaked roof, on the other hand, stands for a country inn of average means; a house with a single-peaked roof means a very modest inn; and so forth. (It is important to emphasize that the Peutinger Table is not drawn to scale, as modern maps are. Instead, it is purposely representational, meant simply to indicate which roads and facilities existed in a given area and the number of miles from one road intersection and facility to another.)

There were also coastal maps (*periploi*) for people traveling by sea. The only one that has survived is the Periplus of the Erythraean Sea, created in the first century A.D. by an anonymous Greek merchant. Meant as a guide for ship captains and merchants, it provides information about two trips, one from the Red Sea to India, the other along the coast of eastern Africa. Fragments of other *periploi* have survived.

No Roman wall maps have survived, though descriptions of them by various ancient writers show that they did exist. Perhaps the most prominent example was a large map of the Empire begun by Marcus Agrippa during the reign of his friend, Augustus. Completed after Agrippa's death, it was displayed in the Porticus Vipsania, a beautiful column-lined walkway near Rome's Quirinal hill. Supposedly the map featured a great deal of detail, although Pliny the Elder (in his *Natural History*) claimed that parts of it were inaccurate.

Another large world map was commissioned by the emperor Theodosius II circa 435. **See** trade; **also** roads (Chapter 6).

marriage

Like the family itself, Roman marriage was an ancient and respected social institution, also crucial because it made one's children legitimate in the eyes of the law and the community. Marriage was always monogamous (consisting of one man and one woman), polygamy (multiple spouses) being frowned on. In early Roman times marriage was seen as so serious and sacred that divorce was virtually unknown. The earliest of several different forms of the marriage union was known as *confarreatio*. It consisted of the bride passing from her father's home (and his authority) into the house and power/control (*manus*) of her new husband (so that she became *in manu,* or under his control and protection almost in the same manner as his children were). If she did not originally belong to his clan (*gens*), she entered it on marrying him. This kind of marriage was at first engaged in mainly by patricians, and the ceremony occurred in the presence of Rome's chief priest (*pontifex maximus*), making it sacred. Divorce was not an option.

The early plebeians married, too; but because they were at first not full citizens, the state did not recognize their marriages. These were of two types. The oldest was called *usus*. It consisted of the man and woman living together continuously, perhaps for some customary period of time, and it evidently often did not involve *manus* (in which case the wife technically remained under her father's authority). The other early type of plebeian marriage was *coemptio,* a fictitious "sale" or "freeing" in which a father transferred his daughter and all of her rights to her new husband (and therefore *manus* was taken for granted).

Over the centuries, Roman marriage customs changed considerably. Marriage between patricians and plebeians, for instance, which had been forbidden in the early days, became legal and eventually fairly common. At the same time, marriages involving *manus* became increasingly less common; and by the first century B.C., *usus* was no longer in use, while *confarreatio* and *coemptio* were fairly rare. *Justae nuptiae,* what might be described as a more "regular" kind of marriage (from a modern viewpoint), had become and thereafter remained the norm. Such marriage required the consent of both parties; the groom had to be at least fourteen and the bride twelve (though in practice both were usually older); and it was forbidden to marry close relatives. Marriage between Roman citizens and foreigners (*peregrini*) was allowed. But any children produced were citizens only if the father was; if the father was a foreigner, so were the children. Marriage between free people and freedmen (emancipated slaves) was long illegal; but in the early Empire, Augustus legalized it (although the prohibition remained for senators).

As to the rituals and ceremonies of marriage, the majority of these unions were not based on falling in love, but rather were arranged by parents for political, social, and business reasons. Love was not seen as essential to a good marriage; yet it did exist in some unions, either from the start or perhaps growing over time. And when love *was* the foundation of a relationship, the feelings of mutual attraction, desire, respect, and tenderness were no less profound than those experienced by modern lovers. "Love, let us live as we lived," wrote the fourth-century A.D. poet Ausonius to his beloved wife, "nor lose the little names that were the first night's grace. And never come the day that sees us old, I still your lad, and you my little lass" (*To His Wife* 1–4).

Whether graced by true love or not, Roman weddings were important and festive occasions. Typically, a couple first became

betrothed, or engaged (a custom that was not obligatory), at a meeting in which the parents discussed the bride's dowry (*dos*), the money or property she would bring into the marriage and from which her husband would benefit. An exchange of gifts and rings and the signing of a contract (also not obligatory) took place at this time. On the night before the actual wedding ceremony, the bride offered her childhood clothes and sometimes her toys (if she was still very young) to the family spirits at the altar in her home.

The following day, the groom, his relatives, and the other guests marched in a formal procession to the bride's home, where she waited dressed in a white tunic and often an orange-red veil, with flowers in her hair. (The groom also often wore flowers in his hair.) As the ceremony began, a bridesmaid stepped forward and joined the couple's hands. Commonly, the bride then recited the following words: "When and where you are, Gaius, then and there I am Gaia," meaning, "I will be at your side from now on no matter where you go." The names Gaius and Gaia were used regardless of the real names of the bride and groom, a custom dating back to Rome's dim past when Gaius was a *nomen* (clan name) and not a *praenomen* (personal name). Thus, the words in the ritual symbolized that the bride was now entering the groom's clan (indicating that this custom probably originated in the formal ceremony accompanying *confarreatio* among early Roman citizens).

After these and perhaps other words had been spoken, everyone took part in a bloodless sacrifice to the gods (and/or said a prayer to them). Then there was a feast that went on well into the evening. Finally, everyone joined in another procession, which led the bride, now a wife (*marita*) and the groom, now a husband (*maritus*), to his house, where he carried her over the threshold. A few close family members and friends were invited to follow. Inside, in front of these guests, the husband offered his wife fire and water (a symbolic act welcoming her into his home) and she lit the hearth using a special marriage torch; she then threw the torch toward the guests, who scrambled to catch it, since it was thought to bring good luck. Other feasts might be held in the days that followed. **See** divorce; family.

materfamilias
For this woman who was either the wife or mother of the male head of a Roman household, **see** family.

medicine
The Romans derived most of their medical knowledge from the Greeks (especially the medical writings of the school founded by the fifth-century B.C. Greek physician Hippocrates). However, largely beginning in the second century B.C. the Romans learned to apply that knowledge with the high degree of practical skill and organization that characterized them as a people. The better Roman doctors (*medici*), who tended mainly wealthy people and soldiers, attempted to treat a wide variety of illnesses. Using specialized instruments (of which more than two hundred designs are known), they removed tonsils; repaired hernias and fractured bones; amputated limbs; removed tumors; performed abortions, simple dentistry, and eye operations; and even did rudimentary plastic surgery. A Roman army surgeon's tomb excavated in Germany has yielded a brain surgery kit containing, among other useful instruments, a bronze drill for opening the skull. During such procedures, turpentine, wine, vinegar, and some herbs might provide a small amount of pain relief; however, effective anesthetics were unknown, so operations were very painful and the patient usually had to be held or strapped down.

Roman physicians were especially skilled at making false limbs (perhaps out of necessity, since many Romans soldiers'

limbs were hacked off in battle). In a tomb at Capua (on Italy's western coast), archaeologists have found a skeleton with an unusually well-made artificial leg. Fashioned of wood coated by thin sheets of bronze (held in place by an iron pin), its top was curved in the appropriate shape to hold the end of the person's severed thigh. It was likely originally accompanied by an artificial foot (which has not survived). In general, only well-to-do people could afford false limbs.

It should be noted that only some Roman doctors were highly skilled and that those who were not caused the death of many patients. Also, many quacks continued to advocate traditional folk remedies, including reciting weird incantations and mystical numbers, or having their patients consume "magic" well water, gladiators' blood, human fat, or other ineffective substances. In addition, religious beliefs conditioned many medical decisions. The Romans believed that the gods, especially the god of healing, Aesculapius, had the power to cure people; so doctors often performed complex religious rituals in hopes of helping patients. Those who got well made offerings of thanks to the gods, including small statues fashioned in the shape of whatever body part had been healed.

Despite such questionable practices, an impressive and reasonably effective medical establishment made up of skilled, caring, and dedicated physicians developed in the Roman Empire, thanks in large degree to state-sponsored medical schools started by the emperor Vespasian in the late first century A.D. The early Empire also saw the growth of more accessible health care for people of average means. Rich persons continued, as they had for centuries, to employ their own personal doctors. But the less affluent could visit doctors paid by town councils to provide treatment in rented rooms or their own homes. These municipal doctors were tax exempt. They could accept extra money if offered by patients who could afford it, but they had to treat the poor at no charge. There were also a few female doctors (*medicae*) (medicine was one of the few skilled professions open to women) as well as many female midwives (*obstetrices*). Meanwhile, army doctors regularly treated soldiers in military hospitals, which existed across the Empire.

Concerning advances in medical knowledge, historically speaking the most noteworthy Roman contributions were those of Aulus Cornelius Celsus, who lived from about 25 B.C. to A.D. 50. He had the distinction of being the only widely recognized medical authority Rome ever produced. His large, detailed book *On Medicine* emphasizes the importance of anatomy, diagnosis and prognosis, and the benefits of proper diet, hygiene, and exercise. It also gives a thumbnail history of medicine up to his time. Celsus was, in addition, a humane individual who criticized the dissection of living people (practiced by some Greek researchers in Ptolemaic Egypt in his own time) as a means of furthering medical knowledge. "To dissect the bodies of men while still alive is as cruel as it is needless," he wrote. "[Dissection] of the dead is a necessity for learners, who should know positions and relations [of the body's parts], which the dead body exhibits better than does a living and wounded man. As for the remainder [of medical knowledge], which can only be learned from the living, actual practice will demonstrate it in the course of treating the wounded in a somewhat slower yet much milder way" (*On Medicine* 1.74–75).

Celsus's frequent reference to his Greek predecessors is a clue to the unfortunate fact that his work was not original. To his credit, he was a highly talented writer who effectively summarized existing medical knowledge in masterful Latin prose. Apparently, however, he was not himself a physician, but mainly collected, collated, and translated, albeit very skillfully, the works of eminent physicians, most of them Greeks. As it turned out, following Celsus's death Roman medicine came to owe a greater debt to the contributions of another Greek, Galen, who became the foremost medical practitioner in Rome. **See** Galen (Chapter 1); **and** Aesculapius (Chapter 3).

metalworking

The Romans used metals, including copper, tin, bronze (an alloy, or mixture, of copper and tin), brass (an alloy of copper and zinc), iron, lead, pewter (an alloy of lead and tin), gold, and silver, for a wide range of items, including coins, tools, weapons, armor, cooking pots, tableware, storage containers, jewelry, statues, water pipes, and much more. They extracted most metals from ores (rocks containing traces of metals) using very hot charcoal-burning furnaces that smelted (melted down) and separated the metals. They then poured the separated metals into molds, producing ingots, and shipped the ingots to various cities and manufacturing centers.

This magnificent silver bowl, made by a Roman metalworker, features a veneer of gold in the center.

Bronze was one of the most widely used and most versatile metals in the Roman world and metalworkers used a variety of casting (molding) techniques. The simplest one was to pour smelted bronze into a stone mold, allow it to dry, and then remove the mold. Another, the "lost-wax" method, involved making a wax model of the object desired, then covering it with clay. When fired in an oven, the clay hardened, but the wax melted away; the bronze was poured into the resulting hollow space; and when the metal solidified, the clay was removed.

A more complex method, called hollow-casting, allowed the casting of larger, hollow bronze objects such as busts and statues (solid versions being too expensive and heavy). Metalworkers made a clay core, surrounded it with a wax model of the object desired, then covered the wax with more clay. When fired, the wax melted, leaving a hollow space with the dimensions and details of the original model. They then poured bronze into the hollow and later removed the clay. To make open vessels, such as bowls, workers sometimes used hammers to beat sheets of cold (unsmelted) bronze into shape around a wooden mold. Also, it was not uncommon to decorate bronze objects with enamel (a substance, such as glass, that can be heated up and fused to the surface of metal or another material).

Ironwork was usually accomplished by blacksmiths in forges, which existed in all but the smallest villages. After softening the iron in a furnace, a smith used hammers and other tools to bend, perforate, or otherwise shape it. A vast array of tools, weapons, and other objects were created this way. (Individual blacksmiths were often immortalized in sculpted portraits on their tombstones; one surviving example, from Noricum, a northern province near the Danube River, shows a smith named Nammonius Mussa holding a hammer and pincers and standing beside his wife.)

Precious metals like gold and silver were much softer than iron, so ingots of these metals were often beaten with hammers into thin sheets. Workers then hammered the sheets around molds or cut the sheets into the desired shapes to form various objects (or into thin strips, some of them wirelike, to make chains and earrings). The hammer marks and rough edges were later polished away. Occasionally, gold and silver were smelted and cast in stone molds. **See** mining; money.

mining

One of the largest industries in the Roman world (agriculture being the largest), mining was also crucial because it produced the ores from which essential metals such as copper, tin, lead, gold, and silver were later extracted. (Copper and tin was mainly mixed to form bronze.) Various kinds of mines existed in numerous Roman provinces; but the area of most concentrated mining was the Iberian Peninsula (now Spain and Portugal), which held very large deposits of gold, silver, copper, tin, lead, and iron. Britain had tin and lead mines and produced a little silver; the island of Sardinia also produced tin and lead; and mines in Greece and Asia Minor produced various metals, including gold and silver, although diminishing supplies in these areas in the late first century A.D. increased the importance of the Spanish mines. By the close of that century, Spanish mines were producing some twenty-nine hundred pounds of gold annually.

Roman mines were almost always owned by the state. They were usually operated and exploited by state officials, who in the Empire were procurators working directly under the emperors. Sometimes the state leased a mine to a private contractor to run and exploit; in such situations, the normal share of the profits that contractors had to pay the government was 50 percent. There is also some evidence that contractors had to provide the state a down payment representing part of its annual share before they could even begin extracting ore.

Mine workers were often slaves and criminals condemned to the mines for years or even for life. However, some miners were free laborers who signed contracts to work for a certain period of time. The surviving contract of a freeman named Memmius, dated to A.D. 164 in what is now Romania, says that he agreed to work from May 20 to November 15 of that year for seventy *denarii* (payable in installments), plus board. He also agreed to pay a fine for each day he took off (whether for sickness or other reasons).

As for mining methods, the most common was to dig a vertical shaft to reach a vein of metal, which could sometimes be quite deep. A shaft from a Roman copper mine near Cordoba, Spain, was over 680 feet deep, for example. Lead and silver mines were also often cut very deep. Apparently, the workers sometimes had to climb up and down such a shaft using small hand- and toeholds cut from its walls. But they might also have the benefit of wooden planks hammered into the walls or ropes operated by windlasses to lower themselves.

At the bottom of a shaft, horizontal galleries, usually only about three feet wide, ran off in various directions. Some utilized timber props to shore up the walls and ceilings; all had niches cut into their ceilings on which oil lamps were placed at intervals. The miners used iron picks, chisels, and other tools to chip away the ore, which they carried to the surface in baskets of woven grass suspended across their backs. In some operations they used metal buckets, handed from worker to worker in a human chain. Such mines could be very dangerous for these workers. Noxious fumes were common, often forcing the operators to excavate extra ventilation shafts, and rockfalls and cave-ins killed many. Archaeologists

have found the skeletons of eighteen Roman miners at the bottom of a mine shaft, victims of a rockfall.

In contrast to the deep mines, some mining, including much gold extraction, took place on the surface. This technique required large amounts of water, which was most often brought into the area via aqueducts and stored in rectangular stone tanks. One method was to release a torrent of water across the area to be mined, washing away the lighter material surrounding the heavier ores. Another method involved washing the area with a less forceful, continuous flow of water. **See** metalworking.

mints
For these facilities where coins were made, **see** money.

money
In the late Republic and all through the Empire, the markets of Rome's Mediterranean realm were extremely widespread and diverse, encompassing dozens of different peoples, languages, and native monetary systems. To make trade simple and reliable, and thereby to keep its economy strong and viable, Rome attempted to maintain a currency made up of coins that were recognized, accepted, and of standard value in all the lands it controlled.

The Romans borrowed the idea of money in the form of coins of standard value from the Greeks, who themselves borrowed it from the Lydians (who inhabited central Asia Minor in the early first millennium B.C.). Lydian coins appeared in the seventh century B.C.; in the sixth century B.C. several Greek cities introduced coinages; and the idea soon spread to the Greek cities of southern Italy, which lay in close proximity to the growing Roman city-state.

Still, the Romans were fairly slow to create a coinage of their own. In the Monarchy and early Republic, they mainly used the barter system (exchanging goods for goods). This fact is reflected in the Roman word for money—*pecunia.* It appears to be derived from the word for livestock, *pecus,* which was a common mode of barter. The early Romans also came to use irregular lumps of bronze (*aes rude*), of varying weight and no standard value. In the late 300s B.C., they introduced bars or blocks of bronze, which over time became more uniform in weight (roughly 3.3 modern pounds).

About 289 B.C., Rome's first true coins began to replace these bars. The principal coin, called an *as,* was made of bronze, weighed one Roman pound (about 0.74 of a modern pound), and featured distinctive markings (ships, or heads of gods) on each side. Other coins of lesser value introduced at this time were the *semis* (worth one-half of an *as*), the *triens* (one-third), the *quadrans* (one-quarter), the *sextans* (one-sixth), and the *unica* (one-twelfth). In 269 B.C., the first silver coin, the *didrachm,* appeared, but this was quickly supplanted by the *denarius* (about 211 B.C.), which remained Rome's principal silver coin for many centuries. Another important silver coin was the *sestertius,* worth one-quarter of a *denarius.* Thereafter, the Romans commonly expressed the value of an item by saying that it was worth so many *sestertii* (or

sesterces). Also introduced in the late third century B.C. was the first gold Roman coin, the *aureus,* which over the next two centuries had various weights and values. Near the end of the Republic, Julius Caesar contributed to the continuing evolution of money by becoming the first person to put his own likeness (rather than that of a god) on a Roman coin.

In the Empire, production of coins was very widespread and numerous types and denominations were produced from various metals. During his long reign, Augustus standardized the coinage in a new system that prevailed, more or less, until the third century A.D. Each coin bore the head of the emperor on its obverse (front) to signify that it was genuine tender guaranteed by the government. The basic coins in this system (ranging from most to least valuable) were: the *aureus,* minted of about one-quarter ounce of gold; the silver *denarius,* worth $^1/_{25}$ of an *aureus;* the bronze (sometimes brass) *sestertius,* equal to one-quarter of a *denarius* ($^1/_{100}$ of an *aureus*); the brass *dupondius,* worth half of a *sestertius* ($^1/_{200}$ of an *aureus*); the copper (sometimes bronze) *as,* worth one-quarter of a *sestertius* ($^1/_{400}$ of an *aureus*); the brass (sometimes bronze) *semis,* worth half an *as* ($^1/_{800}$ of an *aureus*); and the bronze (sometimes copper) *quadrans,* valued at one quarter an *as* ($^1/_{1600}$ of an *aureus*). Modern equivalent values for these coins are difficult or impossible to determine. But some idea of their buying power can be deduced by the fact that the fee for a boy or girl to attend elementary school in the early first century A.D. was about 8 *asses* (or 2 *sesterces*) per month. In that same era a teacher earned probably 15 to 20 *denarii* per month, a soldier about 18 to 25 *denarii,* and an average worker with a small family to support perhaps 20 to 40 *denarii.*

By the late second and early third centuries A.D., bronze coins, including the

A Roman denarius, *minted in 133 B.C., shows the face of a Roman general on the front and his battle elephants on the back.*

sestertius, had become scarce and the silver *denarius* became debased in value as various emperors mixed the silver with bronze. In the reign of Septimius Severus (193–211), for example, this coin was only about 40–50 percent silver. Eventually, the *denarius* became almost completely a bronze coin. In 215, the emperor Caracalla issued a new coin of silver and bronze, the *antoninianus,* which also became increasingly debased in value as the century wore on. (During the chaos of the third-century "anarchy," production of imperial silver currency ceased and the *antoninianus* became a coin of copper with a thin silver coating.) Also during this century of difficulty and confusion for the coinage (as well as for the Empire itself), various imperial usurpers minted their own coins, mainly in Gaul and Britain.

As Augustus had done at the dawn of the Empire, in the 290s A.D., at the start of the Later Empire, Diocletian initiated major currency reform. In general, because of high inflation and the very high cost of precious metals in this period, coins were either reduced in weight or minted in copper with thin coatings of gold or silver (or both). Diocletian issued a gold *aureus;* revived the silver coinage with a *denarius*-like coin called an *argenteus;* and also introduced a large bronze coin, the *follis.* Because of continuing economic problems such as inflation and fluctuating values and standards for money, the *argenteus* was discontinued in 308 and the *follis* had become greatly reduced in size by 318. In 310, trying to contend with such problems, the emperor Constantine I issued a new standard gold coin, the *solidus,* which was lighter and worth less than the *aureus.* Thereafter, various emperors introduced minor revisions of the coinage, but the *solidus* remained its main basis in the west until the sixth century (well after the last western emperor was deposed in 476)

and in the east for several more centuries.

The mints that made these coins were under the control of the Senate during the Republic (specifically a three-man committee called *tresviri monetales*). Most republican coins were minted in Rome or at Capua. In the Empire, the emperors controlled most coinage (although the Senate retained control over some bronze coins and various Greek and other eastern cities were allowed to make their own bronze and copper coins). The capital city remained the site of the main Roman mint at first, supplemented by a mint at Lugdunum (in Gaul); but beginning in the late second century, official mints were established in various other Italian and provincial cities, including Alexandria, Aquileia, Trier, Heraclea, Arles, and Nicomedia. In the west, only the mint in Rome remained in use into the fifth century, while all of those in the east continued to issue coins well after the fall of the western Empire.

The methods of making coins at these mints varied. But the most common method was to smelt bars of the desired metal and pour the liquid metal into small round molds (or onto flat surfaces, as one might pour fixed amounts of pancake batter onto the surface of a griddle). This produced metal blanks—flat, round pieces of the desired size and shape. The blanks were then imprinted on both their obverses and reverses by dies (metal stamps that had been engraved with various designs). A worker heated up a blank in a furnace until its surface was soft, then removed it with tongs, placed it on the top of an anvil, held a die over it, and struck the die with a hammer (the origin of the expression "striking" a coin). In this way, the design of the die was transferred to the coin. **See** metalworking.

munera

For these public combats involving gladiators, **see** public games.

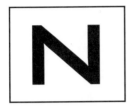

names

Roman names had much more profound meaning and importance than those in modern societies because they denoted social status and family history as well as personal identity. Names evolved from fairly simple forms to much more complex ones, and finally, in the Later Empire, became simple again (although some people, especially in the upper classes, retained longer names). In the Monarchy and early Republic, freemen and -women generally had two names—their *nomen* and *praenomen*. The *nomen* was the name of one's clan (*gens*), which was often a measure of social rank and status. *Nomina* ending in the suffix *-ius* (or variations like *-eius* or *-aius*), such as Fabius, Julius, and Cornelius, were ancient clan names reserved for patricians. Less prestigious *nomina* had endings such as *-acus, -enus,* and *-ca*. The *praenomen,* or first name, identified the individual him- or herself. Principal among the relatively few Roman personal names in general use were Aulus, Appius, Gaius, Gnaeus, Decimus, Lucius, Marcus, Manius, Numerius, Publius, Quintus, Servius, Sextus, Spurius, Titus, Tiberius, and Vibius.

A few Roman men also early used a third name—the *cognomen,* which became much more common in the late Republic and early Empire. The *cognomen* consisted of one and occasionally more extra personal names that at first were like nicknames and reflected personal characteristics; familiar examples include Brutus ("idiot"), Naso ("big-nose"), Pictor ("painter"), Scipio ("stick"), and Rufus ("red-head"). Because these names tended to be handed down from father to son,

they came to be hereditary family names, usually distinguishing individual branches of a clan. The normal order of this sequence of three names (the *tria nomina*) was *praenomen, nomen, cognomen*. Thus, the famous Gaius Julius Caesar was Gaius, of the family of Caesar, in the Julii clan; his equally renowned contemporary, Marcus Tullius Cicero, was Marcus, of the Cicero family, in the Tullii clan. To the frequent frustration of modern historians and students, however, the normal order of these names was often changed for various reasons; official registries of citizens had a different order, for instance, and poets often changed the order to match names to specific rhymes and meters. By late republican times, men with only two names were usually of humble birth. But there were exceptions, a prominent example being Marcus Antonius (Mark Antony), who had no *cognomen*. In common practice, relatives called a man by his *praenomen* at home, friends used either his *nomen* or *cognomen,* and in more formal situations his *praenomen* and *nomen,* or sometimes all three names, were used.

Adding to the complexity and confusion was the frequency of legal adoption in Rome and the name change that went with it. When a man entered another family through adoption, he generally took his adoptive father's three names and added an extra name consisting of his own original *nomen* modified by the suffix *-anus*. Thus, when the young man born Gaius Octavius Caepias (who would later become Augustus, the first Roman emperor) was adopted by Gaius Julius Caesar, he became Gaius Julius Caesar Octavianus. Still another added name, an honorary title called the *cognomen ex virtute,* was often awarded to great statesmen or victorious generals. In this way, after Lucius Aemilius Paulus was adopted by Publius Cornelius Scipio and then distinguished himself as a military commander in

Africa, he became known as Publius Cornelius Scipio Aemilianus "Africanus"!

As for women's names, during the early Republic the custom of giving women two names was discontinued; for several centuries thereafter most young girls went by a feminine form of the father's *nomen,* so that Gaius Julius Caesar's daughter was called Julia and Marcus Tullius Cicero's daughter was known as Tullia. However, later in the Empire, when women's social status increased, the *tria nomina* came into general use by many women. And the same often confusing variations in arrangement prevailed for their names as did those of men in the same period.

The names of slaves and freedmen, except in the early days of the Republic, were no simpler. At first, slaves were called *por,* a slang version of the Latin word *puer,* meaning "boy," and identified with their master's *praenomen.* Thus, Marcipor was "Marcus's boy," Aulipor was "Aulus's boy," and so forth. Later, however, slaves were given individual names, usually of foreign origin, and also the *nomen* and *praenomen* of their masters. Still more complex were freedmen's names, which often consisted of their original slave name, followed by the *nomen* of the former master, then by a *cognomen* assigned at will by the master when freeing the person, and finally by the letter *l,* which stood for *libertus,* the Latin word for freedman. In response to Shakespeare's famous question "What's in a name?", during the early Empire Romans of all walks of life, always conscious of and sensitive about family affiliations and the status of their particular rung on the social ladder, would undoubtedly answer "A great deal!"

Toward the end of the western Empire, however, most people came to use just two simple names, usually a personal name followed by a family name (as is common today); or in the case of a man born in a foreign land, a Roman name followed by a foreign one (an example being the military general Flavius Stilicho). The main exception were many members of the upper classes, who tended to retain the *tria nomina.* **See** family.

navigation
Sailing the waters of the Mediterranean Sea was a difficult, risky business for the small wooden ships of Roman merchants. **See** trade.

oil lamps
For these primary means of interior lighting across the Roman world, **see** heating and lighting.

olives and olive oil
To find out how the Romans produced and used these extremely common products, **see** farming; food and drink.

paterfamilias
For the male head of a Roman household, **see** family.

patricians
The members of Rome's privileged class of landowners who made up the aristocracy of early Roman society and remained a prestigious social group throughout the Republic and, to a lesser degree, during the early Empire (since the number of pa-

trician families had considerably declined by that time). The term *patricians* (*patricii*) came from the word *patres,* which denoted the "fathers" of the original leading Roman clans. Over time, the patricians themselves made a distinction between the most ancient and honored clans (the "major clans") and those clans that came into being later (the "minor clans"). At first, patricians could not marry plebeians, who were seen as social inferiors, but that changed as the result of a law passed in 445 B.C.

In early republican times, the patricians held the major share of government power through their control of the Senate and their influence over the voting members of the assemblies. They also exercised virtual control over the state religion, the law courts, and the army (since generals and other high-ranking officers were for a long time mostly patricians). Patricians were also invariably rich, and land was always the basis of their wealth. This tradition was strengthened by the *lex Claudia,* a law passed in 218 B.C., which forbade senators (most of whom were patricians) from taking part in business, which prompted them to invest even more than before in land; many leased large portions of public land (*ager publicus*) on which they (and others) created huge farming estates (*latifundia*).

patronage

One of the most important and ingrained of Roman social institutions was the patronage system, in which the heads of well-to-do families became the patrons (*patroni*) of less-well-off clients (*clientes*). In the Republic, for example, a patrician patron's dependent plebeian clients usually voted as he directed and supported him in other ways in exchange for his financial and legal protection. In addition, freed slaves were expected to become the clients of their former masters. In general, a relatively few rich patrons controlled various aspects of the lives of numerous less-well-off clients. It should be

emphasized, however, that not all clients were lower-class or poor, for the patronage system extended throughout the ranks of Roman society. Though a well-to-do aristocrat had many clients of his own, he, in turn, was client to someone even more wealthy or powerful. The most obvious example was during the Empire, when Rome's highest elite sought and benefited from the emperor's patronage.

A typical Roman patron expected a great deal from his clients. A client not only supported his patron at election time, but also attended court sessions, dinners and banquets, poetry readings, or any other gatherings where the patron's prestige might be enhanced by the show of a loyal following. By the late Republic and early Empire, a poor or middle-class client typically washed, donned fresh clothes, and visited his patron's house in the morning; then the client, often along with several others, might be expected to accompany the patron on some social or business calls. Afterward, the client might be rewarded with a small amount of money or a dinner invitation. Some clients resented these obligations, feeling that they had better things to do with their time. But other clients, especially during the Empire, became parasites who used their associations with their patrons to better their own social positions; the poets Juvenal and Martial frequently mention such hangers-on in their works.

pets

The Romans kept many kinds of pets in their homes, including dogs (the most common Roman pet); cats (which first became common in the first century B.C.); birds (including pigeons, doves, ducks, geese, crows, and quail); and mice (which, according to the poet Horace, were sometimes attached to toy carts and chariots). Most of these remain common pets in modern Western societies. However, some of the pets that regularly had the range of Roman houses are found today mainly in the wild or in zoos. These included snakes, valued not only for their rodent-killing prowess but also as a fertility symbol. A household snake was thought to represent the spirit of the paterfamilias (or the mater-familias if a female snake); therefore killing a pet snake was considered un-lucky, for it might lead to the father's or mother's injury or death. Monkeys were another exotic pet. They were sometimes seen climbing up and through household colonnades; occasionally one escaped and cavorted across city rooftops.

piracy

The danger posed by pirates had been a fact of life in Mediterranean shipping lanes for centuries before Rome seized virtual control of the whole sea by the middle of the second century B.C. Some pirates boarded, robbed, and sometimes sank ships, while others spe-cialized in illegal trade, especially kidnap-ping free persons and selling them into slav-ery. And some of the areas where their main bases were located became notorious havens for pirates. The coast of Illyria (along the eastern shore of the Adriatic Sea) long fea-tured several such havens, and the largest pi-rate havens of all were located on the coast of Cilicia (in southern Asia Minor). The Cilician pirates had as many as one thou-sand ships by the early first century B.C. and posed an increasing threat to merchant ship-ping and coastal communities in the eastern Mediterranean.

One of the most famous stories about the pirates of this period took place in 75 B.C. While traveling by sea near Greece, the young Julius Caesar was kidnapped and held for ransom for thirty-eight days by a band of pirates. During his stay with them, he fearlessly treated them as inferi-ors and promised that after he was released he would return and punish them. They as-sumed this was an idle threat, which proved a fatal mistake, for after the ransom was paid Caesar did indeed track down, capture, and eventually crucify them.

Pirate kidnappings like that of Caesar continued to increase in number, along with raids on coastal towns in which many people were robbed, raped, and killed. By about 70 B.C., bands of brigands had be-come bold enough to come ashore on Italy's western coast, where they began robbing and burning houses and mugging and seizing travelers on the Appian Way, one of Rome's main roads; pirate ships also sank a small group of Roman war-ships and in 69 B.C. sacked the Greek is-land of Delos (an important marketing center), crippling Mediterranean shipping.

That was the last straw for the Romans. In 67 B.C., they assigned to the popular general Pompey the task of ridding the sea lanes of the pirate menace. In an unprece-dented move, the government gave him supreme (though temporary) command of the Mediterranean Sea and all of its coasts to a distance of fifty miles inland. In a lightning campaign of only forty days, Pompey literally swept the sea of pirates, destroying their strongholds and sinking or capturing more than seventeen hundred of their vessels, all without the loss of a sin-gle Roman ship. This amazing achieve-ment virtually eliminated the danger of pi-rates for many years to come, and made Pompey a hero of epic proportions.

Only much later, in the mid–third cen-tury A.D., did piracy again become a sig-nificant problem in Roman waters. From that time on, many of the raiders were Goths and other so-called barbarians from northern and central Europe. **See** trade; **and** Caesar, Gaius Julius; Pompey (both Chapter 1); **also** Cilicia (Chapter 2).

plebeians

The nonaristocratic common people of Roman society. In the early years of the Republic, the plebeians, or plebs, were not full citizens because they were not allowed to hold public office, sue in court, serve in important priesthoods, or become senators. Moreover, plebs were forbidden by law to marry into the privileged patrician class. The only two major areas in which the plebs could show their abilities were commerce and the army.

Not surprisingly, the plebs became increasingly discontented with their lot and in the fifth and fourth centuries B.C. they gained many civil and social rights in a series of social and legal struggles collectively known as the "conflict of the orders" (the official names of the opposing groups were the patrician order and the plebeian order). The struggles began in about 494 B.C., when the plebs pressed their demands for change by going on strike and refusing to serve in the military. Seeing no other choice, the patricians gave in, and the plebs were allowed to establish the People's Assembly (*concilium plebis*) and to elect tribunes of the people, plebeian officials with veto power over the passage of laws and acts formulated by the patricians. Circa 450 B.C., the plebs demanded that the laws be written down, which resulted in the great legal codification known as the Twelve Tables. Soon afterward, they won the right (through passage of a law called the *lex Canuleia*) to marry patricians. In 409 B.C. the first plebeian quaestors were elected and in 366 B.C. the first plebeian consul took office. Through the consulship, plebs gained access to the Senate (since ex-consuls were allowed to be enrolled in that body).

To be sure, these gains did not afford the plebs complete equality. Even the equites (or equestrians), a small class of plebs that through business dealings became rich and respected, never gained the traditional prestige of the patricians, who continued to dominate the government throughout most of the remaining republican years. In the early Empire, when the old republican institutions were dissolved or became essentially powerless, the lot of the plebs once more declined. Thousands migrated into the large cities and became part of the urban "mob," and in the third

century A.D. most plebs became part of the legal and social underclass known as the *humiliores,* whose members received harsher punishments for the same crimes committed by upper-class people. **See** equites; patricians; **also** assemblies; crime and punishment; laws; Senate; tribune, plebeian (all Chapter 4).

postal service

Ancient Rome did not have a universal postal system that served all members of society, a common feature of modern societies. But certain kinds of postal services developed to meet the needs of specific groups. In wartime, army generals dispatched messengers along Rome's ever-expanding road system; in both wartime and peacetime, government officials did the same. This practice was irregular during the Republic, and the couriers were mostly slaves and freedmen (emancipated slaves).

When Octavian (later Augustus, the first Roman emperor) gained control of the realm about 30 B.C., however, he set up a more regular and official system known as the "government post" (*cursus publicus*). As the service developed, his couriers were drawn mostly from the army, especially from units of highly skilled professional scouts (*speculatores*). For the most part, they traveled in horse-drawn carriages. Noted scholar Lionel Casson here describes a carved relief found on the gravestone of one of these couriers:

We see a *reda,* an open four-wheeled carriage, drawn by three horses, two in the yoke and a trace-horse. On the box [carriage frame] is a driver, who, plying the whip, keeps the team stepping smartly along. On a bench behind is the courier, wearing a hooded traveling cloak and holding what seems to be a riding crop. Behind him, facing rearward, is his servant, who sits on the baggage and clutches a lance with a distinctive head, a special insignia of office showing that his master was attached to the staff of the local governor. (*Travel in the Ancient World*, p.183)

Such a courier ordinarily averaged about forty-five miles a day, but he could cover nearly three times that distance per day in an emergency.

To support the couriers, the *cursus publicus* maintained a network of facilities along the main roads. There were posting stations (*mutationes*), relay points where the carriage riders obtained fresh horses and perhaps a new wheel if one had been damaged, at regular intervals. Evidence suggests that the average interval was between seven thousand and twelve thousand paces. Since a Roman pace (*passus,* the distance between a person's outstretched hands) was about five feet, the relay stations were about seven to twelve miles apart. There were also inns (*mansiones*) at regular intervals—usually between twenty and thirty miles—along the main roads, where the couriers, as well as other travelers, could stay overnight. The government did not build these inns; rather, it selected those that were conveniently placed along the route and ordered the owners to lodge official couriers for free. Thus, some of the financial burden for the upkeep of the government post fell on local communities and businessmen.

Much later (in the early third century A.D.), the emperor Septimius Severus added another official transport service, the *cursus clabularis*. Its purpose was to carry provisions for the army overland using the main roads. Because this system required more people (administrators, handlers, drivers, and so on), large wagons and mule trains instead of carriages, and many more relay stations and inns, it was far more complex and expensive to operate than the government post.

As for ordinary people, they had to rely on a very informal and irregular form of postal service, since the *cursus publicus* was reserved for government correspondence (although well-to-do and influential individuals no doubt managed fairly often to get their personal letters into official pouches). Most commonly, travelers along the roads or high seas agreed to carry letters for various people, some of whom they did not know well or even at all. The usual procedure for the letter writer was to find someone who was headed to or near the destination of the letter's recipient. Therefore the majority of people, who could not afford to hire private couriers (another way wealthy people got their mail delivered), had to rely on the kindness of friends or strangers.

public games

Rome's public games, which included gladiatorial combats, the slaughter of wild animals, staged naval battles, and chariot races, constitute one of the most famous aspects of ancient Roman culture. Of these types of games, all but the gladiatorial fights were called *ludi*. Originally they were connected with various religious festivals (in which people sacrificed to the gods and followed up with feasts and sometimes sporting contests or exhibitions), but by the late Republic they had become more secular in nature.

Though chariot races and fights to the death between gladiators existed in the Monarchy and early Republic, they were small in scale and staged infrequently (as well as privately funded in the case of gladiatorial combats). Not until the late Republic and early Empire did these and other spectacles become large-scale institutions sponsored solely by the government. As late as the early first century B.C., many leading Romans frowned on the idea of staging big public shows on a regular basis, blaming such entertainments as promoting public laziness. The Romans already observed many public holidays (at least fifty-seven by the mid–first century

B.C., a number that continued to grow). Because most work was suspended on these days, large numbers of poor urban Romans were idle for significant periods of time. Many senators and other leaders harbored the paranoid fear that the so-called mob, hungry and having too little to occupy its time, might protest, riot, or even rebel. Especially dangerous, in this view, was allowing large numbers of commoners to congregate in one place, which might lead to civil disturbances and the erosion of state authority; consequently the Senate long refused to approve the construction of large, permanent theaters and amphitheaters.

As public games became increasingly popular, these fears proved groundless. Roman leaders found, in fact, that public spectacles, controlled by aristocrats and/or the state, could actually be potent tools for maintaining public order. So they made these games part of a twofold policy. First, the government sponsored regular large-scale distributions of bread and other food-stuffs to the poor. By the late first century A.D., as many as 150,000 urban Romans received such handouts at hundreds of distribution centers located across the capital city. Senators, military generals, and emperors also spent huge sums subsidizing public festivals, shows, and games. This policy of appeasing the masses through both free food and entertainment eventually became known as "bread and circuses" (*panem et circenses*) in reference to a famous sarcastic remark by the satirist Juvenal. "There's only two things that concern the masses," he said, "bread and games" (*Tenth Satire* 79–80).

Next to the chariot races (*ludi circenses*), the most popular of these games were the gladiatorial combats (*munera*) and wild animal fights staged in amphitheaters like Rome's famous Colosseum. The number of holidays on which *munera* were held each year is unclear. Such games were very expensive to produce and likely took place only on special occasions and therefore on an irregular basis. The Romans borrowed the custom of the *munera* from the Etruscans. The Etruscans believed that when an important man died, his spirit required a blood sacrifice to survive in the afterlife (hence the literal translation of *munera*, "offerings" or "obligations" to the dead); so outside these individuals' tombs they staged rituals in which warriors fought to the death. In Rome, the *munera* were at first relatively small, private affairs funded and staged by aristocrats. Over time, however, both they and the general populace came to view these games more as entertainment than funeral ritual and demand grew for making gladiator bouts part of the public games. Julius Caesar was the first leader to stage large-scale public *munera*, presenting 320 pairs of gladiators in 65 B.C.

It was Caesar who also provided a bridge from the older system of training and managing gladiators to the one that prevailed in the Empire. Before his time, a well-to-do individual who wanted to put on a gladiatorial show went to a professional supplier called a *lanista*, who procured and trained the fighters. Desiring to give the state more control over these fights, Caesar built a gladiator school run by senators and other prestigious Romans. Following his lead, his adopted son, Augustus, and the other early emperors soon made staging the *munera* virtually an imperial monopoly. State control and promotion of the games was a crucial factor in the rapid transformation of their "bread and circuses" policy into an ingrained institution.

The gladiators who fought in these games were mostly prisoners, slaves, and criminals who trained long and hard in schools like the one Caesar built, although a few such fighters were paid volunteers. Some of the latter involved themselves to solve financial difficulties, for the winers received generous prize money. Other volunteers were motivated by the physical challenge and appeal of danger, or the prospect of becoming popular idols and sex symbols who could have their pick of pretty young girls.

There were various types and categories of gladiator. Among the four main types that had evolved by the early Empire was the heavily armed Samnite, later called a *hoplomachus* or *secutor.* He carried a sword or a lance, a *scutum* (the rectangular shield used by Roman legionary soldiers), a metal helmet, and protective armor on his right arm and left leg. The Thracian was less elaborately armed: He wielded a curved short sword, the *sica,* and a small round shield, the *parma.* A third kind of gladiator, the *murmillo,* or "fishman" (after the fish-shaped crest on his helmet) was apparently similar to a Samnite, but less heavily armed. A *murmillo* customarily fought still another kind of warrior, the *retiarius,* or "net-man," who wore no armor at all. A *retiarius* attempted to ensnare his opponent in his net (or used the net to trip the other man) and then to stab him with a long, razor-sharp trident (a three-pronged spear).

In addition to the pairings of these main gladiator types, there were a number of special and off-beat types and pairings. These included *equites,* who fought on horseback using lances, swords, and lassoes; the *essedarii,* who confronted each other on chariots; and perhaps the most bizarre of the lot, the *andabatae,* who grappled while blindfolded by massive helmets with no eye-holes. Women gladiators came into vogue under the emperors Nero and Domitian in the late first century A.D. And evidence shows that Domitian sometimes pitted female fighters against male dwarves, as well as against one another.

On the eagerly anticipated day when *munera* were scheduled at the Colosseum or another amphitheater, the gladiators first entered the arena in a colorful parade known as a *pompa.* Then they proceeded

to draw lots, which decided the pairings, and an official inspected their weapons to make sure they were sound and well sharpened. Finally, the gladiators soberly raised their weapons toward the highest-ranking official present (usually either the emperor or *munerarius,* the magistrate in charge of the spectacle) and recited the phrase, "*Morituri te salutamus,*" "We who are about to die salute you!" After that, the first contest began. Having no rules or referees, the combat was invariably desperate and often savage. It often ended with the death of one of the contestants, but some matches were declared a draw. Another outcome was possible when one gladiator went down wounded. He was allowed to raise one finger, a sign of appeal for mercy, after which the emperor or *munerarius* decided his fate, usually in accordance with the crowd's wishes. The traditional consensus among modern historians has been that if the spectators desired a fighter spared, they signaled that desire with a "thumbs-up" gesture; if their choice was death, they indicated it with a "thumbs-down." This may indeed have been the case. However, several experts have offered other intriguing possibilities, such as a thumbs-down (along with the waving of handkerchiefs) as the signal for the victor to drop his sword and spare the loser; and the pressing of the thumb toward the chest (symbolizing a sword through the heart) to call for death.

Ferocious fights between humans and beasts and between beasts and beasts constituted another large-scale arena attraction. Generally termed *venationes,* or "hunts," they were originally minor spectacles presented mainly in early morning before the bulk of spectators had arrived. By the early Empire, however, the hunts had become popular enough to warrant staging them in late afternoon, when more people attended arena shows. The government imported animals from the far reaches of its realm, and often beyond, including tigers, leopards, lions, bulls, elephants, ostriches, and crocodiles. Often they engaged in mortal combat with a "hunter" (*venator;* the term *bestiarius,* or "beast man," may have referred to a lower-status hunter), who wielded a spear, sword, club, bow and arrow, or some other weapon. The gruesome toll of animals butchered in this manner must have been enormous. The record of nine thousand beasts slaughtered during the one hundred days of the emperor Titus's inauguration of the Colosseum in A.D. 80 was surpassed in 107 when the emperor Trajan presented immense spectacles lasting 123 days. At least eleven thousand animals were killed in these games. Yet in what now seems a strange and grotesque juxtaposition of pitiless slaughter and charming frivolity, a hunt (*venatio*) usually concluded with some comic relief in the form of trained animal acts like those in today's circuses.

Meanwhile, interspersed with the periodic slaughter of nearly helpless animals were shows featuring the massacre of *completely* helpless humans. While various kinds of petty criminals might be sentenced to the gladiator schools, many more serious offenders were condemned to outright execution in the arena. This was certainly not sport by any modern definition of the word; yet as an ever-present component of the general spectacle that the Romans viewed as games, it cannot be ignored. The *munerarius* took charge of the condemned men, guaranteeing that each would be killed within a year. Usually at around noon, before the formal gladiatorial bouts began, guards herded the unarmed criminals up onto the arena floor, where some were quickly hacked down by a troop of fully armed gladiators. Others were crucified, and still others tied to stakes, on which they were mangled and

Though now in an advanced state of ruin, the Colosseum, where gladiatorial and wild beast fights took place, remains an awesome symbol and reminder of Rome's glory days.

devoured by half-starved lions, bears, and other beasts.

Criminals (along with war prisoners) also died in staged naval battles known as *naumachia.* In the roles of sailors and soldiers in rival fleets, they fought to the death in full-size ships, usually on lakes or in special basins (also called *naumachia*) dug to accommodate these spectacles. Often, the men were outfitted to represent the participants of famous historical naval battles. Caesar staged a *naumachia* in 46 B.C. And Augustus held one of the most impressive on record in 2 B.C., later bragging:

> I presented to the people an exhibition of a naval battle across the Tiber [River] where a grove of the Caesars now is, having had the site excavated 1,800 feet in length and 1,200 feet in width. In this exhibition thirty beaked ships [i.e., equipped with rams], triremes [ships with three banks of oars] or biremes [with two banks], and in addition a great number of smaller vessels engaged in combat. On board these fleets, exclusive of rowers, there were about 3,000 combatants. (*Res gestae* 23)

Successful gladiators and arena hunters often became very popular with the crowds and had fan followings. But their popularity rarely compared to that of some of the more winning Roman charioteers, who were on a par with today's most famous sports heroes and movie stars. Some charioteers also became wealthy, though most of them began as slaves or poor commoners. Although the owners of the horses received the purse money, they gave their drivers monetary rewards, and successful charioteers eventually gained their freedom (if they started out as slaves) and began receiving hefty percentages of the purse. Thus, it was not uncommon for the more popular drivers to become rich men. The inscription on a monument erected by one charioteer, Calpurnianus, tells how he won 1,127 victories, including

several that paid him forty thousand *sesterces* (about forty times the annual wage of an average Roman soldier) or more. Another popular charioteer, Crescens, began racing at age thirteen and died at age twenty-four, earning over 1.5 million *sesterces* in his short but glorious career.

The chariots driven by these men were of various types, the most common being four-horse versions called *quadrigae.* Two-horse versions were called *bigae.* Less frequently seen, although not rare, were races for chariots with three (*trigae*), six (*seiuges*), eight (*octoiuges*), and even ten (*decemiuges*) horses. Another race staged only occasionally was the *pedibus ad quadrigam,* in which two men stood in the chariot; when the vehicle crossed the finish line, one of them jumped out and sprinted once around the course. There were also *desultorii,* who probably entertained the crowds in the intervals between the chariot races. More an acrobat than a rider, a *desultor* stood on the backs of two horses that were reined together and performed various jumps and tricks.

Supporting the charioteers were various rival racing organizations, or factions (*factiones*), one of the more important social, as well as economic, aspects of the races. A *factio* was a private stable run by a businessman, a *dominus factionis,* who hired out his horses, equipment, and drivers (many of whom were slaves and therefore his property) to the government magistrate who financed and supervised the races. In a way, the *domini factionum* corresponded to modern owners of professional football and other sports teams. They grew rich from collecting not only their rental fees, but also the often considerable prize money for winning races.

Each faction was identified by the color of the tunics its drivers wore. The four traditional colors—the Whites, Reds, Blues, and Greens—were ancient, dating perhaps from the days of the kings. But there were no factions in that early period. The prob-

A modern engraving accurately captures the size and splendor of the Circus Maximus, where the Romans watched horse and chariot races.

able development was first, that the drivers wearing these colors became fan favorites, prompting the perpetuation of loyal fan support for the colors; that over time the rivalry between the four colors became fierce; and later, when actual racing organizations emerged in the early first century A.D., that each fan following came to identify itself with a faction and vice versa. Some scholars suggest that the first two formal stables were the Reds and Whites, followed by the Blues and Greens.

Both the differences and connections between the racing stables and their fans are further complicated by the common misidentification of the term *factiones* with racing partisans. Besides its regular fan following from the general population, each color/faction had a hard-core group of devotees—the partisans. Relatively few in number (perhaps fewer than a thousand for each color in each major city), they formed clubs; sat and loudly cheered together in the circus; also likely socialized together; and sometimes received the financial support of wealthy individuals seeking to bolster the images of their favorite colors. But the partisans usually had no formal connections with the stables and owners themselves. Whether given by partisans or ordinary fans, public allegiance for the factions was often intense and sometimes even fanatical. Later, in the sixth century, rivalry between the Blues and Greens became so fanatical in Constantinople that their supporters sometimes attacked and killed one another. When the emperor Justinian tried to stem the violence by arresting several faction leaders, it touched off a riot that almost destroyed the city.

An exhibition of chariot racing began with a *pompa,* which in many ways resembled the triumph of a Roman general. When the parade ended and it was time for the first race to commence, four drivers (each usually, though not always, representing one of the four traditional colors) underwent a lottery to determine their starting positions. Then the race began. The charioteers had to complete seven full laps (about two and a half miles), during which time they desperately and ruthlessly vied for every possible advantage. Each attempted to maneuver into the inside lane, against the racetrack's central spine (the *euripus*), since the distance of a lap in this position was somewhat shorter than in the outer lanes. Drivers tried to sabotage one another by breaking a rival's wheels or axles or by other nefarious means. The most spectacular result of such on-track warfare was the "shipwreck" (*naufragium*), in which a chariot and its horses crashed into a mass of twisted debris and broken bones. Such suspense, danger, violence, blood spilling, and death were what kept the crowds coming; indeed, these were the principal themes and common features in all of Rome's public games. **See** circuses; drama; theaters and amphitheaters (all Chapter 6).

quarrying

Because the Romans were such prodigious builders, they used tremendous amounts of fine building stone, including marble and travertine (a durable limestone with a creamy-white texture). Both quarrying and transporting such stones were extremely expensive. So most stone was used in the locality where it was quarried, or else quarries were located near the sea or rivers to facilitate transport by ship, which was much easier, faster, and cheaper than over land. Some quarries were owned by the government, as in the case of mines, while others were privately owned. Most of the workers in the quarries were slaves or condemned criminals, for the work was backbreaking and unrelenting.

To separate the stones from the mountainside, the workers first used picks, mallets, and chisels to cut grooves in the stone. Next, they drove wooden wedges into the grooves and saturated them with water. As the wedges absorbed the water, they expanded, forcing the stone to crack, after which the workers used crowbars and other tools to finish freeing the stones. Often, other workers trimmed and dressed the freed stone blocks right at the quarry.

The task of moving these usually extremely heavy blocks down hillsides and across open land to the building site or docks (if they were to be transported a considerable distance) was daunting, to say the least. Gangs of men used levers, ropes, and pulleys to nudge the stones onto wooden sleds and then, using more ropes, painstakingly maneuvered the sleds down the slopes. To help brake the downward momentum of the heaviest stones, the workers set up posts at intervals, each post bearing a block and tackle, out of which ran a rope tied to a sled. Despite such safeguards, accidents did happen; on occasion the posts or ropes gave way, sending a sled plummeting down the hillside. On a flatter surface, the stones usually moved along a road that had been heavily reinforced to support them. The largest blocks required specially made wagons, each with wheels several feet in diameter and drawn by many oxen.

Quarries also produced other commodities, including clay, sand, gravel, chalk, and crushed limestone. The clay was used for the ceramics (pottery) industry; the sand and gravel went into the making of mortar and concrete, two of the chief materials used in Roman construction; and the chalk and limestone were burned in kilns to make lime, also used in making mortar. **See** trade; **also** building materials and techniques (Chapter 6).

sestertius

For the changing composition and value of this common Roman coin, **see** money.

shipping

For the kinds and sizes of Roman merchant ships, **see** trade.

slaves and slavery

Slavery was an institution common to all ancient societies. Yet no single people in human history kept as many slaves or relied as heavily on slave labor as did the ancient Romans, who practiced the institution throughout their long history. Next to the military, slavery was perhaps the largest, most complex, and most far-reaching Roman institution. Indeed, dependence on the cheap labor of slaves pervaded and helped to shape all areas of Roman life, including the home, agriculture, trade and industry, the arts, the law courts, and the government. Members of all classes, even including slaves and freedmen (emancipated slaves), accepted the institution as an inevitable fact of life.

The numbers and nationalities of slaves varied widely in different eras and regions. The degree of Rome's dependence on slavery also varied, depending on the time period and region. The Romans had the most slaves and were most dependent on them between about 200 B.C. and A.D. 200, roughly encompassing the last two centuries of the Republic and the first two centuries of the Empire. Also, throughout Roman history the largest concentration of slaves could always be found in Italy, the Roman heartland. Far fewer slaves were used in Britain, Gaul, Egypt, and other parts of the realm.

Regarding the sources of slaves, in the first few centuries of the Republic, Roman territory was still confined to the Italian peninsula, so almost all Roman slaves were of Italian birth. A few of these early slaves were Romans who had fallen into debt; at the time, a creditor had the right to enslave someone who was unable to repay a loan. Another important early Roman slave source consisted of the captives taken in skirmishes with neighboring Italian peoples. The capture of the Etruscan stronghold of Veii in the early fourth century B.C., for example, supposedly netted Rome some ten thousand captives. Not surprisingly, war became the main slave source, especially after the Romans abolished debt bondage in the late fourth century B.C. At this point Roman society still had relatively few slaves, who were used mainly to supplement the free workforce. A typical slave-owning household probably owned only one or two slaves and many families had none at all.

This situation steadily changed, however, as Rome's conquests and acquisition of new territories accelerated. In the third century B.C., the Romans took huge numbers of captives in the Punic Wars—perhaps 75,000 in the first of the three conflicts alone. By the end of the Second Punic War (201 B.C.), Roman society had become thoroughly dependent on slaves, in large part to fill a growing labor vacuum created by having so many freemen enrolled in the military. In the second and third centuries B.C., war continued to swell Rome's slave ranks as Roman armies defeated the Greek kingdoms of the eastern Mediterranean. Hundreds of thousands of captives from Greece, as well as Asia Minor, Palestine, and other parts of the Near East, flowed back toward Italy, most of them passing through Rome's chief marketplace for eastern slaves, the tiny Greek island of Delos. The situation was similar near the northern and western Roman borders; as many as 150,000 Germanic tribesmen were captured in 101 B.C., perhaps half a million more when Julius Caesar conquered Gaul a few decades later. By the end of republican times, an estimated one-third of Italy's total population of 6 to 7 million consisted of slaves. During these same centuries, piracy created a lucrative black market for slaves, supplementing the supply of war captives.

Other slave sources grew in importance as the Republic gave way to the Empire. In the first two centuries of the Empire (the *Pax Romana*) war and piracy were less common, so ordinary commerce (buying slaves) and domestic slave breeding became the main slave sources. The city of Rome now became one of the great slave markets of the world, as slaves were imported from many of the imperial provinces and also from foreign lands such as Ethiopia, Arabia, and even faraway India. Only in the last two centuries of the Empire did the demand for and numbers of slaves decrease somewhat, although by how much is uncertain. This was apparently due to a significant rise in the number of agricultural serfs (*coloni*), free tenant farmers who worked small plots of land owned by wealthy aristocrats; because the serfs did much of the work formerly done by slaves, fewer slaves were needed.

It is difficult to ascertain the number of slaves per household, partly because precise evidence is lacking and also because such numbers varied widely from one era and household to another. It appears that before the second century B.C. the average was one slave per household, except in the case of the wealthy who could, of course,

afford to keep more. With the large influx of slaves in the last centuries of the Republic, the average number per household sharply increased. Perhaps a safe estimate for the number of slaves in a Roman household of average means between 200 B.C. and A.D. 200 is between two and ten. Members of the upper classes usually owned many more, several hundred apparently being the norm. And a few wealthy Romans had slaves numbering in the thousands. C. Caelius Isidorus, a rich freedman who Pliny the Elder said owned 4,116 slaves, was a well-known example. But when it came to slave-owning, no private individual could compete with the emperors, each of whom typically owned up to twenty thousand slaves!

A great many of the slaves in large households, at least in the early Empire, reached their masters via the auction block. Public slave auctions were supervised by the aediles, who imposed a sales tax on slaves imported into Italy, which meant that the government profited directly from the slave trade. In certain special cases, slaves were sold privately rather than on the open block. These slaves most often included those who were unusually handsome, beautiful, strong, or highly skilled at some craft, or who could read and write. In such sales, the buyer sometimes negotiated with a dealer, either reputable or disreputable, and sometimes transacted the sale directly with a fellow citizen.

As might be expected, these more desirable slaves were the most costly. In general, the prices of slaves varied considerably from one time period to another and also according to their type and perceived quality. In the late third century B.C., an ordinary unskilled slave probably cost from 50 to 150 *denarii* and highly desirable slaves from 2,000 to 6,000 *denarii.* In the Empire, by comparison, unskilled slaves cost about 500 to 600 *denarii* and educated slaves ran from 8,000 to 200,000 *denarii* or more.

Roman slaves came to be differentiated into two main groups—public slaves (*servi publici*) and private slaves (*servi privati*). Of a master's *servi privati*, his household slaves, known as *familia urbana*, especially the *vernae*, those who had been born and raised in his home, remained an integral part of family life. Regarding household slaves, from a slave's point of view living and working in a private household had certain drawbacks, but also certain benefits. On one hand, like all Roman slaves, the household slave had little or no control over his or her own life and fate. A slave was expected first and foremost to obey the master and do whatever work he assigned without complaint. On the other hand, in a society in which all slaves were exploited in this manner, household slaves were usually better treated and enjoyed more privileges and comforts than most other kinds of slaves.

Slaves in a large Roman household performed an extremely wide variety of tasks. Such jobs ranged from the most unskilled and menial, like chambermaid and food server, to the highly skilled and responsible, like accountant and financial manager. In smaller, simpler households there were naturally fewer tasks to perform and the slaves were correspondingly fewer in number and less specialized. In very wealthy Roman households, such as those of the emperors and the richest senators and military generals, the number, variety, and specialized nature of the *familia urbana* could be staggering. Such workers often included silversmiths and goldsmiths, clothes folders, wool weighers, midwives, architects, cup bearers, food tasters, bakers, barbers, weavers, messengers, gardeners, grooms, actors, and musicians, to name only a few.

Besides performing their many and varied duties in and around the master's abode, some household slaves accompanied the master (and/or mistress) whenever he left the house. Displaying such a retinue of attendants was deemed a sign of social status, the larger and showiest being the most prestigious. Roman writers of more average means poked fun at such displays, which they found pompous. The satirist Juvenal ridiculed "that show-off Tongilius, who's such a bore at the baths with his mob of muddy followers . . . who has eight stout Thracian slaves humping the poles of his litter through the Forum, to go shopping" (*Seventh Satire* 28–32).

A high degree of trust, loyalty, and even love sometimes developed between owners and their personal slaves, especially *vernae*. Writing of the sudden death of a young woman from a wealthy family, for instance, Pliny the Younger remarked how much "she loved her nurses, her attendants and her teachers, each one for the service given her" (*Letters* 5.16). There are also accounts of slaves showing extraordinary loyalty and even voluntarily dying for their masters. It may ring strange in modern ears that people could show such love and devotion to those who had enslaved them. This apparent paradox becomes more understandable when one considers the prevailing beliefs of Roman times. First, slavery was universally accepted as a normal part of life, as evidenced by former slaves' regularly and eagerly acquiring slaves of their own. Another common belief was that fate or the gods had willed some people to be masters and others to be slaves; thus, slavery was seen as a misfortune, rather than an evil, and most slaves felt no resentment toward their masters unless they were mistreated.

In fact, household slaves often were grateful to their masters for feeding, clothing, and protecting them and also for certain privileges granted to them by custom. These included the *peculium*, consisting of money or property given to a slave by an owner, which the slave could spend in any way. Evidence shows that more frugal slaves invested part of their *peculii* in valuable assets such as land, houses, livestock, and shops, or bought slaves of their own (the slave of a slave being called a *vicarius*). Some slaves saved enough to buy their freedom. And an exceptional few actually attained considerable wealth.

In contrast with family slaves in town, farm slaves, termed *familia rustica,* often led very different sorts of lives. Most toiled on large farming estates, and ancient writers paint a generally unflattering and bleak picture of their lives. The skill and intelligence of such workers were seen as secondary to their strength and endurance, the jobs they performed were usually menial and monotonous, and they appear to have led more difficult, grayer lives than their counterparts in the city. Therefore, disciplining slaves was often a bigger problem on farms than in the city.

The best job a slave could expect to have on a farm was manager (*vilicus*) for a rich absentee landlord (although some such managers were free tenant farmers). Of the slaves who worked under a slave *vilicus,* one of the most important, both to

him and the estate, was his female companion (*vilica*), who did spinning, weaving, and other traditional women's work and also acted as a nurse for injured farmhands. Other farm slaves drove the oxen that pulled the plows, dressed vines, herded animals, dug irrigation and drainage ditches, pruned trees, cleaned stables, and so on. The owners and managers imposed strict discipline on these slaves. Vineyard workers and others were sometimes chained to punish them for breaking the rules, for example. Other unruly slaves might be thrown into the farm prison (*ergastulum*).

Beyond the self-contained little worlds of Roman households and farms, slaves were involved in nearly all of society's workaday trades, industries, and business concerns. Some were *servi privati,* either serving as assistants, apprentices, or laborers for masters who owned or ran businesses or assigned by absentee owners to run such businesses themselves. Others were *servi publici,* public slaves owned

A farm slave drives a team of oxen at planting time. The lives of farm slaves were generally more difficult and precarious than those of urban household slaves.

and exploited by the Roman state, individual towns, or the emperor. Because many Romans, especially of the upper class, viewed menial and certain other forms of work as disreputable and beneath their dignity, most tradesmen, craftsmen, industrial workers, business functionaries, and even administrators on the staffs of governors and emperors were slaves or freedmen. Some of these positions entailed considerable responsibility and authority. Ironically, therefore, a number of public slaves came to wield more influence than most of the freeborn Romans who saw them as social inferiors.

The most common arrangement in shops, factories, and other private businesses and institutions was that of a freedman (or sometimes a freeborn person) managing a staff composed primarily of slaves. The freedman might own the shop and the slaves or manage them for an absentee owner, most likely his former master. In either case, slaves filled most of the individual occupations and did most of the work. These included barbers, boot- and shoemakers, fullers, brick makers, tailors, jewelers, carpenters, cloth merchants, metalworkers, bakers, food vendors, and numerous others. Moreover, some slaves actually managed shops and other businesses on a full-time basis for their absentee masters. Such a slave bore the title of *institor* (a term describing any person, free or not, appointed by a business owner to manage that business). In the commercial world, slave *institores* had charge of a wide range of enterprises, from shopkeeping and moneylending to buying and selling all manner of merchandise, including slaves.

Meanwhile, public slaves worked in a wide variety of jobs. Some had difficult, dangerous, and/or unsavory occupations, including those of miner, quarryman, and gladiator. More fortunate slaves served on the staffs of state priests, tax collectors, consuls, and town magistrates; built and maintained roads, temples, amphitheaters, aqueducts, and other public structures; oversaw the public markets and the grain supply; and maintained state libraries, mints, treasuries, and financial accounts. In short, public slaves kept the vital apparatus of the Roman realm in motion.

Still, abundant evidence reveals a darker, meaner, more sadistic side to Roman slavery. Inhumane, brutal masters were probably in the minority, but nonetheless existed throughout Roman history. Moreover, even the kindest, most generous masters routinely exploited and disciplined their slaves. Revoking privileges, boxing the ears, and flogging were among the most common forms of discipline, although some masters employed more brutal forms of punishment such as chaining, branding, starving, breaking the ankles, or even castration. Some masters also took advantage of their household slaves' servile position by exploiting them sexually. These facts, combined with the basic inequity and indignity of slavery as an institution, created an undercurrent of fear and tension that ran always just beneath the surface of slaves' everyday lives. Moreover, the slaves were not the only ones who were afraid. Masters' fear of their slaves often matched and sometimes exceeded slaves' fear of their masters. Thus, in the late Republic and early Empire masters were usually very reluctant to allow slaves access to weapons and there was a ban on slaves serving in the army, where they would receive both weapons and combat training.

The atmosphere of mutual fear and the very real threat of violence and death that sometimes pervaded the master-slave relationship, combined with the serious physical and psychological abuse occasionally meted out by masters, was enough to prompt some slaves to attempt escape. However, a runaway slave (*fugitivus*) was usually easily caught. In a society in which nearly everyone accepted the inevitability of slavery, few people, not even most fellow slaves, were likely to aid a *fugitivus,* for he was seen as a thief who had stolen his master's property, namely himself. Masters often offered rewards for capturing and returning runaways or hired special detectives who specialized in catching *fugitivi.* Another factor that made recapture likely was the common habit of branding and/or collaring slaves who often ran away. Usually, the offender had the letter *F,* for *fugitivus,* branded onto the forehead. And the metal collars riveted around slaves' necks often bore inscriptions identifying the owner; over time, the purpose of such collars became so universally understood that many bore the abbreviation "T.M.Q.F.," which stood for *Tene me quia fugio,* "Arrest me since I am a fugitive." The penalties for running away included beatings or even condemnation to the arena or mines, a virtual death sentence.

On rare occasions, runaways banded together and fought back, initiating a full-scale rebellion. The three major Roman insurrections occurred within a span of about seventy years, the first two in Sicily, from circa 135 to 132 B.C. and from 104 to 100 B.C., and the third in Italy, from 73 to 71 B.C. All three failed. The last and most famous was that of Spartacus, who escaped from a gladiator school and forged a formidable slave army. Though he managed to defeat several small Roman armies, the state eventually crushed him and his followers. The lesson of these insurrections, in which a total of over a million slaves died, was clear to the slaves of succeeding generations. Simply put, slave armies were not large, well-trained, or well-armed enough to stand up to the entire Roman military establishment, which was the most formidable in the world.

The massive and entrenched institution of slavery that supported the fabric of Roman civilization eventually died out. This did not occur through abolition, for despite some improvement in the treatment of slaves, especially through imperial legisla-

tion in the second century A.D. and the humane influence of Christianity in the fourth and fifth centuries, the Romans made no attempt to abolish slavery. Nor did slavery end through the replacement of slaves by free wage earners. Instead, a cheap labor force of serfs replaced the cheap labor force of slaves, a gradual process that continued well past the fall of the western Roman Empire in the late fifth century. Ultimately, neither slave rebellions, nor class struggles, nor the triumph of Christianity, nor even the fall of Rome itself killed what had been the largest, most complex slavery institution in history. Instead, in the final analysis, Europe simply outgrew its need for slaves. **See** family; farming; freedmen; mining; names; piracy; public games; **also** Spartacus (Chapter 1).

snack bars

(*thermopolii*) These small cookshops or fast-food restaurants became very popular in Roman towns and cities in the late Republic and early Empire. More than two hundred have been excavated in the small city of Pompeii, so there must have been several thousand of them in Rome. The cooking was done on metal grills over small charcoal fires or by steaming. Recently cooked food stayed warm for a while in ceramic jars. Typical fare in these snack bars included hot sausages and other meats, bread, cheese, figs, dates, nuts, cakes, and wine. **See** food and drink.

spinning and weaving

Spinning (the making of yarn) and weaving (fashioning it into cloth) were traditionally accomplished by women, both slave and free, working at home. Thus, most families not only made their own clothes but also produced the cloth, although this practice declined somewhat beginning in the early Empire, when increasing numbers of people, at least in the upper classes, turned to buying ready-made clothes from shops. Small spinning and weaving shops also appeared in many towns, representing a sort of expanded cottage industry. (Six such shops have been excavated at Pompeii.) Still, spinning and weaving at home continued, either from necessity or out of reverence for tradition. The first emperor, Augustus, for example, insisted on preserving the tradition and wore only homespun cloth at home. His wife, Livia, had a staff of almost twenty people engaged in spinning, weaving, fulling (finishing the cloth), and making clothes.

The principal tools used in spinning were the spindle and distaff. The spindle was a wooden or bone rod about eight inches long that was slightly thicker toward the lower end; attached to it was a whorl, a small weight that acted on a flywheel to keep it spinning. The distaff was a forked stick that held a bundle of fibers. The spinner pulled a few fibers out of the distaff, twisted them together with her fingers, then tied them to the spindle. Grasping the distaff with her left hand, she allowed the spindle to hang and with her right hand set it spinning; as she pulled more fibers from the distaff, the rotating spindle twisted them into a thread of yarn.

Once a sufficient amount of yarn had been spun, it was possible to begin weaving it. The most common loom in use in the Roman world consisted of two vertical pieces of wood connected at the top by a horizontal beam. The weaver hung a row of vertical threads (the warp) from the beam and weighted them at the bottom using stone or baked clay loomweights. Using a rod (heddle), she moved the odd-numbered warp threads backward and forward, working in horizontal threads (the weft) through a gap (shed) in the frame. The warp and weft threads thus intertwined to produce the cloth. The Romans also began using a two-beam vertical loom from an uncertain date. A more complex horizontal loom came into use in the Later Empire (although it appears to have been used mainly in workshops that made special kinds of cloth, like silk). The cloth that emerged from these looms was still unfinished and many people sent it to a fuller's shop to have it thickened and dyed. **See** clothing; fullers and fulling.

toga
For this common formal garment worn by Roman men, **see** clothing.

trade
Throughout Rome's history, land and the life-supporting crops and livestock it produced remained the mainstay of the Mediterranean economy. Yet while farms and villages might achieve self-sufficiency, cities and armies could rarely be fed on what could be grown and raised locally. Large amounts of grain and other foodstuffs, as well as all manner of luxury goods, had to be imported, and that entailed shipping, trade, and commerce. The Romans quickly learned and exploited this concept as they expanded outward from Italy and won dominion over the whole Mediterranean sphere. By the early Empire, a wide variety of foreign trade goods, along with the agricultural and mineral wealth of Greece, Palestine, Egypt, Spain, Gaul, and many other lands, flowed steadily along the sea's liquid highway and into the Roman heartland. Indeed, that highway was the essential link that tied the Mediterranean world together, inducing all the major cities and cultural and trading centers to cluster along its shores.

The incredible breadth and diversity of this Roman trading network is well illustrated by a partial list of typical Italian imports: wheat from Egypt and North Africa; also from Africa, spices, wild animals for the public games, oil for lamps, and ivory and citrus wood for making and decorating fine furniture; from Spain and Gaul, copper pots and pans, pottery dishes, and fine wines; also from Spain, gold, silver, tin, and horses; from Syria, glassware and fine textiles; from Britain, tin, lead, silver, cattle, and oysters; wool from the coasts of Asia Minor; linen and papyrus parchment from Egypt; from Greece, honey for sweetening foods and magnificent statues and paintings; from the Greek islands, fuller's earth for finishing and cleaning clothes; spices, perfumes, and precious stones from faraway India; and silk and spices from even more distant China. (By the third century A.D., Chinese silk was literally worth its weight in gold in Rome.) Roman traders regularly traversed the Indian Ocean, reaching not only India, but occasionally points as far east as Java and Vietnam. Amazed by the concentration of such a rich variety of goods from so many diverse provinces and countries in Rome, the second-century A.D. Greek writer Aelius Aristides remarked, "If one would look at all these things, he must needs behold them either by visiting the entire civilized world or by coming to this city. . . . Here the merchant vessels come carrying these many products from all regions in every season . . . so that the city appears a kind of supermarket of the world" (*Roman Panegyric* 11).

This vast flow of goods into Italy was the largest but not the only aspect of Mediterranean commerce, for Italy exported products, too. Until the end of the first century A.D., Italian cities sold large amounts of ceramics, metal items, and wine to the provinces; in the following century large quantities of fine marble from the quarries at Carrara, in northwestern Italy, were exported far and wide. These and other Italian products were sold within Italy too, of course. Native vineyards, for example, produced more than fifty kinds of famous wines, of which the capital city alone consumed some 25 mil-

lion gallons per year, enough to supply every man, woman, and child, slave or free, with two quarts a week. Other widespread Italian industries that exported to both local and foreign markets included olive oil production, leather tanning, glassmaking, jewelry making, and furniture making.

Not surprisingly, this huge and constant volume of imports and exports made a growing number of traders and businessmen, many of them freedmen, rich. Some joined the ranks of the equestrian class, although many, despite their relative prosperity, received the cold shoulder from older equestrian families and especially from the patricians. (Because most of Rome's upper-class wealth had originally come from land, most patricians looked down on trade and tradesmen.) By the early Empire, traders who handled export/import businesses, either for themselves or as agents for large trading companies, had come to be called *negotiatores*. The term *mercatores* (from which the word *merchant* derived) generally referred to traders, often locally based, who handled specific commodities.

These traders and merchants rarely used Rome's extensive road system to carry bulky items long distances. Overland transport was very slow and consequently very expensive, and the heavier the items being transported, the higher the cost. Long-range trade was facilitated mainly by shipping, therefore. However, traders did have to get some of their goods from the docks in port cities to inland villages and towns and from one inland town to another. Rivers were used extensively for such trade, including the Rhone and Saone in Gaul and the Rhine along the German border; however, where river transport was not practical, the roads carried this sort of trade.

The chief means of commercial land transport was the pack animal, most often the donkey or the mule (a cross between a donkey and a horse). Horses were rarely used this way, partly because they were more expensive to raise and feed than donkeys or mules. (Of the latter, mules were generally preferable because they were stronger than donkeys, the maximum load of a donkey being about 250 pounds and that of a mule being about 450 pounds.) Mules were also generally superior to carts and wagons for transporting goods along the roads, although the use of such wheeled vehicles remained widespread. First, mules were cheaper; and second, they could easily travel along the many secondary country roads that were too narrow for large wagons. For very small loads, human carriers (porters) were also sometimes used. They commonly employed a wooden neck yoke that ran across their shoulders and held a large basket on each end.

As for shipping, which carried the vast bulk of Roman trade, the cargo ships were all wooden sailing vessels. The hulls were covered with pitch, an oily petroleum residue, to keep them watertight, and painted with a mixture of soft wax and colored pigments. Judging from the remains of wrecks recently excavated from the sea bottom, most of these ships were about 60 to 100 feet long, 17 to 30 feet wide, and carried cargoes ranging from 50 to 250 tons. A few cargo ships, notably those that ferried grain from Egypt to Rome for distribution to the urban masses or that lugged heavy stone artifacts, were much larger. In A.D. 40, the emperor Caligula had a stone obelisk (the one that now stands outside of St. Peter's Basilica in Rome) shipped to the capital from Egypt. The boat that hauled it was specially built to carry a burden of 1,300 tons.

The captains who piloted these ships had no instruments to guide them. For navigation, they relied on observations of familiar landmarks; special nautical books that advised the best routes and sailing times; and, particularly, observations of the sun, moon, and stars. Also aiding them were many coastal lighthouses that employed polished metal plates to reflect light generated by bonfires.

Traders and sailors were often away from home for weeks or months at a time. While docking at ports, they stayed in small inns (*tabernae*) with colorful names like "The Wheel," "The Elephant," and "The Rooster," which featured hard, uncomfortable beds but affordable prices. **See** banking; farming; food and drink; freedmen; glass; mining; money; quarrying.

A Roman mosaic shows a large cargo ship in a city's harbor. Such ships criss-crossed the Mediterranean world for centuries, supplying Rome with thousands of trade goods of all kinds.

vigiles

The members of a permanent professional fire-fighting brigade set up in the city of Rome by Augustus about A.D. 6, following one of the many destructive fires that periodically swept parts of the capital. Before this time, fire fighting was a haphazard, unregulated affair; usually, citizens or untrained brigades hastily organized by the government were left to their own devices to put out blazes using water from the closest fountains. The *vigiles* were divided into seven cohorts of five hundred (later one thousand) men each. A tribune commanded each cohort and these seven men reported to a prefect (the *praefectus vigilum*). There were specialists among the firemen; some operated handheld pumps, others wielded grappling hooks, set up bucket relays, used wet sponges to dampen undamaged walls to keep a fire from spreading, and so forth. After Nero instituted fire safety regulations in the 60s A.D., these firemen sometimes inspected tenement blocks and other buildings to make sure the citizens were complying with the law. Some *vigiles* also had a non-fire-fighting role as community policemen who patrolled the dark, dangerous streets of the capital at night. They could arrest muggers and other wrongdoers and turn them over to the office of the Prefect of the City. Other cities and towns eventually set up their own brigades of *vigiles* (though on a smaller scale than those in Rome). **See** Prefect of the City (Chapter 4); aqueducts (Chapter 6); **and** urban cohorts (Chapter 7).

villas

For these comfortable, often spacious country homes, **see** houses.

water distribution

For an explanation of the complex system that supplied Roman city dwellers with water, **see** aqueducts (Chapter 6).

weights and measures

Roman weights and measures are most conveniently subdivided into units of weight, length, area, and capacity. Weight (*pondus*) was based on the Roman pound (*libra*), which was equal to about 11.8 modern ounces (336 grams). (The term *as,* also a monetary unit, was another common term denoting a pound). The Roman pound had twelve ounces (*unciae*). The pound-scale used to weigh various items in the marketplace and elsewhere consisted of two bronze pans suspended from a metal or bone balance arm. One placed the item to be weighed on one pan, then put standardized weights made of iron, lead, or stone on the other pan until they balanced each other. People measured the weight of wheat and other grains by pouring them into and filling up a bronze bucket (*modius*).

Roman units of length were for the most part based on the Roman foot (*pes*), which measured about 11.6 modern inches (296 mm). (A few other differing foot-units existed in various times and places, including one introduced in the third century A.D. that measured 11.5 modern inches.) Usually, the *pes* was divided into twelve Roman inches (*unciae*). Half an inch was called a *semunica;* and a two-foot length was a *dupondius.* When measuring distances along roads, people used the pace (*passus*) and the Roman mile (*mille passus*). The pace was equal to five feet (*pedes*) and 1,000 paces (5,000 feet) made up a mile. (A Roman mile was equivalent to 4,856 modern feet [1,480 m].) Regional measures of land distances included the league (*leuga*), used mainly in Gaul and some northern provinces; it was equal to 1,500 paces, or 1.5 miles. Roman surveyors, by contrast, mostly used a unit called an *actus,* which equaled 120 Roman feet.

The *actus* was also the basis of units of Roman area. A square *actus* (an *actus quadratus*) encompassed 14,400 square Roman feet (about one-third of a modern acre). Two square *actus* made up a *jugerum* (often spelled *iugerum*). One-third of a *jugerum* was a *triens;* two *jugera* equaled a *heredium;* and 100 *heredia* made up a century (*centuria*), comprising about 125 modern acres.

Units of capacity consisted of wet measures (for wine, oil, and other liquids) and dry measures (for grains). The smallest liquid measure, the *cochlear* (or *ligula*), was equivalent to about one-third of a modern fluid ounce. Twenty-four *cochlearia* made up a *hemina;* two *heminae* equaled a *sextarius;* twelve *heminae* were equivalent to a *congius;* and eight *congii* equaled an *amphora* (about 7.2 U.S. gallons). The *amphora* constituted the principal liquid measurement used in trade and commerce, which also utilized pottery containers of the same name. As for dry measures, one *modius* of grain was equivalent to about 2.4 U.S. gallons. A *sextarius* was $\frac{1}{16}$ of a *modius.*

women

For the social status, home life, duties, rights, dress, and habits of Roman women, **see** clothing; divorce; education; family; marriage; names; spinning and weaving.

CHAPTER 6

ARTS, ARCHITECTURE, LITERATURE, AND PHILOSOPHY

Ab urbe condita libri

For this massive history of Rome composed by the first-century B.C. Roman historian Livy, **see** its English title, *History of Rome from Its Foundation.*

actors

For information about the lives and social status of these entertainers, **see** theater and drama.

Aeneid

Composed in Latin between 29 and 19 B.C. by the poet Virgil, this greatest of Roman epic poems tells, in twelve books, the story of Rome's national hero and founder of the Roman race, the Trojan prince Aeneas. The author intended for the work to celebrate Rome's origins and achievements, as well as to glorify the person and accomplishments of his friend Augustus, the first Roman emperor. Virgil had not quite finished the poem when he died in 19 B.C., and his colleagues, Varius Rufus and Plotius Tucca, edited it on his behalf.

The work is notable not only for the skill and nobility of the writing, but also for its unapologetic conception of the Romans as possessors of a divine destiny to rule the world. Virgil portrays all of Roman history as a continuous narrative leading up to a preordained and inevitable outcome—the accession of Augustus, the "child of the Divine," and the advent of the Roman Empire, which will lead the world into a golden age of peace and prosperity. As historian R.H. Barrow puts it, "The most significant movement of history . . . according to Virgil, is the march of the Roman along the road of his destiny to a high civilization; for in that destiny is to be found the valid and permanent interpretation of all [human] movement and all development. . . . The stately *Aeneid* progresses throughout its length to this theme, the universal and the ultimate triumph of the Roman spirit as the highest manifestation of man's powers" (*The Romans,* pp. 85–86).

The story told in the *Aeneid* begins seven years after the fall of the city of Troy (in Asia Minor) at the hands of the Greeks. After a storm destroys some of his ships near the Italian island of Sicily, Aeneas lands at Carthage (in North Africa) and meets its queen, Dido, who falls in love with him. At her request, he tells her about how he escaped the burning Troy carrying his aged father, Anchises, on his back and how they and their companions built some ships. After several years of wandering through the Mediterranean, during which time the travelers encountered various dangers and Anchises died, Aeneas reached Carthage. Soon after relating this story, Aeneas is commanded by the great god Jupiter to leave Carthage. Dido emotionally pleads with him to stay, but the Trojan informs her that he has no choice but go to Italy. There, according to an oracle he had consulted earlier, his destiny awaits him. As he sails away, Dido curses him and his descendants and then takes her own life.

Aeneas lands at Cumae, in southern Italy. A prophet had earlier told him to seek out the Sibyl, a wise woman who could see into the future. When he finds her, she greets him and tells him that he is destined to fight a war in Italy over the right to marry an Italian bride. He then begs her to help him find a way into the underworld so that he might once more see his beloved father. Granting the request, the Sibyl leads Aeneas into the depths and in time they find the spirit of the old man, who offers to show his son the future of the grand and blessed race he will sire. Anchises reveals that Aeneas's immediate offspring will found the city of Alba Longa in the Italian region of Latium and that the line of Alba's noble rulers will lead to Romulus, who himself will establish a city—none other than Rome. Anchises also shows his son glimpses of several great future Romans, including the divine Augustus.

After Aeneas and the Sibyl return from their journey below, the hero travels northward to Latium to fulfill the destiny that has been revealed to him. He meets the local ruler, Latinus, and soon seeks the hand of that king's daughter, Lavinia. But Turnus, prince of a neighboring people called the Rutulians, has already asked for Lavinia's hand and the rivalry over Lavinia soon leads to a terrible war, thus fulfilling the Sibyl's prophecy that Aeneas would fight over an Italian bride. Eventually, Aeneas defeats Turnus, leaving him free to marry Lavinia and with her to create the noble lineage that will lead to the rise of the Romans, who will one day rule all the world. **See** poetry; **also** Aeneas; Virgil (both Chapter 1); **and** Sibyl (Chapter 3).

alphabet

For the derivation and use of the Roman alphabet, **see** Latin and other languages.

amphitheaters

For these large wooden and/or stone arenas in which gladiator and wild animal fights were staged, **see** theaters and amphitheaters.

Annales Maximi

The Romans began to keep these annals, or important historical records, circa 300 B.C. The state high priest (*pontifex maximus*) carved them onto "the tablets of the priests" (*tabulae pontificum*) and put them on public display outside his official residence. At first, the annals consisted mainly of the names of the annually elected leaders and lists of wars, eclipses, and other especially noteworthy events; later they included more historical information. Roman historians did not begin to make systematic use of these records until the late second century B.C., when the so-called old annalists Calpurnius Piso and Cassius Hemina did so. Their contemporary, P. Mucius Scaevola, who served as *pontifex maximus* in 130 B.C., authorized the publication of all former annals in eighty books. Later Roman historians, including the great Livy, consulted these records heavily in their reconstruction of early Roman events and figures.

Annals/Histories

Of these two major works of the Roman historian Tacitus, the *Histories* was composed first, probably from about A.D. 106 to 108. The complete work covered the period 69 to 96, encompassing the reigns of Galba, Otho, Vitellius, Vespasian, Titus, and Domitian; but of the original fourteen books, only the first four and part of the fifth survive. These cover mainly the turbulent "year of the four emperors" and the accession of Vespasian. The *Annals,* written perhaps between 115 and 117, probably originally consisted of sixteen books, covering the period 14 (the year Augustus died) to 68 (the year Nero died); today, most of Books 5 and 6 and all of Books 7 through 10 are missing.

The surviving portions of these works easily establish Tacitus as a historian of consummate skill and penetrating insight. His format is chronological and his style is logical, concise, brisk, and often dramatic, as shown in this description of a political purge initiated by Tiberius:

> Frenzied with bloodshed, the emperor now ordered the execution of all those arrested for complicity with Sejanus. It was a massacre. Without discrimination of sex or age, eminence or obscurity, there they lay, strewn about—or in heaps. Relatives and friends were forbidden to stand by or lament them, or even to gaze for long. Guards surrounded them . . . and escorted the rotting bodies until, dragged into the Tiber, they floated away or grounded— with none to cremate or touch them. Terror had paralyzed human sympathy. (*Annals* 8.6.19)

A number of modern historians, most notably England's Edward Gibbon (author of *The Decline and Fall of the Roman Empire*) have openly admired and attempted to imitate this style. Tacitus also based most of his information on verifiable records and accounts and rarely includes gossip and rumor, making his works largely reliable sources for modern historians. Although he refrains from undue moralizing, he does consider it his duty to expose and criticize the many vices and "evils" of the imperial court and government; and he makes no secret of his pref-

erence for the defunct republican system, even at its worst. **See** Tacitus, Publius Cornelius (Chapter 1).

Appian Way
For this most famous of Roman roads, **see** roads.

aqueducts
Like people in all times and places, the Romans required supplies of freshwater to exist. To meet this need they built their now world-famous system of aqueducts, channels that conveyed large quantities of water to major towns and cities. They did not always have aqueducts, of course, and even when most of the Roman aqueducts were in place (roughly by the late second century A.D.), many towns and most villages still drew their water from other, more traditional sources. These sources included streams, rivers, and wells, and also cisterns (artificial reservoirs for collecting and storing rainwater; the Romans usually placed them on rooftops, although they sometimes set them up at ground level). All of these nonaqueduct methods of gathering water had the same basic disadvantages—the water had to be drawn and also carried from the place of use, often over long distances. Consequently, as the populations of Rome and other cities in its dominion increased and demand for freshwater grew apace, the Romans began building aqueducts.

In time, Rome's system of aqueducts and water distribution far surpassed any that had come before. The city of Rome was eventually supplied by eleven aqueducts; numerous others were constructed in Italy, Gaul, Spain, Greece, and other parts of the realm. The capital city's eleven aqueducts alone ran for a total of more than 260 miles. (It should be noted that only 30 miles, or about one-ninth, of this distance featured tall rows of stone arches, called arcades. These structures, which were essentially bridges erected to carry the water channels through certain areas, are sometimes confused with the channels themselves, which were the actual aqueducts.) Among the eleven were the Aqua Appia (initiated in 312 B.C.), the first to be built; the Aqua Anio (272 B.C.), later called the Anio Vetus, or "Old Anio," to distinguish it from one with the same name built later (the Anio Novus, or "New Anio," A.D. 38); the Aqua Marcia (144 B.C.), at 58.4 miles the longest of the eleven; and the Aqua Claudia (A.D. 38), today the best preserved of the eleven. With good reason, the Romans were very proud of this unique engineering accomplishment. Sextus Julius Frontinus, who served as water commissioner for the capital city in the late first century A.D., expressed this pride, bragging, "With such an array of indispensable structures carrying so many waters, compare, if you will, the idle [Egyptian] Pyramids or the useless, though famous, works of the Greeks!" (*The Stratagems and the Aqueducts of Rome* 1.16).

A Roman aqueduct was an extensive, complex, and masterfully crafted combination of conduits, tunnels, bridges, pools, reservoirs, pipes, and nozzles. An aqueduct's route was often purposely indirect, with several twists and turns. This design moved water by exploiting the natural force of gravity rather than by placing it under pressure, the method that is more common today. The aqueduct's water channel, called the *specus,* was very slightly inclined (slanted downward from the horizontal), just enough to induce the water to flow downward from its source. The degree of the incline, or vertical drop, varied somewhat from place to place, but averaged about two to three feet per mile. The *specus* was made of stone blocks that measured twenty by fifty inches on aver-

age and was usually about as high and wide as an average doorway. To keep the channel watertight and clean, the inside was coated with a special mortar that was mixed with small pieces of broken tile to give it extra strength. When the mortar was dry, the workmen lowered the top stones into place, sealing the aqueduct. They then buried it, so that it remained underground, except in the short stretches (across ravines, for example) where it emerged to run atop arcades. In the late Republic, the builders began installing milestones, called *cippi,* along the route. This made locating specific sections of the aqueducts much easier when repairs were needed, which turned out to be often. Indeed, maintaining the aqueducts and their water distribution systems turned out to be almost as big a job as building these structures in the first place.

The daily output of (number of gallons supplied by) each of Rome's eleven aqueducts varied, as do modern estimates for these outputs; but a reasonable guess for the total output of the eleven combined is 250 million gallons a day. Since the city of Rome had roughly 1 million inhabitants in the early third century A.D., that yields

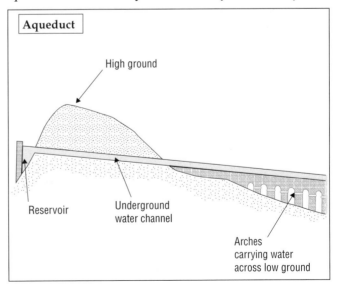

This drawing shows how a Roman aqueduct consisted mainly of a narrow channel running either below or above ground.

about 250 gallons of water per person per day. It should be noted, for comparison, that the water department of the average American town supplies about 125 gallons per person per day.

This enormous volume of water flowing into ancient Rome began at springs and other sources in the hills, what can be thought of as the "back" end of the aqueducts. It then traveled through the countryside within the various water channels until it reached the city. There, on what can be thought of as the "front" end of the aqueducts, the flow entered a complex distribution system that carried the water to fountains, public baths, houses, and so on. The most vital point in the front end of an aqueduct was the main distribution building (*castellum aquae*). It was located near the outer edge of the town it supplied, usually on the highest elevation in the area so that water would flow downward from this structure into the town. There, the water was cleaned by passing it through metal screens and allowing it to rest in settling tanks. Pipes (variously of bronze, wood, ceramic tile, concrete, and lead) then distributed the purified water to the town, including the public fountains, from which most urban dwellers got their daily supplies of water for drinking and cooking.

Although the law forbade private use of the water from the aqueducts, except by a privileged few or by special government permit, many people ignored the law and proceeded to divert water from these channels illegally. Frontinus duly reported such fraud in his book on the aqueducts. The law against water theft penalized a violator with a stiff fine of one hundred thousand *sestercies*—about one hundred times the annual salary of an average Roman soldier—and the obligation to repair any damage inflicted by the thief on the aqueducts.

The vast majority of regular aqueduct maintenance and repair was done by specially trained brigades of slaves. Each slave gang was divided into specialized groups, including managers, inspectors, and various craftsmen capable of necessary repairs. During an emergency, these extremely well-drilled workers rushed into action, diverting water from various regions of the city to the region in need.

Following the third century A.D., the Romans built few new aqueducts, and after the year 500 the existing ones increasingly fell into disrepair. As the centuries wore on, some of the aqueducts were occasionally repaired by the impoverished medieval residents of Rome, but this was done in a haphazard, inadequate manner. All eleven of these once marvelous structures had completely shut down by the eleventh century. Like their distant ancestors, most people now had to rely on the muddy waters of the Tiber River for drinking, cooking, and washing. **See** building materials and techniques; **also** Frontinus, Sextus Julius (Chapter 1).

Ara Pacis

(Altar of Peace) This magnificent monument is often called the crowning artistic masterpiece of the Augustan Age. It was erected, by order of the Senate, in Rome's Campus Martius and dedicated to the emperor Augustus in January 9 B.C. Leading magistrates, state priests, and the Vestal Virgins performed sacrifices on it. Sculpted reliefs from the altar were discovered in the sixteenth century, but at the time no one realized they belonged to the monument mentioned by several ancient writers. Recognition of this fact came in 1879; in the late 1930s archaeologists who had found other pieces of the marble altar managed to reconstruct it. It is U-shaped, its open end facing west and accessed by a staircase. Enclosing the altar is a marble wall about thirty feet square and sixteen feet high. The walls of the enclosure feature horizontal bands of sculptures containing more than one hundred human figures, including Augustus himself (who walks at the head of a procession that includes priests) and members of his family. **See** sculpture; **also** Augustus (Chapter 1).

arch

For this curved structural element of Roman buildings that was so common it became a Roman trademark, **see** building materials and techniques.

Atellan farces

For these short, informal comic skits, **see** theater and drama.

Augustan Age of literature

This greatest of Rome's literary periods, sometimes referred to as its golden age of literature, is usually dated from the death of the great republican writer Cicero in 43 B.C. to the death of the Augustan poet Ovid in A.D. 17. With his keen sense of the power of propaganda, Augustus realized that the written word was a powerful tool he could use to promote his various programs and to emphasize Rome's mission to bring order to the whole world. This motive, coupled with his genuine love of literature and ideas, led him to encourage thinkers and writers. "Augustus gave all possible encouragement to intellectuals," the later historian Suetonius wrote. "He would politely and impatiently attend readings not only of their poems and historical works, but of their speeches and dialogues" (*Augustus* 89, in *The Twelve Caesars*).

However, writers in Augustan Rome received much more than just moral and verbal support. At Augustus's urging, some of his wealthy friends patronized (provided complete financial support for) writers and artists, allowing them to create at their leisure without the worry and distraction of making a living. The emperor's close associate Gaius Maecenas became the greatest literary patron of the age, maintaining an elite literary circle that included Virgil, Horace, Propertius, and other noted poets. Ovid, master of the love letter and love elegy, had a different patron. (Livy, the great Augustan historian, may have been an exception, for he apparently had no patron.) The result of so many talented individuals receiving such generous support from society's highest levels was a literary outpouring greater in scope and quality than Rome had ever produced or would ever again produce.

Indeed, the works of the Augustan writers had a profound and lasting impact, not only on later Roman society, but also on the literature and philosophy of medieval and modern Europe. This was partly because they ably captured the sincere feelings of relief, joy, optimism, and renewal that permeated their times, making their works extremely vigorous and passionate. Most of them also labored diligently, like none before them, to achieve the most perfect and beautiful forms possible. In doing so, they took full advantage of the exceptional qualities of the Latin language; as noted scholar Michael Grant points out, Latin gave these works considerable originality because it "proved able to create both resonant, vigorously compact prose and poetry of stirringly profound, harmonious musicality" (*The World of Rome*, p. 234). Many of the finest of Europe's later writers greatly admired and tried to imitate the preciseness and overall beauty of Augustan literature.

Not surprisingly, among the most prevalent themes employed by the Augustan writers were those that glorified Augustus's special brand of Roman nationalism. These included: peace, emphasizing that it was Augustus who had bestowed it and expressing the hope that it would last forever; the imperial mission of Rome and Italy to rule the world; the beauties of Italy and its fields and farms; praise of Augustus, his family, and his spirits; the revival of religion and traditional Roman virtues and morals (widely seen as having declined in the late Republic); the glories of Rome's heroic pre–civil war past; and the qualities of love and loyalty. Many centuries later, Europeans would marvel at and envy the idealized image of a mighty, noble, and heroic Rome that the Augustan writers created. **See** *Aeneid;* Latin and other languages; *Odes;* poetry; prose writing; *Res gestae;* **also** Augustus; Horace; Livy; Maecenas, Gaius; Ovid; Propertius, Sextus; Tibullus, Albius (all Chapter 1).

Augustan History

The identity of the author of this important collection of biographies of most of the Roman emperors (and some of the imperial usurpers) from A.D. 117 to 284 is uncertain. Supposedly, six different writers compiled it in the late third and early fourth centuries. However, various stylistic features and chronological and other discrepancies have led modern scholars to conclude that the work was written by a single author working in the late fourth century. His reasons for concealing his identity are as mysterious as that identity itself.

The work begins abruptly with the reign of Hadrian (A.D. 117–138) and ends with the accession of Diocletian in 284; however, the period from 244 to 253 is missing. The first half of the *Augustan History,* ending with the reign of Elagabalus (218–222), contains much authentic information, some of it not covered in other ancient sources. However, the second half is filled with fictional episodes and faked documents and speeches and is therefore of dubious quality.

basilicas

The basilica, one of Rome's most important categories of public structure, ap-

peared in the late third century B.C. and rapidly became popular and widespread. Essentially a large rectangular hall, the typical basilica consisted of an open central space (nave) flanked by aisles (the nave rising higher than the aisles), often a high vaulted roof, and a covered entrance porch (*narthex*). A city's basilica was constructed in its forum (main square) and served as a combination meeting hall, law court, and administrative center. In the Later Empire, following Constantine's show of support for Christianity, the Romans adopted the form of the basilica for new Christian churches (such as St. Peter's Basilica, begun by Constantine), while some older basilicas were transformed into churches. **See** building materials and techniques; **also** Constantine I (Chapter 1); **and** Christianity (Chapter 3).

bridges

To carry roads and aqueducts over various natural obstacles, the Romans needed bridges. And as they did in many other areas of engineering and construction, they excelled at the art of bridge building. Incredibly, some of the thousands of bridges they built fully two millennia ago are still in use today and daily bear with ease the tremendous weight of hundreds of modern cars, trucks, and buses. The challenges Roman engineers had to overcome to construct such useful and enduring structures were daunting; had they built nothing else, their bridges alone would rank them among history's most accomplished builders.

Some Roman bridges, including all of the earliest versions, were made of wood. Perhaps the most famous early structure was the Pons Sublicius, which led across the Tiber River and into Rome. Over the years, timber bridges, some built by and for the army and others erected by local towns and individuals, appeared by the hundreds throughout Italy and other Roman territories. They spanned streams, rivers, gorges, and other obstacles and became regular features of Rome's growing road network. Although most such timber bridges were small, some were impressive engineering works in their own right. A famous example is the bridge that Julius Caesar built across the Rhine River (on the border between Gaul and Germany) in 55 B.C. About forty feet wide, some fifteen hundred feet long, and erected in just ten days, it was meant to intimidate the Germans by showing them that the Romans could cross over into their territory any time they pleased. Fortunately for modern scholars, Caesar himself described the construction of this bridge. "Two piles," he begins, "eighteen inches thick, slightly pointed at the lower ends and of lengths varying in accordance with the depth of the river, were fastened together two feet apart; they were then lowered into the river from rafts, fixed firmly in the riverbed, and driven home with piledrivers" (*Commentary on the Gallic War* 4.1). He goes on to provide a good deal more detail. (The Roman army also constructed pontoon bridges, each consisting of a wooden walkway supported by a row of boats placed side by side.)

Caesar had chosen wood because, for strategic purposes, he needed to create a bridge very quickly with whatever materials were most plentiful in the area, but by his day, the Romans had already been constructing more permanent bridges out of masonry (stone or brick) for over two centuries. Many, erected for both roads and aqueducts, consisted of the elegant rows of arches (arcades) that have become a familiar Roman trademark. (Not all bridges were arcades, however; smaller masonry bridges might consist of only one arch.)

Among the finest surviving Roman bridges are the one spanning the Moselle River at Trier (in western Germany) and the one over the Tagus River in western Spain (whose two central arches are about ninety feet in diameter). Another surviving bridge, perhaps the most famous of all

those built by the Romans, has a three-tiered arrangement of arcades. This is the Pont du Gard, which crosses a deep valley near Nimes, in southern France (formerly Gaul). Interestingly, this bridge is not only an excellent surviving example of multiple arcades, but also of a bridge that supported both a roadway and an aqueduct. The tops of the bottom and middle tiers, roughly twenty and fifteen feet wide, respectively, were paved and supported pedestrian traffic; the narrower topmost tier carried the aqueduct. **See** building materials and techniques.

building materials and techniques

The Romans were great builders, overall the most prolific, efficient, and practical in the ancient world. Indeed, the word *practical* perhaps best sums up the driving force behind much of the Roman achievement, for the true Roman artist was not the painter, sculptor, or poet, but rather the engineer. Rome met the needs of its world empire appropriately and impressively by producing a vast network of roads for the swift transport of armies and trade goods; miles of aqueducts to supply life-giving water for hundreds of cities; sturdy bridges to support the roads and aqueducts; as well as temples, giant racetracks (like the Circus Maximus), theaters, amphitheaters (like the Colosseum), public baths, and basilicas, most of which could accommodate thousands of people at a time.

All of these structures were created using a relatively few basic but highly effective architectural concepts and construction materials, devices, and techniques. The two principal architectural concepts, which have become familiar trademarks of Roman construction, were the arch and the vault. A typical Roman arch began with two vertical supports, called piers. Curving inward from the tops of the piers were arcs of wedge-shaped stones, known as voussoirs (VOO-SWARS), which met at a central stone, the keystone, at the top. To keep the wedges from falling while the arch was under construction, the masons used a temporary support called "centering"; this was a sturdy timber framework that carpenters fashioned into a semicircle that fit exactly into the semicircular space directly below the arch. The centering bore the great weight of the stone wedges until the keystone was in place. Then the workers removed the centering, allowing the weight of the stones to be displaced, as intended, through the curve of the arch itself.

A Roman vault was a three-dimensional version of an arch—in effect, a curved or domed ceiling. An extended vault, consisting of a corridor with a curved ceiling running along its length, was called a barrel vault. In Rome's Theater of Marcellus, for example, the outside wall featured elegant arcades (rows of arches), each of which opened into a barrel vault that went halfway around the building. By contrast, the much larger Colosseum had a series of curved barrel vaults running around the full perimeter of the building's ellipse (oval).

Roman building materials included wood; stone, including marble, travertine (a durable, creamy-white variety of limestone), and *tufa* (a lightweight stone composed of compressed volcanic ash); and Roman concrete. Regarding the latter, the Greeks had long before learned to mix lime, sand, and water to produce a hard-drying mortar. It did not take long for the Romans to borrow the idea and, with their usual sense of practicality, to improve on it. Sometime in the third century B.C., Roman builders discovered that adding a special kind of sand to lime, in a ratio of two or three to one, produced a cement of rocklike hardness and great strength. Moreover, this new kind of mortar hardened underwater, which made it ideal for

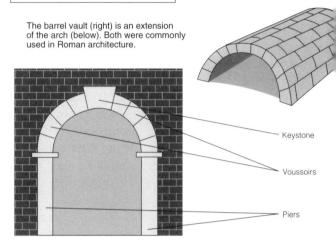

The Arch and the Barrel Vault

The barrel vault (right) is an extension of the arch (below). Both were commonly used in Roman architecture.

Keystone

Voussoirs

Piers

building bridges over rivers. Found near Mount Vesuvius and other volcanoes, the sand in question was actually volcanic ash laid down in prehistoric eruptions. Because the main source of the material was Puteoli, on Vesuvius's slopes, the mortar it produced came to be called *pulvis Puteolanus.* The modern term *mortar* itself derives from the *mortarium,* the wooden trough in which Roman masons mixed the volcanic sand and lime with water. They made the concrete by mixing wet *pulvis Puteolanus* with coarse sand and gravel. The usual method was to lay down a layer of wet mortar, press in a layer of gravel, lay down more mortar, add another level of gravel, and so on, until they had achieved the desired thickness.

Among the various construction devices utilized by Roman builders were surveying and leveling instruments, cranes, scaffolding, and coffer dams. Surveyors (*agrimensores,* often *mensors* for short) had to make sure that foundations were level, piers precisely vertical, roadbeds straight, and aqueducts properly inclined. For leveling, they regularly used a device called a *chorobates,* essentially a long wooden bench with plumb bobs (small metal weights) hanging from it and lines drawn on it. The surveyor kept slipping chocks (wooden wedges) under one end until various lines matched up. Then he looked through two eyeholes cut into the plank and "sighted" the distant terrain or foundation to observe how much it would need to be leveled in order to line up with the instrument's reading.

The manner in which Roman surveyors laid out straight roads whose ends were separated by tens or hundreds of miles of hilly, wooded countryside is still not known for certain. One popular theory holds that they used fire beacons. A series of such beacons set up on hilltops at night may have allowed the surveyors to line up a primary alignment for a road. Once they had established such a primary alignment, they laid out the route on the ground by placing wooden stakes at intervals.

To ensure precise right angles between the vertical and horizontal, surveyors and workmen used a *groma*. It consisted of two boards joined at the middle at right angles to each other and mounted in a horizontal position atop a post. The operator used hanging plumb lines to level the instrument and then sighted along one of the crossed boards to determine the correct angle.

To lift stones and other heavy materials, Roman builders used various devices, including large cranes. One of the most ingenious and powerful of these cranes utilized a circular cage, or drum, in which several workers operated a treadmill. Recommending the device for loads of great weight, the Roman architect Vitruvius described it as having a tall wooden block, or support, surrounded by an elaborate system of ropes and pulleys. Archaeologists have uncovered a sculpted relief of this very machine, with five

men operating the treadmill, in a Roman tomb that archaeologists have dated to the late first century A.D.

To aid in the construction of tall structures, including bridges and the walls of theaters, amphitheaters, temples, palaces, triumphal arches, and so on, the workers used scaffolding not unlike that used today (although the Roman version was made of wood, lighter, and could not support as much weight). The vertical supports (standards) rested on the ground. Attached to them were horizontal planks running parallel to the wall (ledgers), on which the workers stood. Supporting the planks were putlogs, wooden braces often socketed into holes drilled in the wall to give the whole assembly more stability. These holes are still visible in many surviving Roman buildings.

Most Roman masonry construction followed a roughly standard series of steps. The first step was to provide a firm foundation of stone or concrete for the structure. Then stone piers (often topped by arches)

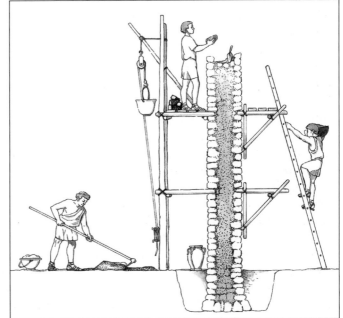

A modern reconstruction of Roman scaffolding shows how the putlogs were inserted into the side of the structure itself, bracing the platforms the workers stood on.

were erected to transfer the weight of the building into the foundation. A building's walls, floors, and other elements, or a bridge's roadway or aqueduct, were constructed on top of the piers. In the case of roadbeds, the foundation consisted of substantial layers of clay, gravel, and stone. Such a firm bed was needed to support the road's surface (which consisted of hard-packed earth, gravel, or paving stones), along with the weight of the traffic that moved along the road. The bed for an aqueduct was laid in a similar manner.

Bridge construction sometimes presented an extra challenge, namely when a bridge crossed over a river or other waterway; the water had to be removed from the work area before the foundation or piers could be installed. Builders managed this seemingly formidable task using a fairly simple and quite effective device called a coffer dam. This was, in essence, a large wooden box that had no top or bottom and whose sides had been sealed to ensure that it was watertight. Workers lowered the box into the water in the place where they desired to place a pier, pushing the wood firmly into the riverbed and making sure that the sides of the box rose several feet above the water's surface. Then they pumped out the water that had been trapped inside the dam using either a chain of men hefting buckets or a waterscrew (a corkscrewlike device that carried water upward when it was turned). When the ground inside the dam was dry, the workers laid the concrete foundation and began building the pier. Once the pier was higher than the water level outside the dam, the workers removed the dam and stood on scaffolding attached to the pier itself to finish its construction. **See** aqueducts; bridges; circuses; orders, architectural; palaces; Pantheon; roads; theaters and amphitheaters; **also** Vitruvius (Chapter 1); temples (Chapter 3); **and** baths, public (Chapter 5).

circuses

(*ludi circenses*) The Romans borrowed the basic concept and style of these chariot-racing facilities from the Greeks and Etruscans, but the Roman versions eventually far surpassed in size and splendor all earlier versions. The earliest Roman circuses were probably little more than flat open areas with temporary turning posts and banks of earth, like Greek hippodromes (where the Greeks held chariot and horse races). It is unknown when the first Etruscan-style wooden bleachers were added, but this development may date to the erection of the first version of the Circus Maximus, in the valley between Rome's Palatine and Aventine hills, about 600 B.C. According to the Roman historian Livy, King Tarquin

> celebrated public games on a scale more elaborate and opulent than any of his predecessors. It was on this occasion that our Circus Maximus was originally planned. On the ground marked out for it special places were assigned to Senators and knights to erect their stands in—or "decks" as they were called. These stands were supported on props and raised twelve feet from the ground. Horses and boxers . . . provided the entertainment. From then onward the games became an annual institution. (*History of Rome from Its Foundation* 1.35)

In the centuries that followed, the Circus Maximus underwent occasional but continuous elaboration and improvement. The starting gates (*carceres*) were added in 329 B.C. And shortly before his assassination in 44 B.C., Julius Caesar undertook a major renovation of the structure. Still, in his day at least three-quarters of the seating section was still of wood (the fewer stone seats being reserved for senators and other important citizens). Not surprisingly, this presented a fire hazard, and indeed, several fires ravaged the facility, one of the worst in 31 B.C. (prompting a new renovation by Augustus). Not until Trajan's renovation, in the early second century A.D., did all of the Circus's seating become stone.

The Circus Maximus in its prime, from Trajan's time until the fifth century (a period in which later emperors continued to improve it), must surely have been one of the wonders of the world. It was about 680 yards (over a third of a mile) long and some 150 yards wide; could seat about 150,000 people (although some ancient writers cite a figure of 250,000, which may have included spectators who stood on the hills overlooking the track); and its racing arena measured about 635 by 85 yards (about twelve times the size of the Colosseum's arena). The Circus featured twelve starting gates and a long, narrow barrier, the *euripus* (sometimes referred to as the *spina*) running down the middle of the track. It was around the *euripus* (which was covered with shrines, altars, and other monuments) that the charioteers drove their teams seven times (about three miles) in a typical race.

Today, large sections of this majestic structure remain buried beneath extensive layers of dirt and debris accumulated over the many centuries following Rome's decline. The site occupied by the Circus has been turned into an archaeological park and excavation continues, but the sheer enormity of the job makes it an extremely expensive and slow process that will take perhaps decades more to complete. For similar reasons, most of the other Roman circuses built across the Empire in ancient times have been only partially unearthed or remain wholly unexposed and uninves-

tigated. A few, however, have been substantially excavated and studied, among these the Circus of Maxentius (one of the capital city's four major racetracks, along with the Circus Maximus, Circus Flaminius, and Circus of Caligula and Nero); the circus at Tyre, on the coast of Lebanon; the circus at Mérida in central Spain; and the circus at Lepcis Magna, on the coast of Libya. Together with the imposing remains of the Colosseum and other surviving amphitheaters, these emerging racetracks clearly demonstrate that Roman builders, the greatest of antiquity, expended some of their greatest energies on games facilities. **See** building materials and techniques; theaters and amphitheaters; **also** public games (Chapter 5).

Circus Maximus
For this giant facility built to present chariot races in Rome, **see** circuses.

City of God
A major work completed about A.D. 426 by the late Roman Christian thinker Augustine, it criticizes pagan ideas and culture and attempts to show how God's purpose is supposedly revealed in the fabric of prior historical events. One of the most important themes of the work is that God's true city is the growing brotherhood of Christian believers, which extends in the spiritual sense from earth into heaven. The earthly, more material city of Rome, says Augustine, is transient and ultimately unimportant in the grand scheme of things; so it matters little whether Rome passes away as long as the heavenly city survives.

The work also helped to redefine and institutionalize a number of doctrinal points that had been developing in the church in the prior two centuries or so, for example the idea of original sin. The author's clarification of this doctrine was part of a theological dispute with a British-born monk and preacher named Pelagius over the concept of free will. Pelagius held that humans are fundamentally good. There is no such thing as original sin, he said, for it would be cruel to deny people, especially innocent babies, entrance into heaven simply because they had not been baptized. Rather, God has given people complete free will to choose between good and sinful behavior; if they choose goodness, they achieve salvation, whereas if they choose sin, they are damned. In response, in an extended series of arguments his *City of God,* Augustine claimed that, being born already tainted by sin, people lack the free will to choose between goodness and sin. Until they receive God's grace, therefore, they can choose only sin. **See** Augustine (Chapter 1).

Colosseum

To find information on this huge arena in Rome where gladiators fought, **see** theaters and amphitheaters.

Commentaries on the Gallic and Civil Wars

The surviving journals composed by Julius Caesar during his conquests of Gaul (58–52 B.C.) and the civil war he fought with his rival Pompey (ending in 48 B.C.). His purpose in writing them was to help maintain his name, reputation, and power base in the capital while he was away on long campaigns; to this end, he sent regular installments to Rome, where his agents saw that they were properly circulated. A combination of historical narrative, personal memoranda, and speeches, the *Commentaries* are written in clear, compact, and at times powerful Latin prose; these strengths, combined with the author's extraordinary authority as an eyewitness to momentous events, makes them literary masterpieces. They are also extremely valuable as historical records, although Caesar's personal biases and political agenda, which sometimes distort the facts, must be taken into account.

Caesar begins the *Gallic War* with the now immortal line: "The country of Gaul consists of three separate parts." He goes on to give a geographical description of Gaul and then tells why and how the Romans came to grips with the Helvetii and Germans and summarizes his campaigns against the Belgic tribes, including the fierce Nervii. Eventually, Caesar's forces put together a makeshift fleet and defeat the tribes on the Atlantic coast, led by the Veneti. Then Caesar defeats some German tribes that had recently invaded Gaul and crosses the Rhine River to demonstrate Roman power (including his building of a wooden bridge across the river). The great general also describes his first, unsuccessful invasion of Britain, as well as the second, successful British campaign. The dramatic climax of the work is Caesar's description of the large-scale Gallic uprising in which he fought the formidable Vercingetorix, of the Averni tribe, and besieged his stronghold of Alesia. (The last section, covering the final events of the Gallic campaign, was written by Aulus Hirtius, one of Caesar's officers.)

The *Civil War* opens with Caesar overrunning Italy after his crossing of the Rubicon River in 49 B.C., Pompey's flight to Greece, and the surrender of Pompey's troops in Spain. Also covered are Caesar's siege of Massilia (on Gaul's southern coast); the campaign against Pompey in Greece, including Caesar's victory at Pharsalus; Pompey's flight to Egypt, where he is murdered; and finally Caesar's arrival there and the beginning of his involvement with Cleopatra. **See** prose writing; **also** Caesar, Gaius Julius; Cleopatra VII; Pompey; Vercingetorix (all Chapter 1); Gaul (Chapter 2); **and** Battle of Pharsalus; siege tactics (both Chapter 7).

Corinthian order

For this ornate and beautiful architectural style used by the Romans in many of their large buildings, **see** orders, architectural.

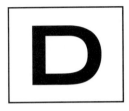

Doric order

For this spare and stately architectural style originated by the Greeks, **see** orders, architectural.

drama

For Roman dramatists (playwrights) and their plays, **see** theater and drama.

epic poetry

For this long, dramatic form of poetry best exemplified in Rome by Virgil's *Aeneid*, **see** *Aeneid;* poetry.

epigram

For this short, witty poetic form, **see** poetry.

epigraphy

The study of inscriptions, words carved or scratched into a durable material such as stone, metal, wood, tile, earthenware, or glass. A few surviving Roman (i.e., Latin) inscriptions date from the sixth century B.C., but most come from the third century B.C. and after. About three hundred thousand Roman inscriptions (excluding those on coins) have been discovered, and new ones are found on a regular basis. Because ancient written documents were often copied many times before reaching the modern world, they were subject to change; whereas an inscription constitutes a sort of original document that captures the lettering, grammar, facts, and ideas of a specific remote period. Thus, the earliest inscriptions give scholars an idea of what archaic Latin was like. The most famous such example is the *Lapis Niger* (Black Stone), the oldest known Roman document, consisting of an inscription on a stone found in 1899 near the site of Rome's old Senate House. The message contained in this inscription is still not completely understood.

Inscriptions were always carved in capital letters and words were divided by stops (sometimes simple dots, other times more decorative designs) rather than spaces, as is the custom today. Also, abbreviations were common, partly to save space and sometimes to be fashionable. Often a single abbreviation stood for several different words and the reader was expected to deduce which one was intended from the context of the message. Some common abbreviations include: AN (year), COS (consul), DISM (to the spirits of the dead), FIL (son), HON (esteemed), LIB (freedman), MAT (mother), OF (workshop), PM (*pontifex maximus,* Rome's chief priest), PR (prefect, praetor, or province), RP (the Roman state), SEN (Senate), TR (tribune), VB (good man), and VET (military veteran). These and the other letters of inscriptions were most often painted red, but traces of the original pigment have only rarely survived. Errors and corrections by the original masons are sometimes visible.

There were numerous kinds of inscriptions. A partial list includes: religious dedications (*tituli sacri,* often containing the abbreviation VSLM, meaning "he willingly and deservedly fulfilled his vow," or some other formula); messages honoring victorious generals and other accomplished individuals (*tituli honorarii*); dedications of public buildings and monuments (*tituli operum publicorum*), which usually included the name of the builder or repairer; military diplomas (*diplomata militaria,* confirming the granting of Roman citizenship), which were engraved on small bronze tablets; and laws, decrees, treaties, and many other political or legal documents (the Twelve Tables, now lost, are a famous example).

By far the most abundant type of inscription consisted of tombstone epitaphs (*tituli sepulchrales*). These often recorded not only the deceased person's name, but also his home city and tribe; longer messages recording the person's deeds, as well as his or her heirs, were not uncommon. The longest such tomb inscription (and indeed, the longest Roman inscription ever found) is the *Monumentum Ancyranum,* containing a copy of the *Res gestae,* composed by the first emperor, Augustus, and listing his main accomplishments. Discovered in Turkey in 1555, it contains some seven thousand letters. **See** Latin and other languages; prose writing; *Res gestae;* writing materials.

forum

A regular feature of Roman towns and cities, a forum was a main square used for social and political gatherings, marketing, and so forth. Fora were usually rectangular and lined with public buildings, including temples. Some cities had several fora, each of which catered to a certain activity, such as a cattle market (*forum boarium*) or fish market (*forum piscarium*). Fora were also often named after emperors and other prominent public figures. **See** names of specific fora.

Forum of Augustus

This magnificent public square was erected just north of the Forum Romanum

and Forum of Caesar, directly bordering the latter, and dedicated by Augustus in 2 B.C. Years before, as Octavian, he had promised that if victorious against Caesar's assassins, he would give thanks by building a temple to Mars. The Forum of Augustus contained the fulfillment of that oath—the Temple of Mars Ultor, which housed Julius Caesar's sword and was surrounded by marble colonnades and statues. In A.D. 19, Augustus's successor, Tiberius, added two triumphal arches, one on either side of the temple. **See** forum; names of specific fora.

Forum of Caesar

This forum was dedicated in 46 B.C. on a plot of land purchased by Julius Caesar just north of the Forum Romanum. It was rectangular, with colonnades on three sides and a large decorative entranceway on the fourth. This forum featured some shops but was dominated by the splendid Temple of Venus. A fire later ravaged much of Caesar's forum; but the emperor Trajan restored it, rededicating it in A.D. 108. **See** forum; names of specific fora.

Forum of Trajan

Completed about A.D. 115, this forum, a true architectural masterpiece, was built by the emperor Trajan along the northern border of the Forum of Augustus. The designer appears to have been the noted architect Apollodorus of Damascus. A magnificent gateway led from the Forum of Augustus into Trajan's forum, which featured curved sides with double rows of colonnaded porches. At the far end was a huge structure, the Basilica Ulpia (which later strongly influenced the design of Christian churches). Just behind this building rose Trajan's Column, covered with reliefs commemorating his exploits, a monument that still stands. Libraries were constructed on each side of the column. Later, the emperor Hadrian added the Temple of the Divine Trajan, honoring

Trajan's memory, near the libraries. **See** forum; names of specific fora.

Forum Romanum

Rome's early marketplace, throughout Roman history it remained the city's administrative heart, main square, and principal forum. It was usually referred to simply as "the forum," and sometimes as the Forum Magnum ("great forum") or Forum Romanum ("forum of Rome") to distinguish it from other fora that rose in the capital over the centuries. It was located in a low basin lying between the Capitoline, Palatine, and Quirinal hills. The area was originally marshy, with a stream running through it; only after the streambed was moved and the marshes drained in the late Monarchy did large-scale building begin there. The Romans erected temples, basilicas, statues, and shops in the forum in republican times, and they gathered in the *comitium,* an open area on one end, to hear

political speeches at various *rostra* (platforms for speakers). Both Julius Caesar and Augustus erected impressive public buildings in the main forum, including the Basilica Aemilia, Basilica Julia, Temple of Castor and Pollux, Temple of Saturn, and Temple of Concord. The Senate House was also located in the main forum. **See** forum; names of specific fora.

The Golden Ass

(or *Metamorphoses*) The only Latin novel that has survived in its entirety, it was written by Apuleius, who flourished in the mid–second century A.D. It may have been based on a story of the prolific

Crowds of citizens and slaves mill about the Forum Romanum, Rome's principal forum, as street entertainers perform.

Greek writer Lucian, but more likely both works are based on a lost earlier work by an unknown Greek. Apuleius's expanded, embellished version is a narrative told in the first person by a young Greek man, Lucius. In his first adventure, he pays a visit to Thessaly (in central Greece), where supposedly practitioners of black magic can be found. Through such black arts, he is transformed into an ass, after which a gang of thieves forces him to become their accomplice in a crime spree. The most famous episode in this section of the book takes place when an old woman tells a story to a young girl whom the robbers have abducted. This tale, the haunting Greek myth of Cupid and Psyche, has survived only in this telling by Apuleius.

Later, Lucius has other adventures, including some temporary service to a band of wandering priests of the goddess Cybele, and a stint performing tricks at public gatherings. Eventually, the goddess Isis takes pity on him and turns him back into a person. He then undergoes initiation rites in the cult of Isis and Osiris. The novel is fast-paced, often quite humorous, and richly detailed, revealing many customs, beliefs, and other aspects of daily life in Apuleius's time. **See** prose writing; **also** Apuleius, Lucius (Chapter 1); **and** Cybele; Isis (both Chapter 3).

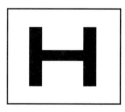

Histories

Written by the Greek historian Polybius in the second century B.C., this historical narrative covers the period of the Punic Wars (264–146 B.C.), during which the Romans defeated Carthage three times and also conquered the Greek states of the eastern Mediterranean. It was composed in Greek and originally consisted of forty books; of these, the first five survive complete, along with fragments of others.

The author states his purpose in the introduction: "The events I have chosen to describe will challenge and stimulate everyone alike. . . . There can surely be nobody so petty or so apathetic in his outlook that he has no desire to discover by what means and under what system of government the Romans succeeded in less than fifty-three years [i.e., from 220 to 167 B.C.] in bringing under their rule almost the whole of the inhabited world, an achievement which is without parallel in human history." Indeed, the relatively sudden eclipse of the Greek lands by Rome was a source of fear, bewilderment, and bitterness for many Greeks. Polybius appears to have meant his history to reconcile his fellow Greeks to the "facts" that much of the fault for their defeat lay with their own mistakes and weakness, and more importantly, that the rise of Rome was inevitable, partly because of the innate strengths of the Roman government and character, and also because Rome had been favored by the gods and fate.

Polybius's writing is clear, straightforward, and free of rhetorical and other literary devices common in other historical works of his era. He deals not only with the historical events and figures themselves, but also digresses to explain to the reader what makes his history superior to many others. A good historian, he says, must not only study the writings of others, but also know firsthand the "cities, places, rivers, harbors, and in general the special features of land and sea and the distances from one place to another." (*Histories* 12.25e). He must also have firsthand experience in politics and war, and he must rely heavily, whenever possible, on interviewing eyewitnesses to the events he describes. For these reasons, modern historians consider Polybius to be an honest and fairly reliable historian who also significantly advanced the art of historical writing. Among the other extremely valuable features of the work are the texts of several ancient documents, the originals of which are lost; the author's detailed analysis of the Roman constitution; and his invaluable comparison of the Greek and Roman fighting systems (the rigid phalanx versus the more flexible legions). **See** prose writing; **also** Polybius (Chapter 1).

History of Rome from Its Foundation

The massive and popular Roman history composed by the great prose writer Livy in the late first century B.C. Of the original 142 volumes, only about 35 have survived—Books 1–10, 21–45 (Books 41 and 43 being incomplete), and a fragment of Book 91. The content of the original work was as follows: Books 1–5 described Rome's legendary founding, the Monarchy, and the Republic's establishment and early years; Books 6–15 Rome's conquest of Italy; Books 16–30 the first two Punic Wars with Carthage; Books 31–45 the subjugation of Greece and other events from about 200 to 167 B.C.; and Books 46–142 (all now lost) subsequent events to 9 B.C., about halfway through Augustus's reign.

Measured by any standard, ancient or modern, Livy's achievement was monumental. Noted scholar J. Wight Duff states: "No Augustan prose writer is for a moment comparable with Livy. His prose-epic is . . . sister to the *Aeneid.* Not even in Virgil has the greatness of the Roman character found a more dignified or more lasting monument than in the colossal ruins of Livy's history" (*A Literary History of Rome,* p. 464). Indeed, Livy's writing style is eloquent, well organized, often dramatic, and very readable.

On the negative side, however, Livy did not set out to write an impartial historical record; rather, his aim was to illuminate the traditions and character traits that had made Rome great in hopes of teaching a moral lesson and thereby helping to reverse what he and many other prominent figures of his day viewed as society's recent moral decay. As he himself summed up his purpose in the introduction to the work: "In history, fortunately, you can find a record of the ample range of human experience clearly set up for everyone to see; in that record, you may discover for yourself and for your country, examples and warnings." Another of Livy's faults is that for sources he relied mainly on written histories (of varying reliability) and consulted few original documents and records; nor was he very critical of his sources. The result was that his facts were often inaccurate or muddled. Also, like most other ancient historians, he paid little attention to economic and social history (to the frustration of modern scholars) and his narrative was riddled with references to omens and fate directing the course of historical events (though to his credit he personally tended to be skeptical about such supernatural forces). **See** Augustan Age of literature; prose writing; **also** Livy (Chapter 1).

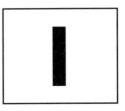

inscriptions

For these letters and words carved into stone, metal, and other durable materials, **see** epigraphy.

Ionic order

For this elegant architectural style originated by the Greeks, **see** orders, architectural.

Latin and other languages

Latin was the predominant written and spoken language in Rome, Italy, and the vast Mediterranean realm the Romans came to administer. However, several other languages remained in use in these regions throughout Roman history. Etruscan, for example, was the principal language of Etruria (the Italian region lying north of Rome) from the eighth to the fifth centuries B.C. and was still spoken by a few people until late republican times. Etruscan was a non-Indo-European language (that is, it did not originate among the Indo-Europeans, early tribal peoples who migrated from western Asia into Europe in the third and second millennia B.C. and gave rise to the Greeks, Romans, and others); it survives only in a few inscriptions; and it has not been extensively deciphered. Greek, on the other hand, was widely spoken in southern Italy beginning in the late eighth century B.C., when colonists from several Greek city-states settled in that area, and Greek remained the principal language of Greece and parts of Asia Minor throughout the Republic and Empire, despite the fact that Latin was the language of government and widely taught in schools (from the late Republic on). Also, various Celtic tongues remained in use in Gaul and some northern border provinces, as well as in Italy's Po Valley, during imperial times. Punic (the Phoenician tongue spoken in Carthage), Syriac, Egyptian, and other languages coexisted with Latin in other Roman provinces and regions.

In central Italy, which became and remained the Roman heartland, a number of Indo-European languages related to but substantially different from Latin were in use during Rome's Monarchy and early Republic. The principal examples were Oscan (spoken by the Samnites and others who inhabited the southern Apennines) and Umbrian (used in central Italy east and northeast of Rome). Oscan remained in wide use in south-central Italy until the first century B.C. and was still spoken by some people in Pompeii and its surrounding region in the late first century A.D.

Latin was itself an Indo-European language. Its exact origins and development are not precisely known. One theory holds that Latin and Osco-Umbrian developed as two separate branches of an Indo-European language that had entered the peninsula long before. Another view suggests that one of the Indo-European languages entering Italy fused with a prehistoric native Italian tongue to form the earliest version of Latin. The Latin alphabet developed much later, perhaps as late as the sixth or fifth century B.C. It was modeled on the Etruscan alphabet, which was itself derived from the Greek alphabet. (The Greek alphabet had emerged some time in the eighth century B.C., based on one used by the Phoenicians, a maritime trading people who inhabited the coasts of Palestine; the Greeks added vowels, since the Phoenician alphabet had only consonants.) Minor changes in Latin letters and their usage occurred in the centuries that followed. For example, the letters *C* and *K* were long similar in that they were both pronounced as *K*, the main difference being that *K* was originally used instead of *C* before an *A*. In time, however, *C* replaced *K* before an *A* and the letter *K* thereafter became redundant; it survived in some retained archaic spellings, such as *Kalendae* (the Kalends, the first day of each month).

In whatever way Latin and its alphabet developed, a form often referred to as "archaic" Latin was the main language of Rome and Latium by the seventh century B.C. and probably earlier. Subsequently, as

Rome expanded its power and influence throughout Italy and eventually the entire Mediterranean world, it promoted the use of Latin as part of its policy of "Romanizing" subject peoples. In this way, Latin came to be used by educated people in most parts of southern Europe, North Africa, and the eastern Mediterranean, although large numbers of people in these regions retained their native languages.

Meanwhile, Latin did not remain fixed and static, but rather underwent a steady evolution over the centuries. By the second century B.C., according to the Greek historian Polybius, archaic Latin (which had been preserved in some documents and inscriptions) had become difficult to understand, even by the best scholars. The form of Latin used for formal documents and much literature in the late Republic and Augustan Age is now referred to as classical or Golden Age Latin. Formal Latin used from the early first century A.D. to about the year 150 is called Silver Age Latin. A less formal kind of Latin, *sermo cotidianus,* used by educated people for everyday (colloquial) speech in these periods, is exemplified in the plays of Plautus and Terence and the letters of Cicero. The Latin spoken by the uneducated classes, especially in the provinces, called vulgar Latin, was even more informal. Characterized by marked variations in pronunciation and spelling, loose adherence to strict grammar, and simpler and more natural word order, from the seventh century on it steadily developed into the European Romance languages, including Italian, French, and Spanish. Meanwhile, more formal Latin remained the language of scholars and the Christian Church well into modern times. **See** poetry; prose writing.

letters of Cicero

A number of ancient writers, including Pliny the Younger (first/second century A.D.) and Quintus Symmachus (fourth century A.D.), left behind collections of letters that reveal much about themselves and the life and thought of their respective times. None, however, can compare in candor, sheer volume, and importance to modern scholars to those penned by Marcus Tullius Cicero. His more than eight hundred surviving letters create the most intimate existing portrait of an ancient person.

These letters are usually divided into four groups. The first consists of those written to his close friend Titus Pomponius Atticus between 68 and 43 B.C.; the second, those to more than ninety friends and acquaintances in roughly the same period (and published by his secretary/friend, the freedman Tiro, after Cicero's death); the third, those to his brother Quintus, mostly between 59 and 54 B.C.; and the fourth, those to Marcus Brutus, all composed in 43 B.C.

Cicero's sincerity and humanity, as well as the casual but direct style of most of his letters, are apparent in the following excerpt from one written on November 7, 50 B.C., while he was away from Rome. It was addressed to Tiro, who was then quite ill. "I am perfectly certain," Cicero begins,

that until you are completely well you should not trust yourself to travel at all, whether on sea or on land. . . . As to your doctor, you write that he is well thought of, and I hear the same. But I am by no means satisfied with the treatment he has been giving you. He ought not to have let you have soup when your stomach was bad. However, I have written to him in detail. . . . I have also written at length to that most agreeable . . . and kindly man, Curius [a friend of Cicero's and Atticus's]. . . . I have asked him to have [i.e., look after] you in his house. . . . Please, Tiro, spare no expense whatever to make yourself well. . . . The services you have done me are beyond all number . . . in my private and public affairs alike. . . . But you will have performed a greater service than any of them, if, as I hope, I am going to see you in good health. . . . I shall measure your regard for me by the amount of care you devote to your recovery. Goodbye, my dear Tiro, good-bye and get well. Lepta [one of Cicero's assistants] and all of us send you every good wish. Goodbye. (*Letters to His Friends* 16.4)

libraries

Long before the Romans established libraries, the Greeks had done so. The largest and most renowned in the Mediterranean world was at Alexandria, founded in the fourth century B.C. and containing possibly as many as seven hundred thousand volumes (mostly in the form of papyrus rolls). Other large Greek libraries existed at Pergamum and Athens. It was collections of Greek books looted and taken back to Italy by Roman soldiers and administrators that formed the nucleus of the first Roman libraries. The first private Roman collection, for example, was the one Lucius Aemilius Paullus seized from the Macedonian king Perseus in 168 B.C. Beginning in the first century B.C., private libraries became fairly common in Rome and other Italian towns. (Excavators have discovered a private library containing the remains of 1,803 papyrus rolls in the town of Herculaneum, buried by the eruption of Mount Vesuvius in A.D. 79.)

Rome's first public library was created by the historian and literary patron Gaius Asinius Pollio during Augustus's reign. Augustus himself established a library in the Campus Martius and another on the Palatine hill. Among the finest of Roman libraries were those erected by Trajan in his forum in the early second century, one featuring manuscripts in Greek, the other in Latin. **See** Forum of Trajan; writing materials; **also** Paullus, Lucius Aemilius (Chapter 1); **and** Alexandria; Athens; Pergamum (all Chapter 2).

Metamorphoses

A long Latin narrative poem (in fifteen books) written by the Augustan poet Ovid over several years beginning about A.D. 2. It contains more than two hundred stories derived from Greek, Roman, and Near Eastern mythology, all supposedly involving some kind of miraculous transformation, hence the title, which means "transformations." Often, however, the transformation has little to do with the tale and Ovid's intention seems primarily to entertain. Included, among many others, are legends about the creation, the flood and Deucalion's repopulating of the earth, Apollo's slaying of Python, the founding of Thebes by Cadmus, Echo and Narcissus, the tragic lovers Pyramus and Thisbe, Jason and the Golden Fleece, Theseus and the Minotaur, the death and deification of Hercules, Venus and Adonis, Midas and his golden touch, the Trojan War, and the love between Aeneas and Dido.

Of all the classical literary works, the *Metamorphoses* had the most influence on later European artists. The Flemish painter Peter Paul Rubens, for example, illustrated 112 of the stories for King Philip IV of Spain in the late 1630s, and in 1931, the Spanish artist Pablo Picasso published 30 illustrations based on tales from Ovid's masterwork. **See** poetry; **also** Ovid (Chapter 1).

mimes

For these informal entertainments, which included short, often bawdy skits and also circuslike acts, **see** theater and drama.

mosaics

These decorative works, made by pressing small stone or glass cubes, tiles, or marbles into wet cement, became extremely popular for floors, walls, and the undersides of arches in the early Empire. Black-and-white geometric patterns were popular, but scenes of landscapes, gods, people, and real and mythical events, rendered in color, were also common; often these had borders or other elements made up of swirls, triangles, Greek keys, and other repeating geometrical patterns.

In many cases, mosaics were copies of paintings. Thus, some surviving mosaics have preserved the look and content of ancient paintings long since lost. A famous example is a Roman mosaic depicting Alexander the Great, found by archaeologists in the House of the Faun at Pompeii (and largely preserved by its burial in the eruption of Mount Vesuvius in A.D. 79). Dubbed the Alexander Mosaic, it is made up of some 1.5 million individual tiny pieces of colored stone and glass. It depicts the climactic moment of one of the young conqueror's battles, probably Issus (333 B.C.), his first victory over the Persian king Darius; many scholars believe it was copied from a late-fourth-century B.C. painting, possibly by Philoxenos of Eretria.

The mosaic technique reached Greece from Persia and the east in the late fourth century B.C., following Alexander's conquests. A bit more than a century later, well-to-do Romans began using mosaics for floors in highly visible rooms such as the atrium, where they came to achieve the same aesthetic purpose as fine carpets. Various distinctive styles of mosaics developed in different parts of the Mediterranean world. Among these, that of North Africa has proven highly valuable to historians because many North African mosaics include very realistic depictions of houses and other buildings, people's clothes, and agricultural scenes. Thus, they reveal details of everyday life that a lack of other hard evidence often makes difficult to ascertain. **See** painting.

music

Various forms of evidence show that music played a prominent role in a number of different situations and aspects of Roman life. Some kind of musical accompaniment regularly figured in prayers and sacrifices; religious, triumphal, and funeral processions; opening ceremonies and dedications; public games (including gladiatorial combats, in which the music backed up the action, not unlike the musical score of a motion picture); theatrical presentations of all types (including poetry recitations); and, by the early Empire, upper-class dinner parties.

The Romans borrowed many of their musical instruments, especially stringed ones, from the Greeks; some others, particularly trumpets and other brass instruments, came from the Etruscans. Besides these brass items, there were reed instruments, such as the *aulos* and *tibia* (double pipes), which were similar to modern clarinets and oboes; lyres and citharas (kinds of harps) and other stringed instruments; percussion instruments such as drums, cymbals, and tambourines; and a water organ with bronze pipes. Sometimes

This detail from the so-called Alexander Mosaic, discovered in a house in Pompeii, shows the Greek conqueror attacking a Persian king.

these instruments were combined into large-scale ensembles like modern symphony orchestras, which usually provided accompaniment for solo singers or entire choruses. Like actors, musicians (many of whom were Greeks and/or freedmen) were looked on as low-class. They often banded together into guilds (*collegia*) for mutual fellowship. **See** guilds (Chapter 5).

Natural History

An encyclopedic compendium of facts and anecdotes composed by Pliny the Elder, dedicated to his friend, the emperor Titus, in A.D. 77, and published shortly after the author's death two years later. Gathering knowledge from many parts of the known world of Pliny's day, the work consists of thirty-seven books, broken down in the following manner: Book 1 contains a table of contents and a list of Pliny's sources; Book 2 covers facts about the cosmos; Books 3–6 information about the lands and peoples of Europe, Africa, and Asia; Book 7 the human body; Books 8–11 land and sea animals; Books 12–19 plants; Books 20–27 the medicinal uses of plants; Books 28–32 medicines derived from animal products; and Books 33–37 geology, including the uses of minerals (and with a long digression on the history of art).

Considering its wide range of topics, great detail, and frequent digressions, Pliny's encyclopedia is extremely well organized. This suggests that he developed an efficient system of collating and indexing many diverse sources, or that he closely followed and paraphrased a small number of well-organized older Greek handbooks, or both. In spite of his vast and diligent research, however, he did almost

no serious independent investigation and usually did not distinguish between reliable and worthless sources and information. The work therefore contains a large number of factual errors and information of dubious reliability.

Still, Pliny must be credited with honest scholarship, as he lists all of his sources up front, an unusual practice for an ancient writer. He cites 473 authors, 146 of them Latin and 327 foreign (mostly Greek); moreover, he readily admits that many of these he found listed in the handbooks he used, rather than having read them in the original. Pliny's encyclopedia remained popular in Rome's final centuries and later become one of the most revered works of the Middle Ages. **See** prose writing; **also** Pliny the Elder (Chapter 1).

Neoplatonism

For this important philosophical movement that developed during the Roman Empire, **see** Plotinus (Chapter 1).

novel

For this popular literary form in which a story is told in a long narrative, **see** *The Golden Ass;* prose writing; *Satyricon.*

Odes

This collection of poems in four books by the Augustan poet Horace was one of the major achievements of Roman literature. Books 1 through 3, comprising eighty-eight poems, were published about 23 B.C.; Book 4, composed of fifteen more, appeared perhaps ten years later. They are in a variety of meters and, by the author's own admission, are modeled on the works of the earlier Greek poets Sappho and Alcaeus.

The themes and subjects of the *Odes* are wide-ranging, some involving public affairs, others private aspects of Horace's life and the lives of his friends. The public ones often express his feelings of relief (presumably shared by a majority of Romans) that an age of strife and uncertainty had begun to give way to one of peace and security under the rule of Augustus. "Jupiter's thunder confirms our belief that he is the lord of heaven," he writes. "Augustus shall be held an earthly God" (*Odes* 3.5). Horace's patriotism also takes the form of praising traditional Roman values of austerity, courage in the face of hardship, and loyalty to country (values widely felt to have been lost in the turbulent years of the late Republic). "Let every Roman boy be taught to know hardship as a friend," one of the odes begins. "Yes, let him live beneath the open sky in danger. . . . For country is a sweet and seemly thing to die for" (*Odes* 3.2).

Horace's more private odes deal with love, the changing seasons, the beauties and virtues of country living, and the need to live life to its fullest, since life is so short. At the same time, he advocates that one should not seek life's extremes, but rather learn to live moderately; that way real happiness is easier to achieve. "He that holds fast to the golden mean," he says, "and lives contentedly between the little and the great, feels not the wants that pinch the poor, nor plagues that haunt the rich man's door" (*Odes* 2.10). Most of these pieces are charming and witty, and some have surprise endings. Overall, the odes display the author's extraordinary talent for expressing himself concisely and always with just the right emotional tone and choice of words. **See** Augustan Age of literature; poetry; **also** Horace (Chapter 1).

On Architecture

A Latin treatise in ten books by the first-century B.C. Roman architect and engineer Vitruvius, it later proved to be one of the most influential surviving Roman literary works. In the preface, the author dedicates the work to his mentor, Augustus:

> I set about the composition of this work for you. For I perceived that you have built, and are now building, on a large scale. Furthermore, with respect to the future, you have such regard to public and private buildings, that they will correspond to the grandeur of our history, and will be a memorial to future ages. . . . In the following books, I have expounded a complete system of architecture.

This last sentence was no idle boast, for the work covers all types of Greek and Roman building, as well as methods of decoration, mathematics, and diverse aspects of civil engineering. Vitruvius discusses the qualifications of an architect, town planning, building materials, temple architecture, and public buildings and how sound propagates within them. He also covers private dwellings and their interior decorations, aqueducts and water systems, geometry and measuring systems, and mechanics and mechanical devices.

Vitruvius's prediction about his conservative "Augustan" style becoming a memorial for future ages turned out to be correct. After Rome's fall, *On Architecture* survived in various medieval handwritten copies. The edition published in 1486 became a sudden sensation among European architects and established the neoclassical building style that dominated Europe for centuries and even influenced American architects such as Thomas Jefferson. **See** orders, architectural; **also** Vitruvius (Chapter 1).

On Duties

The last of Cicero's great works on moral philosophy, *On Duties* (*de Officiis*) was completed late in 44 B.C. Set in the form of a letter to his son, it comprises three books of moral advice derived from Stoic doctrine. In the first book, the author considers the moral duties of the individual, based on the existence of four principal virtues—wisdom, fortitude, justice, and temperance. In Books 2 and 3, Cicero shows how leading a virtuous life might lead to success and holds that personal honor and justice are ultimately more important than wealth and other kinds of material gain. Throughout the work, he emphasizes the importance of public service, as well as one's duty to treat fellow human beings in a just and humane manner. Along with Cicero's other philosophical works, *On Duties* strongly influenced later European theologians and political philosophers. **See** Stoicism; *Tusculan Disputations;* **also** Cicero, Marcus Tullius (Chapter 1).

On the Nature of Things

The only known work of the Roman poet and philosopher Lucretius, it consists of six books of verse. The author's purpose was to help people free themselves from their sense of guilt and fear of death by showing that the soul is not punished following death. Basing his ideas on the atomic theory of the Greek philosopher Epicurus (341–271 B.C.), who was himself influenced by the earlier Greek scientists Democritus and Leucippus, Lucretius maintains that the world and its contents are material in nature and governed by natural laws. Furthermore, the soul too is material and mortal and therefore perishes after death.

In the work Lucretius explains that the universe is composed of invisible, indestructible atoms and describes how these atoms are continually in motion, colliding to form larger masses that form nature's physical objects. He tells how the soul too is composed of atoms and admonishes the reader not to fear death. In addition, the author explains the workings of the human senses and the meaning of dreams; warns that the passion of love is harmful to a

healthy, peaceful state of mind; traces the origins and history of plants and animals on the earth; and discusses natural phenomena such as earthquakes, volcanic eruptions, and plagues.

Though Lucretius does not advocate specific moral conduct, a strong moral sense pervades the work. He follows the Epicurean view that the ideal is to attain peace of mind (that is, the absence of pain and excessive desire) by alleviating human suffering and superstitious fears. **See** Lucretius (Chapter 1).

On Oratory

A famous and influential work in three books by Cicero, who completed it in 55 B.C. Addressed to his brother Quintus, it presents the basic principles of the art of oratory. The author set the work in the form of dialogues supposedly taking place in a previous generation, the main speakers being the renowned lawyer/orators Lucius Licinius Crassus (140–91 B.C.) and Marcus Antonius (143–87 B.C.). **See** Cicero, Marcus Tullius (Chapter 1).

On the Republic

A major work by Cicero dealing with political science, it was published in six books in 51 B.C. Only sections of it survive, among them *The Dream of Scipio,* set in the form of a dialogue modeled somewhat on the *Republic* of the Greek philosopher Plato. The chief aim of Cicero's *Republic* is to discern the best form of government by examining the main types—monarchy, oligarchy, and democracy—one at a time. The author's distrust of pure democracy emerges strongly, although he does advocate combining certain democratic principles with more autocratic ones in a mixed constitution, each extreme serving to balance and check the other. If forced to choose a single system, Cicero goes with kingship, though his version is less a dictatorship and more like the enlightened rule of the "philosopher-kings" advocated by

Plato. Indeed, Cicero insists that rulers and civil institutions should exist primarily to bring the citizenry security and happiness, and the work repeatedly stresses the importance of justice and fairness, both in the government's treatment of its citizens and in its dealings with other peoples. **See** Cicero, Marcus Tullius (Chapter 1).

orations of Cicero

Cicero was, without doubt, the greatest orator Rome ever produced. Fifty-eight of his speeches have survived, including those he composed to defend his clients in the courts (*For Quinctio, For Cluentio, For Flacco,* and so forth); those composed to prosecute Gaius Verres, an administrator on trial for corruption (the so-called Verrine orations); the four speeches he delivered in the Senate denouncing Catiline, who sought to topple the government; and the fourteen *Philippics,* speeches denouncing Mark Antony's seizure of power following Julius Caesar's assassination. The importance of Cicero's speeches has been ably summarized by the noted scholar Michael Grant:

> They are a mine of information about one of the most significant periods in the history of the world. They are transcripts of the most successful and persuasive oratory ever delivered, belonging to an age when oratory was the major activity of civil life and the nucleus of the educational system. They help to reveal the man who was this preeminent orator and who also played a prominent part in the seething, ominous political scene, a person of extraordinary character whom we are able to get to know intimately. Moreover, his works have continued to exercise a decisive influence on the minds of men throughout the intervening ages. (*Selected Political Speeches of Cicero,* p. 7)

One of the principal overriding themes of many of these orations is a steadfast defense of the cherished republican values and virtues that were already crumbling around Cicero and his fellows. The romantic ideal of the Republic that he evokes so often was perhaps just that, only an ideal; but he had come to believe that the country had at least to attempt to strive for its old-fashioned values, or else perish in an orgy of greed, personal ambition, and civil discord. He often emerges in these speeches, therefore, somewhat vainly, as the patriotic champion of the state and the people, placing himself, their shield, in the path of those forces that threaten to destroy them. In the second speech against Catiline, for example, Cicero rails:

> It is impossible for me to forget that Rome is my country and that I am the consul of all you people who are assembled here—with whom I will live, if you live, or die on your behalf! . . . If I detect any move against our government or even the first beginnings or attempts at such a move, its instigator will have good reason to discover that this city of ours is not lacking in vigilant consuls, reliable officials, a courageous Senate, [and] all the weapons that are needed [to defend the state]. . . . The most formidable and horrifying civil war in human memory will be disposed of under the sole and single leadership and command of myself—wearing the clothes of peace. (*Against Catiline* 2.7.26–28)

The same qualities of clarity, boldness, directness, drama, and moral indignation evident in this passage prevail throughout the orations; in them, Cicero is also often clever, amiable, and witty, and he makes frequent references to historical events and figures to illustrate his points. **See** prose writing; **also** Cicero, Marcus Tullius (Chapter 1).

oratory

Public speaking was an essential means of expression for Roman politicians, lawyers, and other influential people. **See** rhetoric.

orders, architectural

The three architectural styles the Romans borrowed from the Greeks, each of which was defined or characterized by the basic features of the columns employed. Columns in the Doric order had simple, flat, rectangular capitals (tops); column capitals in the Ionic order featured volutes (curved scrolls); and in the most ornate order, the Corinthian, column capitals were covered with decorative masonry leaves.

Roman architects did not utilize these orders haphazardly, as many modern builders do. Rather, each order had a symbolic meaning, depending on the kind of building in which it was used, and also produced a specific visual effect. The first-century B.C. architect Vitruvius devoted a great deal of space in his *On Architecture* to the benefits and correct uses of the orders. As a rule, a single building employed the style of a single order. However, there were exceptions. The Colosseum, for instance, features all three orders in its outer façade; the lowest level has half-columns of the Doric order, the second level, Ionic, and the third level, Corinthian. The archless fourth level features forty-five-foot-high pilasters (partial columns embedded in walls) with Corinthian capitals. **See** building materials and techniques; *On Architecture.*

painting

The chief surviving examples of Roman painting (outside of that done on pottery) are the wall murals discovered at Pompeii, Herculaneum, and Stabiae, the three Roman towns buried by the A.D. 79 eruption of Mount Vesuvius. They reveal many details of everyday Roman life. Furthermore,

their abundance in such small communities indicates that most Romans who could afford to do so decorated their homes with such paintings. At least this was the case from the first century B.C. on. The extent and nature of Roman painting before that time is unclear, mainly because no significant examples have survived; however, the art of wall painting, mainly copied from the Greeks, probably began in Rome in the second century B.C.

As the murals at Pompeii and her sister cities show, most Roman paintings were not isolated decorative pieces, as are modern framed paintings; rather, they often covered entire walls, included life-size representations of pillars, furniture, doors, windows, and so on, often purposely and strikingly rendered in three dimensions; and therefore constituted an integral part of the decor. Painted scenes featuring landscapes, vignettes from everyday life, and mythological characters (mostly Greek) were also common. One of the paintings from Pompeii shows Vesuvius, its pre-eruption cone still intact; another depicts a famous riot at the city's amphitheater; an actor resting between shows is the subject of another. One of the true masterpieces found at Pompeii is often called the Lost Ram; it portrays a rustic landscape of hills, stones, and trees, with a small shrine and a man pushing a goat toward the shrine, presumably to sacrifice the animal. The use of successively graduated colors to highlight increasingly distant objects washed by the rays of the setting sun is strikingly effective.

Though some Roman wall paintings were executed on wood panels, the majority were frescoes, worked directly on wet plaster. The artist first applied two or three thin layers of limestone plaster to the wall; then he painted the background, which might include large architectural elements and/or distant landscapes. After the plaster and paint dried, the painter added human and animal figures and other details. When the entire painting was completely dry, the artist added a coating of transparent glue or wax to create a bright, glossy, more durable surface. The paints were made from minerals (such as copper carbonate) and animal and vegetable dyes, which were mixed with soapy limestone and some kind of bonding agent. **See** Pompeii (Chapter 2).

palaces

Although the first emperor, Augustus, chose a rather simple lifestyle and a surprisingly modest residence, his successors quickly abandoned this approach in favor of extreme luxury. They subsequently erected many palaces, at first in the capital city and later in other parts of Italy and also the provinces. The second emperor, Tiberius, built the first palace, the Domus Tiberiana, on the Palatine hill, which became the chief site of the imperial residences in Rome. The third emperor, Caligula, expanded this palace, and Nero, Domitian, Septimius Severus, and others also constructed palaces on the Palatine.

Nero also built one of the most famous of all Roman palaces, the Domus Aurea (Golden House) in another section of the city. After the great fire of A.D. 64 cleared the low, relatively flat expanse lying between the Esquiline, Palatine, and Caelian hills, the egotistical Nero decided to transform the entire area into his own personal pleasure park and palace. The Golden House was essentially a fabulously wealthy country villa set in the middle of the world's most crowded urban center. The living quarters alone covered some nine hundred thousand square feet, about 450 times the floor space of an average modern house. "The entrance-hall," wrote the Roman historian Suetonius, "was large enough to contain a huge statue of Nero, 120 feet high." Outside this palatial residence stretched a vast parkland containing gardens, meadows, fishponds, game preserves, streams, waterfalls, and a pillar-lined, roofed walkway nearly a mile long. Suetonius gave these further details of the emperor's "monument to himself":

> An enormous pool, like a sea, was surrounded by buildings made to resemble cities, and by a landscape garden consisting of plowed fields, vineyards, pastures, and woodlands. . . . Parts of the house were overlaid with gold and studded with precious stones and mother-of-pearl. All the dining-rooms had ceilings of . . . ivory, the panels of which could slide back and let a rain of flowers, or of perfume from hidden sprinklers, shower upon his guests. . . . When the palace had been decorated throughout in this lavish style, Nero dedicated it, and condescended to remark, "Good, now I can at last begin to live like a human being!" (*Nero* 31, in *The Twelve Caesars*)

After Nero's demise, his successors erected large bathhouses on the site of the Golden House.

Some of the palaces that rose outside Rome were no less ostentatious than Nero's lavish abode. The emperor Hadrian's residence and pleasure grounds at Tivoli, fifteen miles outside the city featured swimming pools, bathhouses, gymnasiums, libraries, temples, a theater, warehouses, fountains, and extensive gardens. And at the dawn of the Later Empire, Diocletian erected a massive palace covering some eight acres at Split (or Spalato), in Illyricum. In the shape of a huge rectangle, its sides were fortification walls sixty feet high and seven feet thick. One wall, behind which stretched a grand gallery with forty-two arched windows, bordered directly on the sea. Imperial palaces were also built at Trier, Constantinople, and elsewhere in the realm. **See** building materials and techniques; **also** Nero (Chapter 1); **and** seven hills of Rome (Chapter 2).

Pantheon

The greatest surviving example of Roman architecture and construction, the Pantheon was erected between A.D. 118 and 125 by the emperor Hadrian. It was actually the third version of the building, the first having been built over a century before by Augustus's friend Agrippa. (The features and function of Agrippa's version were obliterated by later construction on the site; however, Agrippa's name still appears in a large inscription on the front of the building.)

The Pantheon consists of two main sections: a porchlike façade in the style of a Greco-Roman temple, and behind it a large spherical rotunda topped by a massive dome. The interior diameter of the rotunda, including the base of the dome, measures 150 Roman feet (44.4 meters). The walls and dome are composed of high-quality Roman concrete, and the entire building rests on a foundation of dense concrete some fifteen Roman feet (4.5 meters) deep.

The exact function of the Pantheon is uncertain. The historian Dio Cassius said that its name (containing the Greek words *pan,* meaning "all," and *theos,* meaning "god") derived from the fact that it contained statues of all the gods, so some kind of worship may have taken place there. He also claimed that Hadrian conducted business in the structure.

Long after the decline of Greco-Roman civilization, the Pantheon became the inspiration for many European and American buildings. The *Il Redentore,* in Venice, and Thomas Jefferson's residence, Monticello, in Virginia, are two prominent examples. British architect Christopher Wren emulated the Pantheon's dome in the dome he designed for St. Paul's Cathedral in London (although Wren's version, having a diameter of 115 feet, is considerably smaller than the Roman one). **See** building materials and techniques.

pantomimes

For these popular, often spectacular ballet-like entertainments that were popular in the early Empire, **see** theater and drama.

papyrus

For this important, widely used parchment made from water plants, **see** writing materials.

Parallel Lives

Plutarch's masterpiece consists of fifty biographies of notable Greek and Roman leaders. His purpose was not strictly historical (he was not a historian by trade) but more didactic (that is, he sought to instruct his readers, especially from a moral standpoint). He strongly believed that the fusion of Greek and Roman civilization following Rome's conquest of the Hellenistic states was a positive development that strengthened both parties. Specifically, then, his main goals in writing the *Lives* were first, to show his fellow Greeks that the Romans possessed qualities that made them more than fit to rule the world; and second, to remind leading Romans that Greece had a tradition of soldiers and statesmen who were on a par with those of Rome. To make his comparisons as clear as possible, he grouped most of the biographies in pairs, each including a famous Greek and an equally renowned Roman whose personalities and careers had certain superficial similarities; hence the title, *Parallel Lives.*

Among the noted Greek figures covered in the work are Solon, Themistocles, Pericles, Nicias, Demosthenes, Alexander, and Pyrrhus; the Romans include Marius, Sulla, Pompey, Caesar, Antony, Cicero, and Brutus. The lives of the Theban statesman-general Epaminondas and the Roman general Scipio "Africanus," which were originally part of the collection, are unfortunately lost. Plutarch's narratives of these men are clearly written, engaging, and often dramatic. They are also filled with historically valuable anecdotes, for he was an honest reporter who used many sources long since lost (although some of these were not as reliable as others, so, like all historical writers, he was only as good as his sources). Among the most vivid of these anecdotes are the disastrous Athenian defeat at Syracuse during the Peloponnesian War; the inventor Archimedes' ingenious defense of Syracuse against the attacking Romans; Caesar's defeat of Pompey at Pharsalus; and Cleopatra's memorable entrance into Tarsus to meet Antony.

Parallel Lives exerted a major influence on later European writers. Its sixteenth-century English translation by Sir Thomas North (retitled *Lives of the Noble Grecians and Romans*) was widely read and popular, and became the main source for Shakespeare's plays *Coriolanus, Julius Caesar,* and *Antony and Cleopatra.* **See** prose writing; **also** Plutarch (Chapter 1).

poetry

With few exceptions, the styles and meters of Roman poetry were borrowed from the Greeks. Unlike the meters of English verse, which are determined by the placement of stressed and unstressed syllables in a line, Greek and Latin meters were quantitative; that is, they depended on the number of syllables in a line and on how many of them were long or short. The only known Roman meter not copied from the Greeks was called *saturnian* (named after the god Saturn). Some of the first examples of Roman literature utilized it, including L. Livius Andronicus's translation of Homer's *Odyssey* into Latin and Gnaeus Naevius's epic poem about the First Punic War, both in the third century B.C. Later Roman poets disliked and avoided this meter and preferred to adapt Greek meters to their own needs and styles.

Though most of the forms of Roman poetry were also adapted from Greek models, the earliest Roman poems were more likely borrowed from the Etruscans. Called Fescennine verses, they were apparently often off-color and humorous and usually recited or sung at festivals and other public gatherings. The main forms of Latin poetry that followed, including bucolic and lyric verse, the elegy, the epigram, and epic poetry, all developed in the late Republic and to one degree or another copied Greek forms. Nonetheless, in the hands of Rome's master poets, especially during the Augustan Age of literature (ca. 43 B.C.–A.D. 17), these older forms found new and often memorable avenues of expression.

Bucolic verse, for instance, was invented by the early-third-century B.C. Greek poet Theocritus. Bucolic means pastoral, and this kind of poetry was intended to capture and glorify the beauty and tranquility of the countryside. Generally, bucolic verse involves herdsmen and other "uncorrupted" rustic types, who sing about love, the hills and forests, farming, and so on. Because the Romans were traditionally a rustic farming people with strong attachments to and nostalgia for the countryside, they readily identified with bucolic poetry. Roman versions of this form reached their height in Virgil's ten *Eclogues,* which later influenced England's John Milton and other European poets. On the peace and joy of napping outside, Virgil writes:

> This night, at least, with me forget your
>   care;
> Chestnuts and curds and cream shall be
>   your fare;
> The carpet-ground shall be with leaves
>   overspread;
> And boughs shall weave a covering for
>   your head.
> For see, yon sunny hill the shade extends;
> And curling smoke from cottages
>   ascends. (*Eclogues* 1.12)

Lyric poetry, as developed by the Greeks, consisted of verses meant to be

A drawing based on a bust of the poet Virgil as a young man. His Eclogues *are widely viewed as the height of Roman pastoral poetry.*

sung to the accompaniment of a lyre (harp) and later other instruments. In adapting lyric meters, however, the Romans rarely used them in this way; instead, most Roman lyric verses were intended to be read or recited rather than sung. Two notable exceptions were a song composed in honor of the goddess Juno by Livius Andronicus in about 207 B.C. and the magnificent *Carmen Saeculare,* written by Horace for the Secular Games in 17 B.C. Gaius Catullus wrote several effective nonmusical Latin lyrics, including this one, in which he describes how the very sight of his beloved turns him to mush:

> No sooner, Lesbia,
> Do I look at you than there's no power
>   (of speech) left me,
> My tongue's paralyzed, invisible flame
> Courses down through my limbs, with
>   noise of their own,
> My ears are ringing and twin darkness
>   covers
> The light of my eyes. (*Poems* 51)

Other Roman poets who sometimes wrote lyric poetry included Horace, Statius, and Martial.

Elegiac poetry was a Greek form used mainly to express personal emotions and sentiments. Common kinds of elegies included laments and epitaphs for the dead, personal reflections on life, and expressions of love; the Roman elegy was most often a love poem. Though they copied basic elegiac form and meters, Catullus and some of the Augustan Roman poets developed a special, distinctive kind—the Latin love-elegy; essentially it consisted of a series of brief verses telling the story of a poet's love for and relationship with a woman, usually his mistress. Roman readers became intimately familiar with the joys and frustrations that Catullus experienced with Lesbia, Ovid with Corinna, Propertius with Cynthia, and Tibullus with Delia. Ovid is often called the master of Roman elegy. Here, he urges his mistress to engage in some subtle, covert interactions with him at a banquet attended also by her husband:

> Your husband? Going to the same dinner
>   as us?
> I hope it chokes him.
> So I'm only to gaze at you, darling?
>   Pretend not to notice
> while another man enjoys your touch? . . .
> Here's my plan. Listen carefully. . . .
> When he takes his place on the couch
>   and you go to join him
> looking angelic, secretly touch my foot.
> Watch me for nods and expressions that
>   speak on their own
> and, unobserved, return my signals
> in the language of eyebrows and fingers
>   wet with wine. (*Amores* 1.4)

An epigram is a short, usually witty poem expressing a specific idea, thought, or observation. Catullus was one of the first Roman poets who wrote epigrams modeled on Greek versions; throughout the remainder of the first century B.C. and on into the early Empire, many other prominent Romans, poets and nonpoets alike, produced epigrams. Most of these have not survived. The culmination of this style in Rome was Martial's large output of epigrams in the first century A.D. Covering every conceivable subject, they often display penetrating observations of human nature and behavior, as well as biting humor, as evidenced by these two examples:

> You ask me what I get
> Out of my country place.
> The profit, gross or net,
> Is never seeing your face.
> (*Epigrams* 2.38)

> Although you're glad to be asked out,
> Whenever you go, you bitch and shout
> And bluster. You must stop being rude.
> You can't enjoy free speech *and* food.
> (*Epigrams* 9.9)

The Romans received their first taste of epic poetry when Livius Andronicus translated Homer's *Odyssey* into Latin in the third century B.C. This inspired Gnaeus Naevius to compose the first original Latin epic poem, about the Punic Wars, soon afterward. In the 180s B.C., Quintus Ennius wrote a long epic (in eighteen books) chronicling Roman history; fewer than six hundred lines survive. Both Homer and Ennius in turn inspired Virgil, by far the master of the Latin epic. His *Aeneid,* telling the story of Aeneas's foundation of the Roman race, is a stately, resplendent work that begins with the famous lines memorized by countless schoolchildren over the ages:

> Of arms I sing and the hero, destiny's
>   exile,
> Who came from the beach of Troy and
>   was the first
> To make the Lavinian landfall, in Italy.

Other Roman epic poets that followed Virgil included Lucan, whose *Pharsalia* (in

ten books, about the civil war between Caesar and Pompey) is perhaps the greatest epic of the first century A.D.; Silius Italicus, whose *Punica* is about the Second Punic War; and Gaius Valerius Flaccus, who composed the *Argonautica* (about Jason and the quest for the Golden Fleece), modeled on a Greek epic of the same title by Apollonius of Rhodes. **See** *Aeneid;* Augustan Age of literature; *Odes;* prose writing; theater and drama; **also** names of specific poets (Chapter 1).

pottery

The making of pottery, or ceramics, was one of the principal industries of the Roman world. Romans used a wide range of pottery vessels and objects for tableware, storing and transporting goods, lighting (as in the case of ceramic lamps and candlesticks), and decoration (ceramic figurines). In fact, pottery objects are the most common artifacts found by archaeologists at ancient Mediterranean sites.

Despite pottery's abundance and importance, however, relatively little is known about how Roman artisans actually made ceramic items, mainly because ancient writers rarely mentioned or described the processes involved. Apparently the clay to be used was first allowed to weather for a while; then, the potter may have mixed it with water to cause pebbles and other coarse particles to settle out. Some of the fashioning of the prepared clay was done by hand. A number of highly decorated vessels were made in molds; however, the majority of ceramics were shaped on potter's wheels of both wood and stone, none of which have survived. Some may have been large and positioned on the ground, while others were likely small and waist-high, with a flywheel below operated by the potter's foot. Once a pot was shaped and allowed to dry, the potter placed it in a kiln and baked it at a high temperature. After firing, some ceramics were left plain; others were painted with intricate floral designs and/or figures of humans and animals.

The types and distribution of Roman pottery fell into two broad categories—native wares, which were made and used mainly locally; and trade wares, made primarily to be shipped far and wide. Native wares were often made in traditional local styles that had been popular in non-Roman areas before the Romans took them over. Many were coarse, plain, and unglazed. Some, however, particularly those made in various parts of Greece, were of much higher quality.

The most abundant type of Roman trade ware was known as *terra sigillata* (translated literally as "clay decorated with figures," although the term is also used to describe unadorned vessels). It is also referred to as Samian, "red-gloss," and "red-coated" ware. As these last two names indicate, it had a reddish hue (partly because it was usually made from a red clay), although marbled and black varieties were also known. Its evolution was as follows. In the fourth century B.C., the Romans began to copy Greek ceramics that used a red clay and had glossy red and black surfaces. The Italian version became known as Campanian ware (after the region of Campania, where many potters worked). Then, in the mid–first century B.C., new firing techniques applied to Campanian ware led to the creation of the first red-gloss ware, which was at first dubbed Arretine ware after the town in which it originated—Arretium, in central Italy. Italy exported Arretine ware across the Mediterranean sphere and into the Near East. In the first century A.D., the red-gloss industry spread to Gaul, which remained the principal center of production for about two centuries, after which pottery-making centers in Spain, Britain, and North Africa superceded it.

Modern scholars often use *terra sigillata* to help date the sites in which it is found. This is possible partly because the form and decorative style of this kind of pottery underwent distinct changes from one era to another. Also, the potters usually stamped the objects they made with their names and sometimes the names of their workshops; when excavators know the era in which a workshop thrived, they can estimate the approximate period when a vessel made at that workshop made its way to the site they are investigating. **See** amphorae; trade (Chapter 5).

prose writing

Unlike Roman poetry, most Roman prose was little influenced by Greek forms. The sources of early Roman (that is, Latin) prose were apparently public oratory (an important aspect of Roman political life and legal institutions); written laws and commentaries on them composed by jurists, judges, and other scholars; and to some degree the early annals kept by Rome's chief priests. Modern scholars are almost unanimous in praising Cicero's speeches and treatises (first century B.C.) as the zenith of Roman prose. His prose works have a natural, graceful flow, free or almost so from the more artificial styles and literary effects regularly used in poetry and rhetoric. Another Latin writer who avoided such artificial effects was the noted teacher Quintilian (first century A.D.). By contrast, the prose writings of Tacitus, Seneca the Younger, Pliny the Younger (all first century A.D.), and Ammianus (fourth century A.D.) are more stylized in one way or another, though still admirable in their own right from a literary standpoint.

The first Roman prose took the form of historical writing (historiography). The earliest Roman historians, among whom Fabius Pictor is perhaps the most famous, worked in the early third century B.C. They wrote in Greek, partly because Latin prose had not yet developed, and also because they wanted to glorify Rome in the eyes of the Greeks, whom the Romans were in the process of subjugating. Latin historical prose began with Cato the Elder in the mid–second century B.C. He composed a large Latin history of Rome based on information from earlier Greek and Roman historians and inspired a new generation of Latin historical writers. They became known as the "annalists," because they consulted the *Annales Maximi,* records long kept by Rome's chief priests. Subsequently, Roman historiography tended to follow the year-by-year chronological approach of the *Annales* (although there were exceptions, such as Suetonius's biographical *The Twelve Caesars*). Later historians, including the great Livy (first century B.C.), also employed a moralistic tone, and most concentrated more on the literary style and quality of their prose than the accuracy of their facts (since very few attempted to verify the information in their sources and freely incorporated hearsay and supernatural elements). Tacitus moralized, too, but his prose was more concise and generally more critical and powerful than Livy's. Also, Tacitus saw history as driven by individual, pivotal figures, so his historical writing has a biographical feel.

Straightforward biography and autobiography as a Roman prose form began with funeral orations and extended tomb inscriptions. In late republican times, some Roman politicians and generals wrote about their own lives and exploits (the most famous example being Julius Caesar's *Commentaries on the Gallic and Civil Wars*). And in the Empire, some emperors and members of their families wrote autobiographies. All of these are lost, with the exception of Augustus's *Res gestae,* a concise and literarily unexceptional synopsis of his major accomplishments. Among the most notable surviving examples of Roman biography are Tacitus's *Agricola* (about his father-in-law) and Suetonius's *The Twelve Caesars* (early second century A.D.); Augustine's *Confessions* (ca. A.D. 400) is an important example of Roman autobiography.

Another important form of Roman prose consisted of letters. Some, like those Cicero wrote to Atticus and other acquaintances, were not written for publication (although Cicero's letters were collected and published after his death), while other letters were composed with publication in mind, a major example being many of those penned by Pliny the Younger. The surviving letters of these and other notable Romans are priceless sources of information, not only about their own lives, but also about the people, events, and customs of their respective eras.

Not much is known about still another kind of Roman prose, the Latin novel. (Ancient novels can be defined generally as lengthy prose narratives that told romantic, fictional stories.) The first known major Latin novel was Petronius's *Satyricon* (first century A.D.), part of which survives. Its style was based on that of Greek novels, which it also parodies to some extent. The only complete surviving Latin novel is *The Golden Ass* (second century A.D.), by Apuleius. Other notable Roman prose works included encyclopedic collections of facts and knowledge, such as those of Varro, Vitruvius, Celsus, and Pliny the Elder. **See** Latin and other languages; poetry; rhetoric; titles of specific works; **also** names of specific writers (Chapter 1).

Res gestae

(*Res gestae divi Augustus,* or "the divine Augustus's achievements") The first emperor, Augustus, began working on this summary of his important deeds circa 8 B.C. and continued to revise it until the end of his reign in A.D. 14. He ordered that after his death the text was to be inscribed on bronze pillars standing outside his tomb. This was done and stone copies were also installed in various parts of the Empire. The most famous copy, found in Ankara, Turkey, is often called the *Monumentum Ancyranum.*

Though clearly intended as propaganda, to justify and glorify the choices and policies Augustus had made as absolute ruler of the Mediterranean world, the text proceeds in a matter-of-fact, concise, rather modest manner. For example, he says: "I was a member of the triumvirate for the settlement of the commonwealth for ten consecutive years. I have been ranking senator for forty years. . . . I have been *pontifex maximus* [high priest], augur, [and a] member of the college of fifteen for performing sacrifices" (7).

For the most part, the author presents a sober, accurate picture of his accomplishments. Yet when it suits his purpose, he generalizes, leaves out pertinent facts and opposing views, and subtly shades the truth, especially in regard to his early career, in which he fought his way to the top using violent and often illegal means. Take, for instance, his opening statement: "At the age of nineteen, on my own initiative and my own expense, I raised an army by means of which I liberated the Republic, which was oppressed by the tyranny of a faction" (1). This painfully brief, ambiguous summary of a period pregnant with crucial events fails to mention that the army he raised was made up mostly of Caesar's veterans, and that Augustus (then Octavian) used these soldiers not to aid the state, but rather to strengthen his own political position in the turbulent months following his adoptive father's assassination. Indeed, far from liberating the Republic, Augustus proceeded in the coming years to transform it into an autocratic state. Conveniently, moreover, he refers to his rival, Antony, as "a faction" rather than by name and says nothing about the nature of their disagreements.

Despite such occasional distortions, for which scholars can easily make allowances, the *Res gestae* remains one of the most important surviving ancient political documents. **See** epigraphy; prose writing; **also** Augustus (Chapter 1).

rhetoric

This form of oratory can be described as the art of persuasive speaking. The Romans borrowed the form from the Greeks, specifically teachers called sophists, who held that skill in public speaking was an essential tool for a man who wanted to take part in politics. By the first century B.C., the study of rhetoric had become an integral component of the education of well-to-do Roman men, especially those entering the two most prestigious public professions, politics and the law. Special schools trained young men in this art, which reached its culmination in the orations of the great republican champion Cicero (d. 43 B.C.).

Rhetoric declined in quality and importance in the early Empire, mainly because speaking in court or before the Senate or assemblies was no longer the primary means for young men of means to get ahead in life. Nevertheless, training in rhetoric continued among the upper classes, and a form of rhetoric called *declamatio,* in which a person gave a public recitation of a literary work, became popular in prosperous circles. Also, formal rhetorical elements and devices came to be used commonly in various forms of Latin literature.

These elements included five basic steps one was expected to follow in preparing a speech. The first was "invention," which consisted of choosing the topic and finding the proper material to craft the presentation; the second, "arrangement," involved arranging the materials in an ordered, logical, and effective manner; the third, "diction," had to do with choosing the most effective tone of voice and manner of delivery (which might be loud and forceful, quiet and subdued, or something in between); the fourth, "memory," involved teaching the orator how to memorize long tracts of material (since it was not customary to use notes or other prompts); and the fifth element, "delivery," provided the speaker with various vocal and strategic techniques, devices, and tricks to use in the actual delivery of a speech. **See** orations of Cicero; prose writing; **also** Cicero, Marcus Tullius (Chapter 1); **and** education (Chapter 5).

roads

The Romans were not the first people in the ancient world to build large-scale roads. The Assyrians, Persians, Etruscans, and Greeks constructed roads, and the techniques they used directly influenced Roman road builders. However, the road systems of these earlier peoples paled in comparison with those built by the Romans. Large numbers of Roman roads were expertly paved and graded for great distances and proved so durable that some are still in use today. Moreover, the sheer size of the Roman road system dwarfed all others constructed in the world until the twentieth century. By about A.D. 300, the Roman Empire had over 370 fully or partially paved major highways, totaling some fifty-three thousand miles in all. Thousands of smaller roads branched outward from these main roads, creating a total mileage, in all likelihood, in the hundreds of thousands. An engineering achievement of the first order, this road system not only facilitated trade and tourism, but also, by allowing the swift movement of armies, proved a crucial tool for maintaining and expanding Rome's vast Mediterranean realm.

The Romans built various kinds of roads, with numerous names and classifications. One of the more familiar road names, *via,* meant a road (or sometimes a city street) wide enough for two vehicles to pass each other; this is the term that became most commonly applied to major highways, such as the first major Roman road, the Via Appia (or Appian Way), begun by and named after the censor Appius Claudius Caecus in 312 B.C. The general term for a city street was *vicus,* while the term *agger,* which meant an embankment or mound, was often applied to a road built atop a raised mound or causeway. A single-lane country road, usually originating as a trackway for cattle and other animals, and almost always having a dirt rather than a paved surface, was called an *actus.*

In addition to these and other individual names for roads, the Romans had general road classifications. A first-century A.D. Roman surveyor named Siculus Flaccus wrote a treatise that lists the four official classes of road recognized in his day. This breakdown was based on which party or parties bore the financial responsibility for the road and included public highways (*viae publicae*); military roads (*viae militares*), which were originally built for the army but later came into general use; local roads (*actus*); and private roads (*privatae*), which were paid for by private parties. Still another way the Romans classified their roads was by the ways these routes were surfaced. The term *via terrena,* for example, referred to a simple dirt road. A *via glarea strata,* on the other hand, had a more durable surface of gravel. More durable still was the surface of a *via silice strata,* a road or stretch of road paved with blocks of stone. By the first century B.C., most of the streets in the larger Roman cities were paved, as were large sections of the Via Appia and other major highways leading to and from the capital city.

During the Republic, the responsibility for the building of public roads fell on the censors, who decided on new construction projects and awarded the contracts for them. On the other hand, resurfacing, cleaning, and otherwise maintaining public roads

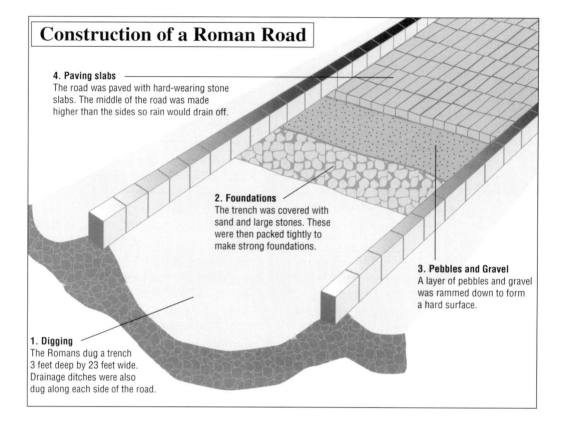

Construction of a Roman Road

4. Paving slabs
The road was paved with hard-wearing stone slabs. The middle of the road was made higher than the sides so rain would drain off.

2. Foundations
The trench was covered with sand and large stones. These were then packed tightly to make strong foundations.

3. Pebbles and Gravel
A layer of pebbles and gravel was rammed down to form a hard surface.

1. Digging
The Romans dug a trench 3 feet deep by 23 feet wide. Drainage ditches were also dug along each side of the road.

were the tasks of the aediles, who maintained public works. In 20 B.C., at the dawn of the Empire, Augustus set up a special board of curators—the *curatores viarum*—to manage public highways in Italy. In the provinces, the governors had overall charge of roads; customarily, a governor contacted a local community and ordered its magistrates either to repair an existing road or to construct a new one in the vicinity of that community.

Roman roads featured many conveniences and amenities. Major roads were cambered (curved so that the middle was slightly higher than the sides) to make rainwater drain away from the surface. Also, in stretches where a road was steep, prone to being slippery, or otherwise dangerous, the builders carved artificial ruts into the surface to guide the wheels of carts and chariots, ensuring that these vehicles would not skid. They also placed high, flat-topped stones at intervals along the roadside so that travelers with horses

could mount their steeds easier (since stirrups, taken for granted today, had not yet been invented). In addition, milestones (*miliaria*) marked intervals of one Roman mile. Like modern road signs, these provided information about distances between towns and cities along the road.

In time, other, more elaborate amenities sprang up alongside the major Roman highways to give aid and comfort to the many kinds of travelers who frequented these roads. Such facilities included posting stations, inns, eating places, stables, markets, chapels, and so on, clusters of which often developed into full-fledged villages and towns. In this way, travel along these roads became more inviting to even more people, who built still more roads, which stimulated the growth of more towns, and so forth, continuing the development of formerly undeveloped regions. Moreover, as the major roads carried their services and amenities to distant parts of the realm, these microcosms of

Roman life and customs spread Roman civilization far and wide. **See** building materials and techniques; **also** weights and measures (Chapter 5) for measurement of road distances.

satire

(*satura*) One of the few literary genres the Romans developed mainly on their own, with little influence from Greek models. Greek literature certainly contained satirical elements, most notably in the Old Comedy (late fifth century B.C.), in which playwrights like Aristophanes poked fun at leading citizens; however, the Greeks never developed the idea of commenting on, criticizing, and ridiculing various aspects of daily life as a separate literary form. The Romans did so, the first important Roman satirist being Gaius Lucilius (ca. 180–ca. 102 B.C.). His satires were in verse; however, the great first-century B.C. encyclopedist Marcus Terentius Varro, who dabbled in satire, introduced a mixture of verse and prose, a style commonly followed thereafter. The noted Augustan poet Horace also wrote satires, although his are more charming and less biting and bitter than most of those that came before and after him.

In this regard, the master of satirical invective and greatest of all Roman satirists was Juvenal, whose sixteen satires were published in the second century A.D. His modern translator, the noted scholar Peter Green, provides this excellent summary of the intent and tone of these pieces:

> The moral dilemma which Juvenal presents . . . lies at the heart of his position as a satirist. . . . [He] finds that the historical process is threatening to sweep him into oblivion. . . . [In the society he describes] lawyers with principles are being ousted by cheap, flashy shysters . . . posts in the army or the civil service are handed out to Greek freedmen . . . writers are at the mercy of ignorant, contemptuous patrons, teachers are despised, bullied, and paid a miserable pittance, [and] the traditional ruling classes are frittering away their money and authority. . . . Like so many writers who feel that the world they inhabit is out of joint, Juvenal is continually harking back to the [good old days of the] distant past. . . . If his solution [to society's ills]—let men pursue virtue and all will be well—seems to us intolerably naïve, at least he saw the crucial flaw at the heart of his society, and expressed it in memorable terms. (*Juvenal: The Sixteen Satires,* pp.33–37)

The following example illustrates Juvenal's tendency to compare the "simpler but purer" past with the "decadent and impure" present. In the old days, he insists, the Romans had not yet been corrupted by luxury, and his own simple lifestyle provides a virtuous contrast with the excesses he perceives around him.

> Our early Republican troops were rough diamonds; they hadn't acquired a taste for Greek material luxuries. When a city was sacked, and their share of the loot consisted of silver antique goblets, quite priceless, they'd break them up to make horse-trappings, or to emboss their helmets. . . . These troops ate their porridge from plain earthenware bowls. . . . But your modern millionaire cannot enjoy his dinner. The fish and venison are equally tasteless, the scent and the roses stink like garbage in his nostrils. . . . To such a man, table-legs of silver are no more special than an iron signet-ring. That's why I blacklist guests who make snobbish comparisons between their means and mine, who despise my non-affluence.

There isn't an ounce of ivory here [in my house], not even in my dice. . . . My cups, too, are the cheapest, picked up at bargain prices. . . . Just forget all your troubles the moment you cross my threshold. (*Eleventh Satire* 93–98, 122–24, 132–35, 145, 188–89)

See poetry; prose writing; **also** Juvenal (Chapter 1).

Satyricon

A long, colorful Latin novel composed by Petronius in the first century A.D., only parts of which (most of sections 14, 15, and 16) survive. The work, which consists of prose interspersed with lines of verse, describes, with considerable humor, the adventures of three young men—Encolpius, who narrates the piece, his buddy Ascyltus, and one Giton. Traveling through the former Greek cities of southern Italy, the three, who have few or no morals, manage to avoid serious trouble by using their considerable native wits. Eventually, they attend "Trimalchio's Feast," the main surviving episode of the novel. Trimalchio, who may have been modeled on a real person, is a rich former slave who tries to show off his wealth through his house's overly ornate decorations and a series of incredibly sumptuous dishes served at the feast. During this repast, he becomes increasingly intoxicated and finally reveals the contents of his will. Moving on, the three young men are involved in a shipwreck, as well as some other misfortunes and amorous adventures. Petronius spices the work throughout with examples of colloquial, often racy Latin, which has helped modern scholars better understand the informal speech of that era. **See** prose writing; **also** Petronius (Chapter 1).

sculpture

Roman sculpture owed much to Greek sculpture. The earliest sculptures that appeared in Rome were Etruscan or executed by Etruscan artisans; but Etruscan sculpture was itself strongly influenced by Greek models as far back as the sixth century B.C. Beginning in the late fourth century B.C., the Romans began to import Greek sculpture, a trend that reached its height in the second and first centuries B.C. when Roman generals looted much Greek art to adorn Roman homes and public buildings. In these years, some new sculptures were created in Italy; but these were often done by Greek artisans and they closely copied Greek originals. These pieces included life-size or larger-than-life-size marbles and bronzes of gods, characters from mythology, and animals, as well as smaller busts and figurines.

The one area of sculpture in which the Romans developed their own style and voice and truly excelled was portraiture, sometimes consisting of full-bodied statues but more often of busts, either three-dimensional or in relief (as frequently seen in tomb sculptures). Roman portraiture developed in the third century B.C. and reached its peak in the early Empire. It was characterized by a unique and powerful sense of realism, as human faces were captured accurately, in minute and sometimes unflattering detail. This style contrasted sharply with that of the Greeks, which tended toward more ideal forms and features.

There is little doubt that Roman portraiture was strongly influenced by the custom of making highly realistic death masks (*imagines*) of deceased relatives. As Pliny the Elder stated, "In the halls of our ancestors, wax models of faces were displayed to furnish likenesses in funeral processions, so that at a funeral the entire clan [including those no longer living] was present" (*Natural History* 35.2). Indeed, one of the finest surviving examples of Roman portraiture, dating from the late first century B.C., shows a patrician man holding two *imagines* of his ancestors. Among the greatest examples of this art are the relief sculptures carved into the walls of the Ara Pacis (Altar of Peace), a magnificent monument erected in Rome by Augustus. The emperor himself is among the figures realistically displayed. **See** Ara Pacis; mosaics; painting.

Stoicism

A philosophical movement founded by the Greek thinker Zeno of Citium circa 300 B.C., Stoicism subsequently became very popular among Roman intellectuals, especially in the first and second centuries A.D. Among the most notable Stoics of that period (often referred to as the Late Stoics), were Seneca the Younger, Gaius Musonius Rufus (who taught Pliny the Younger), the Greek-born philosopher Epictetus (also a pupil of Musonius Rufus), and the emperor Marcus Aurelius. The movement died out in the third century, but its ideas remained influential and eventually contributed to the developing outlook of early Christian thinkers.

According to the main doctrines of Stoicism, the cosmos is endowed with divine purpose or intelligence (*logos*), a tiny spark of divine fire existing in every human. Therefore, all people, from wealthy aristocrats to lowly slaves, are spiritual brothers. The key to happiness is virtue, a form of wisdom exemplified by courage, moderation, and shouldering responsibility. Greed, fear, extravagance, and dishonesty are symptoms of ignorance and will lead to certain misery. Therefore, the wise and virtuous person learns to accept whatever happens in life without complaint, since it happens for a purpose, and to live in harmony with nature. **See** Marcus Aurelius; Seneca the Younger; Zeno 1. (all Chapter 1).

surveying

For the methods the Romans used to select routes for roads and aqueducts and to lay out the sites for structures, **see** building materials and techniques.

theater and drama

Like so many other aspects of Roman culture, including leisure pursuits, the theater was inspired almost entirely by the Greeks, who originated the art form in the sixth and fifth centuries B.C. (The exception appears to be some festive poems, called Fescennine verses, sung and spoken at festivals by performers called *histriones,* an early theatrical form borrowed from the Etruscans.) As usual, the Romans were slow to catch on and formal plays were not presented in Rome until the third century B.C.

Before this time, the chief theatrical fare in Rome consisted of two rather informal kinds of entertainment: the Atellan farces (*fabula Atellana*) and mimes. The Atellan farces, which made their way to Rome from the Greek cities of southern Italy, were short comic skits similar to the sketches on modern TV variety shows like *Saturday Night Live.* Each of these largely improvised pieces revolved around a simple idea or situation, such as getting drunk, overeating, or shoplifting. The actors wore masks representing stock characters. In later centuries, some of these farces were written down, but all that survives are titles, such as *The Bride of Pappus, The Baker,* and *The Pregnant Virgin.* The other early Roman theatrical import from Greece, the mime, was more realistic and more bawdy than the farce. The actors did not wear masks, used facial expressions instead for comic effect, regularly utilized obscene lines and gestures, and even made fun of the gods. Another difference between the two forms was that the mimes also came to feature jugglers, acrobats, dancing girls, magicians, tightrope walkers, and so on, making them similar in many ways to early twentieth-century American burlesque shows.

In the late third and early second centuries B.C., the Romans began to have closer contact with mainland Greece and the Greek kingdoms of the eastern Mediterranean. One result was the adoption of longer, more structured, and more formally presented plays based on the Greek New Comedy (the Greek theatrical form that was popular in the fourth and third centuries B.C.). The first Roman versions appeared about 240 B.C. at the *ludi Romani,* a festival honoring Jupiter; among the authors was a Greek, Livius Andronicus, who strongly influenced the first important Roman playwright, Gnaeus Naevius. Of Naevius's many tragedies and comedies, only a few lines survive.

At the time, and with few exceptions for centuries to come, Roman playwrights turned out copies of Greek originals, imitating their themes, plots, characters, and even giving most of these characters Greek names. Still, some Roman playwrights, particularly Plautus and Terence, who wrote in the third and second centuries B.C., respectively, were very talented, and their works, all comedies (since comedy became much more popular than tragedy in Rome), were widely admired. Plautus, for instance, kept his audiences rolling in the aisles with slapstick comedies such as *The Pot of Gold, The Braggart Warrior,* and *The Comedy of Asses.* These plays featured swift-moving plots and rapid-fire gags and puns. Greek conventions prevailed, including men playing women's roles (although in later times women were allowed onstage), the use of masks, stock characters, and so on. Actors were generally viewed as social and moral inferiors in part because they were mostly foreigners, especially Greeks, and also because many of them had originally been slaves. (A small handful of Roman actors managed to become wealthy and attain some acceptance in high society.)

Although formal written plays continued to be presented in the centuries that followed, during the early Empire the genre declined significantly as a wide array of theatrical events captured the imagination of the masses. On the one hand, mimes, which remained widely popular, still competed with formal plays. Much more popular among all walks of life, however, were the public games, including gladiatorial combats, chariot races, and wild beast shows, with which the plays simply could not effectively compete.

Many former playgoers were also diverted by a new theatrical form. It consisted of pantomimes (*fabula saltica*), balletlike presentations performed by a solo dancer (the *pantomimus*) who was accompanied by musicians and a choir singing a narration of the story the dance portrayed. That the themes were more serious and dignified than those in the mimes is reflected in the titles, which included "Chaos," "Cleopatra," and many named after Greek epics and tragedies. The second-century A.D. Greek writer Lucian praised the art of Roman pantomime, saying that "it sharpens the wits, it exercises the body, it delights the spectator, it instructs him in the history of bygone days, while eye and ear are held beneath the spell of flute and cymbal and of graceful dance" (*On Dancing* 72).

Still another theatrical form that developed in the early Empire was the "tragic recitation," consisting of verses spoken and sung by actors backed up by choruses and musicians. These works, including some notable tragedies by Nero's adviser, Seneca the Younger (including *Medea, Phaedra,* and *Oedipus*), were strictly the province of the upper classes. They were not meant to and never did compete with the more popular forms of theater and drama. **See** prose writing; theaters and amphitheaters; **also** Naevius, Gnaeus; Plautus, Titus Maccius; Seneca the Younger; Terence (all Chapter 1).

theaters and amphitheaters

Roman theaters and amphitheaters underwent the same kind of evolution and were similar in form and structure. The first Roman theaters were makeshift wooden affairs erected for one or more performances and then demolished. Such structures copied the form of the Greek Hellenistic theater, which had a stage five to eight feet high, backed by a wall containing doors for the actors' entrances and exits and painted backdrops. The Romans called such a stage a *pulpitum* and the back wall the *scaenae frons.* By the early first century B.C., some of these temporary theaters had become extremely large and elaborate; one erected in 58 B.C. sat eighty thousand people and was adorned with many bronze statues.

Three years later, Rome's first permanent stone theater, the Theater of Pompey, appeared. It was shaped like a semicircle (hemisphere), with the seating area running along the curve and the *scaenae frons* erected on the inside of the straight wall; it accommodated eight thousand spectators; its stage was made of stone covered by tiles; and its *scaenae frons* was also of stone and decorated with columns, statues, and other finery. The city's other two stone theaters, those named for Balbus and Marcellus, opened in 13 and 11 B.C., respectively. The Theater of Marcellus (which Augustus named after his nephew, who died in 23 B.C.) sat some fourteen thousand people. About 125 similar theaters were constructed around the Empire in the next two centuries. In addition to a *pulpitum* and *scaenae frons,* most featured roofs overhanging the stages, curtains that moved up and down in front of them, and awnings over the seating areas.

Like theaters, amphitheaters (*amphitheatri*) evolved gradually from smaller, less durable, and less impressive structures. In form, these arenas were essentially double theaters, since each combined two hemispheres to form a larger, nearly circular oval. In the early Republic, small-scale gladiatorial bouts and other public shows were usually staged in wide, open areas, most often the fora (main squares) of cities; but in time, the Romans began building wooden arenas to accommodate public shows. Some were dismantled and reassembled as need dictated. Others may have stood intact for several seasons before being demolished to make way for houses, temples, or other structures. Though impermanent, these early arenas were often very large and elaborate, featuring seating for thousands or even tens of thousands of people. In his *Annals,* Tacitus provides a gripping account of the collapse of one such wooden arena at Fidenae (a town just north of Rome) in A.D. 27.

The first stone amphitheater in Italy was erected about 80 B.C. in Pompeii. It is oval in shape and measures 445 by 341 feet. Because the A.D. 79 eruption of nearby Mount Vesuvius encased the town in a protective layer of ash, the amphitheater is well preserved. In fact, it still bears an inscription with the names of the two prominent public

The amphitheater at Pompeii was well preserved after it was buried by the eruption of Mount Vesuvius (visible in the distance).

officials who constructed it, Valgus and Porcius. Because the Latin term *amphitheatrum* had not yet been coined, the inscription refers to the structure as a *spectaculum,* or a "place for spectacles."

Because of the great expense of building and maintaining stone amphitheaters, for a long time few towns attempted to match Pompeii's achievement. Even in Rome, building a properly grand stone amphitheater remained an elusive goal. In 29 B.C., fully half a century after the dedication of the Pompeiian arena, T. Statilius Taurus, one of Octavian's generals, constructed an amphitheater in Rome's Campus Martius. But it was surely far too small to satisfy the needs of a city the size of Rome, which by this time had a population of perhaps nearly a million. Another drawback was that, to save expense, Taurus's builders utilized both wood and stone, leaving the building seriously prone to damage by fire, which in fact eventually destroyed it. Clearly, there was a pressing need in Rome for a large, permanent amphitheater.

That need was met when the Flavian emperors (Vespasian and his sons, Titus and Domitian) erected the mighty Colosseum on the site where Nero had created his pleasure park after the great fire of A.D. 64. The facility's original name was the Amphitheatrum Flavium, or Amphitheater of the Flavians. (Not until early medieval times, well after the Roman Empire had disintegrated, did the name Colosseum come into general use.) Most of the structure's main features were completed by the summer of 80, during Titus's reign; the finishing touches were added after his death by his brother. In its

original majesty, the building's oval bowl measured 620 by 513 feet in breadth and over 156 feet in height. The oval arena floor, outlined by and butting up against a protective wall at the bottom of the seating section (*cavea*), was 287 feet long by 180 feet wide. Because the structure's seating sections no longer exist, the exact seating capacity is unknown, but most historians agree on an estimate of about fifty thousand. A giant awning, the *velarium,* was often rolled out by a gang of sailors to shade the spectators from the hot Mediterranean sun.

In addition to the Colosseum in Rome, other large stone amphitheaters were constructed around the realm. These included the huge amphitheater at Capua, which measured 560 by 460 feet and stood 95 feet high; the arena at Puteoli (across the Bay of Naples from Pompeii), measuring 490 by 370 feet; northern Italy's impressive Verona amphitheater, with dimensions of 500 by 405 feet and a seating capacity of twenty-five thousand to twenty-eight

The stone seating sections were long ago removed from the interior of Rome's greatest amphitheater, the Colosseum.

thousand; and similarly large versions at Nimes and Arles (both in Gaul) and at Thysdrus, in North Africa. Many towns had smaller but no less beautiful and sturdy arenas. Typical was the one at Augusta Treverorum (Trier), which was about 230 feet long and accommodated approximately seven thousand people. **See** building materials and techniques; theater and drama; **also** public games (Chapter 5).

Tusculan Disputations

This work by Cicero, the title of which means "discussions at Tusculum" (an Italian resort town where he had a villa), is one of his most important and emotionally expressive. Completed in 44 B.C., the work, in five books (addressed to Marcus Brutus, one of the leaders of the conspiracy against Julius Caesar), deals with the conditions necessary for true happiness. The literary form is a dialogue between two characters, designated M and A. In the first book, Cicero establishes that death, which is usually viewed as evil, is a natural and necessary process and therefore in and of itself not an impediment to happiness. The themes of the other four books, in order, are: how one can learn to endure emotional pain so that it does not impede happiness; how people can control grief to the same end; how other passions and disorders of the human soul can be controlled; and how leading a virtuous life may in and of itself be sufficient to attain happiness. **See** Cicero, Marcus Tullius (Chapter 1).

The Twelve Caesars

This lengthy and important work by the Roman writer Suetonius contains biographies of Julius Caesar and the first eleven Roman emperors: Augustus, Tiberius, Caligula, Claudius, Nero, Galba, Otho, Vitellius, Vespasian, Titus, and Domitian. Each biography presents the ancestry and principal deeds of its subject, along with numerous personal anecdotes. Though rich in detail and very lively, these works are not straightforward historical writing and have a rather haphazard structure. Perhaps because the author felt the need to take an approach different from that of his great predecessor, Tacitus, who followed a strict chronological progression in his monumental *Annals,* Suetonius arranged his material in an episodic manner, jumping back and forth from year to year and place to place. Suetonius was also much less critical critical than Tacitus, often including much more in the way of gossip, rumors, reports of omens, and other unreliable information. On the positive side, Suetonius refrains from moralizing, unlike so many other ancient biographers, and his writing is frequently dramatic and moving. His biographies are also valuable because he included direct quotes from ancient works now lost, including imperial records and letters. **See** Suetonius (Chapter 1).

vault

For this curved or domed ceiling that graced many Roman buildings, **see** building materials and techniques.

writing materials

A majority of the reading materials used in Roman schools, as well as most letters, treatises, and public documents used in society as a whole, were written on paper made from papyrus. This marsh plant native to Egypt was seen as vital. As the famous Roman naturalist Pliny the Elder put it, "Our civilization—or at any rate our written records—depends especially on the use of paper" (*Natural History* 13.68). We know how the ancients made paper from papyrus partly because some surviving paintings show workers performing some of the steps. A few written descriptions have also survived, including a valuable one by Pliny himself, who says in part: "Paper is manufactured from papyrus by splitting it [the plant's stem] with a needle into strips that are very thin but as long as possible. . . . All paper is 'woven' on a board dampened with water [to prevent the strips from drying out]. . . . The whole length of the papyrus is used and both its ends are trimmed; then strips are laid across and complete a criss-cross pattern, which is then squeezed in presses. The sheets are dried in the sun" (*Natural History* 13.74–77). When dry, the papyrus sheets were joined together to make rolls that were usually about thirty or more feet long. People wrote on the papyrus with a reed or bronze pen dipped in ink made from carbon black (soot), and then rolled it up around a wooden stick. Archaeologists have found numerous ancient Roman papyrus rolls in various states of preservation.

Archaeology has also revealed that the Romans wrote on other materials besides papyrus paper, including vellum (*vellus*), made from the skin of cattle, goats, and sheep. Vellum eventually became the preferred writing material for bound books, which appeared in the first century A.D. and largely replaced papyrus rolls by the late fourth century (although such rolls were still used for public documents). The pages of this kind of early book, called a *codex,* were stitched to a thin spine and bound with thin wooden boards.

Strongly influencing the development of such books was the widespread use of thin sheets of wood called "leaf-tablets." A person either wrote directly on the wood using a reed or quill pen dipped in ink, or covered the surface with wax and inscribed it with a metal pen (*stylus*). Recent excavations of a Roman fort at Vindolanda, in northern Britain, have brought to light more than fifteen hundred late-first-century A.D. documents, many consisting of leaf-tablets. In one, the wife of the commander of a neighboring fort addresses the wife of Vindolanda's commander: "Greetings. I send you a warm invitation to come to us on September 11th, for my birthday celebrations, to make my day more enjoyable by your presence. Give my greetings to your [husband]. My [husband] Aelius greets you and your sons. I will expect you, sister. Farewell sister, my dearest soul, as I hope to prosper, and greetings."

CHAPTER 7
ENEMIES, WAR, AND MILITARY AFFAIRS

Achaean League

This alliance of ten cities situated in the northern Peloponnesus, in Greece, was established in 280 B.C. for purposes of mutual protection against Macedonia. In the latter part of that century, however, the Achaeans joined in an alliance with Macedonia, which brought them into conflict with Rome when Macedonia's Philip V interfered in the Second Punic War between Rome and Carthage. In the Second Macedonian War (200–197 B.C.), the League switched sides and aided Rome. But like many other Greeks, in the years that followed the Achaeans grew antagonistic toward Rome. In 168 B.C., hoping to forestall serious trouble, the Romans deported some one thousand leading Achaeans (the historian Polybius among them) to Italy. Tensions finally came to a head, though, in the early 140s B.C. After Rome intervened in a disagreement between the Achaean League and Sparta, the Achaeans put up a fight; soon afterward a Roman general, Lucius Mummius Achaicus, crushed them and dissolved the League. **See** Greeks; Punic Wars; **also** Polybius (Chapter 1); **and** Achaea (Chapter 2).

Aedui

This ancient Gallic tribe occupied the region that later became Burgundy, in east-central France. The Aedui were long dominated by their neighbors, the Averni and Allobroges; but in the late second century B.C., they formed an alliance with the Romans that allowed them to prosper on their own. They repaid this favor by aiding Julius Caesar in his Gallic campaigns in the 50s B.C. Later, though, the Aedui became resentful of Roman domination. In A.D. 21, they rebelled, but were defeated by a Roman army. In 68, the tribe backed Servius Sulpicius Galba's bid for the Roman throne, one of the key events leading to the brief civil war of 69, the "year of the four emperors." In the third and fourth centuries, invading German tribes overran the Aedui's lands and they ceased to be a factor in Gaul.

Aequi

An ancient Italian people who became rivals of the early Romans, they originally inhabited the region of Reate (or Riete), in central Italy. In the early fifth century B.C. the Aequi invaded the Alban Hills, south of Rome. The Romans drove them away and later subjugated them completely, establishing a Latin colony (Carsioli) in their territory in 302 B.C. Thereafter, the Aequi rapidly became Romanized and their native language, probably Oscan, was largely supplanted by Latin.

Aetolian League

An alliance of towns, most of them in Aetolia, a region of central Greece lying north of the Gulf of Corinth and south of Macedonia. Most of the people of the area had long been organized along tribal lines, rather than in formal city-states, and had wielded little power or influence. Circa 390 B.C., for the sake of mutual protection and advancement, they formed the League and thereafter their territory and influence gradually increased. When Rome entered the Greek sphere at the dawn of the second century B.C., the Aetolians at first allied themselves with the intruders against the Macedonians. But in the late 190s B.C., the League decided to back the Seleucid king, Antiochus III, against Rome. Soon afterward the Romans subdued the Aetolians and forced them to agree to aid Rome against all her enemies ever after. **See** Aetolia (Chapter 2).

Alamanni

A large group of Germanic tribes, the Alamanni threatened the Danube frontier in the early third century A.D. In 213, the emperor Caracalla defeated them, but they soon regrouped. The emperor Maximinus Thrax subsequently crushed the Alamanni. Yet they proved resilient once again, for later they fought the emperors Gallienus and Julian and established a foothold in Gaul. In the fourth century, the Franks finally managed to break the power of the Alamanni. **See** Franks.

aquilifer

For this Roman soldier whose prestigious duty it was to carry the symbol of his legion, **see** army recruitment, training, and personnel.

armor and weapons

The panoply (complete array of armor and weapons) of the typical Roman soldier long consisted of a cuirass (chest or upper-body protection); a metal helmet; metal greaves (lower-leg protectors); a shield (the *scutum,* at first oval but later rectangular); a sword, usually worn on the right side, and sometimes also a dagger; and two throwing spears (javelins, known as *pila;* singular, *pilum*). It must be emphasized, however, that the panoply just described could vary considerably, depending on the kind of soldier and the era in which he lived. Some troops, for example skirmishers like the *velites* of midrepublican times, wore little or no armor and carried only javelins (or slings) and small round shields. Archers, most often hailing from Near Eastern lands, wore little armor and carried a curved composite bow. And by the end of the first century B.C., most soldiers no longer wore greaves (an exception being officers).

Differences and changes in the cuirass constitute an important example of variation in Roman armor. In the Monarchy and early Republic, only well-to-do soldiers could afford upper-body armor, which was usually a cuirass of beaten bronze (in two sections, front and back, held together by leather straps). By about 300 B.C. (or perhaps earlier), cuirasses made of bronze and iron mail (*lorica hamata,* meshes of small interlocked metal rings) appeared, but they were expensive to make, so at first only officers could afford them. Some legionaries did adopt mail cuirasses over time. But another kind of cuirass, the *lorica segmentata,* which appeared in the early first century A.D., became popular because it was easier to make (and therefore cheaper) and lighter in weight. It consisted of laminated horizontal strips of metal held together by buckles or hooks. Still another type, scale armor (*lorica squamata*), came into use in the late first and early second centuries; it was made by sewing rows of small bronze or iron scales onto a linen jerkin. In the Later Empire, some soldiers still wore mail and scale armor. However, armored cuirasses were more or less abandoned, especially among the barbarians who made up an increasingly large proportion of Roman troops.

Shields, swords, and javelins also underwent some change in design and use. The slightly concave rectangular *scutum,* for instance, had been phased out by the mid–third century A.D. in favor of an oval shield. The *gladius,* a sword of Spanish origin with a blade about twenty inches long, was long one of the Roman soldier's main offensive weapons. In the second and third centuries A.D., however, it was gradually replaced by a Celtic-style sword, the *spatha,* which had a blade at least two feet in length. The most important change in the design of the *pilum* was Marius's introduction (in the early first century B.C.) of an improved version equipped with a wooden rivet that broke on impact; this prevented an enemy soldier from throwing the weapon back. In the Later Empire, various versions of the *pilum* were developed with barbed, triangular, and other kinds of tips. **See** army organization and manpower; siege tactics.

army camps

The Romans became masters of the art of constructing marching camps, well-organized and defended resting spots for armies on the move. The Greek historian Polybius describes a Roman camp of the second century B.C., and the Jewish historian Josephus provides a similar tract for a camp of the early Empire. According to Polybius, in the late afternoon, as the traveling army prepared to encamp for the evening, "One of the tribunes and those of the centurions who are in turn selected for this duty go ahead to survey the whole area where the camp is to be placed" (*Histories* 6.41). Surveyors then marked the spot having the best general view of the camp and surrounding countryside with a white flag and measured off a square roughly one hundred feet on a side around it. Here, the soldiers erected the consul's tent (*praetorium*). About fifty feet to one

side of the square, a red flag marked the line where the tribunes' tents would be placed; a hundred feet in front of the tribunes' tents, another red flag indicated where the tents of the legionaries were to be pitched.

Next, the surveyors laid out the camp's two main streets, the *via principalis,* which ran between the row of tribunes' tents and the first row of legionaries' tents, and the *via praetoria,* which interesected the *via principalis* in front of the *praetorium* at a right angle, dividing the camp in half. The rest of the streets, lined with tents, ran off of these two main streets. As Polybius says, "The arrangement both of the streets and the general plan gives it the appearance of a town" (*Histories* 6.31).

If the soldiers were in hostile territory, the entire camp was surrounded by a defensive ditch (*fossa*) about three to ten feet deep. The troops piled up the earth excavated from the ditch to make a rampart (*agger*), a mound forming a protective barrier, on the inner side of the ditch. On top of the mound, the men embedded wooden stakes, creating a stockade fence. In a typical camp, these outer defenses formed a perimeter nearly two miles long, containing between forty and fifty thousand stakes. An ingenious feature of the camp's outer defenses was an empty space (*intervalium*) about two hundred feet wide between the outer row of tents and the stockade. This space served as a sort of corral for cattle, horses, and other animals and also made it difficult for an attacking enemy to set the tents ablaze.

Most of the legionaries shared the duties of setting up (and later striking) the camp. Eight men (making up a platoonlike unit called a *contubernium*) shared each tent, which was typically about ten Roman feet (9.7 English feet) square and made of leather. "Everyone knows exactly in which street and in which part of that street his tent will be situated," Polybius tells us, "since every soldier invariably occupies

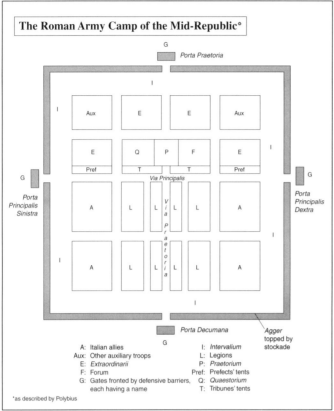

The Roman Army Camp of the Mid-Republic°

Porta Praetoria

Aux | E | E | Aux

E | Q | P | F | E
Pref | T | T | Pref
Via Principalis

Porta Principalis Sinistra

A | L | L | Via Praetoria | L | L | A

A | L | L | L | L | A

Porta Principalis Dextra

Porta Decumana

Agger topped by stockade

A: Italian allies
Aux: Other auxiliary troops
E: *Extraordinarii*
F: Forum
G: Gates fronted by defensive barriers, each having a name
I: *Intervalium*
L: Legions
P: *Praetorium*
Pref: Prefects' tents
Q: *Quaestorium*
T: Tribunes' tents

*as described by Polybius

the same position in the camp, and so the process of pitching camp is remarkably like the return of an army to its native city" (*Histories* 6.41).

After one or more days, the soldiers received the order to strike camp and move on. Fortunately, Josephus's account includes a vivid description of this process:

When the camp is to be struck, the trumpet sounds and every man springs to his duty. Following the signal, tents are instantly dismantled and all preparations made for departure. The trumpet then sounds "Stand by to march!" At once, they load the mules and wagons with the baggage and take their places like runners lined up and hardly able to wait for the starter's signal. Then they fire [burn] the [wooden portions of the] camp, which they can easily reconstruct if required, lest it might some day be useful to the enemy. For the third time the trumpets give the same signal for departure, to urge

on those who for any reason have been loitering, so that not a man may be missing from his place. Then the announcer, standing on the right of the supreme commander, asks three times . . . whether they are ready for war. They three times shout loudly and with enthusiasm "Ready!" hardly waiting for the question, and filled with a kind of martial [warlike] fervor they raise their right arms as they shout. Then they step off, all marching silently and in good order, as on active service every man keeping his place in the column. (*The Jewish War* 3.90–99)

army organization and manpower

The kinds and numbers of units, officers, and soldiers (called legionaries) that made up the Roman army evolved considerably over time, and the military establishment of the mid-to-late Empire was a far cry in size, scope, organization, and effectiveness from the one that defended the Monarchy in Rome's early days.

The exact nature and makeup of the Monarchy's army is unknown. However, writings by later ancient historians suggest that it was a militia, a group of nonprofessionals called into service during an emergency and disbanded after a short campaign. The army was under the direct command of the king, but as it grew larger he needed officers to help him control it. The first such unit commanders were three military tribunes. The Latin word *tribunus* means "tribal officer"; each tribune appropriately commanded one thousand men, all landowners, from one of Rome's three traditional native tribes. The total force of three thousand soldiers was called a legion (from the word *legio,* meaning "the levying"). The various subdivisions of each tribe each supplied one hundred men, a basic unit that became known as a century. The legion was supported by about three hundred cavalry (horse soldiers), who became known as knights.

The way these early part-time soldiers fought is uncertain. But apparently by the early sixth century B.C. they had adopted the hoplite phalanx developed by the Greeks about a century or so before. (For the makeup and tactics of the phalanx, see battlefield tactics.) When Rome's kingship gave way to the Republic, the army came under the command of the two consuls, with the traditional tribunes ranked below them. As the Romans steadily pushed their borders outward, the army also grew in size. By the early fourth century B.C., the legion/phalanx comprised about six thousand men, supported by some eighteen hundred cavalry.

This early Roman army met its greatest test in 390 B.C., when it faced a large force of invading Gauls at the Allia River and suffered an embarrassing defeat. To avoid another such disaster, the Romans decided to institute radical military reforms. Under a strong leader, Marcus Furius Camillus, they abandoned the often inflexible phalanx. In the coming years, Camillus and other reformers created an army in which a legion broke down into several smaller units on the battlefield. These units, called maniples (*manipuli,* meaning "handfuls") were each capable of independent action and could be combined into various configurations, making the army on the whole much more flexible.

By the 360s B.C., the new army consisted of two full legions, each with about forty-two hundred to five thousand men. And by 311 B.C., it had grown to four legions, which thereafter became the standard minimum. Each consul usually commanded two legions. In addition, on campaign, a consul's two legions, in which the legionaries were Roman citizens, were accompanied by two more legions drawn from Rome's allies (Italian peoples it had conquered and signed treaties with). These noncitizen soldiers were collectively referred to as the *alae sociorum* ("wings of allies").

During the third and second centuries B.C., as the Roman realm rapidly expanded across the Mediterranean world, the army continued to increase in size and to become better organized. Campaigns now often lasted many months or more and newly won territories required garrisons (groups of soldiers manning forts) to hold and protect them; so the army developed a hard core of professional soldiers who signed up for hitches lasting several years. The state had no official policy of rewarding these veterans with pensions and land when they retired; by the dawn of the first century B.C. this led to trouble, as the wealthiest and most powerful generals began using their influence to secure such benefits for their men. The result was that many troops began to show more allegiance to their generals than to the state.

The first of these military strongmen to amass a personal army, Gaius Marius, also instituted a new round of far-reaching military reforms. First, he dropped all property qualifications and accepted volunteers from all classes. This not only greatly increased the number of potential recruits, but also initiated profound changes in the army's character. In the past, the majority of soldiers, especially the well-to-do, looked on serving as a necessary but unpleasant duty. Their aim was to discharge that duty as quickly as possible and resume their civilian careers. For the volunteers of Marius's more permanent, professional force, by contrast, serving in the army *was* their career, to which many brought enthusiasm and a sense of purpose and pride.

In addition, Marius reorganized the army into cohorts, groups of about 480 men, each further divided into six centuries of 80 (rather than 100) men, so that a typical legion now had 4,800 men (although apparently it could have fewer or more men under certain conditions). He also taught the soldiers to carry their own supplies rather than rely on cumbersome baggage trains of mules that slowed an army on the march. Thereafter, Roman soldiers were often referred to as "Marius's mules."

Shortly after Marius instituted his reforms, the nature of the auxiliary troops who supported the legions also changed. This was because the Roman government granted citizenship to all the residents of Italy in the 80s B.C. Since Rome's former noncitizen allies (*socii*) were now citizens, the *alae sociorum* ceased to exist. Thereafter, in their place, the army recruited its auxiliaries—including archers, slingers, and other light-armed troops, as well as some cavalry units—from Spain, North Africa, Germany, and other more distant lands.

After the fall of the Republic, the first emperor, Augustus, rightly viewed the imperial army as one of the main pillars supporting his vast autocratic power. Under a new series of reforms he instituted, the reorganized army consisted of twenty-eight legions, each with about 5,500 men (counting cavalry), for a total of over 150,000 men. By the end of his reign, each legion was commanded by an officer called a legionary legate (*legatus legionis*), who was appointed by the emperor; under the legate were the traditional six tribunes; and under them were the centurions (each in charge of a single century), whose position, like that of the tribunes, dated from the fourth century B.C.

The basic organization of the army Augustus created remained largely unchanged during the first and second centuries. But with the advent of the crisis years of the third-century "anarchy," the military showed that it had grown less disciplined and reliable than it had been in the past; often it was unable to stop incursions of var-

ious barbarian tribes into Roman territory. Making matters worse, army units in various parts of the realm swore allegiance to their generals, much as in late republican times, and these leaders frequently and foolishly tried to fight one another while defending against the invaders.

Clearly, new military reforms were needed if the Empire was to survive. These came in the waning years of the third century under the strong emperor Diocletian. His rule brought a general change in the realm's overall defensive strategy, a new outlook that had been developing for some time. Shaped by the sober reality of many decades of relentless barbarian incursions across the northern frontier, it was based on the assumption that it was no longer possible to make the borders (*limes*) completely impregnable; some invaders, the reasoning went, must be expected to get through the line of forts along the frontier. However, these intruders could, hopefully, be intercepted by one or more small, swiftly moving mobile armies stationed at key points in the border provinces. Diocletian stationed such small armies, each accompanied by detachments of cavalry, called *vexillationes,* at key positions on the frontier. He also attached two highly trained legions to his personal traveling court, the *comitatus,* supported by elite cavalry forces, the *scholae,* thus creating a fast and very effective mobile field force.

One of Diocletian's prominent successors, Constantine I, further elaborated on these changes. He also divided his military into both mobile forces, the *comitatenses* (from *comitatus*), and frontier troops, the *limitanei* (from *limes*). However, Constantine withdrew troops from some frontier forts and used them to create several small mobile armies; these patrolled the frontier, traveling from town to town, and when needed hurried to new trouble spots.

The actual size of these armies, as well as of Rome's overall forces in the Later Empire, is difficult to calculate and often disputed. A realistic figure for the combined armies of the first half of the fourth century is perhaps four hundred thousand men. At first glance this sounds truly formidable. But certain realistic limitations must be factored in. First, army lists were frequently inflated with fictitious entries, such as the names of young boys and old men attempting to draw free pay and rations. Also, desertion rates were high, and efficiency was compromised by spotty training and inadequate supplies. Finally, the military was composed of numerous small forces dispersed across a huge realm. Each of Constantine's mobile army units likely consisted of little more than one thousand infantry and five hundred cavalry. These were sometimes combined to form larger armies, of course; but only rarely did generals in the Later Empire field forces numbering in the tens of thousands.

Rome's new grand military strategy, with its frontier forts and small mobile armies, worked well enough as long as barbarian incursions in the north were infrequent and small in scale. However, these invasions soon became both more numerous and much larger in size, and the Roman army proved increasingly inadequate to the monstrous task of keeping all the invaders out. Rome's debilitating defeat at Adrianople in 378, in which more than forty thousand men men were lost, marked a crucial turning point. Thereafter, the barbarian invasions continued to increase, while the quality and morale of the Roman army steadily decreased.

Part of the problem was that by the end of the fourth century many of the soldiers in that army were barbarians themselves. The "barbarization" of the Roman military had begun in prior centuries when the government had allowed Germans from the northern frontier areas to settle in Roman lands. Once these settlers had established themselves, they were more than willing to fight Rome's enemies, including fellow Germans; and Roman leaders, always in need of tough military recruits, took advantage of that willingness. However, as the recruitment of Germans into the military accelerated, this policy began to take its toll, particularly in a loss of discipline, traditionally one of the Roman army's greatest strengths. According to military historian Arther Ferrill, the German recruits "began immediately to . . . show an independence that in drill, discipline and organization meant catastrophe. . . . Too long and too close association with barbarian warriors, as allies in the Roman army, had ruined the qualities that made Roman armies great. . . . The Roman army of A.D. 440, in the west, had become little more than a barbarian army itself" (*The Fall of the Roman Empire: The Military Explanation,* pp. 84, 140).

Other factors contributed to the erosion of the Later Empire's military establishment. The soldiers were not only paid very little, but because of the government's frequent money problems their wages were often months or even years in arrears, which damaged morale. Also, after Christianity became the official state religion in the fourth century, increasing numbers of Christians refused to fight, claiming it violated their moral principles. Because of these and other military problems, the traditional Roman soldier—the tough and tenacious legionary who for centuries had eagerly volunteered to defend family and state—eventually ceased to exist. With him perished the last remnants of the western Empire. **See** armor and weapons; army recruitment, training, and personnel; battlefield tactics; fall of Rome; forts, fortresses, and fortifications; specific battles by name. For a history of the Roman state, **see** Rome (Chapter 2).

army recruitment, training, and personnel

In many ways, these basic aspects of the Roman army were similar to those in modern armies. Soldiers were recruited through either conscription or voluntary enlistment, for example, and then underwent rigorous training not unlike the "boot camp" today's military recruits endure. Also like today, the Roman army comprised numerous kinds of soldiers and officers of varying rank, each with distinct or specialized skills, duties, and privileges.

Roman methods of military recruitment (*dilectus*) varied. In wartime or other national emergencies, the government naturally conscripted however many men it needed to deal with the situation. But on the whole, Rome was at peace more often than at war, and during both wartime and peacetime voluntary enlistment was more common than conscription. In peacetime, not all of those who desired to enlist were accepted, since there were usually only a set number of openings at any given time. It was customary, therefore, for a prospective recruit to obtain a letter of introduction or recommendation (*litter commendaticius*) from a military veteran or other respected citizen to persuade the military to accept him over other applicants. Recruits also had to pass a *probatio,* consisting of an interview and physical examination. The interview mainly determined the recruit's legal status and the branch of the service for which that status qualified him (i.e., army or navy). The physical exam ensured that the recruit met certain minimum height and other standards. The minimum height requirement was at first five feet eight inches; but in the Later Empire, manpower shortages caused it to be lowered to five feet five inches.

If the recruit passed the *probatio,* he took the military oath, which officially made him a soldier. In republican times, he swore to follow the consuls without hesitation in whatever wars might occur during his term of service, never to desert the standards (symbols) of his unit and legion, and to do nothing unlawful. In the Empire, the oath was apparently virtually the same, except that the recruits swore to obey the emperor; in the Later Empire, after Christianity became Rome's official religion, they swore to obey both the emperor and Jesus Christ.

Having sworn the oath, new soldiers were assigned to a post in either Italy or one of the provinces. The term of enlistment varied according to the era. In the Monarchy and early Republic, when the army was a part-time citizen militia, soldiers served short terms, usually only a few weeks or months. In time, however, terms of service became longer, especially during long wars, such as the Punic conflicts, when a legionary might serve as long as sixteen years and a cavalryman as long as ten. In the early Empire, Augustus increased the initial period of service from six to sixteen years, followed by four on call; later he raised these numbers to twenty years of continuous service and five on call; and after his death the standard hitch became twenty-five years of continuous service. (Auxiliaries served up to thirty years, later reduced to twenty-five; sailors, twenty-six years.)

Immediately following a Roman soldier's recruitment process came his training. Little is known about early Roman military training methods, although the Greek historian Polybius describes a Roman general retraining some troops soon after capturing an enemy stronghold in 209 B.C. On the first day of each week, soldiers had to run about 3.7 miles in full armor, an extremely arduous feat; on day two, they cleaned and polished their weapons and underwent an exacting inspection; on day three, they rested; on day four, they endured relentless weapons drills—practicing swordplay, spear throwing, and the like; on day five, they ran another 3.7 miles in armor; on day six, they had another inspection; and on day seven, they rested again. The following week they repeated the process.

As time went on, the training became even more wide-ranging and rigorous.

During the early Empire, new recruits learned to march by engaging in exhausting parade drills twice a day until they were able to cover twenty-four miles in just five hours in full armor. Next, they had to march mile after grueling mile, day after day, carrying a full pack consisting of some sixty pounds of weapons, tools, and rations. They also learned how to build a camp, how to ride a horse, and how to swim. Then came weapons training, which included drills with sword and shield, spear throwing, forced marches, long runs in armor, and practice at jumping and at felling trees. Eventually, the recruits lined up in an open field and practiced shaping the various common battle formations until they could do so quickly and precisely. And finally, they engaged in mock battles, in which the points of their swords and javelins were sheathed to prevent serious injuries.

It goes without saying that nearly every new recruit hoped he would somehow manage to gain promotions and rise through the ranks. Especially desirable was becoming an officer, which carried with it many advantages, including better pay, more authority and respect, and increased prestige and social and political opportunities. In the imperial army, the first step up from an ordinary legionary was the position of *immunis*. The *immunes* were so named because they were immune from normal, and often unpleasant, daily military duties because they possessed special skills. An *immunis* received higher pay than a legionary and generally worked on his own and at his own pace. A small sampling of the more than one hundred kinds of *immunes* known includes: *agrimensores* (surveyors), *aerarii* (bronze workers), *carpentarii* (carpenters), *ferrarii* (blacksmiths), *lapidarii* (stonemasons), *librarii* (clerks), *medicii* (orderlies or doctors), *sagittarii* (arrow makers), *stratores* (grooms), *tubarii* (trumpet makers), and *veterinarii* (veterinarians).

Above the legionaries and *immunes* were the officers, grouped into commissioned (or senior) officers and noncommissioned (or junior) officers. The junior officers (*principales*), were divided into two groups, those in the century and those at the legion's headquarters. Of the century's junior officers, the lowest ranking was the *tesserarius*, a sort of sergeant who made sure the legionaries were doing their jobs. Above him was the *optio,* the deputy centurion who assumed command of his century in the centurion's absence. Another *principalis,* the *signifer,* bore the century's standards, a highly prestigious duty. The headquarters *principales* consisted of a large number of specialized officers, among them the *aquilifer,* who bore the Eagle, the standard for the legion; the *imaginifer,* who carried a portrait (*imago*) of the emperor; and several kinds of *beneficarii* (later called *officia*), head clerks and assistants on the staffs of the senior officers.

The lowest-ranking senior officer was the centurion, a kind of top sergeant or sergeant-major, somewhat equivalent to a company commander in a modern army. The highest-ranking and most prestigious centurion in a legion was the *primus pilus* ("first spear"), who had the right to attend meetings and strategy sessions with higher-ranked officers. In the first century A.D., a centurion's rank was denoted by a horizontal crest on his helmet, usually of either horsehair or feathers. He also carried a vine "swagger stick," with which he sometimes administered corporal punishment. His armor was more richly decorated than that of regular soldiers, and he carried his sword on the left instead of the right side of his body.

Ranked directly above the centurions in both a republican and imperial legion were its six military tribunes. In the Republic, they were usually drawn from the equestrian class and were elected by the people. Beginning in the late first century B.C., the

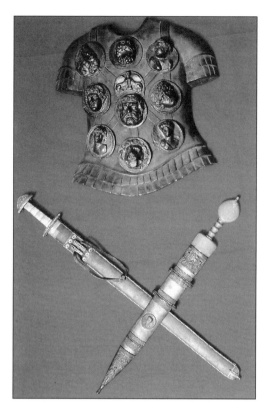

The surviving breastplate and swords of a Roman centurion. Each centurion had charge of a century, consisting of 100 (later 80) men.

administrative and command authority of the tribunes diminished considerably thanks to increased importance of officers called legates. Throughout the Empire, however, the tribunes still held commands among the auxiliary troops.

In the Republic after about 190 B.C., one or more legions might be under the command (usually for a relatively short period) of a higher-ranking officer, the legate (*legatus*), appointed by the Senate. Above the legates were the consuls, until the late Republic, when elected officials no longer commanded the army during their terms of office and legates therefore increased in importance. And in the early Empire, Augustus introduced the position of legionary legate (*legatus legionis*), who had charge of a single legion for several years and reported directly to the general commanding the whole army (who was sometimes the emperor himself). Also at this time the position of camp prefect (*praefectus castorum*) appeared. Similar in rank to a tribune, the camp prefect, supported by a large staff, laid out the army base or encampment and maintained order, sanitation, medical services, and weapons training within it.

This general command structure continued until the Later Empire, when dramatic changes in military organization called for the creation of some new offices. The frontier armies of these times were commanded by *duces* (from which the title "duke" evolved); in charge of the mobile armies were the *magister equitum* ("master of cavalry") and *magister peditum* ("master of infantry"), and small detachments of the mobile armies were led by a *comes* ("count"). Because of a lack of firm evidence, it remains uncertain whether traditional regimental offices and positions, such as tribune, centurion, and *optio*, still existed in this period; but considering the characteristic Roman reverence for military tradition, it is likely that many of them did. **See** army camps; army organization and manpower; *magister equitum; magister militum.*

Averni

(or Arverni) This Gallic tribe became quite prominent by the mid–second century B.C., at which time it dominated much of central Gaul. Long bitter enemies of their neighbors, the Aedui, the Averni fought against an alliance of Aedui and Romans, who delivered them a debilitating defeat in 121 B.C. Subsequently, Averni territory shrank and the Aedui became dominant in the region. During Julius Caesar's Gallic campaigns in the 50s B.C., the Averni made one last bid for supremacy under their talented war chief Vercingetorix. However, Caesar soundly defeated them. Over time the Averni became Romanized along with the other Gallic peoples. **See** Aedui; siege of Alesia; **also** Caesar, Gaius Julius; Vercingetorix (both Chapter 1).

battlefield tactics

Like other aspects of the Roman military, the nature of battlefield tactics evolved over the centuries. In the days of the Monarchy and early Republic, Roman soldiers were hoplites, heavily armored infantrymen who fought in a battle formation called a phalanx. The Romans adopted the phalanx from the Greeks and also from the Etruscans, who had themselves already adopted Greek military methods. In the phalanx, the soldiers stood in ranks (lines), one behind the other, creating a formidable wall of upright shields and forward-pointing spears. When the formation marched forward, it was extremely difficult to stop or defend against.

Yet Rome's phalanx suffered a disastrous defeat at the hands of an invading horde of Gauls in the early fourth century B.C., which inspired the Romans to abandon the old system. Their new tactical system broke down the old phalanx into smaller units—the maniples. On the battlefield, the maniples were arranged in lines with open space separating one maniple from another and one line from another. This allowed individual units to move back and forth with ease, permitting tired troops to fall back and rest while fresh ones pressed forward into the fray. When need dictated, various-size contingents of maniples could also separate from the army's main body and fight on their own.

Because the new "manipular" system was both flexible and effective, it remained in place for a long time. Even after the army's structure underwent another important revision in the late second century and early first century B.C., most generals employed basically the same battlefield tactics as their predecessors. The main difference was that the maniples were replaced by larger units—the cohorts—that were arranged in attack formations of various shapes. Highly gifted generals like Scipio and Caesar, who devised some new and innovative tactics, were rare. Most of their colleagues were content to fall back on the tried and true tactics that had so long and so well exploited the Roman army's greatest asset—its highly disciplined and superbly trained infantrymen.

The most common manipular battlefield array utilized four basic kinds or groups of soldiers. The front of the array consisted of a long line, a few ranks deep, of light-armed skirmishers, the *velites,* very young men usually wearing no armor and carrying throwing spears (javelins). Arrayed behind the *velites* was the bulk of the army, the infantry, assembled in three long lines facing the enemy. Within each line the spaces separating the maniples were the width of a maniple. Also, each line of maniples was staggered in such a way that there was open space in front and back of each maniple, overall rendering a sort of checkerboard effect. (Because this pattern resembled the dots representing the number five on a dice cube, which the Romans called a *quincunx,* they gave the battlefield formation the same name.)

The first line of infantry was made up of the *hastati,* young men with minimal experience but a great deal of vigor and endurance. Each maniple of *hastati* (and each maniple in the other two lines) was composed of two centuries, one positioned behind the other. The front century was termed the "prior" and the back one the "posterior." Each maniple of *hastati* had 60 men to a century and therefore 120 men in all. (The other 20 of a century's standard 80 men were *velites,* who stood in their separate line.) Behind the *hastati* were the *principes,* experienced fighters in the prime of life (probably age twenty-five to thirty). Their maniples were also composed of 120 men each. Finally, the rear line was made up of the *triarii,* older veterans who lacked the physical endurance of the others but possessed more experience. Each century of *triarii* had 30 men, so these rear maniples had 60 rather than 120 men each.

Typically, the *velites* opened a battle by running forward and hurling their javelins, to soften up the enemy before the Roman infantry charged. What most often followed in republican times is termed the manipular tactic. The *velites* suddenly retreated, passing quickly through the open spaces in the three lines of maniples and re-forming their line in the rear, behind the *triarii.* Meanwhile, the posterior centuries of *hastati* swiftly moved from behind the prior centuries and filled the gaps in the line. This formidable solid bank of infantry now charged forward, the men shouting fiercely in unison in an attempt to frighten the enemy. At a distance of about one hundred feet, the *hastati* hurled their light javelins and a few seconds later followed with their heavy ones. Then they drew their swords, rushed forward, and crashed into the enemy ranks with as much impact as possible.

The charge of the *hastati* sometimes damaged and demoralized the enemy enough to force his retreat, giving the Romans an easy victory. On the other hand, if after a while the *hastati* could make no headway or appeared to be in trouble, the Roman commander signaled for them to retreat; and they hurried through the gaps separating the maniples of *principes* and *triarii* and stood behind the *triarii.* Next, just as the *hastati* had done earlier, the *principes* formed a solid line and charged the enemy, who now faced a force of fresh soldiers with even more battle experience than the *hastati.* If the charge of the *principes* was not enough to defeat the enemy, they retreated just as the *hastati* had

done and filled the gaps between the *hastati*'s maniples. Then one of two scenarios played out. If it looked as though the battle could still be won, the *hastati* pressed forward and had a second go at the enemy. However, if the Roman commander decided it was best to quit and fight again another day, he ordered the fresh and very experienced *triarii* to enter the fray. They formed a solid line and pointed their spears forward in phalanx fashion, creating a protective barrier behind which the whole army retreated in an orderly manner.

The manipular tactic helped to revolutionize warfare in the Mediterranean world. The highly disciplined, flexible, and efficient Roman soldiers, trained to deliver one devastating charge after another in battle, conquered many diverse peoples in only a few centuries. And for a long time, the Roman system retained the same flexibility as it evolved. Even when the maniples were abandoned as battlefield units in favor of cohorts in the early first century B.C., battlefield tactics did not change very much, for the following reasons. First, each cohort, made up of six centuries of eighty men, was, like a maniple, a distinct unit that could act on its own. Also, on the battlefield the cohorts typically formed three lines, just as the maniples had. A common arrangement of the cohorts (of which there were ten to each legion) was four in the front line and three each in the second and third lines. One line of cohorts could advance on the enemy while the cohorts of the other lines waited in reserve, as in the manipular tactic.

In fact, the cohorts were even more flexible than the maniples because they could more easily be arrayed in unusual formations. One that proved particularly effective was the "pig's head." It consisted of one cohort in front, two in the second row, three in the third row, and the other four in the fourth row, together creating a massive wedge that was highly effective in frontal attacks. The major difference between the

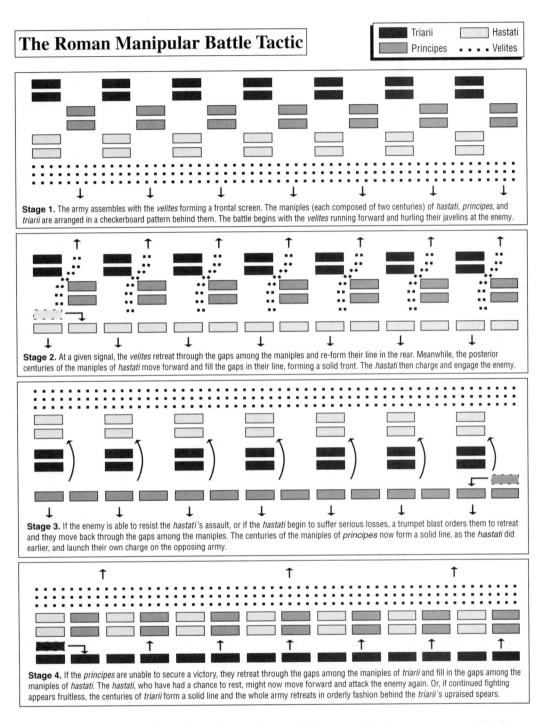

The Roman Manipular Battle Tactic

Legend: ■ Triarii   ▨ Principes   ☐ Hastati   • • • • Velites

Stage 1. The army assembles with the *velites* forming a frontal screen. The maniples (each composed of two centuries) of *hastati*, *principes*, and *triarii* are arranged in a checkerboard pattern behind them. The battle begins with the *velites* running forward and hurling their javelins at the enemy.

Stage 2. At a given signal, the *velites* retreat through the gaps among the maniples and re-form their line in the rear. Meanwhile, the posterior centuries of the maniples of *hastati* move forward and fill the gaps in their line, forming a solid front. The *hastati* then charge and engage the enemy.

Stage 3. If the enemy is able to resist the *hastati*'s assault, or if the *hastati* begin to suffer serious losses, a trumpet blast orders them to retreat and they move back through the gaps among the maniples. The centuries of the maniples of *principes* now form a solid line, as the *hastati* did earlier, and launch their own charge on the opposing army.

Stage 4. If the *principes* are unable to secure a victory, they retreat through the gaps among the maniples of *triarii* and fill in the gaps among the maniples of *hastati*. The *hastati*, who have had a chance to rest, might now move forward and attack the enemy again. Or, if continued fighting appears fruitless, the centuries of *triarii* form a solid line and the whole army retreats in orderly fashion behind the *triarii*'s upraised spears.

old system and the new was the makeup of the soldiers themselves. The distinctions in armor, weapons, and tactics among the *velites, hastati, principes,* and *triarii* ceased to exist; by the first century B.C., all of these fighters had become regular legionaries armed and trained in similar fashion.

The legion/cohort system and its time-proven tactics built around the formidable legionary remained the mainstay of the Roman military until the advent of the Later Empire. In the western Empire's last two centuries, with increasing numbers of enemies pressing on the borders, the burden of defending the realm fell mainly on the mobile armies developed by Diocletian and Constantine. These forces came to emphasize the role of cavalry, which became a principle attack force, while the infantry increasingly fell into a supporting role. One effect of this reduction in the legionary's importance and prestige was a steady decline in the training and discipline of foot soldiers. This in turn contributed heavily to the Roman military's decreased effectiveness in the Empire's last years. **See** armor and weapons; army organization and manpower.

Battle of Actium

(31 B.C.) The last battle of the civil wars of the first century B.C., its outcome signaled the death knell of the Republic and rise of Octavian as supreme ruler of the Roman realm. In the impending war between the former triumvirs Antony and Octavian, the latter could rely on his able commander, Agrippa. Octavian and Agrippa had about 250 warships, perhaps 150 troop transports, and about 80,000 land troops at their disposal. By contrast, Antony had about 60,000 infantry, 70,000 light-armed troops, and perhaps 500 or more ships.

Octavian and Agrippa seized the strategic advantage by advancing on Greece while their adversaries' army and navy were still disorganized and unprepared. Before long, Antony and his lover and ally, Egypt's Cleopatra VII, were trapped at Actium, in western Greece, and had no choice but to fight their way out. The battle took place in the nearby waters on September 2. As it began, the tactics of the opposing sides, which were dictated by the differing sizes of the ships, became readily apparent. Octavian's and Agrippa's smaller and faster ships attempted to ram the larger, less mobile enemy vessels. By contrast, the tactics of Antony's ships were mainly to shoot volleys of arrows, stones, and other missiles at the enemy triremes as they approached in their ramming runs. As

the opposing fleets employed these tactics, the engagement soon came to resemble a land battle.

After the battle had raged for two or more hours, Cleopatra suddenly abandoned the fray, followed soon afterward by Antony. It is likely that the lovers had planned their escape from the beginning, their main objective being to save the treasure they carried and use it to raise new forces and continue prosecuting the war. Whatever the reason for their flight, the move threw their remaining ships and men into disarray. Antony's forces were shattered and the dawn of a new Roman world was at hand. **See** civil wars; navy; **also** Agrippa, Marcus Vipsanius; Antony, Mark; Augustus; Cleopatra VII (all Chapter 1); **and** Rome (Chapter 2).

Battle of Adrianople

(A.D. 378) After the eastern emperor Valens allowed the Visigoths to settle in Roman territory, his representatives unwisely tried to exploit them and they responded by pillaging Thrace. Valens hastened with an army to put down this uprising. But instead of waiting for reinforcements from his nephew, the western emperor Gratian, he imprudently attacked a much larger force of Visigoths and Ostrogoths on his own near Adrianople, in eastern Thrace.

On August 9, the Romans sighted the enemy's wagons (which contained the Goths' families and supplies) and pressed forward. Valens's army was still forming its lines when the commanders of his archers and other light-armed troops prematurely gave the order to attack the enemy. The Goths easily put these troops to flight. Meanwhile the Roman left wing of cavalry penetrated the enemy lines and almost made it to the Gothic wagons. However, these horsemen soon found themselves cut off and overwhelmed. That left the Roman infantry exposed and vulnerable and the Goths quickly and savagely assaulted the legionaries from all sides. On that dark day for Rome, the overconfident Valens died along with at least two-thirds of his army, perhaps as many as forty thousand men. These disastrous losses contributed significantly to the subsequent decline of the Roman army. The Roman historian Ammianus gives a detailed, moving account of the battle in his great *History of Rome*. **See** Goths; **also** Valens, Flavius Julius (Chapter 1).

Battle of Allia

(390 B.C.) A large force of tribal Gauls, who had earlier crossed the Alps into northern Italy, descended through Etruria and marched on Rome. The Roman phalanx assembled near the Allia River (a few miles north of the city), expecting easily to repulse the invaders. But though the Gallic army lacked organization and discipline, its fearsome-looking warriors— nearly naked, long-haired, and wearing war paint—staged a wild, screaming charge that completely terrified the unprepared Roman soldiers. The phalanx fell apart, the Romans were defeated, and the Gauls proceeded to sack Rome. The anniversary of this humiliating defeat, July 18, thereafter became known as the dark "Day of Allia," an unlucky date on the calendar. Moreover, the event convinced Roman leaders to institute new battle formations and tactics. **See** army organization and manpower; battlefield tactics.

Battle of Cannae

(216 B.C.) This stunning victory by Carthage's Hannibal in the early years of the Second Punic War was the single worst battlefield disaster in Rome's long history. A huge Roman army of some seventy-five thousand to eighty thousand men, commanded by the consuls Paullus and Varro, confronted Hannibal's forty thousand troops on a small plain near the village of Cannae, in southeastern Italy. Anticipating an enemy attempt to overwhelm his own

center, the Carthaginian set a trap. Instead of placing his strongest infantry in the center, he held these troops in reserve on the flanks and put his less formidable infantry units in the center.

After the battle opened, the Romans charged the Carthaginian center and easily pushed the enemy back, just as Hannibal had hoped. Meanwhile, the opposing cavalry units engaged, and the Carthaginian horsemen began to drive the Roman horsemen from the field. Before long Hannibal's giant death trap snapped shut on the unsuspecting Romans. The Roman infantrymen drove the Carthaginian center back so far that they passed by and between his elite troops, still standing on the flanks. These completely fresh units now turned inward and attacked. At the same time, the Carthaginian cavalry, having chased away the Roman horsemen, wheeled around and assaulted the Romans from the rear. Surrounded, the Roman ranks crumbled. Rome's losses are estimated at a crippling fifty thousand (including the consul Paullus and some eighty senators), about eight times those of Hannibal. **See** Punic Wars; **also** Hannibal (Chapter 1).

Battle of Cape Ecnomus

(256 B.C.) At the height of the First Punic War, the Romans prepared to invade North Africa by sending some 330 warships, carrying some 140,000 sailors and marines, to Cape Ecnomus, on Sicily's southern shore. The Carthaginians countered this move by hurriedly assembling about 350 ships roughly forty miles west of the Roman fleet.

In his *Histories,* the Greek historian Polybius describes the subsequent battle, which was probably the largest sea fight of ancient times. He says that the Romans arranged their front ships in a wedge formation and smashed through the Carthaginian center. The Carthaginian ships were faster than the Romans vessels, but the former were reluctant to come too close to the latter, which were equipped with "ravens," which the Romans used to hold fast and board enemy vessels. Eventually, the Romans gained the upper hand and their opponents fled. More than thirty Carthaginian ships were destroyed and another sixty or so were captured, while the Romans lost twenty-four ships. The Roman victory left the African coast vulnerable to attack, allowing Rome to carry the war to the Carthaginian homeland. **See** navy; Punic Wars.

Battle of Carrhae

(53 B.C.) Hoping to match the battlefield exploits of his partners in the First Triumvirate (Caesar and Pompey), Marcus Crassus became governor of the province of Syria and launched an attack on the Parthian Empire. In early summer, he crossed the Euphrates River with over thirty thousand infantry and four thousand cavalry. Unwisely, he allowed the much more talented and experienced Parthian general, Surenas, to lure him onto a flat expanse of desert, where, on June 9, the enemy surrounded the Roman legions and for hours poured volleys of arrows into their ranks. Crassus's son, Publius, attempted to break free and launch a counterattack, but his force was wiped out. Almost all of the Romans, including Crassus, were killed and the victors captured the legions' battle standards, which the Romans long afterward looked on as an outrage and a disgrace. **See** Arsacids; Crassus, Marcus Licinius (both Chapter 1).

Battle of Chalons

(or Catalaunian Plain, A.D. 451) Early in the year, Attila the Hun invaded Gaul and pushed toward Orleans. Aëtius, *magister militum* of the western Empire, quickly gathered a combined army of Romans, Franks, Celts, and Visigoths and intercepted Attila near the Catalaunian Plain, in northeastern Gaul, sometime in early summer. According to various ancient ac-

counts, the battle was hard fought by both sides, but ended in a draw when Aëtius refused to press on and destroy the enemy (perhaps because he feared upsetting the balance of power in northern Europe). This mistake came back to haunt the Roman commander when Attila later advanced on Italy. **See** Huns; **also** Aëtius, Flavius; Attila (both Chapter 1).

Battle of Cynoscephalae

(197 B.C.) In this climactic battle of the Second Macedonian War, the Macedonians were led by their king, Philip V, while the Roman commander was Titus Quinctius Flamininus. The two armies approached Cynoscephalae ridge (in central Greece) and made camp, the Macedonians to the north, the Romans to the south. The next morning, each commander, unaware of the enemy's close proximity (mainly because fog blanketed the area) sent out a small covering force of skirmishers and horsemen to take control of the ridge. These forces ran into each other on the hill and a fight ensued that steadily escalated in the coming hours.

Flamininus managed to deploy most of his troops faster than Philip, who could fully assemble only the right wing of his phalanx on the hilltop. As the battle continued, this half-phalanx charged the Romans and drove them partway down the hill. With Philip's right wing now in a commanding position, Flamininus decided to attack the Macedonian left wing, which was still in a state of disarray. During this successful assault, an unknown Roman tribune led twenty maniples away and attacked the rear of the Macedonian right wing. Unable to swing their long pikes around in time, Philip's soldiers were slaughtered where they stood. The Macedonian losses totaled some eight thousand killed and five thousand captured, while the Romans lost only seven hundred men. **See** Macedonian Wars; **also** Flamininus, Titus Quinctius (Chapter 1).

Battle of Lake Trasimene

(217 B.C.) After defeating the Romans at the Ticinus and Trebia Rivers early in the Second Punic War, Hannibal spent the winter in northern Italy. In the spring of 217 B.C., he marched his army southward to Lake Trasimene, just seventy miles north of Rome, and there engaged a Roman force commanded by Gaius Flaminius. Hannibal laid a trap into which Flaminius marched his troops and the Romans soon found themselves surrounded. Some tried to escape along the lakeshore and drowned. The Roman commander was killed along with some fifteen thousand of his men, and another fifteen thousand Romans were captured, while Hannibal lost only fifteen hundred men. According to Plutarch, the noise of fighting and dying men was so loud that no one involved noticed a significant earthquake that struck at the height of the battle. **See** Punic Wars; **also** Flaminius, Gaius; Hannibal (both Chapter 1).

Battle of Magnesia

(or Magnesia-ad-Sipylum, 190 B.C.) After the Romans dislodged the Seleucid king, Antiochus III, from mainland Greece, they pursued him into western Asia Minor; at Magnesia, near Mount Sipylus, Antiochus's 60,000 infantry and 12,000 horsemen met a Roman army of 30,000 commanded by Scipio Africanus's brother, Lucius Cornelius Scipio. The Roman right wing charged and disrupted the Seleucid left wing. Meanwhile, Antiochus led his own right wing against the Roman left wing and drove it back and off the field; however, in doing so he left the rest of his army at the mercy of the enemy. Seeing that defeat was imminent, the king fled. His losses exceeded 50,000, while only about 350 Romans were killed. **See** Seleucid Kingdom (Chapter 2).

Battle of the Metaurus River

(207 B.C.) During the Second Punic War, Hannibal's brother, Hasdrubal Barca, crossed the Alps and threatened northern Italy with an army of thirty thousand. The consul Gaius Claudius Nero swiftly marched northward with seven thousand men and joined a larger Roman army under the command of the other consul, Marcus Livius Salinator, near the Metaurus River in northeastern Italy. The Carthaginians and Romans faced off and the battle began; the fighting was savage and bloody and at first neither side could achieve the advantage. Soon, however, Nero led a force of men around and surprised the Carthaginians from the rear, slaughtering many. Realizing that the battle was lost, Hasdrubal bravely galloped his horse directly into the Roman lines and certain death. Carthaginian losses exceeded ten thousand, compared with only two thousand for the Romans; because the Romans had eliminated Hannibal's only hope of reinforcement, the battle proved the turning point of the war and prelude to Rome's total victory. **See** Punic Wars.

Battle of the Milvian Bridge

(A.D. 312) Intent on unseating Maxentius, who had illegally declared himself emperor and seized the city of Rome, Constantine I led his army toward the city. Maxentius led his own troops across the Milvian Bridge and out onto the Flaminian Way, hoping to intercept the approaching enemy. But he soon found the route blocked by Constantine's soldiers, whose shields bore a strange insignia. Maxentius did not realize that this was a Christian symbol that Constantine had ordered his men to paint on their shields. (Supposedly, Christ had instructed Constantine to do so in a dream the night before.) As Constantine advanced, Maxentius retreated to the Milvian Bridge, where the two armies clashed and Maxentius and several thousand of his men drowned in the Tiber. The next day, October 29, Constantine entered Rome in triumph. **See** Constantine I (Chapter 1); **also** Christianity (Chapter 3); **and** Tetrarchy (Chapter 4).

Battle of Mylae

(260 B.C.) Early in the First Punic War, the Romans were eager to test their new secret weapon, the "raven" (*corvus*), a wooden gangway that allowed them to hold fast and board enemy ships. That test came at Mylae, on Sicily's northeastern coast, in one of the largest sea battles fought up to that time. The Romans had 120 ships and the Carthaginians 130. The latter, who were much more experienced sailors, expected an easy victory. But they soon found themselves unable to cope with the Roman ravens, which proved a huge success; after losing some fifty vessels, the Carthaginians turned and fled. **See** navy; Punic Wars.

Battle of Pharsalus

(48 B.C.) During the civil war that erupted in 49 B.C. when Caesar crossed the Rubicon River, Pompey, Caesar's chief rival, fled to Greece. The following year on August 9, Pompey, commanding at least 40,000 infantry and 7,000 cavalry, engaged Caesar, whose forces numbered only about 22,000 infantry and 1,000 cavalry, at Pharsalus (in central Greece). Pompey's cavalry and archers easily pushed back Caesar's cavalry. But Caesar had foreseen this possibility and now unleashed a contingent of infantry he had hidden in the rear. Many of Pompey's men retreated before this fresh corps, leaving his archers and other skirmishers unprotected. Meanwhile, part of Caesar's infantry managed to outflank Pompey's left wing, which also turned and fled. The Caesarians pursued their opponents to their camp and beyond, while the humiliated Pompey, who had never before tasted defeat in his long and illustrious career, escaped to Greece's eastern coast. The enormity of Caesar's victory is reflected in the casualty figures: Pompey lost some 15,000 dead and 24,000 captured, while Caesar lost just 200 men. **See** civil wars; **also** Caesar, Gaius Julius; Pompey (both Chapter 1).

Battle of Philippi

(42 B.C.) By the summer of 42 B.C., a little over two years after they murdered Caesar, the senators Brutus and Cassius had managed to raise more than eighty thousand troops still loyal to the Republic. The inevitable showdown between these forces and those of similar size commanded by Antony and Octavian took the form of two pitched battles, separated by an interval of three weeks, on the plain of Philippi (in northern Greece). Brutus and Cassius camped their respective forces on hills about a mile apart. Cassius erected a protective stockade between his own camp and a nearby marsh, a barrier that Antony managed to breach on October 3. Antony's men then easily captured the camp, which Cassius had left poorly guarded, and soon Antony engaged and defeated Cassius in a pitched battle.

Meanwhile, less than two miles away, Brutus managed to push Octavian's soldiers back and capture the camp Octavian and Antony shared. However, Cassius was unaware of this development and, thinking all was lost, committed suicide. On October 23, Brutus lined up his troops for another go at his opponents, and this time, despite a valiant effort by his men, he met with defeat. Soon afterward, he too took his own life, and the last credible chance of restoring the Republic died with him. **See** civil wars; **also** Antony, Mark; Augustus; Brutus, Marcus Junius; Cassius, Gaius Longinus (all Chapter 1) **and** Rome (Chapter 2).

Battle of Pydna

(168 B.C.) The concluding battle of the Third Macedonian War took place sometime in the summer. A Roman army led by the consul Lucius Aemilius Paullus faced a phalanx commanded by Perseus, king of Macedonia, at Pydna, near Greece's northeastern coast. At first, the phalanx drove the Romans back. But soon the ground became uneven, hindering the Macedonian pikemen, and Paullus seized the advantage

by ordering contingents of his troops into gaps that had formed in the enemy formation. Many Romans made it to the rear of the phalanx, which, assailed from front and back, quickly fell apart. Perseus lost about twenty-five thousand men and soon afterward surrendered, ending the war; Paullus lost a mere one hundred men. **See** Macedonian Wars; **also** Paullus, Lucius Aemilius (Chapter 1).

Battle of the Teutoberg Forest

(A.D. 9) The worst military disaster of Augustus's reign, it foreshadowed Rome's large-scale losses to Germanic tribes in later centuries. A Roman force consisting of three legions (about fifteen thousand men), commanded by Publius Quinctilius Varus, was ambushed by an army of Germans led by Arminius in Germany's dense Teutoberg Forest, about eighty miles east of the Rhine River. The battle lasted for three days and the Romans fought with desperate courage, but they were surrounded and heavily outnumbered. The Germans wiped them out almost to the last man, and in the final moments the disgraced Varus committed suicide. Augustus was said to have taken the news of the catastrophe badly, tearing his clothes, beating his head on a door, and crying out for Varus to return the lost legions. **See** Augustus; Varus, Publius Quinctilius (both Chapter 1); **and** Germany (Chapter 2).

Battle of Thapsus

(46 B.C.) Though Caesar had defeated Pompey at Pharsalus in 48 B.C., many of Pompey's supporters carried on the war. Early in 46 B.C. Caesar landed in North Africa intent on dealing with some of these hostile forces, led by Quintus Caecilius Scipio, who was reinforced by Juba, king of Numidia. In April, Caesar camped near the coastal town of Thapsus with about 50,000 men. Scipio and Juba arrived with a total of some 70,000 infantry, 40,000 cavalry, and 90 elephants.

After a series of minor skirmishes, the two armies finally lined up for a major battle. Seeing that his opponents had placed their elephants on the wings, Caesar arrayed his own wings with archers, slingers, and cavalry, who proceeded to unleash a deadly rain of missiles on the befuddled beasts. The elephants turned and ran, after which Caesar's infantry charged and sent the Numidian cavalry packing. Perceiving that their side was losing, Scipio's troops also fled, with the Caesarians in pursuit. Caesar's men killed all those they managed to catch. Casualty figures are uncertain, but the Pompeians likely lost over 5,000 men, compared to only 50 dead on Caesar's side. **See** civil wars; **also** Caesar, Gaius Julius (Chapter 1).

Battle of Trebia

(218 B.C.) Shortly after Hannibal surprised the Romans by crossing the Alps into northern Italy in the opening of the Second Punic War, the consul Publius Cornelius Scipio rushed a small cavalry force to the Ticinus River (a tributary of the Po). There, Scipio engaged Hannibal's cavalry in a skirmish in which the Roman commander was wounded and had to order a retreat. Soon, however, the other consul, Tiberius Sempronius Longus, commanding fresh troops, met Scipio at the nearby Trebia River; because Scipio was still recovering, Longus assumed sole command.

Early one morning, Hannibal, who had set a clever trap, sent a cavalry force to coax Longus out of his camp and the Romans took the bait. To reach the enemy, the Roman troops had to wade through the river's icy waters, so that by the time the battle started they were wet and numb. The Carthaginian cavalry immediately pushed back the Roman wings, exposing the infantry's flanks. Then Hannibal sprang the trap, signaling a force led by his brother, Mago, to emerge from its hiding place and attack the Romans in the rear. A few Romans managed to break free and escape, but most were killed. **See** Punic Wars.

Battle of Zama

(202 B.C.) The climactic battle of the Second Punic War, it pitted two of history's greatest generals—Hannibal and Publius Cornelius Scipio "Africanus"—against each other. Scipio had landed a large force in North Africa in 204 B.C. He had laid siege to the town of Utica, pillaged the Carthaginian countryside, and made an alliance with the Numidian prince Masinissa. These events forced Hannibal to leave Italy and return to Africa to stop Scipio.

The opposing armies met at Zama, about eighty miles southwest of Carthage. Hannibal had forty thousand or more troops and eighty elephants, compared with Scipio's forces of thirty-six thousand or so (counting Masinissa's Numidian cavalry). Each general arrayed his men in three lines. Hannibal first sent in his elephants, but Scipio ordered his trumpeters to blast away, creating a din that frightened the beasts, and they proved largely ineffective. Then the Roman and Numidian cavalry, stationed on Scipio's wings, charged and drove Hannibal's horsemen from the field, leaving his infantry exposed. When the Roman infantry attacked, it drove the Carthaginian first line back, but the men in Hannibal's second line refused to help their struggling comrades. The Roman infantry cut through this second line and finally faced Hannibal and his veterans in the third line. The sides were evenly matched until Masinissa suddenly returned to the field with his cavalry and attacked the Carthaginians from behind. This tipped the scales in Scipio's favor. Carthaginian losses were some twenty thousand killed and close to that number captured, while Scipio lost only about two thousand men. Hannibal escaped; but his cause was lost and Carthage soon surrendered, ending the war. **See** Punic Wars; **also** Hannibal; Scipio, Publius Cornelius "Africanus" (both Chapter 1).

Belgae

This collection of tribal peoples inhabited Belgica, the northern region of Gaul bordering the Rhine River. They included the Remi, Bellovaci, Suessiones, Ambiani,

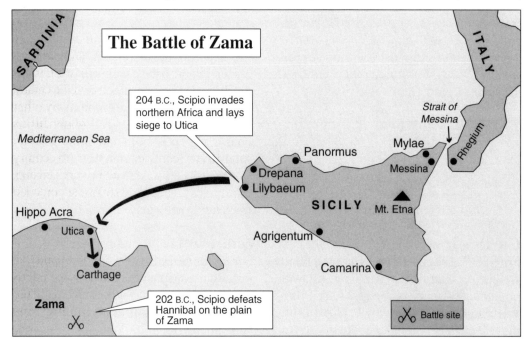

The Battle of Zama

204 B.C., Scipio invades northern Africa and lays siege to Utica

Mediterranean Sea

Panormus

Strait of Messina

Mylae

Drepana
Lilybaeum

Messina

Rhegium

Hippo Acra

SICILY

Mt. Etna

Utica

Agrigentum

Carthage

Camarina

Zama

202 B.C., Scipio defeats Hannibal on the plain of Zama

Battle site

SARDINIA

ITALY

and Nervii, among others. By the early first century B.C., they had managed to extend their influence across the English Channel to Britain's southern coast, although they did not launch a major invasion. In 57 B.C., during his Gallic campaigns, Julius Caesar led a force of nearly fifty thousand troops into Belgica. Some of the tribes recognized his superior strength and submitted without a fight, and he was able to pick off those that did resist one by one.

One Belgic tribe, however, severely tested Roman might and nerve. The Nervii staged a resistance so savage and courageous that Roman historians recalled it vividly for generations. As Caesar approached their territory, they laid an ambush for him. While the Romans were casually making camp, thousands of nearly naked Nervii warriors suddenly burst forth from their hiding places and fell on the camp. In the desperate, hand-to-hand struggle that ensued, Caesar hurried to and fro, organizing and encouraging his men. Roman arms and training finally proved superior, but the defiant Nervii refused to retreat. In a terrible bloodbath, they died by the thousands, until the last of them stood fighting atop mounds formed by the bodies of their slain comrades. In his war commentaries, Caesar called these native warriors heroes and cited their extraordinary bravery.

Carthaginians

For the inhabitants of Carthage, the North African–based city and empire that opposed Rome in the three bloody Punic Wars, **see** Battles of Cannae, Cape Ecnomus, Lake Trasimene, Metaurus River, Mylae, Trebia, and Zama; Punic Wars; **also** Hannibal (Chapter 1); **and** Carthage; Rome (both Chapter 2).

catapult

For this artillery device that hurled large stones great distances, **see** siege tactics.

cavalry

For information about horsemen who fought in the Roman army, **see** army organization and manpower; battlefield tactics.

Celts

A general term used to describe the collection of tribal peoples who spread across most of northern and central Europe in the Bronze and Iron Ages. Celtic cultures arose in Spain, Gaul, Britain, northern Italy, Illyria, northern Macedonia, along the Danube River, and in Asia Minor. Those Celts who crossed the Rhine River and occupied Gaul became known to the Greeks and Romans as Gauls; those who settled in central Asia Minor were called Galatians. Most Celts spoke dialects springing from a common language and shared a common culture, which featured rule by kings and chieftains; a religious system known as Druidism (which advocated reincarnation and human sacrifice); and primitive, largely undisciplined military organization and tactics. Germanic tribes, including the Cimbri and Teutones, eventually pushed the central European Celts westward, and many other Celts were Romanized following Julius Caesar's conquest of Gaul in the 50s B.C. After Rome lost Britain in the fifth century A.D., the island's Celtic culture survived and, along with invading Germans, superceded Roman culture there.

centurion

For this junior officer who commanded a Roman century and dealt with the needs and discipline of the soldiers on a daily basis, **see** army recruitment, training, and personnel.

century

For this military unit consisting of one hundred (later eighty) soldiers, **see** army organization and manpower.

Cimbri and Teutones

Large Germanic tribes that had long inhabited Jutland (the northern European peninsula now occupied by Denmark). In the late second century B.C., both peoples began a massive migration, disrupting many of the Celtic groups in Gaul. They marched southward and invaded the region directly north of the Alps, then inhabited by Roman allies, the Taurisci. After defeating a Roman army that came to the Taurisci's aid, the Germans turned westward and approached Rome's Gallic province, the Narbonese. Between 109 and 106 B.C., the invaders defeated several more Roman forces sent against them, then some entered Spain while the rest prepared to invade Italy. To deal with this dire threat, the Romans sent their greatest general, Gaius Marius, who decisively defeated the Teutones in 102 B.C. and then nearly destroyed the Cimbri a year later in a large battle fought in northern Italy. The name Teutone (or Teuton) thereafter became a common term denoting any German. **See** Marius, Gaius (Chapter 1).

circumvallation

For the details of this technique of surrounding an enemy camp or town with elaborate siege works, **see** siege tactics.

civil wars

(first century B.C.) These conflicts spread death and devastation throughout the Mediterranean world and eventually brought the Roman Republic to its knees. They can be conveniently grouped into five episodes. The first was the so-called Social War. Upset by the Roman government's refusal to grant them citizenship and civic rights, a large number of Italian towns, mostly in the central and southern sectors of the peninsula, rebelled in 90 B.C.; thousands died on both sides before the state gave in and granted citizenship to all adult men in Italy.

The second round of civil strife pitted two Roman strongmen, Marius and Sulla, against each other. In 88 B.C., Sulla was elected consul and the Senate assigned him an army to quell a threat to Roman interests in Asia Minor. But the leaders of the popular party wanted their own favorite, Marius (who had been born a commoner), to lead the campaign. As tensions between the popular and aristocratic factions swiftly rose, Sulla struck first; he marched an army into the capital, marking the first time that a Roman consul had seized control of Rome by force. Soon after Sulla left for the east, fighting erupted in the streets and Marius massacred many in the aristocratic faction. Now an old man, Marius died soon afterward. But his supporters remained in power and faced Sulla when he returned from the east in 83 B.C. Marching on Rome a second time, Sulla regained control and then took the unprecedented action of making himself dictator. After murdering many of his opponents, he died in 78 B.C. Sulla's civil war and dictatorship had shown that the government was not able to maintain order, whereas the army, under a charismatic individual, clearly was. An ominous precedent had been set, pointing the way for other ambitious, powerful men to manipulate the apparatus of state.

The next civil war, which erupted in 49 B.C., involved two such ambitious and powerful men—Caesar and Pompey. After crossing the Rubicon River (separating Cisalpine Gaul from Italy proper), Caesar marched on Rome and Pompey fled, along with many senators, to Greece. In August of the following year, Caesar delivered his adversary a crushing defeat at Pharsalus, in central Greece, after which Pompey fled to Egypt, only to be murdered there by the boy-king, Ptolemy XIII. Once Caesar dealt with the Egyptian court and placed the young Cleopatra on the throne, he proceeded to deal with Pompey's many supporters, who were raising armies in Africa and Spain. In December 47 B.C., Caesar crossed to North Africa, where he defeated the Pompeians at Thapsus (April 46 B.C.); then he traveled to Spain and destroyed the forces of Pompey's eldest son, Gnaeus, at Munda (March 45 B.C.). After this, all resistance to Caesar's rule collapsed.

The fourth episode of civil strife was the short-lived resistance put up by Brutus and Cassius, the leading conspirators in Caesar's assassination in 44 B.C. Caesar's chief military associate, Antony, and heir, Octavian, marched on Greece, where Brutus and Cassius had raised a large army, hoping to restore the dying Republic. In 42 B.C., at Philippi (in northern Greece), two hard-fought battles ended with the total defeat of the republican forces and the triumph of Antony and Octavian.

But the victors' celebration was short-lived, for Antony (backed by his lover and ally, Cleopatra) and Octavian soon came to grips in a struggle for supremacy. The contest was decided largely by a single battle, the great sea fight at Actium (September 31 B.C.), which Octavian won (largely through the services of his associate, Agrippa). The following year, Antony and Cleopatra took their own lives, leaving Octavian sole ruler of a shattered, war-weary Roman world. The Republic was dead and he proceeded, with his new name of Augustus, to erect the Empire on its ruins. **See** Battles of Actium, Pharsalus, Philippi, and Thapsus; Social War; **also** Agrippa, Marcus Vipsanius; Antony, Mark; Augustus; Brutus, Marcus Junius; Caesar, Gaius Julius; Cassius, Gaius Longinus; Cleopatra VII; Marius, Gaius; Pompey; Sulla, Lucius Cornelius (all Chapter 1); **and** Rome (Chapter 2).

cohort

For this battlefield unit comprising 480 men, which was introduced in late repub-

lican times, **see** army organization and manpower; battlefield tactics.

corvus

("raven" or "crow") For this ingenious device that allowed Roman marines to board enemy ships, **see** navy.

cuirass

For this kind of armor designed to protect the chest and other parts of the upper body, **see** armor and weapons.

Etruscans

The inhabitants of Etruria (the region lying north of Rome) during the Monarchy and early Republic, the Etruscans fought the Romans at intervals over a span of several centuries. All the while, especially at times when relations between the two peoples were cordial, the inhabitants of Rome felt the cultural influence of these more advanced neighbors. The Etruscans were an energetic, talented, highly civilized people who lived in well-fortified cities featuring paved streets laid out in logical, convenient grid patterns. Most of what is known about them comes from excavations of their tombs, which began in earnest in the nineteenth century. In the twentieth century, thousands of Etruscan tombs were discovered using advanced archaeological devices. In one area alone—Tarquinii, a few miles northwest of Rome—archaeologists found over five thousand Etruscan tombs in the 1960s. Many of those explored have revealed beautiful wall paintings, sculptures, weapons, pottery, and other grave goods, all providing evidence of a culture that both impressed and inspired the Romans.

The origins of the Etruscans are still uncertain and disputed by scholars. They may have migrated to Italy from Asia Minor in the early first millennium B.C., or they may have been indigenous to Italy. In any case, by the early sixth century B.C. a loose confederation of independent Etruscan city-states controlled much of northern and central Italy. Some of Rome's kings were said to be of Etruscan lineage (although the idea that Rome was long under direct Etruscan rule is a matter of debate). Over the following two centuries, however, Etruscan power waned as Greeks, Romans, and invading Celts chipped away at Etruscan territory. The Romans captured the Etruscan stronghold of Veii (ten miles north of Rome) in 396 B.C.; by the close of the fourth century B.C., most of Etruria had been absorbed into the growing Roman realm. **See** Etruria (Chapter 2); **also** Latin and other languages (Chapter 6).

fall of Rome

Modern historians generally view the dissolution of the western Roman Empire in A.D. 476 as the beginning of the end of what we now call ancient times, or antiquity. In the coming centuries, some of the "barbarian" states that superceded Rome grew into medieval kingdoms, and a few of these in turn evolved into some of the more familiar nations of modern Europe. (The medieval era is often referred to as the Middle Ages because it fell between antiquity and modern times.) The passing of Rome's ancient, long-lived, and grand civilization was therefore a major watershed in the pageant of Western history.

Modern historians have churned out thousands of books and essays attempting to account for the cause or causes of this great historical turning point. The first major modern study, which remains the classic of the genre, was *The Decline and Fall of the Roman Empire,* published in six volumes between 1776 and 1788 by the great English historian Edward Gibbon. This large, well-researched, and beautifully written work eventually delineated four major causes for Rome's decline and fall. These were its "immoderate greatness," or its having become too large and complex to govern itself efficiently and safely; too much indulgence (by upper-class Romans) in wealth and luxury at the expense of the state; the devastating invasions of the so-called barbarians (Germanic and other peoples from northern Europe); and the rise of Christianity, whose ideas supposedly weakened Rome's traditional martial spirit. To these causes, later scholars added many more, including climatic changes that triggered a decline in agriculture; class wars between the poor and the privileged; depopulation as the result of plagues and wars; race mixture with "inferior" peoples; the moral and economic ravages of slavery; and brain damage from lead poisoning.

Today, most historians favor two broad views of Rome's decline and fall. The first stresses military factors, the most crucial being the accumulative effects of one devastating barbarian incursion after another and the steady deterioration of the Roman army, which became less and less capable of stopping the invaders. The second view (which does refute or preclude the first) contends that only Rome's political and administrative apparatus fell in the fifth century, and that many aspects of Roman institutions, culture, and ideas survived, both in the Byzantine Empire in the east and in the barbarian kingdoms in the west. Through such continuity, this view holds, Roman language, ideas, laws, and so forth survived to shape the modern world.

Whatever causes for Rome's passing one accepts, it is important to avoid a common misconception often portrayed in movies and other popular media, namely that the fall was a fairly sudden and calamitous event. Typical are visions of hordes of uncouth savages suddenly sweeping out of the north and looting and burning the cities and countryside. In reality, although some such pillaging did occur from time to time, the process was a very gradual one lasting several centuries. Moreover, the Germanic and other northern European peoples who took over the Roman world were mostly civilized and some already partly Romanized tribes who for various reasons needed new lands to occupy. Most often their intentions were either to become part of the Roman state or to coexist with it, not to destroy it. Over time, however, the Roman areas they occupied became increasingly less Roman in character. More importantly, the central government steadily lost control of these regions, causing the Empire to shrink until there was practically nothing left. For an overview of the main historical events of Rome's decline and fall, **see** Rome (Chapter 2).

federates

(*foederati*) A term coined in the Later Empire to refer to "equal allies" living within the Roman realm. As various barbarian tribes threatened Roman borders, the government periodically and unwisely struck deals with them, giving them pieces of Roman territory. The policy began in earnest shortly after Rome's disastrous defeat at Adrianople (in 378). In 382, the eastern emperor Theodosius negotiated a deal with the Visigoths, the victors of the battle, allowing them to settle in Thrace permanently. In return for providing troops for the Roman army, they were free from taxation and could serve under their own leaders. This set an ominous precedent, for it marked the first time that a section of the

realm was no longer under direct Roman control. Over the next several decades, one barbarian tribe after another acquired federate status in the western provinces, a trend that steadily weakened the authority of the government and reduced the size of the Empire.

forts, fortresses, and fortifications

The Romans utilized defensive walls and fortified bases for various reasons and in various ways over their long history. Archaeological evidence shows that some of the original seven hills of Rome were fortified by mounds of earth topped by stockade fences and fronted by ditches, similar to the outer defenses of later Roman marching camps. The residents apparently relied on these simple barriers, along with the steepness of the hills, to discourage large-scale attacks. In 378 B.C., the Romans began work on the so-called Servian Wall, a more formidable stone barrier that ran around the city's entire perimeter. (The emperor Aurelian erected a similar but much larger wall around Rome in the third century A.D.) The Servian Wall was backed (and strengthened) by an enormous rampart of earth and fronted by a wide, deep ditch (or moat). As time went on and Rome's territory expanded, other Roman cities, as well as forts, were protected by similar protective barriers.

The only significant innovation the Romans made in the art of fortification during the remainder of the Republic and early Empire was the portcullis, which later became a familiar feature of medieval European castles. This was a heavy door, usually made of wood, and shod with iron for extra strength, that protected a wall or fortress's gateway. A system of ropes and winches located in a chamber above raised and lowered the door.

By the reign of the emperor Hadrian, in the early second century A.D., the Romans had come to perceive a need to fortify not just individual cities and forts, but the realm as a whole. So they began building defensive walls, fortresses, and forts in larger numbers and on a grander scale than ever before. The most spectacular surviving example of a fortification wall meant to keep enemies out of Roman territory is Hadrian's Wall, begun in 122. In its heyday, it stretched for some 73 miles (117 km) across the north-central section of the province of Britain. It was about 16 feet (5 m) high; had a ditch 26 feet (8 m) wide and 10 feet (3 m) deep running along its outer side; and was defended by 80 small castles spaced at intervals of about a mile. Beginning in about 140, Hadrian's successor, Antoninus Pius, erected a similar but smaller wall several miles north of Hadrian's. The new fortification was intended to replace the old one and guard an expanded Roman frontier. But about six or seven decades later, the Romans abandoned the Antonine Wall and fell back to the one Hadrian had built.

Both Hadrian's and Antoninus's walls had roads running behind them, and along these roads were forts where most of the soldiers assigned to man the walls lived. In the case of Hadrian's Wall, the forts were spaced about 6 miles (10 km) apart. Beginning in the late first century, the Romans constructed a much larger network of forts linked by roads along the Rhine and Danube frontiers with Germany. Significantly reinforced and expanded by Hadrian in the second century, this defensive line stretched for some 2,500 miles, from the North Sea in the northwest to the Black Sea in the east. The line became the basis for an even more formidable network of frontier defenses installed by Diocletian and his successors in the Later Empire. The forts were eventually spaced about 5 to 6 miles apart (or closer in some places); between them loomed numerous imposing *burgi* (solidly built, free-standing, square watchtowers from 20 to 40 feet on a side) and intermittent sections of stockades and ditches, all guarded by sentries.

For added security, a system of fortresses backed up the forts. The major factors that distinguished the fortresses from the forts were their size and the kinds of soldiers who manned them. Generally, the forts were relatively small, each covering about 2 to 14 acres and accommodating a few hundred to perhaps a thousand men. Some housed only auxiliary troops, almost always inhabitants of the provinces or noncitizens, while Roman legionaries or a mixture of legionaries and auxiliaries garrisoned the others. Fortresses, by comparison, were much larger. Each covered 50 or more acres and housed at least one legion, up to 5,000 or more men, usually Roman (rather than auxiliary) troops. There were obviously fewer fortresses than forts at any given time.

Despite these differences, Roman forts and fortresses, which can be classified together as fortified military bases, had much in common. First, they were structurally similar, being more permanent versions of the traditional and temporary Roman marching camp. Like marching camps, permanent bases had outer defenses, including ramparts and ditches. However, the defenses of the bases were much more elaborate, like those of fortified towns, including towers at intervals in the walls and wider and deeper moats. Also like towns, the larger permanent bases had various civilized amenities, including bathhouses, small amphitheaters, and taverns. **See** army camps; army organization and manpower; **also** Hadrian (Chapter 1).

Franks

A Germanic people who settled along the lower and middle reaches of the Rhine River at least by the early third century A.D., when Greek and Roman writers first mention them. In the middle of that century, various groups of Franks began penetrating Rome's northern frontiers. The emperor Probus pushed them back, but they persisted and in the century that followed various emperors, including Constantine I and Julian, fought them. Julian eventually made a deal with the Salian Franks, allowing them to settle in northeastern Gaul. They subsequently became Roman allies and supplied troops for the imperial army. In the fifth century, the Gallic Franks launched aggressive campaigns to gain territory at the expense of the weakening Roman government. After the decline of the western Empire, they came to occupy most of Gaul, which in time became known as France ("land of the Franks").

Gauls

A general term used by the Greeks and Romans to denote some groups of European Celts, especially those that settled in Cisalpine Gaul (northern Italy's Po Valley) and Transalpine Gaul (modern-day France). Thus, the Celtic warriors who defeated the Romans at Allia in 390 B.C. were referred to as Gauls, as were the tribesmen Caesar fought in his Gallic campaigns. **See** Battle of Allia; Celts; **also** Gaul (Chapter 2).

Goths

A numerous and strong Germanic people, the Goths were among Rome's most formidable enemies and played a crucial role in the Empire's history and decline over the course of two centuries. The Goths originally inhabited the region around the Vistula River, south of the Baltic Sea in what is now Poland. Sometime in the late second century A.D., they began a mass migration that led them to the Roman Empire's northern borders by the early 230s. A series of emperors, among them Philip the Arab and Decius, fought them. But the Goths proved too strong and determined; in 251 they defeated and killed Decius, and in the next twenty years they raided the Balkans and Asia Minor at will, inflicting widespread damage.

The tide turned against the Goths during the reigns of Claudius II (268–270), who earned the name "Gothicus" for defeating them, and Aurelian (270–275), who beat them severely and pushed them back to the Danube. For a century thereafter, the Goths posed no serious threat to Roman territory. During this interval, they split into two distinct groups, the Ostrogoths (or Eastern Goths) and Visigoths (Western Goths). The Ostrogoths created a large kingdom that stretched from the Black Sea's northern shores through what is now Ukraine. Meanwhile, the Visigoths remained in the area of Dacia, north of the Danube, where they settled into an agricultural lifestyle.

Then, circa 370 the Huns came sweeping out of western Asia and set in motion a momentous chain of events. They crushed the Ostrogoths in battle, killing the great Ostrogothic king Ermanarich, and overran his kingdom. Realizing that they were the Huns' next target, the Visigoths appealed to the eastern Roman emperor Valens to allow them to settle in Thrace; soon afterward, a group of Ostrogoths made the same appeal. Troubles with the Romans led to Valens's catastrophic defeat at Adrianople in 378 by the Visigoths, aided by the Ostrogoths. After their victory, the Visigoths plundered Thrace and settled in Moesia (just south of the Danube), while the Ostrogoths invaded Pannonia (now Austria), where they settled.

A few years later, the emperor Theodosius struck a deal with the Visigoths, granting them the status of federates ("equal allies" living within the Empire). However, this did not satisfy many of the tribesmen, especially Alaric, who became their king in 395. He fought the Romans off and on until marching into Italy and sacking

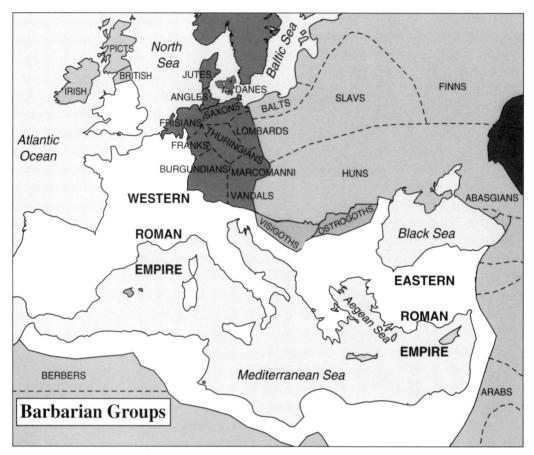

Barbarian Groups

Rome in 410. Alaric died soon afterward and his brother-in-law, Athaulf, led the Visigoths into southern Gaul and later into Spain. There, they built a powerful kingdom that thrived until the invasion of the Muslims in the eighth century. Meanwhile, the Ostrogoths, under their able king, Theodoric the Great, entered Italy in 493 and deposed Odoacer, who had himself deposed the last Roman emperor seventeen years before. The Ostrogothic Italian kingdom lasted until 553, when the Byzantines and Lombards took control of the peninsula. **See** Battle of Adrianople; **also** Alaric; Aurelian; Claudius II; Decius, Gaius Messius Quintus; Odoacer; Valens, Flavius Julius (all Chapter 1); **and** Rome (Chapter 2).

Greeks

The Romans borrowed more aspects of their culture from the Greeks than from any other single people, despite the fact that the Romans and Greeks were often at violent odds during a period of almost three centuries. The two peoples first had marginal contacts in the seventh century B.C. after a number of Greek cities planted colonies in southern Italy (which became known as Magna Graecia, or "Greater Greece"). Periodic cultural and commercial exchanges occurred over the course of the next few centuries. As Roman territory and influence expanded in the fourth and early third centuries B.C., the Italian Greeks found themselves threatened, and in 280 B.C. they appealed to Pyrrhus, king of the Greek kingdom of Epirus, for aid. He fought the Romans to a standstill, but was unable to beat them decisively, and five years later he vacated Italy. A mere decade later, all of Magna Graecia was under Roman control.

New Greco-Roman hostilities ignited half a century later, during the Second

Punic War, when another Greek kingdom, Macedonia, allied itself with Carthage against Rome. This led the Romans to strike back at the Macedonians and to become heavily involved in the eastern Mediterranean. The Roman military system of legions and maniples proved superior to the Greek system, based on the phalanx, and by 146 B.C., Rome had come to dominate most of the Greek lands. The last major Greek state to fall to Rome was Ptolemaic Egypt, in 30 B.C.

All the while, as well throughout later centuries, Greek artistic, religious, and philosophical ideas had a profound impact on Roman life and thought. The cultural fusion between the two peoples came to be called "classical" civilization; and the classical ideal in turn exerted a powerful influence on later European thinkers and artists. For Greek opposition to and cultural influences on Rome, **see** Battles of Cynoscephalae and Magnesia; battlefield tactics; Macedonian Wars; **also** Cleopatra VII; Flamininus, Titus Quinctius; Plotinus; Plutarch; Pyrrhus (Chapter 1); Athens; Corinth; Macedonian Kingdom; Magna Graecia; Ptolemaic Kingdom; Seleucid Kingdom (Chapter 2); afterlife; Eleusinian Mysteries; temples (Chapter 3); athletic games; medicine; trade (Chapter 5); Latin and other languages; libraries; orders; architectural; painting; poetry; pottery; rhetoric; sculpture; Stoicism; theater and drama (Chapter 6).

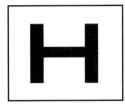

Hadrian's Wall

For the famous defensive wall the Romans built across northern Britain in the second century A.D., **see** forts, fortresses, and fortifications.

Helvetii

This rugged, numerous tribal people originally lived in the western sector of what is now Switzerland. In the early 50s B.C., they decided to migrate into the more expansive and fertile region of southern Gaul, but Julius Caesar, who had recently acquired governorship of that area, repelled them with heavy losses and forced them to return to their homeland. Subsequently, the Helvetii became increasingly Romanized. In A.D. 69 (the "year of the four emperors"), the would-be emperor Vitellius passed through their territory and devastated it, after which the tribe more or less faded from view.

Huns

A fearsome, nomadic people of central Asia, at first they tried to overrun China, but after the Chinese built the Great Wall to discourage them, the Huns turned westward and slowly but steadily made their way to Europe. About the middle of the fourth century A.D., the Hun hordes attacked the Ostrogoths, Alans, and other eastern European tribes, setting in motion the vast folk migrations that pushed hundreds of thousands of "barbarians" into Rome's northern border provinces. The Roman historian Ammianus's graphic description of the Huns explains why they appeared repulsive and frightening even to the Germanic barbarians:

> The Huns are quite abnormally savage. . . . They have squat bodies, strong limbs, and thick necks, and are so prodigiously ugly and bent that they might be two-legged animals, or the figures [gargoyles] crudely carved from stumps which are seen on the parapets of bridges. . . . Their way of life is so rough that they have no use for fire or seasoned food, but live on the roots of wild plants and the half-raw flesh of any sort of animals, which they warm a little by placing it between their thighs and the backs of their horses. . . .

When they join battle they advance in packs, uttering their various war-cries. Being lightly equipped and very sudden in their movements they can deliberately scatter and gallop about at random, inflicting tremendous slaughter. (*Histories* 31.2)

In the late fourth and early fifth centuries, the Huns consolidated their gains, which included much of eastern Europe. Then, in the 440s, a new war chief, Attila, assumed control and launched an invasion of Rome's eastern Danube frontier. After threatening Constantinople, he turned westward and began to overrun Gaul, but a combined Roman-barbarian army stopped him in 451 at Chalons. Attila next attempted to invade Italy, but he left as quickly as he had come and died soon afterward. His sons were unable to hold together the various Hun factions; and in 454 the various Germanic tribes then dominated by the Huns rebelled and

A modern engraving depicts the Huns arriving in Europe. The Roman historian Ammianus called them an "ugly" people who ate raw animal flesh.

drove them away. **See** Battle of Chalons; **also** Attila (Chapter 1).

Iceni

A tribe of northeast Britain, in the area of modern Norfolk, who became Roman allies very soon after Claudius's general, Aulus Plautius, invaded the island in the 40s A.D. In the early 50s, the new governor, Publius Scapula, advanced into central and northern tribal territories and demanded that the natives, including the Iceni, surrender their weapons. The Iceni refused and rebelled, but the Romans quelled the insurrection. In 61, the Iceni king died, leaving his kingdom to the Romans in hopes of pacifying them, but they responded by plundering his domain and flogging his wife, Boudicca. She subsequently led the Iceni, along with neighboring tribes, in a new revolt, but it too failed and the tribal lands were absorbed into the Roman province of Britannia. **See** Boudicca (Chapter 1); **also** Britain (Chapter 2).

imperator

At first, this honorific was conferred on a victorious general by his soldiers and held until he celebrated his triumph. In the late Republic, Julius Caesar held onto the title permanently, and his heir Octavian, on becoming Augustus, adopted it as part of his official name (Imperator Caesar Divi Filius Augustus), so that thereafter *im-*

perator came to signify the supreme military authority of the emperor. **See** emperor (Chapter 4).

Jews

For these proud and courageous residents of Palestine who challenged the might of Rome in the first and second centuries, **see** Herod; Jesus Christ; John the Baptist; Josephus; Paul; Peter; Titus; Vespasian (all Chapter 1); Judaea (Chapter 2); **and** Christianity; Judaism (both Chapter 3).

Jugurthine War

This conflict erupted in 112 B.C. in the kingdom of Numidia (in North Africa), which had been on friendly terms with Rome ever since its colorful king, Masinissa, aided the Romans in fighting his neighbor, Carthage. In 118 B.C., Rome arranged a settlement whereby three young Numidian princes would share the rule of their realm. One of these young men, Jugurtha, eventually rejected the settlement, killed one of his rivals, drove away the other, and in 112 B.C. massacred all of the Roman residents of the town of Cirta. Rome declared war and its police action against this upstart became known as the Jugurthine War.

The first Roman commanders sent to Numidia were unsuccessful in stopping "the lion of the desert," as Jugurtha came to be called; but in 109 B.C., a much more capable general, Quintus Metellus, became consul and took charge of the war. Metellus pushed Jugurtha back, forcing him to resort to guerrilla tactics, at which, as it turned out, he excelled. Meanwhile, one of Metellus's deputies, Gaius Marius, who would later become one of Rome's great-

est generals, made a name for himself in the campaign. Marius's big break came in 107 B.C., when he managed to get himself elected consul and the tribal assembly gave him command in Numidia in place of Metellus.

Marius vigorously attacked one enemy stronghold after another, but he was unable to capture the crafty Jugurtha. It was Marius's rival, Cornelius Sulla, who finally managed to get some of Jugurtha's allies to hand him over to the Romans. Marius humiliated Jugurtha by marching him in chains in his victory triumph, after which the government executed the Numidian. **See** Marius, Gaius; Sulla, Lucius Cornelius (both Chapter 1); **and** Numidia (Chapter 2).

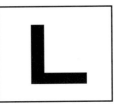

Latin League

An early association of Latin towns, including Rome, clustered around the plain of Latium. It formed sometime in the seventh century B.C., in part because the residents of these communities shared a common language as well as the same gods and religious traditions, and also because they long met once a year to celebrate the festival of Latin Jupiter (*Jupiter Latiaris*), held atop the Alban Mount in Latium. The League also came to have a military dimension. The neighboring Etruscans and various Italian hill tribes posed a threat common to all the Latins, who sometimes banded together for mutual protection.

Rome early became dominant in the League. In the early 400s B.C. it fought the other members, defeated them at Lake Regillus (near the Alban Mount), and then formed an alliance with them. In 340 B.C., the other towns in the League rose against Rome once more, which defeated them again. This time, the Romans dissolved the organization, incorporated five of the former members into the Roman state, and forced the others to become allies obliged to furnish troops for Rome's armies. **See** Latium (Chapter 2).

legion

For this large Roman military battalion, usually numbering about five thousand soldiers, **see** army organization and manpower; battlefield tactics.

legionary

For this common Roman soldier, **see** army organization and manpower; army recruitment, training, and personnel.

Liburnian

For this small, fast Roman ship, **see** navy.

Macedonian Wars

These three conflicts between Rome and Greece's Macedonian Kingdom took place in the late third and early second centuries B.C. and ended with the dissolution of that kingdom and the advent of Roman domination of Greece. The First Macedonian War (214–205 B.C.) was, from the Roman standpoint, a subconflict of the greater Second Punic War. The Macedonian king, Philip V (grandson of Antigonus Gonatas, the founder of the Macedonian Antigonid dynasty), allied himself with Rome's enemy, Carthage, and attacked various Roman outposts in Illyria (west of Macedonia). Because the Romans did not then possess the manpower and resources to open a new front in Greece, they formed alliances with some of Macedonia's Greek enemies, including the Aetolian League, Sparta, and Pergamum. And fighting these states kept Philip too busy to launch further campaigns against Rome.

When the Second Punic War ended (in 201 B.C.) with a resounding Roman victory, Rome wasted no time in mounting a punitive expedition against Philip. In the first year or so of the Second Macedonian War (200–197 B.C.), the Romans spent most of their time consolidating Illyria. Then, in 198 B.C. the consul Flamininus took charge of the war and pushed into Thessaly (in central Greece). There, the following year, he delivered Philip a debilitating defeat at Cynoscephalae, after which the king sued for peace. Macedonia was forced to surrender most of its warships, pay a large indemnity, and become a Roman ally.

Over time, Philip's bitterness toward Rome and its interference in Greek affairs increased. When he died in 179 B.C., his son, Perseus, who inherited the throne, intrigued with various anti-Roman Greek factions, hoping to stir up trouble. Aware of the danger Perseus posed, the Romans took the initiative and forced him into the Third Macedonian War (172–168 B.C.). In 168 B.C., the consul Aemilius Paullus crushed Perseus at Pydna and took him under guard back to Rome, where he soon died. The Romans dismantled the Macedonian Kingdom, and in 146 B.C. annexed it as a province. **See** Battles of Cynoscephalae and Pydna; **also** Macedonian Kingdom (Chapter 2).

magister equitum

(initially "master of the horse," later "master of cavalry") In the Republic, the *magister equitum* was the principle assistant and deputy of the dictator (on those rare occasions when the state appointed a dictator). Augustus eliminated the position of master of the horse and assigned most of its duties to the Praetorian Prefect. In the Later Empire, however, Constantine I decided to revive the title; this time it referred to the leading general of Rome's cavalry, while the leader of the infantry was the *magister peditum*. Soon, their titles and duties merged into one overall military leader—the *magister militum*. **See** army recruitment, training, and personnel; *magister militum*.

magister militum

("master of soldiers") The supreme commander of Rome's military forces in its last century or so, the office grew out of a merging of the positions of "master of the infantry" and "master of cavalry," which had been established by Constantine I. In the western Empire, the *magistri* often came to dominate not only military affairs, but also their supposed masters, the emperors. This was because Roman troops, who were increasingly Germanic or otherwise foreign in character, tended to show more allegiance to their generals (who were often of "barbarian" extraction themselves) than to the government. These powerful generals frequently made decisions on their own that were not in the best interests of the already deteriorating western Roman state.

In the east, at Constantinople, by contrast, the emperors eventually managed to exercise control over their *magistri*. In 471, for instance, the eastern emperor Leo I executed his barbarian *magister militum*, Aspar, and set the precedent of appointing local, rather than foreign, generals, a move that helped the eastern realm to survive the fall of the west.

magister peditum

For this commander of Roman foot soldiers during the Later Empire, **see** army recruitment, training, and personnel; *magister equitum*.

maniple

For this basic and important battlefield unit of Rome's midrepublican armies, **see**

army organization and manpower; battlefield tactics.

Marcomanni

Originally a branch of the Suebi, the Marcomanni were a numerous and powerful Germanic tribe that fought the Romans on and off for about three centuries. At first they inhabited northern Germany, but in the early first century B.C. population migration within that sphere led them to an area on the Main River (a tributary of the Rhine). Some Marcomanni apparently fought alongside the Suebi chief, Ariovistus, whom Julius Caesar defeated in Gaul in 58 B.C. A few decades later, in Augustus's reign, the Marcomanni fought a Roman army led by Drusus the Elder, after which Rome installed a client king in their territory. Throughout most of the first century, fighting with German neighbors and internal political rivalry kept the Marcomanni weak. But in the 90s, they engaged the Romans again, requiring the emperors Domitian and Nerva to expend considerable effort in containing them.

There then followed another period of relative quiet among the Marcomanni. In 166, however, they once more burst forth to threaten Roman lands, this time at the head of a coalition of other tribes (including the Quadi and Vandals). This ignited the so-called Marcomannic Wars (166–175 and 177–180). In the first conflict, the Germans entered Italy and boldly besieged the Roman city of Aquileia. The emperor Marcus Aurelius managed to push them back, but spent the next few years fighting new waves of invaders. A temporary peace from 176 to 177 ended when the emperor launched a massive and successful campaign against the Marcomanni and Quadi. He was on the verge of literally annihilating them when he died in March 180. His son, Commodus, decided not to pursue Aurelius's plans to absorb and Romanize central Germany and instead made peace with the Marcomanni.

This ultimately allowed them to regroup for later attacks on Rome, for the Marcomanni were among the barbarian tribes the Romans fought in the following century. **See** Commodus; Marcus Aurelius (both Chapter 1); **and** Germany (Chapter 2).

Mithridatic Wars

Three bloody conflicts initiated against Rome by Mithridates VI, king of Pontus (on the southern shore of the Black Sea). In the first war (89–85 B.C.), his forces suddenly overran much of Asia Minor and in 88 B.C. he gave the order to execute without trial perhaps as many as eighty thousand Romans living in the region. He sacked and briefly occupied Athens in 86 B.C. until the Roman general Sulla defeated him twice in rapid succession. The second war (83–82 B.C.) pitted the Roman governor of the province of Asia against Mithridates, who easily fended off his opponent. The king then steadily built up his stores of money and supplies and invaded Bithynia, igniting the third Mithridatic war (74–63 B.C.). The Roman generals Lucullus and Pompey expelled him first from Bithynia and then from Pontus itself, forcing him to flee to Armenia (east of Asia Minor). After failing to raise more armies to regain his kingdom, Mithridates committed suicide in 63 B.C. **See** Lucullus, Lucius Licinius; Mithridates VI; Sulla, Lucius Cornelius (all Chapter 1); **and** Bithynia; Pontus (both Chapter 2).

navy

Because the Romans were not originally a maritime people, Rome had no appreciable navy of warships in the Monarchy and early Republic. Only when they perceived an urgent need did they build such ships and then they did so with amazing speed and on a grand scale. (These were the 120 warships that the Greek historian Polybius tells us they produced in only two months to meet the challenge of fighting Carthage in the First Punic War.) Rome's military tradition as a land power was so ingrained, in fact, that even after its navy became an institution, it was for the most part viewed as secondary to and considerably less prestigious than the army. Thus, for a long time young Roman men aspired to be soldiers rather than sailors.

As for those who did become sailors, ships' rowers and other crewmen were mostly noncitizens or foreigners who were organized as auxiliaries rather than legionaries. (The rowers were not slaves, nor were they chained to their oars, as so often depicted in Hollywood films.) In the Republic most of these seamen were members of Rome's Italian allies, while in imperial times they tended to be Greeks, Egyptians, Phoenicians, Syrians, and others from societies with long-established maritime traditions. Often their major motivation when signing on for long hitches was to be granted Roman citizenship as a reward on discharge.

Rome's first warships were a handful of small craft built in 311 B.C. to police the local waters of western Italy against pirates who periodically raided the area. About twenty years later, some of these Roman ships made the mistake of getting into a fight with the war fleet belonging to the still independent Greek city of Taras (in southern Italy). The Romans were beaten so badly that they scrapped their ships, and for the next several years they relegated the task of policing their coast to ships from nearby Greek cities that were already subjects of Rome.

Faced with the naval might of Carthage in the First Punic War, however, the Roman Senate reluctantly concluded that Rome would have to construct a large fleet of warships. Using a Carthaginian warship that had accidentally run aground as a model, they built an entire fleet and trained thousands of landlubbers to be sailors and rowers. By 256 B.C., the Romans had some 330 warships. Many of these were lost in battle or in violent storms, so they continually built new warships and fleets. Incredibly, during the First Punic War, which was fought mostly at sea, Rome lost an estimated 700 warships and troop transports and over one hundred thousand crewmen, the largest naval losses ever suffered by a single nation in one war. Yet they still managed to win the war, and by 201 B.C. Rome was the mightiest sea power in the Mediterranean.

In the centuries that followed, Roman navies came and went as need and circumstances dictated. With Carthage's navy

The chaos and destruction of an ancient sea battle are captured in this modern rendering of the Battle of Actium, which ended the civil wars of the first century B.C.

out of the way, the only other fleets posing the slightest threat to Rome's belonged to a few Greek states in the eastern Mediterranean. Rome quickly gained control of this region though, and with the seaways largely at peace, its war fleets were allowed to decline. Not until the civil wars of the late first century B.C. did the Romans require fleets of warships again, and this time they commandeered most of them from Greek cities under their control.

Once the civil wars were over, these same ships became the nucleus of the imperial fleets organized by Augustus. In the first century A.D. he and his successors established fleets on the coasts of Italy, Egypt, Syria, the Black Sea, the English Channel, and the Rhine and Danube Rivers. In the second century, the fleets began to decline again, however. Sea power had almost no role in warfare in the Later Empire; by the end of the fourth century, the once mighty Roman navy had virtually ceased to exist.

In their prime, these fleets featured a wide variety of vessels; yet the Romans

predominantly used four kinds of war-ship—triremes ("threes"), quadriremes ("fours"), quinqueremes ("fives"), and Liburnians. The original designs of the first three types were Greek. As its name suggests, the trireme had three banks of oars, with one man to an oar. A Roman trireme probably carried a complement of about 220 to 250 men, including about 170 rows (with between 50 and 60 in each oar bank), about 15 to 20 crewmen, and a few dozen marines (fighters). Adding to-gether the hull, decks, mast, oars, men, weapons, and supplies, such a vessel would have weighed, or in nautical terms "displaced," 80 to 90 tons. Yet it was rela-tively quick for its time. In short spurts, when attacking for instance, it could attain a speed of perhaps 7 to 8 knots (8 to 9 miles per hour).

The quadrireme and quinquereme were both somewhat larger than a trireme. A quadrireme appears to have had two banks of oars, with two men to each oar. The quinquereme likely took this design a step further, so that it had three oar banks, the top two having two rowers to an oar and the bottom one having one man to an oar. Per-haps the most common warship in Roman navies during the mid-to-late Republic, the quinquereme was up to 120 feet long and carried some 270 rowers, 30 crewmen, and from 40 to 120 marines.

By contrast, the Liburnian, invented by a tribe of pirates in Illyricum, was much smaller. A fast, lightweight, very maneu-verable ship, it was useful for pursuit or carrying messages, and it became the most common vessel in Rome's provincial fleets. It was likely single-banked at first, but later had two banks of rowers. The Liburnian became so popular that in time the word was accepted as a general term meaning warship.

The Romans acquired knowledge of naval affairs from the Greeks and Carthaginians during midrepublican times, adopting the basic naval battle tactics then widely in use. The first of these was the employment of a bronze-coated beak mounted on the ship's bow to ram an en-emy vessel. The object was to open a hole in the enemy's side and sink it. Among the tactical maneuvers a fleet used to gain the advantage was the *periplus,* in which an attacking fleet managed to outflank (en-velop the sides of) the enemy fleet; this al-lowed some of the attacking ships to ram the exposed sides of the outer ships in the enemy's line. Another common maneuver was the *diekplus.* One ship attacked an en-emy vessel at an angle, shearing off most of its oars on one side and thereby immo-bilizing it; then a second attacker, stationed directly behind the first, moved in for the lethal ramming run.

Although the Romans sometimes used these maneuvers, they much preferred the second basic naval battle tactic—board-ing an enemy ship and taking control of it via hand-to-hand fighting. Perhaps it was the long and prestigious record of their army that led to their increased em-phasis of land warfare techniques in naval battles. The first major advance in this di-rection was their invention of the *corvus* ("crow" or "raven") in the early years of the First Punic War. This was a long wooden gangway with a spike attached to its end. The crow stood in an upright po-sition on the front deck of a Roman ship until the vessel pulled alongside an en-emy ship, at which time sailors dropped the device onto the enemy's deck. The spike pierced the deck, holding the gang-way in place, and Roman marines charged across and attacked the enemy vessel's crew. In the Republic, marines who boarded enemy ships were not sailors but army legionaries who had been trained to adapt their weapons and tactics to the narrow confines of ships' decks. Therefore, the *corvus* made a naval battle more like an infantry battle on land.

In time, however, the Romans abandoned the *corvus* because its weight made their ships unbalanced, unsteady, and more prone to capsizing in stormy conditions. However, they continued to develop and use devices that allowed them to hold fast and board enemy ships. These included long poles or lengths of chain with large grapnel (hooks) attached to the ends; when one of their ships maneuvered close enough to an enemy vessel, Roman sailors tossed the grapnel, snagging the enemy's deck, and the marines boarded on wooden planks or ladders.

The Roman naval command structure was no less complex than that of the land army. The topmost naval leader, the admiral, was always a Roman citizen from a prominent family; in the Republic, admirals were usually senators, while in the Empire they held the rank of prefect and tended to be well-to-do, high-ranking army officers. The Romans borrowed the terms used to describe most of the other naval officers from the Greeks. The commander of a squadron, perhaps about ten ships, was a *navarch,* and the captain of an individual ship was a *trierarch*. In the early Empire, both positions were filled mainly by experienced Greek sailors.

Under a *trierarch* ranged a number of junior officers who made up the captain's staff. These included a chief administrator (*beneficarius*) and various kinds of clerks with specialized jobs, such as making reports to the admiral's office and keeping financial records. The *trierarch* also had deck officers to help him run his ship. Among them were the *gubernator,* who supervised the steersmen from his station on the aft (rear) deck; his assistant, the *proreta,* stationed on the prow (front); the *celeusta,* who used wooden mallets to pound out a beat for the rowers to follow; two or three *velarii,* experts at raising and lowering the sails; and a *nauphlax,* in charge of the ship's physical upkeep. Usually, these junior officers and

specialists received double or more the pay of an ordinary sailor.

In addition, each warship had its complement of marines. Since an individual warship was, for organizational purposes, designated as a naval century, these fighters were trained and commanded by a centurion. As in an army century, he was assisted by an *optio.* The relationship between the centurion and the *trierarch,* including who had more authority in specific areas, remains unclear. But it is almost certain that the centurion made all the important decisions concerning actual combat. **See** Battle of Actium, Cape Ecnomus, and Mylae; Punic Wars; **also** piracy (Chapter 5).

Nervii
For this formidable and courageous Gallic tribe that offered Julius Caesar fearsome resistance, **see** Belgae.

Notitia Dignitatum
A list of Roman political and military offices, providing information about the duties, staff, and military units of each. It was compiled by an unknown person or persons some time around A.D. 400 or perhaps a bit later. Most of the information concerns officials in the western part of the realm. Modern scholars find the *Notitia* an invaluable aid in understanding how the deteriorating late Roman government and army worked.

Ostrogoths
For this large and important "barbarian" tribe that fought the Romans on numerous occasions and occupied much Roman land, **see** Goths.

Parthians

For these inhabitants of the Near Eastern region once controlled by Persia, who fought the Romans off and on for several centuries, **see** Arsacids (Chapter 1).

Persians

For these inhabitants of the region now occupied by Iran and Iraq, who were frequently at odds with the Romans, **see** Arsacids; Sassanids (both Chapter 1).

phalanx

For this battlefield formation (composed of rows of spearmen) the early Romans adopted from the Greeks, **see** army organization and manpower; battlefield tactics.

Picts

The Roman name applied to the various wild, warlike tribesmen who inhabited Caledonia (now Scotland, in northern Britain) in the early first millennium A.D. (The term *Pict* came from the Latin word *pictor,* meaning "painter," a reference to their habit of painting their bodies with colorful symbols and designs.) The culture and language of the Picts apparently consisted of a mixture of Celtic and pre-Celtic elements, suggesting that at least some of them were descended from the original Stone Age inhabitants of Britain. They began raiding southward into the Roman province of Britannia shortly before A.D. 300 and remained a periodic menace in the century that followed. After the Romans abandoned Britain in the early fifth century, the Picts joined with the Germanic Saxons and other tribes in overrunning the island. **See** Celts; **also** Britain (Chapter 2).

pilum

For this throwing spear employed by Roman soldiers, **see** armor and weapons.

Praetorian Guard

This elite force of bodyguards, which the first emperor, Augustus, created in the 20s B.C. to protect his person, became an influential and often ominous and brutal factor in the subsequent history of the imperial regime. The original force consisted of nine cohorts, each having from five hundred to one thousand men. Some patrolled the Palatine hill (where Augustus lived) and other parts of Rome, while others were stationed in surrounding towns. Their leader was called the Praetorian Prefect.

From the reign of Augustus's successor, Tiberius, on, the Guard became a significant political force in its own right, as its leaders and members intervened in imperial affairs at will, usually when paid to do so by one ambitious faction or another. In A.D. 41, for example, the Guards joined in the conspiracy to kill the emperor Caligula, and they then placed Claudius on the throne. In an even more audacious display, following Commodus's assassination in 192 the Guards murdered his successor, Pertinax, after a reign of only eighty-seven days because he had paid them only half of a promised bonus; they then auctioned off the throne to the highest bidder. Some emperors took steps to rein in the Guards. Septimius Severus, for instance, disbanded them and created a new bodyguard from scratch. Finally, in the early fourth century Constantine the Great abolished the Praetorian Guard altogether and demolished its barracks.

Punic Wars

Three monumental conflicts fought between Rome and the maritime empire of Carthage, centered in what is now Tunisia, in North Africa. (The term *Punic* comes from the Latin name meaning "Phoenician," a reference to the fact that the

Phoenicians were the original founders of Carthage.) Once the Romans had become masters of all Italy in 265 B.C., it was inevitable that their ambitions could not be contained on that peninsula. A year later, Carthage made the mistake of occupying Messina (on the northeastern tip of Sicily), only a few miles from the southern Italian shore. Considering this a violation of an agreement Rome and Carthage had made in the preceding century, in which they had promised to stay clear of each other's spheres of influence, the Romans declared war.

The First Punic War (264–241 B.C.) was the largest, most destructive conflict ever fought up to that time. It consisted mostly of sea battles, as the Romans, who had never possessed war fleets of any consequence, manufactured them literally overnight and boldly challenged the Carthaginians, who had a long naval tradition and controlled the western Mediterranean sea-lanes. The Roman fleets initially had a secret weapon, the "raven," a gangway that held fast an enemy ship and allowed Roman infantrymen to board it. This gave them the upper hand and won them victories in the huge engagements of Mylae (260 B.C.) and Cape Ecnomus (256 B.C.). Rome then invaded North Africa, hoping to capture Carthage. But its army was defeated by a Greek general hired by the Carthaginians. A series of violent storms then sank hundreds of Roman ships, inflicting horrendous losses of life. Somehow, Rome, seemingly on the brink of ruin, managed to pull its remaining resources together, built still another fleet, and shattered the enemy off the coast of Sicily in 241 B.C., after which Carthage sued for peace. The Romans gained control over Sicily and Sardinia as a result.

Embittered by Carthage's defeat, its leading general, Hamilcar Barca, spent years turning southern Spain into a military base from which he hoped eventually to strike back at Rome. After he died in a drowning accident in 229 B.C., his son, Hannibal, one of the greatest military commanders of all time, attacked Saguntum (in 219 B.C.), a Roman ally on Spain's eastern coast, and once more Rome declared war. The Second Punic War (218–201 B.C.) was a truly enormous conflict that almost brought Rome to its knees.

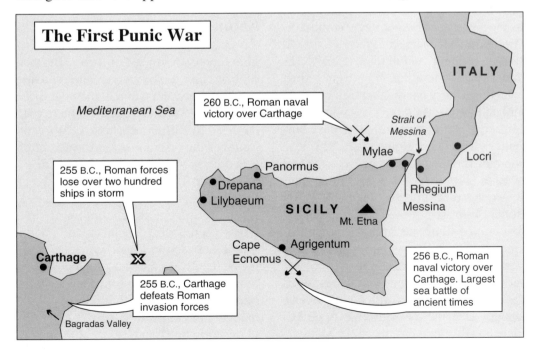

The First Punic War

ITALY

Mediterranean Sea

260 B.C., Roman naval victory over Carthage

Strait of Messina

Mylae

Locri

255 B.C., Roman forces lose over two hundred ships in storm

Panormus

Drepana

Lilybaeum

Rhegium

SICILY

Messina

Mt. Etna

Carthage

Cape Ecnomus

Agrigentum

256 B.C., Roman naval victory over Carthage. Largest sea battle of ancient times

255 B.C., Carthage defeats Roman invasion forces

Bagradas Valley

Hannibal boldly crossed the Alps with an army and attacked northern Italy. One by one, he crushed every force the Romans sent against him, winning huge victories at the Trebia River (218 B.C.) and Lake Trasimene (217 B.C.). His greatest triumph, however, was at Cannae (216 B.C.), where he delivered the Romans their worst single battlefield loss ever (over fifty thousand dead). At this point, Hannibal seemed on the verge of total victory. Yet he was unable to win over most of Rome's Italian allies, whom he needed to capture and hold the Roman heartland. As the years went by, the dauntless, resourceful Romans rebounded, as they had done so often in the past. In 202 B.C., they once more attacked North Africa and there, at Zama, Publius Cornelius Scipio (later called "Africanus") handed Hannibal his first defeat, ending the war in Rome's favor. The Carthaginians had to give up all but ten of their ships and cede Spain and most of their other territories to Rome.

After its second defeat, Carthage watched nervously as the Mediterranean steadily turned into a Roman lake. Yet the Carthaginians carefully honored the terms of the treaty and tried not to provoke Rome's wrath. However, several conservative Roman leaders still viewed their old rival as a threat, and in the late 150s B.C. they secretly plotted its final destruction. Using the flimsy excuse that Carthage had violated the terms of the treaty when it defended itself against an attack by Numidia's Masinissa, Rome declared war in 149 B.C. The final conflict between the two peoples (149–146 B.C.) was a brutal affair in which Roman forces, eventually led by Scipio Aemilianus, mercilessly besieged and burned Carthage. This once magnificent city was leveled and its inhabitants were killed or sold into slavery in 146 B.C., the same year that Rome totally destroyed the Greek city of Corinth. In just over a century, the wings of the Roman eagle had come to stretch across the entire Mediter-ranean world. **See** Battles of Cannae, Cape Ecnomus, Lake Trasimene, Metaurus River, Mylae, Trebia, and Zama; navy; **also** Cato the Elder; Fabius Maximus; Hannibal; Scipio, Publius Cornelius "Africanus"; Scipio, Publius Cornelius Aemilianus (all Chapter 1); **and** Carthage; Numidia; Rome; Sicily; Spain (Chapter 2).

quinquereme

For this large warship utilized by the Carthaginians, Greeks, Romans, and other ancient peoples, **see** navy.

Sabines

An early Italian people who lived in the region directly northeast of Rome. Because of their close proximity to Rome, and also because they were culturally similar to the Latins, the Sabines appear to have contributed to Rome's early development. Some of the original noble Roman families may have had Sabine roots, for instance. The famous story about the Roman founder, Romulus, inviting the Sabines to a celebration and then kidnapping their women is probably legendary, although it might be based to some degree on a real incident between the two peoples. What is more certain is that the Romans fought the Sabines on occasion until decisively defeating them in the mid–fifth century B.C. In the early third century B.C., the Sabines and their territory were absorbed into the growing Roman state.

Samnites

A sturdy, often warlike people who inhabited the valleys of the central and southern Apennines, they consisted of four large tribes (or cantons) that sometimes banded together for mutual protection. In the middle of the fourth century B.C., Samnite territory and population were probably twice the size of Rome's and the largest of any single Italian people. Both the Romans and Samnites were aggressive, ambitious, and had strong military traditions, so it is perhaps inevitable that they would eventually come to blows over land and other issues.

And indeed, Rome fought three wars with the Samnites. The first one (343–341 B.C.) was a short, rather inglorious affair that arose when the Samnites attacked Capua (in the Campania, south of Rome) and the town asked the Romans for assistance. At one point, the Roman army mutinied because it felt it was fighting too far from home. However, the war ended with Rome in control of northern Campania.

The Second Samnite War (326–304 B.C.) resulted when the Samnites again intruded in the Campania, this time occupying the town of Neapolis (Naples). The Romans drove the Samnite garrison out and were at first successful in other military encounters. In 321 B.C., however, the enemy trapped a Roman army at the Caudine Forks (near Capua), forcing the Roman troops to surrender, a humiliation the Romans never forgot. Still, the Romans rebounded and eventually defeated the Samnites, who had to vacate the Campania for good.

In the Third Samnite War (298–290 B.C.), the Romans carried the fighting directly into Samnite territory. Despite a dogged, courageous defense put up by the local towns, the Romans ravaged one Samnite valley after another until the enemy had no choice but to surrender. Rome absorbed a good deal of Samnite territory and forced the Samnites to become Roman allies, thereby removing the greatest single obstacle to Rome's conquest of the Italian peninsula.

Saxons

This large and active tribal people originated near the Elbe (in ancient times the Albis) River, in eastern Germany. After fighting and defeating some of their neighbors in the late second century B.C., they came into contact with the Franks and Romans about a century later and began raiding Gaul. In particular, bands of Saxon pirates ravaged Gaul's northern coasts, making it difficult for Rome to maintain its British provinces. After Rome abandoned Britain in the fifth century, the Saxons, along with the Angles and Jutes, invaded Britain and stayed permanently. Eventually, the fusion of their cultures came to be called Anglo-Saxon.

scutum

For this large, effective shield long wielded by Roman soldiers, **see** armor and weapons.

siege of Alesia

This famous operation, supervised by Julius Caesar, took place in the summer of 52 B.C. after Vercingetorix, chief of the Averni tribe, took charge of a large native rebellion against Rome's presence in Gaul. Following a pitched battle that went badly for the tribesmen, Vercingetorix fell back with some sixty thousand men to the huge Averni fortress-town of Alesia in eastern Gaul.

Surrounding the town, Caesar ordered his men to circumvallate it with ditches, mounds, booby traps, and guard posts. He described these siege works in his personal journal:

> Tree trunks or very stout branches were cut down and the ends were stripped of bark and sharpened; long trenches, five

feet deep, were dug and into these the stakes were sunk and fastened at the bottom so that they could not be torn up, while the top part projected above the surface. There were five rows of them in each trench, fastened and interlaced together in such a way that anyone who got among them would impale himself on the sharp points. The soldiers called them "tombstones.". . . When these [and the other] defenses were completed, I constructed another line of fortifications of the same kind, but this time facing the other way, against the enemy from the outside. These additional fortifications had a circuit of thirteen miles. (*Commentary on the Gallic War* 7.5)

These outward-facing defenses proved vital, for a huge force of Gallic reinforcements arrived during the siege and attempted to break the Roman lines. For four days, Caesar led a brilliant defense against enemy troops attacking from both inside and outside his perimeter. He was ultimately successful, Alesia fell, and Vercingetorix was forced to surrender. **See** Averni; siege tactics; **also** Caesar, Gaius Julius; Vercingetorix (both Chapter 1).

siege of Jerusalem

After the start of the Jewish revolt against Rome in A.D. 66, Vespasian, then a general, arrived in Judaea, subdued many of the rebels, and was about to besiege Jerusalem in 68 when news came of civil strife in Italy. After returning to Rome and becoming emperor, Vespasian sent his son, Titus, to finish quelling the Jewish insurrection.

The siege of Jerusalem began in the early spring of 70; by May the Romans had penetrated the first of the city's three defensive walls. Late in August, they reached the great, sacred Temple, which, despite Titus's desire that it should be spared, caught fire and was destroyed. Fierce fighting continued and the attackers

were unable to capture the entire city until late September. What they did not burn, they demolished later, and there was much indiscriminate killing and plunder by Roman troops. **See** siege of Masada; siege tactics; **also** Titus (Chapter 1); Judaea (Chapter 2); **and** Judaism (Chapter 3).

siege of Masada

The siege of Masada proved a classic demonstration of the Roman approach to siege warfare, combining methodic patience, enormous muscle power, the technique of circumvallation, and a huge siege ramp. This was the last of three major sieges conducted by the Romans against the Jews in their rebellion of A.D. 66–73. After the general collapse of the revolt in 70–71, a few militant diehards retreated to Masada, a seemingly impregnable fortress at the summit of an imposing rock plateau overlooking the western shore of the Dead Sea. There, the leader of the group, Eleazar ben Ya'ir, and some 960 men, women, and children bravely determined to resist, to their dying breath, the might of Rome.

In 72, the new Roman military governor, Flavius Silva, set about capturing Masada. He had two full legions (ten thousand men) and several thousand Jewish prisoners, whom he used to create a vast supply train of men and mules to carry food, water, timber, and equipment into the desert to prosecute the siege. Then Silva began circumvallating the fortress in the usual Roman fashion. He surrounded the plateau with a six-foot-thick stone wall having guard towers spaced at intervals of about eighty to one hundred yards. Next, he constructed a huge assault ramp (of earth and stone, reinforced by large timbers) on Masada's western slope. Once the ramp was finished and the attackers had breached walls, they received an unexpected and eerie surprise. All of the defenders (excepted for two women and five children) had killed themselves in a suicide pact, preferring death to surrender. **See** siege tactics; **also** Judaea (Chapter 2); **and** Judaism (Chapter 3).

siege tactics

Very little is known about Roman siege warfare before the time of the Punic Wars (third century B.C.). According to later ancient historians, the Romans besieged the Etruscan city of Veii in the late fifth century B.C. and finally captured it by digging a tunnel under its walls; however, although we know that Veii did fall to the Romans, the details of the siege remain unconfirmed.

The first Roman siege for which details are known was that of the Sicilian town of Agrigentum in 262 B.C., near the start of the First Punic War. Here, the besiegers used a technique they borrowed from the Greeks which became the standard Roman siege system. This was circumvallation, basically blockading a town or fort by surrounding it with camps and wooden towers connected by lines of trenches and earthen mounds. These barriers sealed off the town and prevented anyone from getting in or out. To counter a threat of relief or reinforcements from the outside, the besiegers set up a second line of mounds and ditches (called bicircumvallation), facing outward. They also placed forts and sentry posts at intervals along the perimeter. This was the method Julius Caesar employed in his famous siege of the Gallic fortress of Alesia in 52 B.C.

The considerable time and patience needed to make circumvallation a success illustrates the main difference between Roman siege techniques and those of the Greeks, from whom the Romans learned the art of siege warfare. In the Republic's last few centuries, the Greeks developed numerous clever, sophisticated, and often enormous siege machines. These included giant drills that could pierce stone walls and monstrous siege towers that moved on rollers and held dozens of catapults and

other mechanical missile throwers (artillery). The Romans did employ siege towers and artillery. (Their artillery most often consisted of large bolt throwers, a bolt being essentially a huge spear, and catapults and other stone throwers. In the early Empire, each legion carried about fifty or so of these machines.) However, Roman artillery pieces were generally smaller and used less frequently than those of the Greeks. More often, the Romans preferred to exploit the nearly limitless muscle power of the thousands of soldiers making up their legions. The men took weeks, or even months, to build elaborate defenses and booby traps, or to erect gigantic earthen ramps or long underground tunnels to gain access to the town or fortress they were besieging. In almost every Roman siege, therefore, dogged persistence and patience, along with sheer manpower, won the day.

In those situations in which Roman besiegers did erect large earthen ramps, as in the case of the siege of Masada (in Judaea in A.D. 72), the defenders usually rained missiles down on the workers in an at-

During a siege, Roman attackers use their shields to protect against stones and other missiles hurled down by the defenders.

tempt to thwart the effort. To counter this danger, the Romans employed screens of thickly woven wicker covered by layers of animal hides. Similar kinds of screens, often on rollers, were used to protect the men operating battering rams, which sometimes smashed the gates of forts or cities.

Another common device the Romans used to protect themselves while they attacked enemy defenses was the "tortoise" (*testudo*). It consisted of a minimum of twenty-seven (but sometimes more) soldiers crouching side by side and holding their shields either outward or upward, forming a solid protective barrier. The formation moved along in unison as arrows and rocks bounced harmlessly off the shields. (Usually, a rain of boiling oil was the only way to break up a tortoise.) **See** sieges of Alesia, Jerusalem, and Masada.

slave rebellions

For the major insurrections of slaves against the Roman state, including the famous war with Spartacus, **see** Crassus, Marcus Licinius; Spartacus (both Chapter 1); **and** slaves and slavery (Chapter 5).

Social War

(90–88 B.C.) This conflict resulted from the refusal of the upper-class men who ran the Republic to deal with growing unrest among Rome's Italian allies (various independent communities dominated by Rome). Though they had long contributed many soldiers to Rome's armies, the allies were denied both a voice in Roman government and a share in the wealth gained by Roman conquests.

The Social War began in 90 B.C. when a praetor and several other Roman citizens were murdered by rebels in the town of Asculum (in south-central Italy). Emboldened by the news, many other towns in the southern half of the peninsula rebelled; some of them formed their own collective government and even established a new

capital, which they called Italica. The surprised and outraged Senate sent several Roman commanders against the rebels in the following year, overall to little effect.

By early 88 B.C., after thousands on both sides had died in bitter fighting, the senators conceded the practical necessity of granting the former allies citizenship. A sweeping decree declared that all free adult males in Italy south of the Po Valley were hereby full Roman citizens. This move had the desired effect of inducing most of the rebels to lay down their arms. A few towns held out against government forces for a few months, but by early 87 B.C. all of these, including Asculum, had been recaptured. **See** civil wars.

Suebi

(or Suevi) This collection of Germanic tribes originally occupied large sections of eastern and central Germania. In the mid–first century B.C., one band of Suebi, under the war chief Ariovistus, reached the Rhine River and raided parts of Gaul. Julius Caesar summarily defeated them in 58 B.C., but they continued to threaten Roman lands on a periodic basis for several more centuries. The emperor Marcus Aurelius fought them in the late second century A.D., and they were among the barbarians who invaded Gaul in the fifth century, helping to bring about the fall of the western Empire. **See** Germany (Chapter 2).

"tortoise"

For this effective battle formation in which a group of Roman soldiers huddled together beneath their upraised shields, **see** siege tactics.

tribune, military

For this important military officer, who was elected by the people during the Republic, **see** army organization and manpower; army recruitment, training, and personnel.

trireme

For this standard ancient warship, which had three banks of oars, **see** navy.

triumph

A celebration honoring a victorious general, consisting of his grand entry into Rome, usually accompanied by troops under his command. The parade began at the Campus Martius and wound through the city to the Capitoline hill, where the sacrifice of two white bulls took place. The general wore a purple toga (*toga picta*) and laurel leaves in his hair, carried an ivory scepter, and rode in a magnificent chariot. Meanwhile, a slave who stood behind him in the vehicle periodically whispered to him, "Remember that you are but a mortal man."

During most of the years of the Republic, a general had to fulfill strict requirements to merit a triumph. The battle he won could not be part of a civil war, for example; his victory had to result in peace; and only a man who had served in high public office was eligible. In the final few republican years, however, powerful men often broke these rules. Julius Caesar celebrated triumphs during civil conflicts, for instance. In the Empire, only the emperors were allowed to receive triumphs.

urban cohorts

(*cohortes urbanae*) Three units of policemen created by the first emperor, Augustus, for the city of Rome. There were three co-horts, each composed of one thousand men and commanded by a tribune, who reported to the Prefect of the City. The urban cohorts were stationed in a barracks on the Viminal hill until the late third century A.D., when their headquarters moved to the Campus Martius. A normal hitch for members of these units was twenty years, and they received considerably better pay than ordinary legionaries. Over time, other cities in the realm, including Lugdunum and Carthage, instituted their own urban cohorts. **See** Prefect of the City (Chapter 4).

Vandals

One of the most resilient and successful of the Germanic tribes that fought against the Romans. The Vandals' original homeland appears to have been northern Germany, near the Baltic Sea, but by the mid–second century A.D. they had migrated southward to the region now occupied by Hungary. In the years to come, they periodically raided Roman border provinces. But they posed a much bigger threat beginning in the early fifth century when they joined other Germans in crossing the Rhine River into Gaul. Soon, feeling pressure from other barbarian groups entering Gaul, the Vandals moved farther south into Spain. There, they acquired federate status from the Roman government, but this proved a short-lived arrangement, for the Visigoths, led by King Wallia, invaded Spain in 416 and made war on the Vandals.

In 418 or 419, the Vandals decided that they must find still another new home. They built a fleet of ships and landed in the Balearic Islands (off Spain's eastern coast). Then, in 429, shortly after the unusually capable, ambitious, and far-sighted

Gaiseric became their leader, they landed in Africa. His forces (which included some Alans and Suebi) swept eastward, overrunning the region's Roman provinces; soon Gaiseric established a new and very powerful Vandal kingdom, with its capital at Carthage. Not satisfied with these gains, in 455 the Vandals sailed north to Italy's western coast, sacked Rome, and also terrorized the coasts of Sicily, Sardinia, and Corsica. The Vandal kingdom survived Rome's fall in 476 and prospered until the 530s, when an expedition sent by the eastern emperor Justinian destroyed it. **See** Rome (Chapter 2).

Visigoths

For this large and prominent "barbarian" tribe that challenged Rome in the Later Empire and sacked the eternal city in A.D. 410, **see** Goths.

Volsci

An ancient Italian tribe, they inhabited the region west of the Fucine Lake (in central Italy). Under pressure from neighboring tribes, they moved westward, and by the mid–fifth century B.C. they occupied part of southern Latium. This inevitably brought them into collision with the Romans and other Latins who lived nearby. The Volsci allied themselves with another Italian people, the Aequi, against the Latins and intermittent fighting went on for over a century. The Volsci switched sides and joined the Latins when they rose against Rome in 340 B.C., only to share in the Latins' defeat at Roman hands two years later. Not long afterward, Rome absorbed and quickly Romanized the Volsci. **See** Aequi; Latin League.

"year of the four emperors"

In A.D. 69, following the death of the emperor Nero, a power struggle erupted among various Roman generals. **See** the final winner of that struggle, Vespasian (Chapter 1).

B.C.

ca. 1000 (and probably well before) Latin tribesmen establish small villages on some of the seven hills marking the site of the future city of Rome.

753
Traditional founding date for the city of Rome by Romulus (as computed and accepted by Roman scholars some seven centuries later).

753–717
Supposed years of Romulus's reign as Rome's first king.

534–509
Supposed years that Tarquinius Superbus, Rome's last king, reigned.

509
The leading Roman landowners throw out their last king and establish the Roman Republic.

496
The Romans defeat the other members of the Latin League at Lake Regillus.

ca. 451–450
The Twelve Tables, Rome's first law code, are inscribed and set up.

445
The Romans pass a law allowing patricians (aristocrats) and plebeians (commoners) to marry one another.

396
After a long siege, the Romans capture the important Etruscan town of Veii.

390
At the Allia River, a Roman army suffers a major defeat at the hands of a force of invading Gauls, who proceed to sack Rome.

366
The first plebeian consul is elected.

343–341
The First Samnite War, fought in the Campania (south of Rome).

340–338
Rome defeats the Latin League, dissolves it, and incorporates the territories of some of its members into the growing Roman state.

321
During the Second Samnite War, a Roman army surrenders to a force of Samnites at the Caudine Forks.

312
The building of Rome's first major road, the Appian Way, and its first aqueduct, the Aqua Appia, begins.

ca. 300
Rome's high priests begin keeping historical records known as the *Annales Maximi;* the Greek thinker Zeno founds the Stoic philosophical movement, which in succeeding years will become extremely popular among Roman intellectuals.

ca. 289
Rome mints its first coins.

280–275
The Romans fight several battles with the Greek Hellenistic king Pyrrhus, who has come to the aid of the Greek cities of southern Italy; his victories are so costly that he abandons the Italian Greeks to their fate.

265
Having gained control of the Italian Greek cities, Rome is master of the entire Italian peninsula.

264–241
The First Punic War, in which Rome defeats the maritime empire of Carthage.

218–201
Rome fights Carthage again in the Second Punic War, in which the Carthaginian general Hannibal crosses the Alps, invades Italy, and delivers the Romans one crippling defeat after another.

216
Hannibal crushes a large Roman army at Cannae (in southeastern Italy); Roman fatalities exceed fifty thousand.

202
After the Romans weather the storm and rebound, their greatest general, Scipio "Africanus," defeats Hannibal on the plain of Zama (in North Africa).

200–197
The Romans defeat Macedonia in the Second Macedonian War.

190
A Roman army defeats the Seleucid king, Antiochus III, at Magnesia (in Asia Minor).

168
The Third Macedonian War comes to a close as the Romans defeat Macedonia's King Perseus; the Macedonian Kingdom is dismantled.

153
The Romans change the first month of their year from March to January.

149–146
Rome annihilates Carthage in the Third Punic War.

135–132
The Romans put down a large slave rebellion in Sicily.

133
Death of the social reformer Tiberius Sempronius Gracchus.

112–105
Rome fights and defeats a North African prince, Jugurtha.

107
The Roman general Marius, who will soon initiate important military reforms, wins the first of his several consulships.

102
Marius defeat the Teutones, a large Germanic tribe that has invaded Gaul and threatened northern Italy.

100
Birth of Julius Caesar, one of the greatest statesmen and military generals in history.

90–88
Years of the Social War, in which many of Rome's Italian allies resort to violence to acquire full citizenship.

88–82
A civil war rages between the supporters of Marius and Sulla.

ca. 80
The first all-stone Roman amphitheater opens in the town of Pompeii.

74–63
Rome defeats Mithridates VI of Pontus in the Third Mithridatic War.

73–71
The Thracian slave Spartacus leads the last of Rome's large slave rebellions; the Roman nobleman Marcus Crassus eventually defeats the slaves.

67
The noted general Pompey rids the Mediterranean sea-lanes of pirates in only forty days, becoming a national hero.

65
Caesar stages the first large public gladiatorial combats in Rome.

63
The senator/consul Cicero exposes a plot by the disgruntled nobleman Catiline to topple the government.

60
Caesar, Pompey, and Crassus form a strong political alliance later referred to as the First Triumvirate.

58–51
Caesar conquers the peoples of Transalpine Gaul.

55
The Theater of Pompey, seating some eighty thousand people, opens in Rome.

53
Crassus is defeated and killed by the Parthians at Carrhae, in the Near East.

49
Caesar crosses the Rubicon River, initiating a new civil war; the following year he defeats Pompey at Pharsalus (in Greece).

46
Caesar defeats some of Pompey's supporters at Thapsus (in North Africa).

44
After declaring himself "dictator for life," Caesar is assassinated by a group of senators; Cicero completes his great work dealing with moral philosophy, *On Duties.*

43
Caesar's associate, Antony, Caesar's adopted son, Octavian, and a powerful general, Lepidus, establish the Second Triumvirate; they proceed to murder their political enemies, including Cicero, the last great republican champion.

42
Antony and Octavian defeat the leaders of the conspiracy against Caesar at Philippi (in northern Greece); at this point, the Republic is effectively dead.

31
Octavian defeats Antony and Egypt's Queen Cleopatra at Actium (in western Greece) and gains firm control of the Mediterranean world.

ca. 30 B.C.–A.D. 180
The approximate years of the so-called *Pax Romana* ("Roman peace"), a period in which the Mediterranean world under the first several Roman emperors enjoys relative peace and prosperity.

29–19
The Roman poet Virgil composes the *Aeneid,* which becomes Rome's national epic.

27
The Senate confers on Octavian the name of Augustus (the "exalted one"); historians usually mark this date as the beginning of the Roman Empire.

ca. 23
The poet Horace publishes his *Odes.*

20
Augustus sets up a board of curators (the

curatores viarum) to manage Italy's public highways.

9

Augustus dedicates the Ara Pacis (Altar of Peace), one of Rome's architectural masterpieces.

4

Jesus is born in Bethlehem (in the Roman province of Judaea).

2

Augustus dedicates a magnificent new forum, named for himself, in Rome.

A.D.

ca. 6

Augustus establishes a fire-fighting force (the *vigiles*) to protect the Roman capital.

9

A Roman army commanded by Publius Quinctilius Varus is annihilated in the Teutoberg Forest (in western Germany); thereafter, the Romans abandon their plans to absorb the German lands.

14

Augustus dies, plunging the Roman people into a period of deep mourning; he is succeeded by Tiberius.

17

Death of the poet Ovid, marking the close of the Augustan Age of literature, Rome's greatest literary period.

20

The first large state-run public bathhouse opens in Rome.

ca. 30–33

Jesus is executed on the orders of Pontius Pilate, the Roman governor of Judaea.

64

A great fire ravages large sections of Rome; the emperor Nero blames the disaster on the Christians and initiates the first of a series of persecutions against them; he also begins to erect a fabulous new palace for himself, the Golden House.

69

The so-called "year of the four emperors," in which several Roman generals vie for supremacy; Vespasian emerges the victor and founds the Flavian dynasty.

70

Titus, Vespasian's son, besieges and captures the Jewish city of Jerusalem.

79

The volcano Mount Vesuvius erupts, burying the towns of Pompeii and Herculaneum; the great naturalist Pliny the Elder dies while observing the disaster up close.

80

Titus inaugurates the Colosseum.

98–117

Reign of the emperor Trajan, in which the Roman Empire reaches its greatest size and power.

107

Trajan stages public games lasting 123 days, during which some eleven thousand animals are slaughtered.

ca. 115–117

The distinguished Roman historian Tacitus writes the *Annals*.

ca. 122

The emperor Hadrian visits Britain and plans the construction of the massive defensive wall that will bear his name.

166

A terrible plague spreads across the Empire; the Marcomanni and other Germanic tribes invade Rome's northern border provinces.

180

Death of the emperor Marcus Aurelius, marking the end of the *Pax Romana* and the beginning of Rome's steady slide into economic and political crisis.

192

The corrupt emperor Commodus is assassinated.

193–235

Period of the combined reigns of the emperors of the Severan dynasty, beginning with Septimius Severus and ending with Severus Alexander.

212

The emperor Caracalla extends citizenship rights to all free adult males in the Empire.

215

Caracalla issues a new coin of silver and bronze, the *antoninianus*.

235–284

The Empire suffers under the strain of terrible political upheaval and civil strife, prompting later historians to call this period "the anarchy."

284

Diocletian ascends the throne and initiates sweeping political, economic, and social reforms, in effect reconstructing the Empire under a new blueprint; modern historians often call this new realm the Later Empire.

293

Diocletian establishes the first Tetrarchy, a power-sharing arrangement in which two emperors (with the title of Augustus) reign, one in the east, the other in the west, each with an assistant (with the title of Caesar).

305

Diocletian abdicates and retires, the first Roman emperor to do so; the Second Tetrarchy he had engineered to replace him soon falls apart as its members and some of their sons begin to fight one another.

306–337

Reign of the emperor Constantine I, who carries on the reforms begun by Diocletian.

312

Constantine defeats his rival, the usurper Maxentius, at Rome's Milvian Bridge.

313

Constantine and his eastern colleague, Licinius, issue the so-called Edict of Milan, granting religious toleration to the formerly hated and persecuted Christians.

330

Constantine founds the city of Constantinople, on the Bosphorus, making it the capital of the eastern section of the Empire.

337

Constantine dies; he converts to Christianity on his deathbed.

361–363

Reign of the emperor Julian, who, in the face of Christianity's growing popularity, tries but fails to reestablish paganism as Rome's dominant religion.

ca. 370

The Huns, a savage nomadic people from central Asia, sweep into eastern Europe, pushing the Goths and other "barbarian" peoples into the northern Roman provinces.

374

The Roman state passes a law banning the exposure of unwanted infants.

378

The eastern emperor Valens is disastrously defeated by the Visigoths and Ostrogoths at Adrianople (in Thrace).

391

At the urgings of Christian leaders, especially the bishop Ambrose, the emperor Theodosius I closes the pagan temples, demolishing some and turning others into museums.

395

Theodosius dies, leaving his sons Arcadius and Honorius in control of a permanently divided Roman realm.

ca. 407

As Rome steadily loses control of several of its northern and western provinces, Britain falls under the sway of barbarian tribes.

410

The Visigoths, led by Alaric, sack Rome.

426

The great Roman Christian thinker and writer Augustine completes his monumental *City of God*.

438

The eastern emperor Theodosius II completes the Theodosian Code, a large compilation of Roman laws.

451

After terrorizing and pillaging Roman lands for more than a decade, Attila, war chief of the Huns, is defeated by a combined army of Romans and barbarian federates at Chalons, in what is now northern France.

455

Rome is sacked again, this time by the Vandals, led by Gaiseric.

476

The German-born general Odoacer demands that the western emperor, the young Romulus Augustulus, grant him and his men federate status; when the emperor refuses, Odoacer deposes him and no new emperor takes his place. The succession of Roman emperors continues in the eastern realm, which steadily evolves into the Byzantine Empire.

EMPERORS

(including major illegal or unsuccessful claimants to the throne)

Pax Romana
Augustus, reigned 27 B.C.–A.D. 14
Tiberius, A.D. 14–37
Caligula, 37–41
Claudius, 41–54
Nero, 54–68
Galba, Otho, Vitellius, Vespasian, 69 ("year of the four emperors")
Vespasian, 69–79
Titus, 79–81
Domitian, 81–96
Nerva, 96–98
Trajan, 98–117
Hadrian, 117–138
Antoninus Pius, 138–161
Marcus Aurelius, 161–180
Lucius Verus, 161–169 (coemperor with Marcus Aurelius)

Transition from *Pax Romana* to Third Century
Commodus, 180–192
Pertinax, 193
Didius Julianus, 193

Severan Dynasty
Septimius Severus, 193–211
Pescennius Niger, 193–195 (claimant)
Clodius Albinus, 195–197 (claimant)
Caracalla, 211–217
Geta, 211–212 (brother of and coemperor with Caracalla)
Macrinus, 217–218 (not a Severan)
Diadumenian, 218 (son of and coemperor with Macrinus)
Elagabalus, 218–222
Severus Alexander, Marcus Aurelius, 222–235

"Anarchy"
Maximinus I Thrax, 235–238
Gordian I, 238
Gordian II, 238
Balbinus, 238
Pupienus, 238
Gordian III, 238–244
Philip the Arab, 244–249
Philip II, 247–249 (son of and coemperor with Philip the Arab)
Uranius, 248–254 (claimant)
Pacatian, 248 (claimant)
Jotapian, 248 (claimant)

Decius, 249–251
Herrenius Etruscus, 251 (son of and coemperor with Decius)
Gallus, 251–253
Hostilian, 251 (son of Decius and coemperor with Gallus)
Volusian, 251–253 (son of and coemperor with Gallus)
Aemilian, 253
Valerian, 253–260
Gallienus, 253–268 (son of and coemperor with Valerian)
Saloninus, 260 (son of and coemperor with Gallienus)
Macrianus, 260–261 (claimant)
Quietus, 260–261 (claimant)
Regalianus, 260 (claimant)
Postumus, 260–268 (claimant)
Laelianus, 268 (claimant)
Marius, 268–269 (claimant)

Military Recovery
Claudius II, "Gothicus," 268–270
Victorinus, 269 (claimant)
Quintillus, 270
Aurelian, 270–275
Vaballathus, 271–272 (king of Palmyra and claimant)
Zenobia, 271–272 (queen of Palmyra, mother of Vaballathus, and claimant)
Tacitus, 275–276
Florian, 276
Probus, 276–282
Saturninus, 280 (claimant)
Carus, Marcus Aurelius, 282–283
Carinus, 283–285 (son of and coemperor with Carus)
Julian, 283–285 (claimant)
Numerian, 283–284 (son of and coemperor with Carus)
Diocletian, 284–305

Later Empire Initiated by Diocletian

West	East
First Tetrarchy	
Maximian (Augustus), 286–305	Diocletian (Augustus), 284–305
Constantius I Chlorus (Caesar), 293–305	Galerius (Caesar), 293–305
Carausius, 286–293 (claimant)	
Allectus, 293–296 (claimant)	
Second Tetrarchy	
Constantius I Chlorus (Augustus), 305–306	Galerius (Augustus), 305–311
Severus (Caesar), 305–306	Maximinus Daia (Caesar), 305–309
Civil Wars	
Severus, 306–307	Maximinus Daia, 309–313
Constantine I, 306–324	Licinius, 308–324
Maxentius, 306–312	Valens, 314 (coemperor with Licinius)

West	East
	Martinian, 324 (coemperor with Licinius)

Constantine I and His Successors

Constantine I, sole ruler, 324–337

West	East
Constans, 337–350	Constantius II, 337–350
Constantine II, 337–340	
Magnentius, 350–353 (claimant)	
Vetranio, 350 (claimant)	
Nepotian, 350 (claimant)	

Constantius II, sole ruler, 350–361
Julian, sole ruler, 361–363
Jovian, sole ruler, 363–364

West	East
Valentinian I, 364–375	Valens, 364–378
Gratian, 367–383	Procopius, 365–366 (claimant)
Valentinian II, 375–392	Theodosius I, 379–392
Magnus Maximus, 383–388 (claimant)	

Theodosius I , sole ruler, 392–395

West	East
Eugenius, 392–394 (claimant)	
Honorius, 395–423	Arcadius, 395–408
Constantine III, 407–411 (claimant, no relation to Constantine's heirs)	Theodosius II, 408–450
Maximus, 409–411 (claimant)	
Priscus Attalus, 409–410 (claimant)	
Constantius III, 421 (coemperor with Honorius)	
John, 423–425	
Valentinian III, 425–455	Marcian, 450–457
Petronius Maximus, 455	
Avitus, 455–456	
Majorian, 457–461	Leo I, 457–474
Libius Severus, 461–465	
Anthemius, 467–472	
Olybrius, 472	
Glycerius, 473	Leo II, 473–474 (son of Zeno and coemperor with Leo I and Zeno)
Julius Nepos, 473–475	
Romulus Augustus, 475–476 (western throne hereafter vacant)	Zeno 2., 474–491 (eastern throne continues to be occupied until 1453)

Ancient Sources

Paul J. Alexander, ed., *The Ancient World: to 300 A.D.* New York: Macmillan, 1963.

Ammianus Marcellinus, *History,* published as *The Later Roman Empire, A.D. 354–78.* Trans. and ed. Walter Hamilton. New York: Penguin, 1986.

Appian, *Roman History.* Trans. Horace White. Cambridge, MA: Harvard University Press, 1964; also excerpted in *Appian: The Civil Wars.* Trans. John Carter. New York: Penguin, 1996.

Apuleius, *The Golden Ass.* Trans. P.G. Walsh. Oxford: Oxford University Press, 1994.

Augustan History, published as *Lives of the Later Caesars, The First Part of the Augustan History, with Newly Compiled Lives of Nerva and Trajan.* Trans. Anthony Birley. New York: Penguin, 1976.

Augustine, *The City of God.* Trans. Marcus Dods. In Mortimer Adler, ed., *Great Books of the Western World.* Vol 18. Chicago: Encyclopaedia Britannica, 1952.

Julius Caesar, *Commentary on the Gallic War* and *Commentary on the Civil War,* published as *War Commentaries of Caesar.* Trans. Rex Warner. New York: New American Library, 1960.

Catullus, complete poems, in *The Poems of Catullus.* Trans. and ed. Guy Lee. New York: Oxford University Press, 1990.

Cicero, various works collected in: *The Basic Works of Cicero.* Ed. Moses Hadas. New York: Random House, 1951; *Cicero: Murder Trials.* Trans. Michael Grant. New York: Penguin, 1990; *Cicero: The Nature of the Gods.* Trans. Horace C.P. McGregor. New York: Penguin, 1972; *Cicero: On Government.* Trans. Michael Grant. New York: Penguin, 1993; *Cicero: Selected Works.* Trans. Michael Grant. New York: Penguin, 1971; *Letters to Atticus.* 3 vols. Trans. E.O. Winstedt. Cambridge, MA: Harvard University Press, 1961; *Letters to His Friends.* 3 vols. Trans. W. Glynn Williams. Cambridge, MA: Harvard University Press, 1965; *On Duties.* Trans. Walter Miller. Cambridge, MA: Harvard University Press, 1961; *Selected Political Speeches of Cicero.* Trans. Michael Grant. Baltimore: Penguin, 1979; and *Verrine Orations.* 2 vols. Trans. L.H.G. Greenwood. Cambridge, MA: Harvard University Press, 1966.

Columella, *On Agriculture.* 3 vols. Trans. H.B. Ash et al. Cambridge, MA: Harvard University Press, 1960.

Basil Davenport, ed. and trans., *The Portable Roman Reader: The Culture of the Roman State.* New York: Viking Press, 1951.

Dio Cassius, *Roman History: The Reign of Augustus.* Trans. Ian Scott-Kilvert. New York: Penguin, 1987.

Diodorus Siculus, *Library of History.* Vol. 3. Trans. C.H. Oldfather. Cambridge, MA: Harvard University Press, 1961.

Dionysius of Halicarnassus, *Roman An-*

tiquities. 7 vols. Trans. Earnest Cary. Cambridge, MA: Harvard University Press, 1963.

J. Wight Duff and Arnold M. Duff, trans., *Minor Latin Poets.* Cambridge, MA: Harvard University Press, 1968.

Eusebius, *Ecclesiastical History.* 2 vols. Trans. Roy J. Deferrari. Washington, DC: Catholic University of America Press, 1955.

Frontinus, *The Stratagems and the Aqueducts of Rome.* Trans. C.E. Bennett. Cambridge, MA: Harvard University Press, 1993.

Fronto, *Correspondence.* 2 vols. Trans. C.R. Haines. Cambridge, MA: Harvard University Press, 1965.

Francis R.B. Godolphin, ed., *The Latin Poets.* New York: Random House, 1949.

Horace, *Satires, Epistles, Ars Poetica.* Trans. H. Rushton Fairclough. Cambridge, MA: Harvard University Press, 1966; and *Complete Odes and Epodes.* Trans. Betty Radice. New York: Penguin, 1983.

Jerome, *Letters,* excerpted in F.A. Wright, trans., *Select Letters of St. Jerome.* Cambridge, MA: Harvard University Press, 1963.

Josephus, *The Jewish War.* Trans. G.A. Williamson. Rev. E. Mary Smallwood. New York: Penguin, 1970, 1981.

Juvenal, *Satires,* published as *The Sixteen Satires.* Trans. Peter Green. New York: Penguin, 1974.

Lactantius, *The Deaths of the Persecutors,* in Sister Mary Francis McDonald, trans., *Lactantius: Minor Works.* Washington, DC: Catholic University of America Press, 1965.

Mary R. Lefkowitz and Maureen B. Fant, eds., *Women's Life in Greece and Rome: A Source Book in Translation.* Baltimore: Johns Hopkins University Press, 1992.

Naphtali Lewis and Meyer Reinhold, eds., *Roman Civilization, Sourcebook I: The Republic,* and *Roman Civilization,*

Sourcebook II: The Empire. Both New York: Harper and Row, 1966.

Livy, *The History of Rome from Its Foundation.* Books 1–5 published as *Livy: The Early History of Rome.* Trans. Aubrey de Sélincourt. New York: Penguin, 1971; Books 21–30 published as *Livy: The War with Hannibal.* Trans. Aubrey de Sélincourt. New York: Penguin, 1972; Books 31–45 published as *Livy: Rome and the Mediterranean.* Trans. Henry Bettenson. New York: Penguin, 1976.

Lucretius, *On the Nature of Things,* published as *Lucretius: The Nature of the Universe.* Trans. R.E. Latham. Baltimore: Penguin, 1951.

Marcus Aurelius, *Meditations.* Trans. M. Staniforth. New York: Penguin, 1964.

Martial, *Epigrams.* 2 vols. Trans. Walter C.A. Ker. Cambridge, MA: Harvard University Press, 1993; and excerpted in *The Epigrams of Martial.* Ed. and trans. James Mitchie. New York: Random House, 1972.

Cornelius Nepos, *The Great Generals of Foreign Nations.* Trans. John C. Rolfe. Cambridge, MA: Harvard University Press, 1960.

Ovid, *Metamorphoses.* Trans. Rolfe Humphries. Bloomington: University of Indiana Press, 1967; and selected poems in *Ovid: The Love Poems.* Trans. A.D. Melville. New York: Oxford University Press, 1990.

Petronius, *The Satyricon.* Trans. J.P. Sullivan. New York: Penguin Books, 1977.

Plautus, plays excerpted in *Plautus: The Rope and Other Plays.* Trans. E.F. Watling. New York: Penguin, 1964.

Pliny the Elder, *Natural History.* 10 vols. Trans. H. Rackham. Cambridge, MA: Harvard University Press, 1967; also excerpted in *Pliny the Elder: Natural History: A Selection.* Trans. John H. Healy. New York: Penguin, 1991.

Pliny the Younger, *Letters.* 2 vols. Trans. William Melmouth. Cambridge, MA:

Harvard University Press, 1961; also *The Letters of the Younger Pliny.* Trans. Betty Radice. New York: Penguin, 1969.

Plutarch, *Parallel Lives,* published complete as *Lives of the Noble Grecians and Romans.* Trans. John Dryden. New York: Random House, 1932; also excerpted in *Fall of the Roman Republic: Six Lives by Plutarch.* Trans. Rex Warner. New York: Penguin, 1972; and *Makers of Rome: Nine Lives by Plutarch.* Trans. Ian Scott-Kilvert. New York: Penguin, 1965.

Polybius, *The Histories,* published as *Polybius: The Rise of the Roman Empire.* Trans. Ian Scott-Kilvert. New York: Penguin, 1979.

Procopius, *Works.* 7 vols. Trans. H.B. Dewing. Cambridge, MA: Harvard University Press, 1961.

Quintilian, *The Education of an Orator.* Trans. H.E. Butler. Cambridge MA: Harvard University Press, 1963.

Sallust, *Works.* Trans. J.C. Rolfe. Cambridge University Press, 1965; also, *Sallust: The Jugurthine War/The Conspiracy of Catiline.* Trans. S.A. Handford. New York: Penguin, 1988.

Seneca, *Moral Epistles.* 3 vols. Trans. Richard M. Gummere. Cambridge, MA: Harvard University Press, 1961; *Moral Essays.* 3 vols. Trans. John W. Basore. Cambridge, MA: Harvard University Press, 1963; and assorted works collected in Moses Hadas, trans. and ed., *The Stoic Philosophy of Seneca.* New York: W.W. Norton, 1958; and C.D.N. Costa, trans. and ed., *Seneca: Dialogues and Letters.* New York: Penguin, 1997.

Jo-Ann Shelton, ed., *As the Romans Did: A Sourcebook in Roman Social History.* New York: Oxford University Press, 1988.

William G. Sinnegin, ed., *Sources in Western Civilization: Rome.* New York: Free Press, 1965.

Statius, *Works.* 2 vols. Trans. J.H. Mozley. Cambridge, MA: Harvard University Press, 1961.

Suetonius, *The Twelve Caesars.* Trans. Robert Graves. Rev. Michael Grant. New York: Penguin, 1979.

Tacitus, *The Annals,* published as *The Annals of Ancient Rome.* Trans. Michael Grant. New York: Penguin, 1989; *The Histories.* Trans. Kenneth Wellesley. New York: Penguin, 1993; and *Germania,* in H. Mattingly, trans., *Tacitus on Britain and Germany.* Baltimore: Penguin, 1954.

Terence, complete surviving works in *Terence: The Comedies.* Trans. Betty Radice. New York: Penguin, 1976.

Virgil, *The Aeneid.* Trans. Patric Dickinson. New York: New American Library, 1961; also *Works.* 2 vols. Trans. H. Rushton Fairclough. Cambridge, MA: Harvard University Press, 1967.

Vitruvius, *On Architecture.* 2 vols. Trans. Frank Granger. Cambridge, MA: Harvard University Press, 1962.

Thomas Wiedemann, ed., *Greek and Roman Slavery.* London: Croom Helm, 1981.

Garry Wills, ed., *Roman Culture: Weapons and the Man.* New York: George Braziller, 1966.

Modern Sources

Archaeological Rediscovery of Roman Civilization

Paul G. Bahn, ed., *The Cambridge Illustrated History of Archaeology.* New York: Cambridge University Press, 1996.

Joseph J. Deiss, *Herculaneum: Italy's Buried Treasure.* Malibu, CA: J. Paul Getty Museum, 1989.

Maurizio Forte and Alberto Siliotti, eds., *Virtual Archaeology: Re-Creating Ancient Worlds.* New York: Harry N. Abrams, 1997.

Michael Grant, *The Visible Past: Recent Archaeological Discoveries of Greek *and Roman History.* New York: Scribner's, 1990.

———, *Cities of Vesuvius: Pompeii and Herculaneum.* New York: Macmillan, 1971.

R.R. Holloway, *The Archaeology of Early Rome and Latium.* New York: Routledge, 1994.

Paul MacKendrick, *The Mute Stones Speak: The Story of Archaeology in Italy.* New York: St. Martin's Press, 1960.

Claude Moatti, *The Search for Ancient Rome.* New York: Harry N. Abrams, 1993.

Art, Architecture, and Engineering

Jean-Pierre Adam, *Roman Building: Materials and Techniques.* Trans. Anthony Mathews. Bloomington: Indiana University Press, 1994.

Raymond Chevallier, *Roman Roads.* Trans. N.H. Field. Berkeley and Los Angeles: University of California Press, 1976.

L. Sprague de Camp, *The Ancient Engineers.* New York: Ballantine, 1963.

Michael Grant, *Art in the Roman Empire.* London: Routledge, 1994.

Martin Henig, *Architecture and Architectural Sculpture in the Roman Empire.* Oxford: Oxford Committee for Archaeology, 1990.

———, *A Handbook of Roman Art: A Survey of the Visual Arts of the Roman World.* Oxford: Phaidon, 1983.

A.T. Hodge, *Roman Aqueducts and Water Supply.* London: Duckworth, 1992.

Alexander G. McKay, *Houses, Villas, and Palaces in the Roman World.* Baltimore: Johns Hopkins University Press, 1998.

Colin O'Connor, *Roman Bridges.* Cambridge, England: Cambridge University Press, 1993.

Peter Quennell, *The Colosseum.* New York: Newsweek Book Division, 1971.

Donald Strong, *Roman Crafts.* London: Duckworth, 1976.

J.B. Ward-Perkins, *Roman Imperial Architecture.* New York: Penguin, 1981.

Mortimer Wheeler, *Roman Art and Architecture.* New York: Praeger, 1964.

Augustus and the Augustan Age

Donald Earl, *The Age of Augustus.* New York: Crown, 1968.

John B. Firth, *Augustus Caesar and the Organization of the Empire of Rome.* Freeport, NY: Books for the Libraries Press, 1972.

A.H.M. Jones, *Augustus.* New York: W.W. Norton, 1970.

Don Nardo, *The Age of Augustus.* San Diego: Lucent Books, 1996.

Henry T. Rowell, *Rome in the Augustan Age.* Norman: University of Oklahoma Press, 1962.

Ronald Syme, *The Augustan Aristocracy.* Oxford: Clarendon Press, 1986.

C.M. Wells, *The German Policy of Augustus.* London: Oxford University Press, 1972.

Games and Leisure Pursuits

Roland Auguet, *Cruelty and Civilization: The Roman Games.* London: Routledge, 1994.

J.P.V.D. Balsdon, *Life and Leisure in Ancient Rome.* New York: McGraw-Hill, 1969.

Carlin A. Barton, *The Sorrow of the Ancient Romans: The Gladiator and the Monster.* Princeton, NJ: Princeton University Press, 1993.

Richard C. Beacham, *Spectacle Entertainments of Early Imperial Rome.* New Haven, CT: Yale University Press, 1999.

James H. Butler, *The Theater and Drama of Greece and Rome.* San Francisco: Chandler, 1972.

Alan Cameron, *Circus Factions: Blues and Greens at Rome and Byzantium.* London: Clarendon Press, 1976.

Michael Grant, *Gladiators.* New York: Delacorte Press, 1967.

John H. Humphrey, *Roman Circuses: Arenas for Chariot Racing.* Berkeley and Los Angeles: University of California Press, 1986.

Don Nardo, *Games of Ancient Rome*. San Diego: Lucent Books, 2000.

———, *Greek and Roman Theater*. San Diego: Lucent Books, 1995.

Vera Olivova, *Sport and Games in the Ancient World*. New York: St. Martin's Press, 1984.

Michael B. Poliakoff, *Combat Sports in the Ancient World*. New Haven, CT: Yale University Press, 1987.

General Roman History and Culture

Lesley Adkins and Roy A. Adkins, *Handbook to Life in Ancient Rome*. New York: Facts On File, 1994.

R.H. Barrow, *The Romans*. Baltimore: Penguin, 1949.

John Boardman et al., *The Oxford History of the Roman World*. New York: Oxford University Press, 1991.

T.J. Cornell, *The Beginnings of Rome: Italy and Rome from the Bronze Age to the Punic Wars (c. 1000–264 B.C.)*. London: Routledge, 1995.

Tim Cornell and John Matthews, *Atlas of the Roman World*. New York: Facts On File, 1982.

J.F. Drinkwater, *Roman Gaul*. Ithaca, NY: Cornell University Press, 1983.

Charles Freeman, *Egypt, Greece, and Rome: Civilizations of the Ancient Mediterranean*. Oxford: Oxford University Press, 1996.

———, *The World of the Romans*. New York: Oxford University Press, 1993.

Michael Grant, *History of Rome*. New York: Scribner's, 1978.

———, *The World of Rome*. New York: New American Library, 1960.

Edith Hamilton, *The Roman Way to Western Civilization*. New York: W.W. Norton, 1932.

Robert B. Kebric, *Roman People*. Mountain View, CA: Mayfield Publishing, 1997.

Peter Salway, *Roman Britain*. Oxford: Clarendon Press, 1981.

Chris Scarre, *Historical Atlas of Ancient Rome*. New York: Penguin, 1995.

Chester G. Starr, *A History of the Ancient World*. New York: Oxford University Press, 1991.

L.P. Wilkinson, *The Roman Experience*. Lanham, MD: University Press of America, 1974.

Gods, Worship, Burial Customs, and Mythology

Peter Brown, *Power and Persuasion in Late Antiquity: Towards a Christian Empire*. Madison: University of Wisconsin Press, 1992.

John Ferguson, *The Religions of the Roman Empire*. London: Thames and Hudson, 1970.

Jane Gardner, *Roman Myths*. Austin: University of Texas Press and British Museum Press, 1993.

Michael Grant, *The Jews in the Roman World*. London: Weidenfeld and Nicolson, 1973.

———, *The Myths of the Greeks and Romans*. New York: Penguin, 1962.

Martin Henig, ed., *Pagan Gods and Shrines of the Roman Empire*. Oxford: Oxford Committee for Archaeology, 1986.

———, *Religion in Roman Britain*. London: Batsford, 1984.

Georg Luck, *Arcana Mundi: Magic and the Occult in the Greek and Roman Worlds*. Baltimore: Johns Hopkins University Press, 1985.

Ramsay MacMullen, *Christianizing the Roman Empire, A.D. 100–400*. New Haven, CT: Yale University Press, 1984.

Don Nardo, ed., *The Rise of Christianity*. San Diego: Greenhaven Press, 1999.

R.M. Ogilvie, *The Romans and Their Gods in the Age of Augustus*. New York: W.W. Norton, 1969.

Stewart Perowne, *Roman Mythology*. London: Paul Hamlyn, 1969.

H.J. Rose, *Religion in Greece and Rome*. New York: Harper and Brothers, 1959.

H.H. Scullard, *Festivals and Ceremonies of the Roman Republic*. London:

Thames and Hudson, 1981.

Marta Sordi, *The Christians and the Roman Empire*. Trans. Annabel Bedini. London: Croom Helm, 1983.

J.M.C. Toynbee, *Death and Burial in the Roman World*. Baltimore: Johns Hopkins University Press, 1996.

Robert L. Wilken, *The Christians as the Romans Saw Them*. New Haven, CT: Yale University Press, 1984.

Government, Politics, and Law

J.A. Crook, *Legal Advocacy in the Roman World*. Ithaca, NY: Cornell University Press, 1995.

———, *Law and Life of Rome*. Ithaca, NY: Cornell University Press, 1984.

David Daube, *Roman Law*. Edinburgh: Edinburgh University Press, 1969.

M.I. Finely, *Politics in the Ancient World*. Cambridge, England: Cambridge University Press, 1983.

Jill Harries and Ian Wood, eds., *The Theodosian Code*. Ithaca, NY: Cornell University Press, 1993.

A.W. Lintott, *Imperium Romanum: Politics and Administration*. New York: Routledge, 1993.

Friedrich Munzer, *Roman Aristocratic Parties and Families*. Trans. Therese Ridley. Baltimore: Johns Hopkins University Press, 1999.

O.F. Robinson, *The Criminal Law of Ancient Rome*. Baltimore: Johns Hopkins University Press, 1996.

H.H. Scullard, *Roman Politics, 220–150 B.C.* Oxford: Clarendon Press, 1973.

R.J. Talbert, *The Senate of Imperial Rome*. Princeton, NJ: Princeton University Press, 1987.

Lily Ross Taylor, *Party Politics in the Age of Caesar.* Berkeley and Los Angeles: University of California Press, 1968.

Alan Watson, *International Law in Archaic Rome*. Baltimore: Johns Hopkins University Press, 1993.

———, *Roman Slave Law*. Baltimore: Johns Hopkins University Press, 1987.

Later Roman Empire, Barbarian Invasions, and Fall of Rome

Timothy D. Barnes, *The New Empire of Diocletian and Constantine.* Cambridge, MA: Harvard University Press, 1982.

Peter Brown, *The World of Late Antiquity, A.D. 150–750*. New York: Harcourt Brace, 1971.

J.B. Bury, *History of the Later Roman Empire*. 2 vols. 1923. Reprint, New York: Dover, 1958.

Averil Cameron, *The Later Roman Empire: A.D. 284–430*. Cambridge, MA: Harvard University Press, 1993.

John Drinkwater and Hugh Elton, eds., *Fifth-Century Gaul: A Crisis in Identity?* Cambridge, England: Cambridge University Press, 1992.

Arther Ferrill, *The Fall of the Roman Empire: The Military Explanation*. New York: Thames and Hudson, 1986.

Edward Gibbon, *The Decline and Fall of the Roman Empire*. 3 vols. Ed. David Womersley. New York: Penguin, 1994.

Walter Goffart, *Barbarians and Romans, A.D. 418–584: The Techniques of Accommodation*. Princeton, NJ: Princeton University Press, 1980.

Michael Grant, *The Fall of the Roman Empire*. New York: Macmillan, 1990.

Peter Heather, *The Goths*. Cambridge, MA: Blackwell Publishing, 1996.

A.H.M. Jones, *Constantine and the Conversion of Europe*. Toronto: University of Toronto Press, 1978.

———, *The Decline of the Ancient World*. London: Longman Group, 1966. Note: This is a shortened version of Jones's massive and highly influential *The Later Roman Empire, 284–602*. 3 vols. 1964. Reprint, Norman: University of Oklahoma Press, 1975.

Solomon Katz, *The Decline of Rome and the Rise of Medieval Europe*. Ithaca, NY: Cornell University Press, 1955.

Justine Davis Randers-Pehrson, *Barbarians and Romans: The Birth Struggle of*

Europe, A.D. 400–700. Norman: University of Oklahoma Press, 1983.

E.A. Thompson, *Romans and Barbarians: The Decline of the Western Empire*. Madison: University of Wisconsin Press, 1982.

Literature, Philosophy, and Ideas

A.J. Boyle, ed., *Roman Epic*. New York: Routledge, 1993.

Gian B. Conte, *Latin Literature: A History*. Trans. Joseph B. Solodow. Rev. Don P. Fowler and Glenn W. Most. Baltimore: Johns Hopkins University Press, 1999.

J. Wight Duff, *A Literary History of Rome*. New York: Barnes and Noble, 1960.

Elaine Fantham, *Roman Literary Culture: From Cicero to Apuleius*. Baltimore: Johns Hopkins University Press, 1996.

Michael Grant, *Greek and Latin Authors, 800 B.C.–A.D. 1000*. New York: H.W. Wilson, 1980.

G.O. Hutchinson, *Latin Literature from Seneca to Juvenal: A Critical Study*. New York: Oxford University Press, 1993.

R.O.A.M. Lyne, *The Latin Love Poets from Catullus to Horace*. Oxford: Oxford University Press, 1980.

Chester G. Starr, *Civilization and the Caesars: The Intellectual Revolution in the Roman Empire*. New York: Norton, 1965.

Neal Wood, *Cicero's Social and Political Thought: An Introduction*. Berkeley and Los Angeles: University of California Press, 1988.

Prominent People

A.E. Astin, *Cato the Censor*. Oxford: Oxford University Press, 1978.

Timothy D. Barnes, *Constantine and Eusebius*. Cambridge, MA: Harvard University Press, 1981.

Anthony A. Barrett, *Agrippina: Sex, Power, and Politics in the Early Empire*. New Haven, CT: Yale University Press, 1996.

———, *Caligula: The Corruption of Power*. New York: Simon and Schuster, 1990.

Anthony Birley, *Septimius Severus: The African Emperor*. London: Batsford, 1989.

———, *Marcus Aurelius: A Biography*. London: Batsford, 1987.

Peter Brown, *Augustine of Hippo: A Biography*. Berkeley and Los Angeles: University of California Press, 1967.

Robert Browning, *The Emperor Julian*. Berkeley and Los Angeles: University of California Press, 1976.

M.L. Clarke, *The Noblest Roman: Marcus Brutus and His Reputation*. Ithaca, NY: Cornell University Press, 1981.

Gavin de Beer, *Hannibal: Challenging Rome's Supremacy*. New York: Viking Press, 1969.

Michael Grant, *Constantine the Great: The Man and His Times*. New York: Scribner's, 1994.

———, *Caesar*. London: Weidenfeld and Nicolson, 1974.

Peter Greenhaulgh, *Pompey: The Roman Alexander*. Columbia: University of Missouri Press, 1981.

Miriam T. Griffin, *Nero: The End of a Dynasty*. New Haven, CT: Yale University Press, 1984.

———, *Seneca: A Philosopher in Politics*. Oxford: Clarendon Press, 1976.

B.W. Jones, *The Emperor Titus*. London: Croom Helm, 1984.

Phillip A. Kildahl, *Gaius Marius*. New York: Twayne, 1968.

Barbara Levick, *Claudius*. New Haven, CT: Yale University Press, 1990.

———, *Tiberius the Politician*. New York: Routledge, 1986.

Sara Mack, *Ovid*. New Haven, CT: Yale University Press, 1988.

Ramsay MacMullen, *Constantine*. New York: Dial Press, 1969.

Christian Meier, *Caesar*. Trans. David McLintock. New York: HarperCollins, 1996.

Thomas N. Mitchell, *Cicero: The Senior*

Statesman. New Haven, CT: Yale University Press, 1991.

Don Nardo, ed., *Cleopatra.* San Diego: Greenhaven Press, 2000.

Stewart Perowne, *Hadrian.* Westport, CT: Greenwood Press, 1976.

————, *The Caesars' Wives.* London: Hodder and Stoughton, 1974.

E.P. Sanders, *The Historical Figure of Jesus.* New York: Penguin Books, 1993.

Alaric Watson, *Aurelian and the Third Century.* London: Routledge, 1999.

A.N. Wilson, *Paul: The Mind of the Apostle.* New York: W.W. Norton, 1997.

————, *Jesus.* London: Sinclair-Stevenson, 1992.

Roman Empire

Matthew Bunson, *A Dictionary of the Roman Empire.* Oxford: Oxford University Press, 1991.

Michael Grant, *The Roman Emperors.* New York: Barnes and Noble, 1997.

————,*The Climax of Rome.* New York: New American Library, 1968.

Chris Scarre, *Chronicle of the Roman Emperors.* New York: Thames and Hudson, 1995.

Chester G. Starr, *The Roman Empire, 27 B.C.–A.D. 476: A Study in Survival.* New York: Oxford University Press, 1982.

Colin Wells, *The Roman Empire.* Stanford: Stanford University Press, 1984.

Roman Republic

E. Badian, *Roman Imperialism in the Late Republic.* Ithaca, NY: Cornell University Press, 1968.

Mary Beard and Michael Crawford, *Rome in the Late Republic: Problems and Interpretations.* London: Duckworth, 1985.

F.R. Cowell, *Cicero and the Roman Republic.* Baltimore: Penguin, 1967.

Michael Crawford, *The Roman Republic.* Cambridge, MA: Harvard University Press, 1993.

Jean-Michel David, *The Roman Conquest of Italy.* Trans. Antonia Nevill. London: Blackwell, 1996.

Erich S. Gruen, *The Last Generation of the Roman Republic.* Berkeley and Los Angeles: University of California Press, 1974.

Don Nardo, *The Collapse of the Roman Republic.* San Diego: Lucent Books, 1997.

Ronald Syme, *The Roman Revolution.* New York: Oxford University Press, 1960.

Society, Economic Institutions, and Daily Life

Keith R. Bradley, *Slavery and Society at Rome.* New York: Cambridge University Press, 1994.

————, *Discovering the Roman Family: Studies in Roman Social History.* New York: Oxford University Press, 1991.

————, *Slaves and Masters in the Roman Empire: A Study in Social Control.* New York: Oxford University Press, 1987.

Lionel Casson, *Travel in the Ancient World.* Baltimore: Johns Hopkins University Press, 1994.

————, *The Ancient Mariners.* New York: Macmillan, 1959.

M.H. Crawford, *Coinage and Money Under the Roman Republic.* London: Methuen, 1985.

A.M. Duff, *Freedmen in the Early Roman Empire.* Oxford: Clarendon Press, 1928.

M.I. Finley, *The Ancient Economy.* Berkeley and Los Angeles: University of California Press, 1985.

M.I. Finley, ed., *Slavery in Classical Antiquity.* New York: Barnes and Noble, 1968.

Jane F. Gardner, *Being a Roman Citizen.* New York: Routledge, 1993.

————, *Women in Roman Law and Society.* Indianapolis: Indiana University Press, 1986.

Peter Garnsey, *Social Status and Legal Privilege in the Roman Empire.* Oxford: Clarendon Press, 1970.

Michael Grant, *A Social History of Greece and Rome.* New York: Charles Scribner's Sons, 1992.

Erich S. Gruen, *Culture and National*

Identity in Republican Rome. Ithaca, NY: Cornell University Press, 1995.

Ralph Jackson, *Doctors and Diseases in the Roman Empire.* London: British Museum, 1988.

Harold W. Johnston, *The Private Life of the Romans.* New York: Cooper Square, 1973.

Naphtali Lewis, *Life in Egypt Under Roman Rule.* Oxford: Clarendon Press, 1983.

Mima Maxey, *Occupations of the Lower Classes in Roman Society.* Chicago: University of Chicago Press, 1938.

Don Nardo, *Life of a Roman Slave.* San Diego: Lucent Books, 1998.

T.G. Parkin, *Demography and Roman Society.* Baltimore: Johns Hopkins University Press, 1992.

Sarah B. Pomeroy, *Goddesses, Whores, Wives, and Slaves: Women in Classical Antiquity.* New York: Schocken Books, 1995.

Beryl Rawson, ed., *Marriage, Divorce, and Children in Ancient Rome.* Oxford: Oxford University Press, 1991.

John E. Stambough, *The Ancient Roman City.* Baltimore: Johns Hopkins University Press, 1988.

Susan Treggiari, *Roman Freedman During the Late Republic.* New York: Oxford University Press, 1969.

K.D. White, *Roman Farming.* London: Thames and Hudson, 1970.

War and Military Affairs

M.C. Bishop and J.C. Coulston, *Roman Military Equipment.* Princes Risborough, England: Shire, 1989.

Brian Caven, *The Punic Wars.* New York: Barnes and Noble, 1992.

Peter Connolly, *Greece and Rome at War.* London: Macdonald, 1998.

Roy W. Davies, *Service in the Roman Army.* Ed. David Breeze and Valerie A. Maxfield. New York: Columbia University Press, 1989.

Michael Grant, *The Army of the Caesars.* New York: M. Evans and Company, 1974.

Sir John Hackett, ed., *Warfare in the Ancient World.* New York: Facts On File, 1989.

Lawrence Keppie, *The Making of the Roman Army.* New York: Barnes and Noble, 1994.

J.F. Lazenby, *The First Punic War: A Military History.* Stanford: Stanford University Press, 1996.

Edward N. Luttwak, *The Grand Strategy of the Roman Empire.* Baltimore: Johns Hopkins University Press, 1976.

Simon Macdowall, *Late Roman Infantrymen, 236–565* A.D. London: Osprey, 1994.

E.W. Marsden, *Greek and Roman Artillery.* Oxford: Clarendon Press, 1969.

Valerie A. Maxfield, *The Military Decorations of the Roman Army.* London: Batsford, 1981.

Don Nardo, *Life of a Roman Soldier.* San Diego: Lucent Books, 2000.

———, *The Punic Wars.* San Diego: Lucent Books, 1994.

Nick Sekunda, *The Roman Army, 200–104* B.C. London: Osprey, 1996.

Pat Southern and Karen R. Dixon, *The Late Roman Army.* New Haven, CT: Yale University Press, 1996.

Chester G. Starr *The Roman Imperial Navy, 31* B.C.–A.D. *324.* Ithaca, NY: Cornell University Press, 1941. 2nd ed., Cambridge, England: Heffe, 1960.

G.R. Watson, *The Roman Soldier.* London: Thames and Hudson, 1969.

Graham Webster, *The Roman Imperial Army.* Totowa, NJ: Barnes and Noble, 1985.

Terence Wise, *Armies of the Carthaginian Wars, 265–146* B.C. London: Osprey, 1996.

INDEX

PICTURE CREDITS

ABOUT THE AUTHOR

Historian Don Nardo has written extensively about the ancient world. His studies of ancient Greece and Rome include *Life in Ancient Athens, The Age of Augustus, Greek and Roman Sport,* and *Life of a Roman Soldier;* he is also the editor of Greenhaven Press's massive *Complete History of Ancient Greece* and *The Encyclopedia of Greek and Roman Mythology.* He lives with his wife, Christine, in Massachusetts.